POWER PLAY

The Life and Times of Peter Hall

STEPHEN FAY

Hodder & Stoughton

First published in 1995 by Hodder and Stoughton
A division of Hodder Headline PLC

10 9 8 7 6 5 4 3 2 1

A CIP catalogue record for this title is available
from the British Library

ISBN 0 340 50844 2

Typeset by Palimpsest Book Production Limited,
Polmont, Stirlingshire
Printed and bound in Great Britain by
Mackays of Chatham PLC, Chatham, Kent

Hodder and Stoughton
A division of Hodder Headline PLC
338 Euston Road
London NW1 3BH

To the memory of my grandfather
Frank Fay,
a founder of the Abbey Theatre,
the first National Theatre
in the British Isles

Contents

List of Illustrations

George Hall and His second wife Edith (*Elsie Hall*); Father and son: Reg and Peter on the beach at Kessingland (*Derek Lawrance*); Grace Hall, with her mother and son (*Vera Pamment*); Peter Hall as a baby with the family dog; in the company of his father's animals; and in school uniform at Barnham (*Elsie Hall, Vera Pamment and Derek Lawrance*); Peter Hall as head boy and as Hamlet at the Perse School in Cambridge (*National Theatre Archive*); Sergeant Instructor (Acting) Hall, P.R.F. (*National Theatre Archive*); An undergraduate worth knowing (*Theresa Robertson*); *Waiting for Godot* (*Theatre Museum*); Hall takes over at Stratford, aged twenty-nine (*Camera Press*); A memorable marriage: Peter Hall and Leslie Caron (*Camera Press*), (*Hulton Deutsch Collection*); Stratford legends (*Shakespeare Centre Library*); Sir Fordham Flower, Chairman of the RSC (*Lady Flower*); Peggy Ashcroft and Hall on the terrace at the Memorial Theatre in Stratford in 1962 (*Theatre Museum, V&A*); A second wife: Hall marries Jacky Taylor, attended by his two children, in 1965 Daily Express).

Directors of the National Theatre: Hall with his predecessor, Laurence Olivier (*Hulton Deutsch Collection*); The Queen Mother and her daughter Margaret at the unofficial opening of the South Bank theatre in 1976 by Hall and the architect, Denys Lasdun (*Camera Press*); Hall and the building he boosted (*Camera Press*); Peter Hall rehearses *Moses and Aaron* at the Royal Opera House (*Reg Wilson*); Teamwork at Glyndebourne: Hall with Moran Caplat, Glyndebourne's benevolent administrator, John Bury, his designer, and the conductor, Raymond Leppard (*Guy Gravett*); A Mozart debut: Hall directs Ileana Cotrubas, who sang Susanna in *The

Marriage of Figaro in 1973 (*Guy Gravett*); A growing family (*Hulton Deutsch Collection*), (*Jacky Hall*); Third wife: Hall with opera prima donna Maria Ewing (*Camera Press*); Max Rayne's farewell, with Hall and his successor Richard Eyre (*National Theatre*); Rayne and former Treasury mandarin, Sir Derek Mitchell (*National Theatre*); Besieged: Hall at the stage door during an NT strike (*Hulton Deutsch Collection*); Hall rehearses *Oresteia* (*Nobby Clark*); Hall rehearses *Jean Seberg* (*Nobby Clark*); Rehearsing Pinter's *Other Places* at the National Theatre in 1982 (*National Theatre*);, Hall rehearses *Antony and Cleopatra* with Anthony Hopkins (*John Haynes*); Anthony Hopkins and Judi Dench (*John Haynes*); Young Turks and an old Turk (*Camera Press*); Julie Walters in William's *The Rose Tattoo* (*John Haynes*); Dustin Hoffman as Shylock in *The Merchant of Venice* (*John Haynes*); Venessa Redgrave in Tennessee Williams's *Orpheus Descending* (*John Haynes*); Sephen Dillane as Hall's fourth Hamlet (*Ivan Kyncl*); A wonderful marriage and a tribe of children (*Steve Shipman Photography*).

Acknowledgements

I should like to thank Sir Peter Hall for many kindnesses; for permission to quote from his *Diaries*, and from his autobiography, *Making an Exhibition of Myself*; and for reassuring friends and colleagues that he had no objection to their speaking to me, nor to their letters being published.

Before their deaths in 1988, Reginald and Grace Hall were generous with hospitality and information. Each of Hall's wives – Leslie Caron, Jacky Hall, Maria Ewing and Nicki Hall – has spared me time to talk. I thank them all.

Among Hall's former colleagues, John Goodwin and Jan Younghusband provided me liberally with documentary information, as well as with their own recollections. Maggie Sedwards, the administrator of the Peter Hall Company, has been a good-natured and efficient go-between.

Lady Flower gave permission to quote from Sir Fordham Flower's collection of papers at the Shakespeare Centre Library, and illuminated a rich period in theatre history by her reminiscences. I am indebted to her.

For permission to quote from letters, I am grateful to: Lady Olivier, Sir John Gielgud, the estate of Tennessee Williams, and Harold Pinter.

Lady Soames and the Board of the Royal National Theatre generously gave me permission to read and to quote from the minutes of the Board and its Finance and General Purposes Committee. Nicola Scadding, the archivist at the RNT, helped me find the relevant papers in their collections. I am particularly obliged to Sir Derek Mitchell for the time he took to put flesh on the bones those minutes reveal.

I should like to thank the librarians at the Shakespeare Centre Library in Stratford-upon-Avon (Marion Pringle); at Glyndebourne (Rosy Runciman); and at the Royal Opera House (Francesca Franchi); and at the London Library, the Garrick Club, and Cambridge University. Patrick Masters proved to be an invaluable guide to the files at Companies House.

Finally, I would like to thank the people who took time to talk or write to me: Lisa Aronson, Alan Ayckbourn, Lord Birkett, John Barton, Sally Beauman, Yolande Bird, Kitty Black, Michael Blakemore, Ronald Blythe, Howard Brenton, David Brierley, John Bury, Mel Calman, Moran Caplat, Mary Counsell, Paul Daneman, Judi Dench, Gillian Diamond, Floy Donnell, Richard Eyre, Trader Faulkner, Kate Flanagan, William Gaskill, Suzanne Goodwin, Elsie Hall, David Hare, Jeremy Isaacs, David Isitt, Parin Janmohamed, Michael Kustow, Derek Lawrance, the Very Revd Michael Mayne, Jonathan Miller, Lord Mishcon, Christopher Morahan, John Mortimer, Trevor Nunn, Tarquin Olivier, Timothy O'Brien, Vera Pamment, Richard Pearson, Harold Pinter, The Revd Dr John Polkinghorne, Stanley Price, Lord Rayne, Theresa Robertson, Toby Robertson, Toby Rowland, Barrie Rutter, George Rylands, Donald Sinden, Barbara J. Smith, John Tanfield, Sir John Tooley, Dorothy Tutin, Rowena Webster, Sir Hugh Willatt, Peter Wood, and Stephen Wood. Irving Wardle, who read the manuscript, made many helpful suggestions; any errors are, of course, my responsibility.

The initial enthusiasm of Ion Trewin, when he was editorial director of Hodder and Stoughton, and the patience of his successor, Richard Cohen, were important to me. When both had gone from the firm, Rowena Webb picked up where they had left off. Beth Humphries was a diligent copy editor.

Finally, I am most indebted, as usual, to Prudence Fay's shrewd comments, and for her dextrous editing of the manuscript.

Foreword

This biography of Peter Hall is not an authorised version. The book has been written with his consent and co-operation, but from the outset Hall recognised that it would be 'warts and all'. When the *Evening Standard*'s Londoner's Diary suggested in 1988 that Hall had 'appointed' me as his biographer, he wrote to the editor: 'I have no control over what he writes . . . I know he will say what he thinks about me, and that is not necessarily what I would like him to say.' This is an unusually generous attitude for the subject of a biography to take, and I am most grateful to him.

Because Hall has held public positions, a pile of documentary material about his life has already built up. It now includes a cache of letters written by theatrical luminaries in the 1950s and 1960s, which came to light unexpectedly and which he believed had been irretrievably lost. In these letters the voice of theatre people speaking privately to each other comes across with great clarity. Along with long conversations with his former wives and his family, and with his contemporaries in the theatre, these letters and other documents have helped me set Hall's complex personality and remarkable achievements in the exhilarating story of his times.

Prologue

'A Dramatiser of His Own Life'

Shakespeare made a good joke out of Owen Glendower's claim that, when he was born, the frame and huge foundation of the earth shook like a coward. ('So it would have done at the same season if your mother's cat had but kittened.') Too much can be read into auguries.

On 22 November 1930, the day Peter Hall was born in Bury St Edmunds, there was a gale off the Suffolk coast, but, in fact, the significant portent for his life was the announcement a couple of days earlier by Philip Snowden, Labour's chancellor of the exchequer, that the government would make an annual grant of £17,500 towards the cost of grand opera. This modest sum – worth £570,000 in 1994 pounds – was the first regular government subsidy ever to be given to the arts in Britain. As auguries go, it is uncommonly meaningful for a man who became the great impresario of the subsidised theatre.

The reaction to Snowden's announcement is interesting because it begins a story of patronage, parsimony and philistinism that was to provide some of the themes for Peter Hall's life. On 21 November, the day before Hall's birth, a leader writer in *The Times* was particularly tart:

Mr Snowden has taken the first step in a policy, firmly resisted by all his predecessors, of giving a subsidy to the theatre out of taxation . . . Direct taxation for Opera means a new expenditure on something which very few people want at a moment when expenditure of any sort should be most jealously scrutinised. That the amount in itself is small does not alter the fact that it is an extravagance, and moreover it is not likely to be allowed to remain small. For what demand on behalf of the more popular arts, the 'legitimate theatre' for example, could be reasonably refused when Covent Garden draws its annual income from the Treasury?[1]

The *Times* parliamentary correspondent's report was also remarkably prescient: 'While members of all political parties are anxious to ensure the continuance of Grand Opera at Covent Garden . . . those members who hope to obtain further information . . . are anxious lest the decision should be regarded as a precedent. They doubt, for instance, whether it would be easy to resist a claim for financial aid from those who are trying to establish a national theatre.' It was forty-five years later that Hall finally led the National Theatre company into its new theatre on the South Bank of the Thames.

Right from the start, the opponents of state subsidies for the arts insisted that there were better things to spend the money on. An early day motion proposed that the House of Commons reject the subsidy in view of 'the present industrial situation and of the growth of unemployment'. For many years (thirty-three in the case of the National Theatre) every attempt merely to establish the principle of government subsidies for the arts was to be met by the refrain that was first heard in November 1930: they were imprudent, extravagant, the nation could not afford them, and the time was not right. Yet a good case for subsidy could be made just by reading *The Times* for the day of Hall's birth.

The West End theatre was then dominated by stars playing light comedy: Gertrude Lawrence in Noël Coward's *Private Lives* at the Phoenix, Tallulah Bankhead in *Let Us Be Gay* at the Lyric, Ralph Lynn in an Aldwych farce, Charles Laughton in an Edgar Wallace thriller. There were two of those in town, as well as plays by Somerset Maugham and Emlyn Williams. Beatrice Lilley was appearing at the Coliseum and Gracie Fields at the Holborn Empire.

The Lord Chamberlain, acting as official censor, was in his pomp, able to decree that Pirandello's *Six Characters in Search of an Author* would not be licensed unless it was performed in Italian. A play about Charles Stewart Parnell, whose political career had ended some fifty years earlier, had been banned by the Lord Chamberlain on the grounds that it dealt with people and events of too recent a date. No modern English or European classics were to be seen, for the London theatre was given over mostly to a middle-class audience with middlebrow tastes. There was, however, a new production of *Antony and Cleopatra* at the Old Vic; and Ivor Brown, critic of the *Week-end Review*, declared that, despite the disdain of academic critics like A.C. Bradley, he considered *Antony and Cleopatra* to be the equal of *Hamlet*. Brown judged that, as Antony, John Gielgud was too young for the part, but a great joy none the less. Enobarbus was Ralph Richardson ('admirable').[2] This production was an augury, too.

Since 1930, almost everything has changed utterly, much of it for the better. Political parties squabble over the sums that should subsidise the arts, and the Treasury never stops looking for cuts, but the principle is rarely questioned. The Lord Chamberlain's long run ended in 1968, his authority undermined first by small companies like the Arts and the Royal Court that could be turned into club theatres where the censor's writ did not run, and then by the full majesty of the Royal Shakespeare Company. New theatres have been built for the new subsidised companies: the RSC and the National Theatre. These were Hall's empires.

In the decade after the Second World War there was loose talk about the death of the theatre in England, but the mid-1950s saw a renaissance that flourished for twenty-five years. This was one of the most exhilarating periods in the English theatre since the seventeenth century. No single person presided over it, but Hall was closer to the centre of it for longer than any other individual.

Peter Hall was twenty-four in August 1955 when he directed the first performance in English of Samuel Beckett's *Waiting for Godot* at the Arts Theatre, an event which 'irreversibly changed the face of the British theatre'.[3] He was fifty-seven in 1988 when he directed three of Shakespeare's late plays before retiring as director of the National Theatre. For the first part of this rich period Hall concentrated on the Royal Shakespeare Company, emphasising the company concept, insisting on clear verse-speaking, and demystifying Shakespeare. Hall then was left-wing, contemptuous of the West End theatre, and of established figures like the Lord Chamberlain. He was a hero of his time.

By the 1970s, the radicals, led by Hall, were occupying the new theatres on the South Bank and at the Barbican. But the mood had changed, and those theatres became derided symbols of giganticism in the arts. Hall, the impresario, was now cast as a member of the establishment. The outsider was now on the inside; he was brutally made over from hero into villain. Jonathan Miller, for instance, said it must be awful to wake up each morning and find that you were Peter Hall. He was known by a variety of spiteful nicknames. Miller's own contribution was Genghis Khan; others were Dr Fu Manchu (John Osborne), Lord Vestibule (John Dexter), Toad Hall and Tammany Hall.[4] All these names refer to Hall's power. One of his worst offences has been never to apologise for liking power.

Four wives, all being much the same age when he married them – late twenties to very early thirties – plus (by his own account) two long-term relationships that amounted to marriage, ensured that the gossip columnists never became bored by him. And although Hall claimed to be shy, he published his diaries of the first years in the National Theatre in 1983, and his autobiography, *Making an Exhibition of Myself*, in 1993. Regular newspaper, magazine and radio interviews, and the knighthood, made him a public figure. Hall was the first theatre and opera director to become a fully fledged showbusiness celebrity.

Despite this, his personality has remained opaque. His acquisition and deployment of power, the loyalty of a small group of friends, the alienation felt by some of his professional colleagues, and his marital musical chairs have made him an object of envy and curiosity, of mystery even. Hall believes that people are defined by the masks they wear: 'Life is just a question of wearing or changing masks,' he once said. 'I think that's true of all of us at all times, whatever profession we're in . . . I think that from the moment we begin to talk and learn about social behaviour, we learn the use of masks.'[5]

Michael Birkett, one of Hall's old friends, puts this in a different way: 'Peter is a dramatiser of his own life,' he says.[6] Peter Wood, another friend, speaks of Hall's personal 'psycho-drama'.[7] Disentangling the appearance from the reality is one of the most tantalising tasks he sets a biographer. But, besides that, the crowded story of Peter Hall's life is a compelling history of his times.

1

An East Anglian Childhood

'A little bit above themselves'

Grace Hall did not have an easy pregnancy. Six weeks before her first child was due, she was severely nauseous and was ordered by the doctor to spend the rest of her pregnancy in bed.[1] Her son was born, like most working-class children then, at home. After the birth on 22 November 1930, the doctor advised Grace not to think about having another child for the time being. She did not mind; she was happy with the one she had: a bonny baby weighing 8lb. 7oz. He was named Peter Reginald Frederick Hall.

Shortly after Peter was born, a professional photographer in Bury St Edmunds took a picture of him with his mother, and it stayed on the sideboard wherever she went. The look on her face is of fulfilment and adoration. When he was still a babe in arms, the relations were already commenting that she lived for her son. Peter Hall's feelings about his mother were not so straightforward. After he had grown up, he strung together a number of strong adjectives to describe her: pretentious, wayward, bossy, moody, emotional.[2]

Grace Hall had good taste, and a sharp mind. Since she had been disappointed by her own life and her husband's, she invested her hopes in her son. Hall found the need to please his mother hard to bear as a child; and for most of his adult life he told the people he was close to that he had not loved her.[3] Even when she grew old there was never complete peace between them. Hall tucked away his explanation for this at the end of his autobiography; he said he supposed they were too alike.[4] Some of the adjectives he applied to her, then, must apply to him.

Grace Florence Hall's maiden name was Pamment. She described her family as town people, but she had long family memories of life on the land. Two generations earlier, the Pamments had been smallholders in Suffolk; her grandfather was an ostler, who had thirteen children and lived in Hartest, on the outskirts of Bury St Edmunds. Grace's parents lived in small towns around Bury; her father ran a modest pork butcher's shop in Norton before taking a job as a decorator on a country estate at Shimpling. Peter, who recalled the smell of the old collie in his grandparents' kitchen, disapproved of his grandfather, who retired from decorating with sciatica at the age of fifty, and spent the next twenty years reading the *Daily Mirror*, smoking his pipe and listening to the radio. Peter Hall did not inherit his work ethic from his Grandfather Pamment.

By 1930 the Pamments had moved into Bury St Edmunds, but the land was still part of their life. In time, Peter Hall filmed *Akenfield*, Ronald Blythe's story of a Suffolk village, and when Grace saw it she recalled the four years she had spent as a child at a country school in Shimpling. It was true, she said, that children were given time off school to pick stones in the fields, as the film showed; true, too, that they looked miserable, cold and frightened.[5]

Grace always described her own family as poor. There were four children: her elder brother Ted, her elder sister Jean (or Gee), and a cheerful, good-natured younger brother called Bill. The family was close, and argumentative; Hall wrote of the Pamments: 'They believed that life owed them a better living than it had provided, and were moody, introspective, and always seeing implied insults in each other's behaviour. They loved to be proud of their grievances.'[6] A breach between Ted and his father went so deep that Ted watched his father's funeral procession standing by the entrance to the cemetery, and left as soon as it had passed. When he grew up, Peter Hall tended to blame any personal failings on his Pamment blood.

The Pamments wept easily, and Grace had an innate sense of

drama. Leslie Caron, Hall's first wife, watched Grace cry at the slightest pretext – at the television news, for instance, if it was bad enough.[7] Believing that the worst was likely to happen, Grace was suspicious of enthusiasm, and when Leslie wanted to tease her she would simply say things were wonderful. To Grace, that was tempting fate.

Grace was a victim of a time when girls didn't matter as much as boys. When she was young, she was usually in the company of her mother or her grandmother, and when she went to school none of the men in the family cared much whether she did well or badly. In fact, she was head of the form. She read a good deal, and hoped to go on to secondary school; but no one in the family was strong enough to contest her father's veto.

With her sister Gee, Grace went to work in Lindsey's drapery store in the Buttermarket in the centre of Bury St Edmunds, and stayed there for thirteen years. She worked as a window-dresser and a buyer, ending up on £2 10s. a week, which she considered a poor wage, considering her experience and skill. She was not tempted to stay on after her marriage. Lindsey's did, however, encourage her artistic streak. Leslie Caron – whose taste was expensive, French and impeccable – observed that Grace immediately recognised quality and, although her means were limited, she always dressed well.

Grace and Reg both attended St Mary's, the fine fifteenth-century parish church just up the street from the Bury cathedral. Reg was an attractive man, six foot tall. A baritone, he was good enough to win medals at Suffolk music festivals, and he sang in amateur performances of Gilbert and Sullivan, as well as in St Mary's choir for seventeen years. He and Grace had music in common: Grace's grandfather had written music, and her uncle was the organist at St John's church in Bury St Edmunds. Grace had a good voice too, although girls were not allowed to sing in a church choir then, but she never joined Reg in his amateur opera and dramatics ('I didn't want anything to do with a crowd like that'). All his family and in-laws recall Reg's sense of fun; he was well known and well liked in Bury. Reg had lived alone with his mother, and when she died, in February 1929, he and Grace, who had already been engaged for three years, married as soon as was decently possible, on 11 July 1929. They moved into the family home.

Reg Hall was the opposite of Grace in virtually every way: calm and secure, tolerant and easygoing. Reg's sister-in-law, Elsie Hall, thought that Grace tried to keep him down a bit, but Reg was not easy to subdue. She nagged him; Reg put up with it. Grace was ambitious for her men, and although Reg himself was not without ambition, it was not strong enough to satisfy hers. But they were a devoted couple, and died within a week of each other. Peter was certain that his father died because he was unable to bear the idea of life without his mother.

Towards the end of his life, in 1983, Reg Hall decided that his son ought to know more about his background, and, in a spidery hand, wrote a family history:

My father (your great grandfather [sic]) was born in 1846 (in Suffolk) and died in 1917 (aged 71). His education consisted of part time attendance at school for which he paid 1d (one old penny) per week. His teacher made coffins in between lessons. Although my father received very little education from outside sources, he was eventually, through self-education, a fairly learned man. He left Suffolk and became Gamekeeper on Lord Penryn's estate in North Wales where he met and married my mother (your great grandmother [sic]). After a period he left this job and became landlord of the Royal Oak Hotel, Bangor. After a few years he returned to Suffolk to carry on the business ['work' is crossed out] of his father which was Vermin Destroying. He had contracts with the leading Aristocracy on their estates and mansions in England, Scotland, Ireland, and Wales to which places he travelled regularly to give advice. One of the most important customers was Her Majesty Queen Victoria (his Majesty King Edward VII) at Sandringham where he often went, travelling 50 miles from Suffolk by pony and cart (cars were not efficient in those days). My mother had 11 children in all, I being second youngest. Only [crosses out '2 of us are'] myself is alive today ['my sister Dottie and me' is crossed out]. All these are recorded in the family Bible which I have in my possession today. Referring back to my father, he received invitations to the Garden Parties at Sandringham & the invitation cards were treasured by my mother & I do not know where they are now.

My mother Edith Kate (nee Mitchell) was born in Yorkshire & taken as a babe to Bangor, North Wales where she was educated at local schools & was fluent with the Welsh language. My father was born in 1846 and died in 1917 having been married twice as his first wife died young after having one son, my stepbrother Jonathon. My mother was several years younger than my father, she was born in 1865 & died in 1929 aged 64.

My father was successful in business in his early life & became the owner of several pieces of property, but unfortunately ill health forced him gradually to dispose of most of this. This affected me most of anybody as I was attending the West Suffolk County School having won a scholarship. This school was also the Pupil Teacher Centre & it was intended I should with luck be a school teacher. My father's health deteriorated & the family became poorer

& it was decided I would have to leave school & get employment. I therefore obtained a position as a clerk on the Great Eastern Railways and I started at the salary of 8/- (eight shillings) per week.[8]

George Hall came from Horham, near Eye, in the depths of Suffolk, and although Grace always preferred to call him a vermin destroyer, George Hall was a rat-catcher, known as 'Ratty' to his neighbours in Bury St Edmunds. Peter Hall took Grace's preference for the term 'vermin destroyer' as an example of his mother's 'distinct aura of piss-elegance'. In fact, being the rat-catcher was a good job for a skilled, self-employed man, working with his dogs and ferrets. There were always spaniels in the Hall household.

A photograph of George Hall, taken in Sandringham, shows a sturdy figure with a full, barbered moustache and mischievous eyes, dressed in good tweeds, with a watch-chain in his waistcoat. His home in the village of Fornham All Saints, not far from Bury St Edmunds, was a substantial, double-fronted Georgian house set in a carefully cultivated garden. A portrait of his wife shows an ample woman with strong features, dressed in silk and brocade.

By the turn of the century, however, George Hall had moved into a much less agreeable house in town, and Reg was born on 4 October 1901 in 62 Avenue Approach, a nondescript street on the edge of Bury St Edmunds, beyond the railway station. A decade or so after that the family's finances had deteriorated badly, and Reg's mother was forced to send him out to ask the neighbours to spare a pint of gooseberries and some eggs. Some of the children had already emigrated to Australia, and by 1914 the Halls were poor. Gradually, the land George had accumulated was sold off to meet bills, and when he died in 1917 only one small piece nearby, which he had used as a garden, remained in the family. His will was not proved, and by the time the lawyers had finished with the estate, Mrs Hall received just £15.

Like Grace's, Reg's education ended sooner than he wished. In 1916, when he was fifteen, his mother still had two children to support, and decided it was time Reg earned a living. She got him a job as a trainee clerk on the railways, a promising occupation that offered security, a uniform, the prospect of promotion and a railway house. Reg, as he noted, would have preferred to stay on at West Suffolk County School in Bury and train as a teacher, but he was not asked, and did as he was told. His education was not quite over; boys leaving school at fifteen were given lessons, but these were confined to shorthand and typing and Morse code, in preparation for the railway promotion examinations.

After the death of his father, Reg and his mother moved up the street to 24 Avenue Approach, where Edith Hall suffered her stroke in February 1929. Within four months of her death, Reg had decorated the house from top to bottom. The redbrick terrace house is a modest two-up, two-down, with grey brick courses on the lintels above the door and the windows. The lavatory was outside and there was no bathroom (a hip bath hung in the kitchen), but there was running water and electricity, and a yard stretched fifty feet from the kitchen at the back of the house. The front room was always neat, and the living-room leading to the kitchen was always untidy; upstairs there were three bedrooms. The house was comfortable enough for a family of three.

Bury St Edmunds is a market town, with a cathedral, assembly rooms and a pretty Georgian theatre, the Theatre Royal (where the first night of *Charley's Aunt* was staged in 1892). By the 1930s the Theatre Royal had become a barrel-store for the neighbouring Greene King brewery; to explore it, Hall once had to break in. There were rows of elegant Georgian houses in the town centre, and the Playhouse cinema, where Reg Hall had sung Giuseppe in *The Gondoliers*. But it was a dull place; even in the surrounding Suffolk countryside people would say: 'It's always early closing in Bury.'

Around Bury were some great shooting estates: not far north was the Duke of Grafton's Euston estate (the London railway station is named after it). Lord Iveagh and Lord and Lady Islington were familiar figures in the town, which was also the home of the professional people who looked after their interests. Politics then was about deference: Bury was barren ground for trade unionists and Labour men like Reg Hall. Having polled less than 10 per cent of the votes in the 1929 general election, the Labour Party did not bother to put up a candidate against the Tories in 1931 or 1935.

There was no shortage of musical life, however. Besides the church choirs and Gilbert and Sullivan at the Playhouse, the band of the Suffolk Regiment led the parade from the barracks to St Mary's on Sundays, and the band of the Salvation Army performed regularly in the market-place. As a small child, Peter Hall was particularly fond of drums and cymbals.

Bury St Edmunds was well ordered, and law-abiding; it was

also acutely class conscious and insensitive to poverty. Bury was not a bad place to grow up in, but it was the kind of town that ambitious men, and families with ambitions for their children, were happy to leave if they got the chance.

After the birth of their son, Grace bought a pram. Not just any pram, but the brand leader, a Silver Cross. Only the best was going to be good enough for Peter, no matter how much scrimping was involved. Reg Hall was doing well on the railways, passing his exams and climbing step by step up the ladder of promotion; but Peter could not be brought up in the style they wanted for him on a weekly wage of £3 16s. Fortunately, Reg Hall had a flair for making extra money.

Before he married, he and his younger brother Ted would buy clapped-out bicycles in Bury market, and tart them up in the shed in the garden, before selling them on. 'I was always one to try to make an extra shilling,' Reg said towards the end of his life. By the early 1930s Reg had another source of income. The alley at the bottom of their back yard in Avenue Approach led to a lane, and at the bottom of the lane were two fields, amounting to seven acres in all. Reg managed to acquire them, and there raised pigs, goats, a cow and some chickens.[9] The cow was milked twice a day, and the eggs were sold locally. As an infant, even at the height of the Depression, Peter always had enough to eat, though unfortunately he soon developed an aversion to the principal products of Reg's smallholding – milk, eggs and meat. The fields also came in useful when Peter announced that he wanted a pony. Because he had the space to break it in himself, Reg was able to buy an untrained animal. At Christmas, he always made sure the family had enough money for chicken and oranges.

Reg also bought chests of tea which he repackaged and sold, as Railway Tea, from door to door. One of the sales team was the daughter of a neighbouring railwayman, Elsie Glading, who recalls that, as a girl, she thought the Halls a little bit different from the other railway families in the street: 'Reg would have been thought well off. They were always a little bit above us. The Halls were just a little bit above themselves.'[10]

Elsie Glading was a regular visitor at the Halls' house, especially when Grace was ill in hospital with peritonitis. Elsie was twelve when Peter Hall was born, and during the first five years of his life she doted on him. Grace trusted her to play with Peter when she was poorly or busy; together they would listen to Henry Hall's band on the radio playing 'The Changing of the Guard' and 'The Teddy Bears' Picnic'. Peter would march around the kitchen table, and, if the weather was fine, out into the yard, playing the drum or blowing a bugle. Elsie recalls that Peter always insisted on leading the procession, even when it included her mother: 'He always led from when he could walk.' As an only child, he grew used to being the centre of attention. Elsie Glading's mother, having been led in procession round the kitchen table, told him: 'We'll see your name in lights one day.'

Elsie was a constant companion. Indeed, her recollection is that she was Peter's only playmate. As a child he showed no interest in sports and games, preferring to be read to by his mother or Elsie. This was partly because he was a sickly child: before his adolescence he had had typhoid fever, appendicitis and shingles. Shingles struck twice, and dogged him throughout his life.

The adjectives used to describe Peter as a child are 'adored', 'idolised' and 'worshipped'. 'Mollycoddled' is Elsie's word for it: 'His mother wrapped him in cotton wool. He would complain if his socks or his vest were tickling him, and he would have them changed.' Since Grace had few friends, there was nothing to distract her attention: she fed Peter, read to him, played with him, bathed him daily, and said his prayers with him each night. His passion for bananas mashed in cream was satisfied regularly on Saturdays when they were sold cheaply just before the market closed.

Hall had inherited his mother's deep brown eyes. Photographs of him as a child show a chubby infant with pale brown hair on the beach at Kessingland, the Suffolk seaside town where, his mother reported, he cut his first tooth. There is a picture of Reg holding his baby, prettily dressed in a woollen outfit and hat, surrounded by pigs and goats; others show him in a smart cap and double-breasted coat or dungarees amid the piglets or clutching a collie dog. His varied wardrobe was made for him by his Grandmother Pamment. When he wanted a cowboy outfit, it arrived complete with broad-brimmed hat, waistcoat, scarf and chaps. In another photograph he is dressed as a guardsman, with a tunic and a woolly 'bearskin'. In all the photographs he has a pleasant, open smile. Dressing up was the first clue he gave that he had inherited his mother's sense of drama. Grace recalled a neighbour, remembering Peter when he was a little boy, who said that she couldn't talk to him when he was dressed up because he didn't see anybody: 'He wasn't Peter Hall, he was somebody else.'[11]

By the age of four, he had already been taken to see *Robinson Crusoe* at the Playhouse and had been captivated by the darkness, the audience and the music. Bored and lonely on a rainy day, he pestered his mother to make him a stage out of a shoebox. It was the first of many. His interest was further aroused two years or so later by a performance of *The Sleeping Beauty* done with string puppets at his school. After that, he converted a model railway station, a present from his Uncle Bill, into a theatre. When he wanted a fretwork set, his parents sent away for one at a cost of £5. With that he made bigger and more complex stages, and his first home-made puppets. This new model stage had a decorated proscenium arch, a curtain on rings that could be drawn open – made by his mother – and lights. His first performers were members of a Negro band. Later Hall's repertoire expanded to include puppets made from drawings of Mickey Mouse characters, and Snow White and the Seven Dwarfs. The first public performances were given at his school.

Grace did not make friends in the street, and when the Halls went visiting it was usually to their Pamment relations. For many years Peter was not just the only child of Reg and Grace; he was the only child in the whole extended family. He hated the family lunchtimes when feuds would surface, and refused to eat anything outside his own home until he was eight. But he loved his Uncle Ted. He describes Ted Pamment as 'a Heathcliffian genius'[12] who could brood and sulk better than any other Pamment, but who could be funny, warm and generous too. Like Henry Straker, George Bernard Shaw's New Man, Uncle Ted was a gifted, self-taught mechanic. Since he understood motorbikes and refrigeration, he was employed by the first shop in Bury to deliver ice-cream by motorbike. By the 1930s Ted was working for Mann Egerton, selling and repairing cars, but what he liked best was making them. He had lathes and tools in the workshop in the back garden; there he built a two-seater car, worked on a succession of motorbikes, and pored over the *Model Engineer* with his nephew.

It was his Uncle Ted's mechanical skill that left Hall with his most vivid childhood memory. At Christmas 1936, at his Pamment grandparents' house, the voice of Father Christmas spoke out during a radio programme wishing a Happy Christmas to Peter Hall of Bury St Edmunds. Father Christmas was actually Ted Pamment speaking from his workshop into a microphone, but it confirmed Peter Hall's belief that Father Christmas spoke with a Suffolk accent. It also confirmed the notion that the universe revolved around him.

Peter learned from Ted's wife Vera that he could get what he wanted by being persistent. He had told her about a brass band of toy soldiers he had seen in Ipswich, and explained how he could make them perform such wonders in his newest toy theatre that they would change his life. He vaguely grasped that he was begging, and was a bit guilty when he recalled how manipulative he could be, but Aunty Vera bought the toy soldiers for him.[13]

Already he was thoroughly spoiled. Hall says that, from the age of about seven or eight, he found it irksome to attend to the ordinary things of life. His mother would ask him to help with the washing up, but if he was reading he was excused. This was a working-class household in which men were not really expected to do the chores. Reg's sister-in-law, Elsie, remembers Reg being waited on hand and foot: 'He never washed a plate, and I doubt whether he could open a can of sardines.'[14]

By Christmas 1936 Peter Hall was attending the East Anglian School kindergarten in Bury. Years later he could still recall the plasticine, the percussion band, and a kindly maternal teacher called Miss Cook. He also remembered feeling that school and family were socially miles apart. In the first school report that his mother kept, dated 26 July 1938, his reading was excellent; he was very good at arithmetic, dictation, composition, handwork and tables, and good at writing and drawing. (He was excused needlework.) His conduct was very good; only in gymnastics was he no better than average. A certificate, dated 28 October 1938, states that he had won the kindergarten prize. The East Anglian School was a private school for girls which admitted boys to the kindergarten, but Reg had earned the money needed for the fees. In principle, he was willing to go on doing so, but Peter's education was continued in a state school. It was also in Bury, but he had to commute to this one.

They had moved deep into the Suffolk countryside, nine miles due north of Bury St Edmunds to the outskirts of a village called Barnham on the railway line to Thetford, just short of the border with Norfolk. Reg was the new stationmaster. The only one of thirty of his contemporaries from the Ipswich area who had passed all his exams, when the job at Barnham came up, he was the only applicant. Until 1938 Barnham was so small there there was no stationmaster, but an RAF aerodrome was to be built nearby at Honington, a couple of miles to the north, so supplies were routed through Barnham sidings.

At home in Bury St Edmunds the Hall family had had three bedrooms, electricity and running water. At Barnham, where they lived above the shop, there was no electricity and water had to be pumped from a well; there was an outside lavatory. When Reg told them they were moving, Grace and Peter both wept. But Reg sold the fields down the lane, and, decades later, was still sure the move to Barnham was the best thing he had ever done. It was the first job in which he had blossomed. His hat proclaimed his rank, and his pocket watch checked the four passenger trains and the goods train that passed through Barnham each weekday. When he travelled, he went first class.

Grace and Peter arrived at Barnham determined to hate it, but the son of the stationmaster was a freeman on a branch line, and Peter rode with the driver and fireman on the shunting engine, playing them his ukulele. He had enjoyed days in the Fens with his Grandfather Pamment when they lived in Bury, but at Barnham he became a country boy, collecting birds' eggs and gleaning ears of corn to feed to their chickens.

He also met a gamekeeper on the Grafton Estate named Charlie Kent, who dug the station garden. With sandwiches packed by his mother, Peter and Charlie would spend the day together. Charlie taught Peter, aged eight, about the birds and their eggs, and about animals in their natural woodland habitat. Later Hall would say that this interlude at Barnham was the most formative of his life, and one which explains why he prefers the country to town. (He always claims not to be happy in London.) There were other perks in the countryside, such as an occasional brace of pheasant from the Duke of Grafton. Grace learned to skin rabbits, and Peter grew used to eating them. There was even, that year, a white Christmas.

Reg Hall never forgot what happened to Charlie when he reached pensionable age. He was then earning 26 shillings a week as a gamekeeper, and assumed that, at the age of sixty-five, this would be boosted by an extra 10 shillings from his pension.

'I remember the payday after he was due for his rise. He came up our drive to the house, his head hung down, and he told me that since he was now getting his pension, the estate office was stopping 10 shillings from his wages,' Reg said. Reg knew whose side he was on, and so did Peter.[15]

Before they left for Barnham, Peter had been put down for Culford School, but that would have meant a five-mile bus journey out of Bury after the nine-mile journey from Barnham to Bury. In various interviews, Hall has said that after the East Anglian kindergarten, 'it was village schools all the way'.[16] But his next school was his father's old school in Bury St Edmunds, the West Suffolk County School. It was not far from the railway station, which made it convenient for Peter to commute. Reg Hall told how he telephoned the headmaster, who wanted to know Peter's age. He was eight; the school did not take boys until they were ten. Reg said that since he was himself an old boy, the headmaster might make an exception. The headmaster asked if the boy was bright. 'All parents think their children are bright,' Reg replied. After a short interview with the boy, the headmaster agreed to admit Peter Hall, who was the youngest child in the school by two years. The daily journey to Bury was a pleasure because of the splendour of that local train – shining leather straps to open and close the window, brass handles and teak were standard on the Great Eastern.

But Reg was in charge at Barnham for no more than nine or ten months: 'We did the Honington job so well that I made myself redundant,' he said.[17] He was promoted to relief stationmaster at the district office in Cambridge. With the job went a semi-detached, bow-fronted house at 15 per cent of his railway wage: number 121 on a quiet street called Blinco Grove on the outskirts of Cambridge. It even had indoor plumbing. In retrospect, Peter Hall could see that the move to Cambridge provided him with opportunities available to no country boy; but at the time, when his father announced the move, he wept for two days and two nights, and it was transformed into one of the dramas of his youth.

For his ninth birthday, in November 1939, Peter Hall was given a black Raleigh bicycle. It was too big, so his father attached wooden blocks to the pedals, and on it he cycled all round Cambridge. The more he saw, the less he liked it. He found it bleak, and windy; even the long, single platform at Cambridge station had no charm for him. He records that he frequently burst into tears: 'A passion not to go on has obsessed me on several occasions of my life. This was the first time it struck, and because I had less inner resource and less to distract me than when I was grown up, it was perhaps the worst time of all. I was very near the brink.'[18] His aunts and uncles worried that his depression might be the result of reading too much, but in fact it seems more likely that it had more to do with the streak of melancholia that Leslie Caron detected in his mother.

War broke out four months after the Halls arrived in Cambridge. Hall remembers that he was sitting on the front doorstep shelling peas when Neville Chamberlain announced that the country was at war with Germany. On moving from Barnham, Hall's parents had looked for a suitable private school, where he could prepare for the entrance and scholarship exams he would take when he was ten. Nothing could be found, so Reg and Grace walked down Blinco Grove to the local state school – a redbrick, single-storey building with an asphalt playground, called the Morley Memorial Junior School – and decided it would do. But Hall was in no mood to enjoy it. He was intimidated by town manners, and found the Morley Memorial much rougher than anything he had experienced before. His Suffolk accent was mocked, and for the first time he became conscious of his father's railwayman's earnings.

Not everything about the school was disagreeable, however: he says he fell in love here for the first time, with a blonde girl called Emma. But his mother did not actively encourage him to bring other children home from school, and he rarely did so. He preferred listening to music on the radio to playing with friends. In the public library not far from Blinco Grove he discovered Charles Dickens and Richmal Crompton's *Just William*. He also began to learn to play the piano properly. He had first had lessons when he was seven, and now he wanted to learn on his own piano with an experienced teacher. His parents heard of an instrument that was being evacuated from London and snapped it up; their next-door neighbour, a Mr Spinks, who had formerly been an organist in Lowestoft, began to give Hall lessons, at sixpence a time. Hall's depression slowly lifted, and by the time he was ten he had begun to enjoy living in wartime Cambridge.

When his parents asked what he would like to do on his tenth birthday, Hall announced that he wanted to go to a concert. Years later he told the psychiatrist Anthony Clare that everything that happened to him from about eight years old divided him from his parents, and a good example of this was the concert he chose for his birthday treat: it was not Gilbert and Sullivan, as sung by his father, but Mozart's Requiem, which was being performed on 22 November 1940 in the King's College Chapel. In the same week his mother also took him to hear *The Marriage of Figaro*, performed in English by the Sadler's Wells company, which had just been evacuated from London.

Grace was absorbed by everything Peter did. When he came home from school, she wanted a debriefing on the lessons he had done and what the teachers had said. He found this irritating and would go straight to his room, saying he had homework to do. Hall told his second wife, Jacky, that he felt he had nothing in common with his mother, and did not like the way she bullied his father. 'He said he had hated his mother since he was eight,' Jacky Hall recalls. Although he could be sharp with her, Grace had no inkling of her son's strength of feeling. Later in life he attributed his persistent determination to provoke, to startle and to challenge to the practice he had as a child in provoking his mother.

It was her fault, he thought, that he was an only child.

> *All she said to me about it was that they decided not to have another because if you can't do it for two properly, you should only have one. I never quite believed that. All mothers always tell their children what they went through, but [in their case] it was always based on economics. I was always terribly jealous of other children who had brothers and sisters. I hated being an only child.*[19]

A cousin called Derek Lawrance remembers how Peter's role in the family differed from his own: 'You couldn't have had a more encouraging couple than Reg and Grace. Anything Peter needed for advancement, he'd get. I thought to myself at the time that, although he was doing very well, it was costing them a lot.'[20] They were always on the lookout for ways of making an extra bob or two. Grace took in a lodger once they had moved into Blinco Grove; and at harvest-time Peter would cycle into the surrounding countryside to find food for the rabbits that they bred to sell in the market.

Reg Hall was a Labour man, but his and Grace's ambitions for

Peter subtly distorted the family's place in the English class system. His working-class parents made sure Peter had all the attributes of a middle-class upbringing: private education, music lessons, a pony, a bicycle, books in the house. Writing in 1966, Peter accepted that, as a ten-year-old, he had already become extremely adept at getting his own way. He was the type categorised by psychologists as 'oral' because it is through the mouth that a baby's earliest needs are met. As a solitary child, he never had to make the adjustments that come naturally to children with brothers and sisters. 'Oral' children tend to be demanding, insensitive to the feelings of others, and greedy.[21]

In a discursive interview in the mid-1960s, Hall suggested that his precocious interest in the arts could be explained by his upbringing.

I was avid for art, hungry for culture. A lot of it was showing off – a fault that I have learnt to disguise a little but not to cure. And some of it was because I was quickly and delightedly aware of the right highbrow thing to do. Yet I believe most of the enthusiasm was because I was a misfit in my school, a misfit in my town, and a misfit in my family. So my love of the arts was partly neurotic: they gave me security. I wanted to pass on my pleasure and organise it.[22]

To achieve that meant getting the best available education, and in Cambridge the young Peter Hall was already acutely conscious of the importance of getting a place in the right school. 'I think the pressure to win the educational rat-race was something I was aware of at eight or nine, and that declassed me progressively from that moment on . . . I'm of that generation that allowed themselves to be declassed . . . We were conditioned and altered by the educational process.'[23]

His school report for July 1940, one year before he was due to sit his county scholarship exam, suggests that his getting into grammar school was not a foregone conclusion. Although he was 'very good' at reading, general English, history and scripture, and a marked improvement was noted in both English and arithmetic, he came only thirteenth in a class of forty-two children – not obvious scholarship material.

In later years, Peter Hall was to describe his childhood as poor and terribly bare. It always seemed to be bitterly cold when he was a boy: 'One was aware of being poor partly because my mother was always telling me that we were.'[24] For many years Hall described himself as a lonely, working-class, scholarship boy who had gone from village school to grammar school. He cast himself as the outsider. In fact, that version of his childhood betrays the legacy of that family of congenital moaners, the Pamments. But this conviction that he was a rejected working-class boy spurred him to win the scholarship that would get him away from the unlovely children at the Morley Memorial School.

2

Public Schooldays
at the Perse

'A pretty, gangling Hamlet'

War broke out, and Peter Hall did gas-mask drill at school, helped his father to black out the windows at home, and dug the allotment. As a university town, Cambridge was allowed to keep its distance from the war. Air raids there were sporadic, although a house near to Blinco Grove was hit. And on the night after the retreat from Dunkirk in 1940, a company of tired and silent soldiers arrived in Blinco Grove; each house took one of them in for a bath and a meal. Aircraft from the aerodromes of East Anglia, like Honington, the new airfield near Barnham, were on the front line in the Battle of Britain in September 1940, and Hall could soon distinguish a Hurricane from a Spitfire. But at the outset the only real privations were food rationing, and the absence of new toys in the shops.

Hall worked hard to get a county scholarship, and in the summer of 1941 he did well enough in the exams to be offered a place in any one of three schools in Cambridge: the County, the Central, and the Perse. When Reg Hall asked a colleague, who had children at both the Perse and the County, which school Peter should choose, the friend replied that since it cost as much for a term at the Perse (£9) as it did for a year at the County, the Perse ought to be the better school. The Hall family decided on the Perse.

The Perse, founded in 1615, was proud of its high standards. The handbook for 1941 gives an impression of old-fashioned confidence in the education the school provided. 'The classrooms are large, well lit and airy, and are so arranged that they are protected from noise and disturbance of any kind.' Discipline was designed to uphold the school's reputation: 'The Headmaster wishes to remind parents and boys that the good name of the school is dependent as much upon the conduct of the boys who wear the cap as upon any other factor.'[1] Boys were required to wear the school cap on the streets of Cambridge in term time, and were expected to be neatly turned out in suits of medium grey, with black and purple ties. School hours were 8.55 a.m. to 3.45 p.m., with the cadet force on Tuesday and games on Thursday; homework was designed to last from one to one and a half hours. As it was wartime, the price of school dinners fell from a shilling to eightpence.

When the headmaster asked Hall what he wanted to be, he replied that he wanted to be an aeronautical engineer. In fact, aged ten, rising eleven, he already fancied himself as a musician – but there was a war on. It is mildly surprising that the headmaster did not ask Hall which Cambridge college he wanted to go to, since that is what the Perse was for: to get bright boys into Cambridge University. Since its foundation, there had been a symbiotic relationship between the school and the university. Its governing body was dominated by dons, who had a personal interest in its educational standards because many of their children were enrolled there. Pupils who were not clever enough for university, or had no desire to go there, were second-class citizens.

There is some disagreement about the exact status of the Perse. Hall always says he was a grammar school boy, but contemporaries of Hall's are sceptical, suspecting that he says so because, by the late 1950s and 1960s, it was modish to have been to a state school.[2] The Perse received money from the County Council in return for taking a number of local boys – like Hall. But it was an established member of the Headmasters' Conference, making it a public rather than a grammar school (to those who care, the Perse is a minor public school). An accurate description of it would, however, have nothing to do with these symptoms of class and cultural confusion. In the 1940s the Perse was a meritocracy in which the cleverest boys rose to the top. 'We knew that his father was a stationmaster, but there was nothing very odd about that. There was a wide social mix, and the Perse wasn't socially conscious. It was intellectually conscious,' says John Polkinghorne, who became, successively, a Professor of Physics, a priest, and President of Queens' College, Cambridge.[3]

The masters did not like boys to lounge about ('Keep your hands out of your pockets, boy'), but the Perse had a liberal reputation (only the headmaster and his deputy were allowed to beat boys), and a tolerant one (there was a boarding-house, called Hillel House, for Jewish boys from Orthodox families, where dietary laws were observed). Naturally, the Perse was for boys only. There was a Perse School for Girls, but its premises were separate.

When Hall arrived in September 1941 he was acutely conscious of his status as a working-class scholarship boy. He took exception to being called a minor scholar – 'so that none of us should forget our non-paying status . . . I burned with resentment'. His scholarship provided him with free tuition and free books – there were extras, like his uniform and games, but his father paid for those without difficulty or complaint – and the books were a second irritant. Stamped with the words 'Minor Scholar', they were old, dog-eared, and written in: 'It made me absolutely furious, because we were much brighter than everyone else,' says Hall.[4]

But while the Pamment genes fuelled his resentment, the Hall genes cloaked the strength of his feelings. The late Mel Calman, the cartoonist, who won a minor scholarship to the Perse a year after Hall and felt no bitterness about it at all, remembered Hall well: 'He was very popular. I should have thought he had an absolutely delightful time at school.'[5]

The younger teachers had been called up by September 1941, so the impact of war on Perse was to increase the average age of the teachers, and narrow the curriculum. Hall had to choose between geography and Latin. But English and history, the two subjects he did best at, were consistently well taught. The report at the end of his first year shows that he got 94 per cent in his English exam, and his form master commented on his commendable keenness. In the fourth form he won the prize for English and history, and the prospect of taking School Certificate in July 1946 was hardly forbidding: he passed in seven subjects. In the string of school reports that were lovingly kept by his mother, his behaviour is criticised on only a couple of occasions. In 1942 his homework book is 'a disgrace', and in 1944 he 'does not always behave if not watched'. The only subject for which his marks were consistently disappointing was French. Despite his good ear and keen intelligence, it was clear from the beginning that he had no gift for languages. He was never better than 'quite good' at physical training ('He seems to have no energy to spare'), or at games, until he took up tennis. By the time he reached the fifth form, aged fifteen – seven months younger than the average for his class – he was scoring straight A's in English and history, and his teachers regarded his work as 'very satisfactory'.

But Hall first made his mark at the Perse as an impresario. He was only eleven when he organised a band among the boys in the second form. As a gifted pianist, he was a skilful enough musician to be able to arrange the instrumental parts of tunes like Glenn Miller's 'In the Mood' for his violinist, cornet player and drummer. When the band was ready, Hall asked his father to sound out the secretary of the local Conservative Club about the hire of the hall (it would cost nothing), and then to discover from the Red Cross whether he could use its name to publicise the concert in return for a share of the profits (he could). There was a good house at the performance, and, besides organising the programme and arranging the supporting acts, Hall displayed admirable sang-froid by ad-libbing while the band was removing its black make-up during the change from Nigger Minstrel Players to Perse Boys' Band. Grace Hall took the ticket money at the door, and £12 was raised for the Red Cross. The boys' names appeared in the local paper, and when the butcher met Grace in the bank the following day he told her that her boy would go a long way.[6] Hall himself says he discovered then how much he liked organising people.

In his early teens, Hall displayed exceptional, almost prodigious, musical flair. He practised the piano in the dining-room with his mother listening while she sewed or knitted. Within a year or so of beginning his piano lessons, his teacher from next door, Mr Spinks of Lowestoft, asked Reg Hall if Peter could learn the violin as well. Reg replied that there was a limit to what the family budget could stand, but Mr Spinks said he already had a small violin. Next, having already learned to play the piccolo, Hall decided he wanted a flute, and saved up for a second-hand instrument. When he wanted a clarinet, he saved £8: the one he wanted cost £12, but the family budget stood the difference. It often did. The only instrument Hall learned without actually owning one was the organ.

Hall's parents regarded his music as a way of expressing his talent. For them it was a means to an end. To the adolescent Hall, it seemed to be much more than that: it might eventually provide him with an occupation. When he thought to himself that he would much rather be a conductor or concert pianist than an aeronautical engineer, this was not a total fantasy. The rest of the family, who visited the Halls at Blinco Grove and heard him play, also thought he might eventually become a concert pianist. The idea was attractive enough to Hall for his parents to warn him that music was too precarious a business to provide him with a living.

Aged thirty-eight at the beginning of the war, Reg Hall was too old to join the services. Stationmasters were working in a reserved occupation anyway, and were not available for conscription. Reg joined the Home Guard instead, and continued to work as a relief stationmaster. Twice when he was in charge of Newmarket station a bomb destroyed the signal box. He was temporarily stationmaster in his home town, but the greatest turmoil of the war years was caused by his successful application for a substantial promotion. The job was relief stationmaster at a busy London terminal, King's Cross, and it paid £270 a year. In the Hall and Pamment families, a weekly wage of £6 was the definition of having it made; so Reg – at £5 4s. a week – had very nearly made it. However, he soon discovered that the money was earned at the cost of intolerable disruption to family life. Leaving home in Cambridge on Monday at 6.30 a.m., he never knew when he would get back. If it was the same day, it was rarely before 11 p.m. London was bombed constantly and the dreaded doodlebugs (the V1 rocket bombs) were becoming common. 'Well, it began to tell on everybody,' he recalled in 1987.[7]

In 1944 a vacancy occurred for a stationmaster at Shelford, a village four miles south of Cambridge on the main line to London. It was the kind of job Reg had always had his eye on. He would be the man in charge; the station was close enough to Cambridge for Peter to be able to commute to school each day; and the family would be together. The problem was the wage – because it was graded below his King's Cross post, Reg would have to take a pay cut. But, despite having earlier criticised Reg's lack of ambition, Grace did not mind that: 'We'd eat bread and cheese as long as we were together.' A number of applicants were attracted by the calm of Shelford and some were senior to Reg, but he got the job and the family settled in comfortably. Peter had his own room and a growing sense of independence. Grace remembered that when his young friends would shout to him to see if he wanted to come out, he would ask them what they were going to do. If it did not appeal, he would say he was busy.

He extended his repertoire of musical instruments by starting to pump the church organ at Stapleford, a short distance from Shelford, and then by learning to play it. Although he and Grace always said prayers before bedtime when he was small, church had not played a part in the Halls' life after Reg stopped singing in the choir at St Mary's. Hall wrote that, as a child, his vision of God was the portrait of the energetic, smiling young countrywoman who advertised Ovaltine; but at St Andrew's, Stapleford, he did not just play the organ. Although he may have remained more interested in the sound of music than the word of God, in January 1946, aged fifteen, he was confirmed.

While many of the residents of Shelford took the train each day to Cambridge, it was still a detached village with a life of its own. Reg Hall became vice-chairman of the parish council and of the Horticultural and Allotment Society. He grew vegetables by the signal box; Rhode Island Reds laid eggs in the goods shed, and he kept three pigs, named Faith, Hope and Charity. Reg enjoyed the sense of his importance: 'The vicar, the doctor and the stationmaster were the three most important people in the village,' he said. But he voted Labour in 1945 and was a fervent advocate of the nationalisation of the railways; even as a stationmaster, he thought of himself more as working class than managerial class.

In subsequent years, the area manager of British Railways would observe that he never saw applications for promotion from Reg. 'I told him that we only had one son,' Reg said after Peter had gone to university, 'and we'd decided to give him the best education we could. There were only two of us. We'd put up with any inconvenience. My boss said that was admirable, but not to let it ruin my career.' The move to Shelford served its purpose as far as Peter's upbringing was concerned: the station proved to be a stable home for the next eight years, beginning with his final impressionable time at the Perse.

Hall believes that education is a lottery: whether you win or lose depends on whether you meet one or two good teachers. He was in luck, and the best of it was that his good teachers were all interested in the theatre. Already there was a strong theatrical tradition at the Perse. The school handbook emphasised the special attention that was paid in English lessons in the lower forms to speaking, lecturing and acting: 'It is found that in this way boys do not become so self-conscious and acquire much accuracy and clearness in expression.' Hall soon discovered a musty room called the Mummery with a little stage and curtains that jammed: 'It smelt like a deserted house.' This was where a legendary teacher at the Perse named Caldwell Cook had once encouraged boys to act and to make speeches. Hall remembers: 'I was bored in the class by Shakespeare, for we sat imprisoned by footnotes while the master intoned his way through the leading part. But I can't forget the excitement of shouting *Macbeth* at each other, clad in purple cloaks and waving wooden swords. I recognised something that made me completely sure and happy.'[8] He had a shrewd idea by the time he was fourteen of what he wanted to do when he grew up, and it was no longer a musical career. He was prudent enough to keep it to himself.

In 1944 he began to make regular visits to the theatre in London. In some respects, Hall was privileged in his teens: he travelled on the railways either free or for a quarter of the fare. Hall claims, facetiously, that this railwayman's fringe benefit dictated the course of his life: 'Without those travel facilities, I would not have found my profession.' He had one more advantage over many other Cambridge boys: one of his aunts – Mahalia, an elder sister of his father's – lived in Lewisham, and would put him up when he wanted to stay for two or three days in London.

It was a wonderful year to fall in love with the theatre. On 31 August 1944 the Old Vic company opened its momentous season at the New Theatre. Ralph Richardson played Peer Gynt with Laurence Olivier as the Button-maker. In the middle of September, Olivier's Richard III was so brilliant that John Gielgud presented Olivier with the sword, given to him by his mother, that had been used by Edmund Kean in his own performance of Richard III. Richardson was his Richmond, and they played together again in *Uncle Vanya* during the winter. Later they were to do *Henry IV, Part One*, with Richardson as Falstaff and Olivier as Hotspur. The two great men would hold the curtain for each other at the end of each performance, and whoever was playing the lead would make the curtain speech that night: 'The sheer excitement of their work, with Richardson's Peer and Olivier's Richard, the uniformly high quality of the ensemble playing – all heralded a new golden age of the English theatre.'9 Another augury of the golden age was to be seen at the Haymarket Theatre, where John Gielgud had assembled a company to play the classics in repertory. Hall took the train from Shelford to see Gielgud's Hamlet (it was Hall's second and Gielgud's fourth); Peggy Ashcroft had agreed to play Ophelia so that she might perform the Duchess of Malfi later in the season. She made a vivid impression on Hall: 'What was striking was the way her English containment and decency contrasted with a wild passion. That has always been the extraordinary thing about her as an actress.'10

The other intense adolescent experience in the theatre happened in the summer holiday of 1946 when Hall cycled from Shelford to Stratford-upon-Avon. He pitched his tent across the river from the Memorial Theatre and queued for standing seats. In 1946 Sir Barry Jackson, the celebrated director of the Birmingham Rep and the Malvern Festival, had become artistic director, and had been bold enough to ask a promising young director to work in Stratford. What Hall saw in 1946 was Peter Brook's famous production of *Love's Labour's Lost*. 'It was played fast . . . it had a delight in artifice as great as that of any of the characters, and it was *funny*, belying the play's reputation for difficult-to-comprehend jokes. The whole affair, wrote *The Times*, had a "puff-ball lightness".'11 The fifteen-year-old Hall confessed that he was actually jealous of Brook, who was all of twenty-one; later he declared that it was on this visit to Stratford that he decided he wanted to run the Shakespeare Memorial Theatre.

His love of the theatre was reinforced at the Perse, where the three teachers who shared his enthusiasm had the expertise to cultivate Hall's passion. The most influential member of this trio was a young man called Douglas Brown. He had been educated at the Perse before going to St Catharine's College, Cambridge where he took a remarkably good degree in English (a double-starred first-class; there is none better). Brown eventually taught at Reading and York universities and could have become a fellow at a college in Cambridge as soon as he graduated. Instead he decided that he could be more useful as a teacher at his old school. His friend, the poet and critic Donald Davie, describes Brown as 'brilliantly scholarly, devoutly low-church Anglican, ascetic, chaste and pacifist'.12 Brown was a slight man with dark hair, and spectacles; he was religious, musical and conscientious.

The first thing he did at the Perse was to restore and redecorate Caldwell Cook's Mummery. One of the boys who volunteered for this task in the summer of 1947 was Peter Hall, who had completed School Certificate and then was in the modern lower sixth. Brown's benevolent influence on Hall was to last for the next seven years.

Cecil Crouch was the second of these influential teachers. He had been at the Slade School and taught art, but was also a good enough pianist to have performed in public; he was a pleasant man who became a real friend of Hall's, says Polkinghorne. Crouch was Hall's form-master during the war, and years afterwards Leslie Caron said that she thought Crouch and John Tanfield, his history master, were both people whom Hall thought of as father-substitutes. Crouch himself said later in life that if he had had a son he would have liked to have had Hall because, as a child, 'he gave so much back'. Tanfield recalls that Crouch had friends in unusual places, like the ballet and the circus: 'He was lively, entertaining and temperamental.'[13] Crouch cast Hall as Petruchio in the Perse Players' production of *The Taming of the Shrew*, which was performed in February 1948. The *Cambridge Daily News* critic, who thought it the best production he had seen at the Perse in twenty-five years, singled out Hall's performance for its vigour, authority and swagger: 'unusually good for a youth'.

Although he was now teaching history, John Tanfield, the third of the trio of influential teachers, had actually worked in the theatre: after graduating from Cambridge, where he was president of the Marlowe Society, Tanfield had worked in repertory. The theatre was no idle matter at the Perse; boys had to audition, even for walk-on parts like the Third Player in *Hamlet* (Mel Calman's début role). All the parts were played by boys, and the teacher's wives made the costumes. Hall's Petruchio was also praised by a fellow member of the cast, the author and playwright Stanley Price, although not without qualification: 'He didn't have a light touch.'[14] But the performance gave Hall's mentors the confidence to cast him as Hamlet in the following year's school play. John Tanfield was to direct *Hamlet*, and, after a career spent directing schoolboys, he said: 'Hall was one of the few boys I've known who I'd trust with the part. It's not in the range of most adolescents.'

At the Perse, the text of Shakespeare was not tampered with lightly. Hall was taught by people who were familiar with the work of William Poel and the Shakespearian revival at the turn of the century, when the bowdlerisations of generations of English actors were expelled from acting editions. Scholars like W.J. Lawrence, in extensive pre-Restoration stage studies, were describing how Shakespeare might have played Hamlet. Harley Granville-Barker's prefaces to Shakespeare were textbooks for directors who wished to scrape away the layers of custom and practice in the acting profession that obscured much of Shakespeare's own work from the audience. 'Hall grew up in the Poel/Granville-Barker tradition,' said Tanfield. There were a few cuts in the Perse Players' *Hamlet*, but, according to Douglas Brown, 'We lost nothing but a certain wealth of reference in the verse.'[15]

Tanfield imposed no directorial interpretation on *Hamlet*, and concentrated on drawing performances out of his schoolboy actors. Forty years on he could recall Hall's attitude: 'For a schoolboy in particular, he took a curiously professional approach, realising what the problems were and reacting with an instinctive understanding of the theatrical solution. He was nice to work with, always willing to accept suggestions, not in any sense a prima donna.'

Mel Calman, who kept a diary, captured the excitement of a school play:

> The stage had been erected right across the far end of the brick and panelled hall. Across the linen proscenium the school arms and motto were pinned. A cleaner was giving a final rub to the chairs the headmaster and the governors were to reside in. The art master [Cecil Crouch], music master, and history master [John Tanfield] were furiously making people up. The air smelt heavily of greasepaint and tan lotion and powder. I quickly changed myself, put on the No 5 and No 4 and queued up to have my eyes mascara'd. There was an atmosphere of genial panic everywhere. I felt ever so slightly sick.
>
> The producer as he feverishly worked was reminiscing in an expansive mood. He had for a time been a rep producer in Birmingham and he chatted of theatrical first night superstitions. A boy began to whistle and was curtly silenced. The headmaster himself, a short, fat complacent man, came in to wish us all the best of luck. Our call boy ran round collecting the first-scene actors. You could feel the tension. As soon as the play started, it would be all right, but until the first words were spoken and it was under way, it was unbearable. Faintly we could hear the opening gramophone music, and the play had begun.[16]

In the school magazine, the *Pelican*, Douglas Brown, reviewing

Hall's Hamlet, called it 'remarkable'. The local Cambridge news-paper, the *Daily News*, wrote: 'Eighteen-year-old P.R.F. Hall made an extremely good attempt at the part.' Under the headline A DIGNIFIED HAMLET, an anonymous reviewer in *The Times Educational Supplement* wrote: 'Hamlet himself occasionally seemed a little more flexible in movement than mood, but gave his performance consistently, gracefully and with feeling.'[17] Even the magazine of the British Drama League, *Drama*, referred to Hall's part in the Perse Players' *Hamlet* in its Summer 1949 issue: 'A remarkable performance of Hamlet was given by an eighteen-year-old boy.'

Word of mouth about the performance reached some under-graduates at Cambridge, and Julian Slade, the young composer, took time out to see this schoolboy Hamlet. Simon Raven mentioned Hall's 'pretty, gangling Hamlet' in his autobiography written thirty years later.[18] But what Hall remembered, because it seemed to please him most, was that the Provost of King's College, J.T. Sheppard, went backstage to congratulate him. As for Grace Hall, she went to all five performances. Both his parents were immensely proud. This was the first time that Reg was really surprised by Peter's talent.

In his school report, the headmaster wrote that he believed Hall had enough common sense not to let his great success go to his head. He need not have worried. Hall was single-minded about the theatre to the point of being self-important, and later he judged his performance by higher standards than those of any of the reviewers: 'I was giving a lecture on the part; I wasn't *being* it. I don't believe I could ever act.'

Hall was free to do *Hamlet* in his last year instead of concentrating on exams because he had already been awarded a university place. Later in his life Hall claimed that as a schoolboy he had his own agenda for his future, part plan and part instinct. John Tanfield remembers Hall talking about having a career in the theatre when he was at the Perse. 'Very naturally, I discouraged it,' he said. Reg Hall hoped Peter would succeed where he had failed, and become a teacher. Peter appeased his parents and teachers by saying that he would go to London University and take a commerce degree. Because he had chosen not to study Latin at school, one of the attractions of this university was that, unlike Cambridge, Latin was not an entry requirement. But, before long, he had changed his mind and was taking private tuition in Latin. The attraction of Cambridge had proved too strong.

Hall's sixth-form reports contain regular references to his breadth of reading, maturity and depth of understanding, and his teachers decided to try him out for a university scholarship early. Douglas Brown was a graduate of St Catharine's College, which held its scholarship exams in February and March, unlike most colleges, where they were held in November and December, and he and his cronies in the common room decided to put Hall in for that exam early in 1948. 'It was to get me limbered up,' Hall says.[19] At St Catharine's he wrote papers on literature and Shakespeare, before being interviewed by a prominent don named Tom Henn, who asked Hall to give some of Petruchio. The recitation evidently pleased him because a telegram arrived at Shelford shortly afterward to announce that Hall had won a scholarship. Brown and his colleagues then debated whether Hall should accept the offer, or try for a more prestigious college, like King's, at the end of the year. Hall settled it: he would accept St Catharine's, and give his schoolboy Hamlet.

But there was much more to his final year than that. First there was the Headmaster's Prize for Orations. The winner was required to learn and deliver a substantial speech from the classical repertory. Hall's winning performance was Jaques' speech about the seven ages of man from *As You Like It* ('All the world's a stage, / And all the men and women merely players . . .') The list of Hall's achievements in the school magazine the *Pelican* for July 1949 shows that Orations was only the icing on the cake: besides editing the *Pelican*, Hall was honorary secretary of the Games Committee, honorary chronicler of the Perse Players, president of the Literary Society, captain of East House, and sergeant in the RAF section of the School Corps. A friend who worked with Hall in Stratford once commented on Hall's need to assert his strength in all departments at all times. This trait would have surprised no one who had been with him at the Perse.[20]

There was only one serious omission from this list: he had never won a place in any of the school's sports teams, and never seemed likely to. He couldn't run fast or play rugby with the required violence. The poor performances of Hall's East House in school sports were a running joke. As house captain, he began his term report in the *Pelican* with a quotation from Garrick – 'Prologues precede the piece – in mournful verse; / As undertakers walk before the hearse' – and continued: 'Garrick supplies us with a prologue; now follows the hearse. We were fourth in the Hockey House

Matches, the Boxing Competitions, and the Senior Cross Country Races.' (There were five houses.) In fact, sport played no part in his life. It was not that he rejected the spirit of competition; Hall just did not like team games. The sole exception was tennis, and in 1948 he made the Perse School tennis team. The team comprised three pairs, and the competition to win a place on the third pair was not fierce. 'He scraped into the third pair as a result of sheer application and dogged consistency,' says Stanley Price. The team photograph shows a tall boy in the second row with thick dark hair combed back from his forehead, neatly turned out in white.

Adding a sporting colour to his c.v. made Hall the ideal candidate for head boy. Former head boys pop up regularly in establishment positions such as governor of the Bank of England or editor of *The Times*, and they are an interesting English phenomenon. Having first accepted the merit of authority in others, they become youthful figures of authority themselves. They are not outsiders by behaviour, nor true radicals by nature. Head boys like and are liked by adults; they are level-headed, charming, and willing to take responsibility, though they are only really successful if the charm works on the younger boys as well. They exhibit precocious powers of leadership; indeed, a wish to become a head boy is one of the most reliable indicators of an ambitious nature. Of course Peter Hall became head boy at the Perse, and, as John Barton, who was to become a close friend of his at Cambridge, observes, 'Head boys direct.'[21]

Becoming accustomed to public speaking is another of the skills a head boy develops while at school. In Hall's case he had demonstrated an instinctive skill for this even before he was a teenager. According to his father, the first time Grace grasped exactly how accomplished her son had become was when she heard Peter make an extempore speech at a dance at which the boys from the Perse were allowed to mingle with girls from the Perse Girls' School, from whom they were normally segregated. Grace told Reg of a conversation she had had with the kitchen staff: 'The cook had said: "Listen to him. He's the best one we've ever had." I could not believe it was my son talking.'

As head boy, Hall was expected to speak at the Old Persean Society dinner, and his skill is evident in the notes he made:

Well wishers advice for little speech.
1. Doesn't matter what you say – after dinner.

2. *Quote Lewis Carroll.*
   So preparation sketchy. But does matter what one says – different angle.
   With feeling of inadequacy, many thanks to Society for all kindnesses
   to school.
   And now for Lewis Carroll, and the perfect advice to all speakers: 'Begin
   at the beginning,' the King said gravely, 'and go on till you come to the end:
   THEN STOP'.[22]

Hall claimed he made no friends at school, but this did not include his teachers. He continued to meet them while he was an undergraduate. He had also discovered the difference between the sexes. As head boy, he took out the head girl of the Perse Girls' School, the biology master's daughter; but he seemed to prefer the racier girls at the County School. Stanley Price recalls feeling envious when Hall started to go out with a glamorous, well-developed girl called Elizabeth King; Price thought this the mark of a real man.

Price also observed Hall's attitude towards the homosexual schoolboys who belonged to the Perse Players. Since Hall's charm was indiscriminate, they trusted him. 'That's a plus in the theatre: to be a heterosexual who has the gift of getting on with homosexuals. It's a trick Hall was born with,' Price said. When he was older and more experienced, Hall realised that two of his favourite teachers, Cecil Crouch and Douglas Brown, were probably homosexual. Brown lived with his parents, and was a keen Boy Scout; when he thought about it many years later, Hall assumed that Brown had preferred to stay in the closet. ('He's not a ladies' man,' his mother used to say.) The passion that drove Brown was broadening the culture of the boys he liked.

On Friday evenings Brown would invite a few boys to his parents' house in Sedley Tayor Road for a 'feast of exotic culture'.[23] The boys were fed cocoa and biscuits in his study, which was candlelit on dark nights. Then he would read or play music from his extensive collection of 78 r.p.m. records. Hall first heard the music of Benjamin Britten, Michael Tippett and William Walton at Brown's house. He would read from authors like Dostoevsky and Tolstoy, who were not to be found on the curriculum for School Certificate, and make pronouncements that lingered in the memories of boys who heard them: 'One really ought to set aside a week-end a year to read Keats's letters from start to finish.' In his last year, Hall was a privileged member at the centre of Brown's circle, free to issue invitations to younger boys like Mel Calman.

Calman recalls the skin tightening on the back of his neck when he first heard Sibelius's *Finlandia*. 'Brown communicated the notion that education was not just facts,' Calman said.

The books Hall read in his last two years at school – most memorably those of Shaw, H.G. Wells and Samuel Butler – were full of reason, and rapidly eroded his faith. By the time he left the Perse, he was an agnostic. He might have needed reassurance, but he did not seek it either from God or his parents. He thoroughly enjoyed his last two years at school, but this did not counter his introspective, somewhat morbid streak of self-analysis. Recalling the end of his schooldays in 1966 he wrote: 'I still felt I might be found out for the fraud I was: not an empire-builder but a low class interloper.'[24]

Peter Hall may not have been the stuff of which earlier generations of public school head boys were made. A career in India, the Civil Service, or the armed forces would not have crossed his mind. But he was the very model of a modern young man: interested in the arts rather than the empire; capable of seizing the educational opportunities that would, if he so chose, make him classless. He was fluent, charming, and intelligent; he showed qualities of leadership; he was not ashamed of his feelings; he liked girls. It seems almost too good to be true.

That is not how he chose to see himself. In his autobiography, Hall emphasised his mother's East Anglian puritanism, and his father's simple origins ('He always remained a peasant, despite his reasonable education').[25] But while he might plausibly be described as an empire-builder, his self-portrait as a fraudulent low-class interloper is melodrama.

3

Sergeant Instructor
(Acting)

'A very mature eighteen-year-old'

It is instructive to discover what sticks in the memory. Having won all the prizes at school, Peter Hall left the Perse in March 1949 after only two terms of his final year so that he could get national service over as quickly as possible. His basic training for the RAF was done at West Kirby, near Liverpool and the moment he got leave, Hall made for the Liverpool Playhouse. During those weeks in West Kirby in April and May 1949, Hall can remember exactly what plays he saw (*Uncle Vanya*, *The Magistrate* and *The Tempest*) and rattle off the names of the casts (Cyril Luckham, Gladys Boot and Michael Aldridge). When he was transferred to RAF Wellesbourne on the outskirts of Stratford, he would catch the bus that left the base at 6.30 p.m. on most nights and arrive in town at 7.10 p.m., in time to buy a standing ticket for the Shakespeare Memorial Theatre. He reels off the names and plays in the repertory he had seen in three Stratford summers: 'Paul Scofield and Robert Helpmann alternating Hamlet, with Tony Quayle as Claudius; Diana Wynyard as Gertrude. There was *King John*, *The Merchant of Venice*, *The Winter's Tale*, *Pericles*, and *Cymbeline* for the first time.'

Theatre was an escape. Having had no experience of the survival courses provided for boarders at public school, Hall had exchanged the cosseting of home and the respect of school for the foul-mouthed intolerance and casual cruelty of basic training. He had never been north before, the food was awful, the discipline was harsh and no one read a book. He felt like a country boy, though that was not the impression he gave: 'They thought I was an intellectual and a snob.'[1] Since there was not enough time for the charm to work, and since he lacked the instant popular touch that might have endeared him to the other recruits, he never made friends with whom to share the misery. His father had begun to ask him to join him for a pint in Shelford, but Hall did not enjoy the *bonhomie* of the pub, and the RAF was not going to change that. Quite the reverse.

On paper, Hall ought to have been a candidate for officer training. Besides everything else, he had been the sergeant in the RAF section of the school cadet corps and had a Certificate of Proficiency. But he was not considered officer material. Because he had a Cambridge scholarship, he was sent to the Education Branch of the RAF instead, and that meant promotion to the senior non-commissioned rank of Sergeant Instructor (Acting).

To be taught to teach, he was transferred to the RAF Education School at Wellesbourne Mountford in Warwickshire, where he learned that he was unlikely to do much teaching. The likelihood was that he would occupy a comfortable billet as the education sergeant at an air base, looking after the library and the newspapers, organising a few current-affairs sessions, and playing some improving records; perhaps arranging a play-reading. He was looking forward to reading from lists given to him by Douglas Brown. The more he could read in the RAF, the more time he would have for the theatre when he got to Cambridge. Waiting in transit camp to be posted, he consumed *War and Peace*, and when the posting came, he was lucky that it was Germany – closer to home than the Far East.

He made a small drama of his arrival in Germany by feeling sick with apprehension as his train crossed into enemy territory.[2] He was posted first to the headquarters of the RAF Education Branch at Bückeberg not far from Hanover, and his immediate future was determined by an officer who taught economics and business management, and who had got a German girl pregnant. Despite his B.Sc. (Econ.) from the London School of Economics, this officer was transferred forthwith. Since Hall had studied economics in the sixth form, the Squadron Leader announced that he would take over the economics and business course. Hall pointed out that economics had been a subsidiary subject, but it did not matter; there was no one else. The advantage of spending the rest of his National Service at Bückeberg was the interesting company he found among the teachers. The drawback was the sergeants' mess at night.

Hall, who turned nineteen that winter, was twenty years younger than the next youngest sergeant. His new colleagues were skilled technicians, toughened by war and coarsened by service life. Promotion had been hard, and they did not welcome a keen, baby-faced boy just out of school. Their revenge suggests a shrewd appreciation of what would make Hall most miserable. He was appointed mess barman. One of his fellow teachers at Bückeberg says: 'He didn't whine about it, but one was aware that he was having a fairly rough time in the mess.'[3] By his own account, the sergeants were a bunch of alcoholics whose conversation was bigoted and reactionary: 'To me, it was a grotesque version of the English pub.' To judge by their reactions to him, Hall's mask must have slipped in the mess. He recalls his room-mate returning drunk one night and, while pissing in Hall's boots, muttering, 'Who does this young fucker think he is? . . . Pretending he knows better than us.'

But he was well fed, and for the first time he was warm in winter. At Christmas he was taken care of by his Uncle Ted and Aunty Elsie not far away from Bückeberg at Dettmold where Ted Hall, Reg's youngest brother, who had become a policeman in 1929, was an officer in the Military Police. Hall shared an office with a young graduate called Kenneth Ewing, who also shared his passion for the theatre. (Ewing became a literary agent, specialising in plays.) When Ewing returned to England, his place was taken by another graduate who had just come down from Cambridge: David Isitt, who shared Hall's love of music. Shortly after his arrival the Education Branch moved into the servants' quarters of the Schloss Bückeberg, a princely residence dating from medieval times, which, since her governess had lived there, had provided Queen Victoria with a carp from its moat each Christmas. In the splendid servants' quarters there were big sitting-rooms and two grand pianos, a Bechstein and an Erard. 'Hall was quite a good pianist, better than me, but, as the superior officer, I got the Bechstein,' says Isitt. Their repertoire included Mozart's sonata for two pianos, for which Hall had bought the music. The population of the pretty little town was normally about 5,000, but in 1949 that was swollen by 15,000 or so refugees. One of them, named Seufert, had been a colleague of the composer Paul Hindemith, and Hall took lessons from him.

There was theatre, too, at RAF headquarters nearby. Hall signed on for the amateur dramatic society straight away, and was cast as Robert Browning in *The Barretts of Wimpole Street*. He made no secret of his ambition to be a director, and Isitt agreed to write the music for a proposed production of *The Man with the Load of Mischief*. An early demobilisation aborted that plan.

Because he never learned German (local Germans wanted to speak English to improve their chances of getting jobs on the base), Hall spent more time at the opera than the theatre. Hanover was not far away and he saw *Tristan und Isolde* there; he travelled to Oberammergau to see the Passion Play, and to Hamburg to see the work of the great German director, Gustav Gründgens. According to regulations, officers and non-commissioned officers were not permitted to fraternise off-duty, but Hall and Isitt stole off together to see a German production of *Albert Herring*, and Mozart's *Die Entführung aus dem Serail*. They went gliding together, too; it was the only flying they managed in the RAF.

Isitt was left with a strong impression of Hall: 'He was still physically gauche; hadn't quite grown into himself. He talked quite a bit about the Perse, but not about Suffolk or his parents (there wasn't much Suffolk accent) . . . a little *déclassé* . . . coped remarkably with people of different ages . . . enormous self-possession; a very mature eighteen-year-old.' Isitt kept a photograph he had taken of Hall in Germany. He is tall, slim, with thick black hair combed back from his forehead. His cheeks are still plump, and for the first time he is not giving his obliging smile.

Everyone leaving the RAF was entitled to be taught courses in any subject, from bricklaying to astronomy or economics, the object being to ease their re-entry into civilian life. Some already had economics degrees. Sergeant Instructor Hall fobbed these graduates off with reading lists and the odd seminar. The hard work was the lectures, he says, but a crash course in Keynesianism enabled him to stay one lesson ahead. He learned about handling groups, kindling enthusiasm, and retaining attention. Before he finished, he thought he had become quite good at it.

Until he was given a room of his own and relieved of his barman's duties, Hall hated the sergeants' mess, and could detect no virtues at all in the RAF. He believed it was beset by idleness and pomposity and obsessed with detail and precedent. When North Korea invaded the South in June 1950, national service was increased from eighteen months to two years, and Hall feared he would be stuck in Germany. Then the War Office announced that anyone who had a university place that autumn would be demobbed immediately. He served just seventeen months.

The real legacy of his interlude in Germany was the taking root of his belief in state subsidy for the arts. The economic privation of post-war Germany, he saw, had not prevented governments from being patrons of the arts, and it lent conviction to a new English model that had been outlined by a theatre director, Norman Marshall, in a book published in 1947 called *The Other Theatre*.[4] Hall eagerly read the book's attack on the intellectual poverty of the West End, its failure to fund new plays, and its passive tolerance of state censorship. Marshall admired alternative theatres from the 1930s like the Festival Theatre in Cambridge and the Maddermarket in Norwich, as well as Anmer Hall's seasons at the Westminster Theatre, the club theatres and the Sunday Societies' play readings. 'It was a state of affairs which existed in no other country,' wrote Marshall.

> *In Paris, in pre-Nazi Berlin, in Prague, in Vienna they had no need of theatre clubs and play-producing societies. There the ordinary commercial theatre was adventurous and contemporary in the best sense of the word. The reasonably intelligent playgoer and the more enterprising actors and producers found no need for their own organisations in self-defence against the standards of commercialisation . . . The theatre in 1946 is even more unhealthy than in 1919.*

The solution was subsidy:

> *The subsidised theatre, relieved of the . . . necessity for showing large profits, can take greater risks than it is reasonable to expect a profit-making organisation to undertake, and by producing the works of dramatists which seem risky propositions to the commercial manager, the subsidised theatre will increase the number of plays which the commercial managers require to keep their theatres open.*

Like Marshall, Hall believed this must mean government-subsidised theatres in each major city in Britain. In London, there would be a National Theatre.

Post-war Britain was a curate's egg, but the good parts were bold and new. Listeners to the BBC's Third Programme were becoming a significant lobby for the arts, and the audience for fresher and more imaginative theatre than the West End provided was growing. A National Theatre, fed by a network of provincial repertory companies, was not near the top of the political agenda, but it was not pure fantasy either. Hall could reasonably hope to see a National Theatre in his lifetime, and at Cambridge he intended to obtain the necessary qualifications for running it, or a company that was something like it. There was only one problem, and she was called Jill.

Jill was a secretary in the Women's Royal Air Force (WRAF), presumably at RAF headquarters and she belonged to the Amateur Dramatic Society there. She and Hall had acted together in an historical romance called *The Rose without a Thorn*. She is, however, a figure in his life that has been sketched in very lightly indeed. Hall's memory of that time is photographic only for the theatre. When asked the surname of the woman to whom he was engaged for a year or so and with whom he lost his virginity, he confessed he could not remember: he thought it was Mortimer. Nor is it any use asking his friends about her. David Isitt, his piano-playing partner with whom he shared an office and travelled widely at that time, did not know that Hall had been engaged until he read it in Hall's autobiography. Michael Birkett, who became a close Cambridge friend a year after Hall's return to England, did not know he had been engaged.[5] Hall never took Jill to meet his Aunty Elsie in Dettmold; she heard about the engagement from Reg and Grace. His first great romance was a very private affair.

Hall describes her as porcelain-faced, and shy. He says they spent much of the summer of 1950 together, boating, swimming and visiting the Harz mountains. Hall resists the idea that they became engaged so they could make love: 'It was all frightfully serious. It was months before we went to bed together . . . after I'd left the RAF.'

Hall attributes the loss of his virginity to the family Austin 7, known as the Dilly. It had been bought either by him (his account) or by the family (his mother's version), for either £40 (Hall's memory) or £80 (Grace's). But whoever bought it, Hall had the use of a car when that was still rare, and he used it to drive with Jill to North Wales. The affair was consummated in Leamington Spa.

By his account, Jill (which seems to have been short for Gillian) deeply influenced the mood of his first year at Cambridge, but once he had left Germany their meetings must have been infrequent. When they met again, she was about to become an officer: 'She was very high-powered.' He says she was commissioned during the summer of 1951, and the Air Force List shows that 2810758 Mortimer, G. was promoted to the rank of pilot officer in the Secretarial Branch on 5 July 1951.[6] Hall says they met whenever they could during a 'spring and summer of cramped cars, cold tents and rain-soaked trees'. Since she must have on leave from Germany, these damp couplings must have been fairly few. His travels in Europe that summer were to France and Italy, not to Germany, and were made in the company of a university friend named Tom Burgner, not Jill Mortimer.

Not long afterwards, Jill moved out of his life and out of the range of biographers. The RAF Personnel Management Centre at RAF Insworth in Gloucestershire has mislaid her record card. Hall did hear from her once more: she wrote to him around 1958 to say she was pleased he was doing well, and that she herself was married with two children. But she has a part to play in his story. It was Jill who set up the dramatic conflict Hall wrestled with in his first year as a Cambridge undergraduate.

4

A Cambridge Apprenticeship

'Good practice for the future'

When Peter Hall arrived at Cambridge University to study for an English degree in October 1950, one of his first duties was to take his food rationing book to the bursar at St Catharine's. But apart from this, Cambridge had not changed much in a hundred years. John Vaizey described the university then as being like a dilapidated country house: the undergraduates were treated like young gentlemen, and their rooms were cleaned by college servants.[1] Well-educated grammar school boys, products of a state education improved by R.A. Butler's Education Act of 1944, were jostling for places at Cambridge, but the majority of undergraduates were public school boys. Women were still comparatively few, and did not share all the men's privileges. In Hall's second year, the Cambridge Union voted by 148 to 85 to continue to exclude women from membership. Considering the prevailing attitude of misogyny, the remarkable thing was not that the motion was lost but the size of the 'no' vote.

The romantic view of Cambridge was perfectly expressed by one of the dons who influenced Hall most. George Rylands, known as Dadie, was at King's College, and in his autobiography Simon Raven, who was an undergraduate at King's in the late 1940s,

writes about Rylands as though he were a character in one of his
novels. Raven's Rylands believes:

> It [is] recognised that it is better to give a place to an amusing or beautiful
> boy who will only get a third class degree (or may perhaps even fail) than
> to give it to some boring swot who might manage a second with the wind
> behind him. There will be diversity, and a certain amount of wealth. Wide
> interests will be encouraged as much as specialised studies; there will be
> tolerance and civility; in a word, there will be civilisation.[2]

But these were precarious times, and Rylands went on to describe
to Raven the people who would betray traditional values: 'There
is a kind of new man who will surely come to us . . . I suspect in
about 20 years. This sort of new man will be a scientist, or possibly
a practitioner of what I believe are called social studies; he will be
a philistine and a prig; he will be left-wing . . . He will destroy and
expel and pervert. For all I know, he may even let in women.' It
was less than twenty years before this kind of new man began
to dominate Cambridge (although many such men proved to be
Conservatives, and ended up in Margaret Thatcher's government).
Even in 1950, there were bits of the new man about Peter Hall.

A few eccentrics at that time chose not to wear Harris tweed
sports coat and flannels, with a shirt and tie. But when Michael
Birkett and Tony White, both theatrical friends of Hall's, bought
a cheap earring each to wear in a production of *Titus Andronicus*,
many students were scandalised when they did not bother to take
them off between performances. The rules were old-fashioned,
strict, and generally adhered to. Students were locked into their
colleges by 10.30 p.m.; virtually everyone had a short haircut;
hardly anyone had a car. In Hall's final year, Mark Boxer – who
became Marc, the celebrated cartoonist – at that time the editor of
Granta, was expelled from Cambridge for printing a blasphemous
poem. (This read, in part: 'You drunken gluttonous seedy God,
You son of a bitch, you snotty old sod' – more a demonstration
on Boxer's part of bad literary judgement than of bad taste.) The
authority of the proctors did not go completely unchallenged:
besides sending Boxer down, *Granta* was banned for a year, but
it reappeared straight away as *Gadfly*, with identical format and
contributors, including Boxer.

When Hall went to Cambridge, Clement Attlee's Labour government was still in power, and by the time he left Churchill was in

office. But the political passions aroused by the reforming Labour government were mostly spent by the early 1950s, and the one event that raised the political temperature was the opposition of Ambrose Reeves, the then Bishop of Johannesburg, to the passage of the Bantu Education Act, a cornerstone of apartheid. Douglas Hurd and Greville Janner were the flashy undergraduate politicians, but a higher premium was put on artistic talent. In Hall's first term, a playwriting competition netted Keith Dewhurst, Frederic Raphael and John Arden among the runners-up; the winner was Hugh Thomas, the distinguished historian and Thatcherite peer. Julian Slade was writing musicals; Thom Gunn and Karl Miller were writing poetry; Raymond Leppard was conducting; Nicholas Tomalin was writing for *Varsity*, the student newspaper; Peter May and David Sheppard were batting at Fenners.

As an English student, Hall had a truly privileged education. On the one hand there was Dadie Rylands's worldly classicism, an expression of his intimacy with John Maynard Keynes and Bloomsbury. On the other, there was the puritan radicalism of F.R. Leavis. In Hall's own college, St Catharine's, Tom Henn, who had interviewed Hall when he applied for a scholarship, became his tutor. An Anglo-Irishman who had had a good First World War, Henn was tweedy and pipe-smoking. Two spaniels sat steaming in front of his gas fire while he talked of W.B. Yeats. Hall describes Henn as moody and periodically petulant, but also watchful and tolerant.

Of this considerable trio, Hall admired F.R. Leavis most of all. Leavis taught at Downing College, and although he was at the height of his power and the leader of a cult which took his name, he cultivated the role of the outsider at Cambridge. He cycled through the town in an open-necked shirt and sandals; his politics were left-wing, and his uncompromising opinions were intended to cause discomfort, especially among the reputable grandees at fashionable colleges like King's. Leavis charged Keynes and his friends with frivolity, with overvaluing articulacy, with callowness and with being too fond of irony. His heroes were writers like D.H. Lawrence, who had been formed in a working-class culture, and he was contemptuous of the lack of feeling and 'reverence' among Keynes's friends.[3] Others who met with Leavis's approval were Jane Austen, George Eliot, Henry James and Joseph Conrad, and his preferences affected the reading habits of a generation of young

English students, including Hall, who wrote copiously about D.H. Lawrence, and whose favourite novelist is George Eliot. Leavis edited a critical magazine called *Scrutiny*, aptly named since textual scrutiny is what he taught his students. They were to ask how a line reverberated, and what it suggested; why it was structured as it is; what was underneath it; what it was all about? Leavisite students were text oriented.

Leavis's were the only lectures Hall bothered to attend. He liked listening to Leavis undermining the reputations of writers like T.S. Eliot and F.L. Lucas, but, he says, there was more to it than mere subversive pleasure. 'I learned from Leavis that literature and art have a moral weight, and that, in social terms, art is more important than religion; that it is the only way of passing the past on to the future.'[4] It did not matter to Hall that Leavis held the theatre in contempt, as lacking integrity. By emphasising the high moral significance of art, Leavis gave his students an intellectual justification for working for a living in the arts. Hall was always grateful to him for that.

Rylands had come to personify the King's set that Leavis disapproved of. Rylands was homosexual; Leavis heterosexual. Rylands lived in splendour in rooms at King's; Leavis lived in a family house with his wife, Queenie. Rylands had a wide acquaintance among London actors and theatrical producers whom Leavis would have found juvenile. But it was Rylands who taught Hall about verse-speaking.

Rylands had come to Cambridge in 1921, only fourteen years after the Marlowe Society had been founded to revive and restore Elizabethan play texts, and he established his academic reputation by rediscovering John Webster's *The White Devil*. From the beginning, the Marlowe Society was a radical force. Its productions stripped the stage of the accumulation of scenery that featured in nineteenth-century designs. The text was sacrosanct: no cuts were allowed. And, since it mattered so much, the text had to be spoken properly – especially if it was verse. University actors were expected to know how to speak that as if it were music.

Rylands's influence spread beyond the university. His friends included John Gielgud, Peggy Ashcroft and Irene Worth, who had appeared in Marlowe Society productions and in its recordings of Shakespeare plays, but his most influential friend was Hugh 'Binkie' Beaumont, who ran H.M. Tennent, the dominant West End production company. Beaumont's preoccupation was the commercial theatre, but he dabbled on the fringe as well, and was one of the founders of the Company of Four, which played at the Lyric, Hammersmith and the Arts Theatre in Cambridge and staged a number of influential productions in the late 1940s and early 1950s. These included Benjamin Britten's *Let's Make an Opera*, Paul Scofield's *Richard II*, directed by John Gielgud, and, in 1950, a play called *Point of Departure* by a little-known French playwright, Jean Anouilh, which helped spread the idea that the fashionable avant-garde was to be found in Paris.[5] His friendships meant that Rylands was more than a teacher. He became an exclusive employment agency for actors and directors as well – another of the privileges of a Cambridge education.

When Peter Hall went to Cambridge just a few weeks short of his twentieth birthday, he did not see himself as a gilded youth, careless and fancy free: he felt frightened, lost, inadequate and anxious. Jill was in Germany, so the only solace available was home, which was now in Wittlesford, a station one down the line from Shelford, where Reg was the new stationmaster. Since he did not like the digs the college had allocated him, Hall went to live at home in his third term. He was deeply disgruntled when the Ministry of Education reduced his maintenance grant by £23 6s. 8d. a term and he threatened to turn his appeal into a test case. In the end they compromised.

His grant and his scholarship were enough to live on, but the Pamment in Hall was conscious of having less money than boys from affluent families, who could drink wine and wear fashionable clothes. (It was no comfort that he had no great delight in drink or fashionable clothes.) His friends knew where he came from: indeed, he would take them to Wittlesford station for tea. John Barton, the Old Etonian among them, claims the class thing made no difference.[6]

Another cause of his low spirits was his engagement: marriage, Hall thought, must put an end to his theatrical ambition. Apparently, Jill did not discourage the view that a good degree and a secure teaching job was the proper way to begin adult life. Reg and Grace, of course, shared this view: 'My parents were distraught at the idea of me going into the theatre; they were terrified that I was going to waste my time at university instead of working. The rest of the family was just horrified.' Hall knew that he had to choose; and he was inevitably influenced by the fact that, while his early

efforts as a student actor met with only limited success, his tutor
thought he could get a first-class degree.

He played King Magnus in Bernard Shaw's *The Apple Cart* at the
Amateur Dramatic Club (ADC) 'nurseries' where new students
display their wares. Directed by Hall's new friend, Tony Church,
a Londoner with a broad cockney accent, his performance did
not cause a stir. None the less, Dadie Rylands never forgot the
first time he saw Peter Hall at Cambridge. The Marlowe Society's
production was then auditioning for *Coriolanus*, and when Hall
appeared Rylands suggested to John Barton that they ask him
to do a little bit from the First Citizen. Barton said afterwards
that he didn't think Hall was going to be any good, but Rylands
contradicted him: 'Peter had a feeling for it.' Barton never changed
his mind about Hall's acting: 'He wasn't a bad actor, but he wasn't
very good either. I think there was something physically wrong
with him.'

Chatting at the time to Stanley Price, who had been in his *Hamlet*
at the Perse and who was now a fellow undergraduate, Hall said
mournfully that he hadn't made it as an undergraduate actor; the
competition was so much fiercer than at school, and he was not in
the same league as Tony Church. Cambridge was full of schoolboy
Hamlets; Hall knew at least two others personally. He knew what
was wrong: he acted in bold strokes and made his characters seem
too simplistic. By the end of his first year Hall had done promising
academic work (a first in Prelims, the preliminary exam) but had
as yet left no perceptible mark on Cambridge.

A small case of nepotism eased his first long summer vacation.
His father knew that British Rail hired temporary level-crossing
keepers for the summer and that there would be a vacancy on
the Cambridge to London line at Grantham's Road crossing not
far from Wittlesford. He recommended his son for the post, but
this was a responsible job, and candidates had to be examined on
the rules. Peter's attitude to the exam was so casual that his father
feared he would let him down. To his pride and astonishment,
Peter learned in a couple of days the 200 rules it would have taken
railwaymen of Reg's generation months to learn.

Like his father, Hall was good at odd jobs. Besides working on
the railways, he picked fruit, and worked for the Post Office at
Christmas. When he had finished on the railway in the summer of
1951, he had enough money to take the family's Austin 7 to Italy. He
and his companion, a fellow undergraduate named Tom Burgner,

ate sparingly, but they saw Florence: Hall declared that it was his favourite city in the whole world. And there was money left over. In his second year, he discovered a 1793 Broadwood piano in an old piano shop, and bought it for £40 – the equivalent of £590 in 1994 prices.

By the end of his second year Hall had committed himself to making his début as a director at the beginning of his third year, in October 1952. A slight deterioration in his exam results (2:1 in part one of his Tripos after a first in Prelims) was an indication that he was concentrating more on the theatre than studying. During his second year at Cambridge his engagement ended; Hall says that he and Jill did not so much break up as drift apart. Their ambitions were incompatible. One consequence of this was the end of an intermittent sex life. The few women undergraduates were idealised, since for most of the young male students they were unobtainable. A Zuleika Dobson-like figure named Sasha Moorson was an object of his unfulfilled desire: 'We were obsessed by girls,' says Hall, although Birkett contradicts this: 'We weren't very amorous at all.'

For his first eighteen months at Cambridge, Hall loitered sulkily on the theatrical fringe. Or so he says; his contemporaries in the first two undergraduate years recall his charm and his smile. Years afterwards Hall said he had found early in life that if he smiled at people he got rather better results than if he shouted at them. His smiling mask, in prototype at the Perse, was being perfected at Cambridge.

Dedicated theatre people spent most days at the Amateur Dramatic Club, the ADC, on Park Street, where they could eat and drink as well as talk about who would do the scenery, and where they would get the costumes, and who could be persuaded to lend props. The theatre had a capacity of 200, the stage was small and the lighting was primitive, but it belonged to the students, who formed the committee that ran it, and financed it out of revenue. It was a competitive environment with elections for the committee and its officers. 'There were a lot of very talented, energetic people,' Hall recalls.

It wasn't just a question of throwing on a play and being approximate. We weren't very good, but we were very serious and very hardworking. It was terribly professional. You had to get your ideas accepted by committees –

good practice for the future. You had to justify what you put on stage –
more good practice for the future. If you could survive the university-drama
rat-race, you stood a fair chance in Shaftesbury Avenue.[7]

Hall's own position on this greasy pole was precarious. He was
a candidate for one of three places on the committee on 11 May
1952 and was narrowly elected. The first vote put him in equal
third place, and, in a run-off, he beat his opponent, Shirley Davis,
by the nerve-racking margin of 21 to 20. The highest ADC office
he achieved was librarian.

From his place on the fringe, Hall observed Peter Wood, who
was, by his own admission, fairly noisy and flamboyant as an
undergraduate. He had directed *Cymbeline* and *Henry IV, Part Two*.
As with Peter Brook, Hall was envious of Wood's assurance: 'He was
so bloody patronising. I hated him.' Michael Birkett remembers that
Wood frightened them because he was already much bitchier than
they were. Actors thought Wood liked his cast to be in tears, but the
final product was often much praised. Wood's productions were
elegantly designed by a contemporary named Timothy O'Brien.

Wood's only rival was John Barton, a lanky, bearded protégé of
Dadie Rylands at King's, where he had become a junior dean after
his graduation. Barton was an eccentric ('he was an eccentric in his
basinette,' says Wood), whose best-known habit was chewing razor
blades. Birkett identifies them as Gillette Blue: 'I think he liked the
danger and the control it required,' he says. At moments of stress
blood would trickle out of the corner of Barton's mouth.

Barton was more academic than Wood, who was already preparing his entry to the West End. In Hall's second year, Rylands
and Barton produced *Julius Caesar* for the Marlowe Society, in what
they conceived to be the accent of Shakespeare and his actors. This
was a combination of West Country Mummerset, Liverpool and
Belfast, in which the most striking aspects were the long 'a's' (as
in the dogs of 'waare'), and the pronounced 'k's' (as in 'kerneel').
Hall could still speak the lines that way decades later. He thought
they made him sound like Ian Paisley.

Other student directors were Toby Robertson and Michael
Birkett, who did *Cyrano de Bergerac* with Hall as the Duke de
Guiche. 'He was not bad; I was awful,' says Birkett. Toby Robertson
remembers that Hall was now 'beavering to get into productions'.
He was cast as Tybalt in the Marlowe Society's summer festival
production of *Romeo and Juliet*, which was directed by Dadie

Rylands, assisted by Barton. Since Tybalt dies in Act III scene i, Hall asked if he could also play the First Musician. This is a bit part with a memorable opening line ('Faith, we may put up our pipes and begone') and Hall played the musician as a simpleton, bewildered, moved and embarrassed by the grief at Juliet's death, to Rylands's lasting admiration.[8]

Romeo was played by Tony White, the star actor during Hall's years at Cambridge, but because there were so few women undergraduates, Juliet was played by a professional actress imported from London. This was Toby Robertson's sister Theresa, or Toppet, whose stage name was Theresa Moore. She found disconcerting Rylands's habit of rehearsing with his eyes on the text, calling out instructions only when the rhythm of a line of poetry was at fault. The actual staging was left to Barton. Toppet recalls a black set, and passionless scenes with Romeo, who was deliberately tough and rather callous. 'It was a rather cold production,' she says.[9]

It was memorable too. At the dress rehearsal, Barton's Mercutio died so spectacularly after falling down a staircase and sliding off a balcony that Rylands burst into tears and had to be helped home. Barton's ferocity in his carefully choreographed duel with Tybalt caused Rylands to fear for Hall ('more cut fingers,' he said when Barton was organising the fights). But when Hall fumbled a move, it was Barton who was impaled. He bled so copiously that he had to be taken to Adenbrookes Hospital.

In the summer of 1952, *Romeo and Juliet* transferred to London, to the Scala Theatre on Charlotte Street; the notices were sufficiently good for it to run for another fortnight at the Phoenix. Winston Churchill was in the audience at the Scala one evening, and like Rylands, he kept his head buried in the text. Later, meeting the cast, Churchill commented on a couple of dropped lines he'd noticed. But what made that summer memorable for Hall was a chance to direct. Barton had agreed to produce a double bill of a short version of *Two Gentlemen of Verona* and Terence Rattigan's *The Browning Version*. Thinking he had taken on too much, Barton asked Hall to help with *The Browning Version* ('a masterpiece; the best play Rattigan ever wrote,' Hall says). A taste of directing confirmed Hall's determination to try to do it for a living. He joined Equity that summer.

Hall also visited Stratford-upon-Avon in the summer, in the company of Barton, Wood, Robertson and Michael Birkett, whose Morris 8 provided the transport. They saw the season of Shakespeare's histories, including a particularly fine *Henry IV, Part One*, with Richard Burton (Prince Hal), Anthony Quayle, the company's artistic director, as Falstaff, and Michael Redgrave as Hotspur; smaller parts were taken by Robert Hardy and Alan Badel; Bolingbroke was Harry Andrews. The five were especially fond of Andrews, who befriended them and joined them for a drink at the Swan Hotel before the performance. 'He was our man,' says Birkett. They also made the acquaintance of Cyril Keegan Smith, who ran the costume department, and who took a liking to intense young men; he agreed to lend them costumes for their Cambridge productions.

Michael Birkett also took Hall to Glyndebourne in 1952. Birkett was a comparatively worldly figure, the son of a distinguished barrister who had prosecuted Nazis in Nuremberg before becoming a judge, and a peer. The Birketts lived comfortably in Buckinghamshire; as a house guest, Hall developed a taste for sweet, scented Château Yquem at the Birketts' dinner table, and a taste for country house opera in the panelled auditorium at Glyndebourne. The Birketts were fond of a German refugee named Dr Wilcken who edited the ICI technical journal and took a pair of front-row centre seats for each performance of the season. He took Birkett to hear his first Mozart, and, after they had been introduced, asked Hall to join him too. The dinner jacket was no problem; his father owned one, and Peter borrowed it.

The first ADC production of each university year was open to bids from undergraduate directors, and the ADC committee would select the most promising offer. On 7 June 1952 *Varsity* announced that a group of ADC members under the leadership of Peter Hall had been chosen to perform Jean Anouilh's *Point of Departure*. This is one of the most telling episodes in Hall's own story of his life; he says that at the start of his first year he put down his marker as a future director by reserving the ADC for the start of his third year, and he financed his bid by obtaining promises of financial support from two of his teachers at the Perse, John Tanfield and Cecil Crouch.

Explaining the apparent contradiction between this bold piece of forward planning and his determination to get a decent degree so as to be a good husband to Jill, Hall says it was 'a contingency plan . . . born of calculation and desperation'.[10] John Barton, who was on the ADC committee, recalls it somewhat differently. He says that there were two contenders for the independent slot in October 1952. Although the minutes for the meeting at which it was agreed that Hall would direct that production have been lost, the evidence of similar minutes strongly suggests that it was not possible to 'reserve' the ADC. Independent directors were asked to apply, and the committee then made its selection. 'I got him the slot against another director because I thought he was more talented,' says Barton.

Moreover, the ADC committee reserved residual rights over the selection of the play. Hall's preferences reflected current fashion for the French avant-garde: he proposed Jean Cocteau's *The Infernal Machine*, and Henri de Montherlant's *The Master of Santiago*, and both were turned down. Subsequently, he proposed *Point of Departure*, the Anouilh play, and the committee liked this idea better. To confirm the booking, Tanfield and Crouch each put down £20: 'a not inconsiderable sum,' noted Tanfield.[11]

Point of Departure is an updating of the Orpheus legend, in which Orpheus meets Eurydice in Marseilles railway station. Donald Beves, a crony of Rylands's at King's, joined a promising group of undergraduate actors in the cast. (Beves later gained brief public notoriety when he was incorrectly named as the Fifth Man in the Philby spy ring.) One of the undergraduates, Michael Mayne, was impressed by Hall's authority over Beves, a much older man. Mayne was in awe of Hall:

> He struck me as a quiet, contained, caring person who knew exactly what he wanted. He didn't chew razor blades, or show off, or lose his cool. I enjoyed the rehearsals and was impressed . . . he encouraged and affirmed, giving you confidence . . . I remember him going over and over, line by line, a particularly difficult speech I had in the last act. I felt enormous gratitude . . . one actually believed in him.[12]

In his last year at Cambridge Hall exhibited a range of the talents that were to serve him well as a professional director.

Point of Departure was an example of his ability to set the critical agenda before the first night. *Varsity* for 11 October 1952 was a bumper issue for Hall. On page eight he was named as one of six 'People Worth Knowing' in Cambridge that year, and on page five he wrote an article on 'Problems of Producing *Point of Departure*'.

'The producer's approach to the play,' he wrote,

> is clearly marked by the dramatist. The railway station where Orpheus and

Eurydice meet has a definitely indicated locale . . . Too much reliance on impressionistic settings would, therefore, rob this re-telling of the myth of its chief power – its literal modernisation . . . But this treatment has its danger . . . It is essential that the passion of a man for a woman be put into striking theatrical terms . . . In this production, therefore, I have tried to intensify the mysterious power of the love which Orpheus and Eurydice feel for each other by the constant use of music and occasional impressionistic lighting.[13]

The article shows how little the way he was to work changed over the following decades. (Peter Wood immediately noticed the use of music; Hall was taking advantage of new technology – long-playing records and tape recorders.)

The first paragraph of *Varsity*'s review on 18 October referred to Hall's preview, and Peter Firth, the reviewer, judged: 'As a first production, Mr Hall should be justly proud . . . He has brought modern emotional drama to Cambridge on a large scale.'[14] Years afterwards Hall retained a vivid memory of his state of mind after *Point of Departure*: 'A lot depended on it, he said.

I didn't imagine it was very good, but it was good enough . . . and I got a terrific sense of freedom and release . . . like a duck who'd found water and could swim. It's a physical feeling I want to recapture with every production. I suppose that is the reason I do it . . . the elation that comes out of something happening creatively that wasn't there before . . . also the sense of total security and ease you have when you see a really good piece of work in the theatre.[15]

Hall was learning by doing; and, in making up for lost time, he virtually abandoned his academic work. His next production opened only a month later, and it was the sort of play that was to make him famous. *Saint's Day* by John Whiting was an ambiguous mixture of symbolism, realism and reverie. Reviewing the production, John Wilders defined Hall's approach precisely:

In this, as in his production of Point of Departure *a few weeks ago, Peter Hall has wisely chosen to follow the playwright's intentions without imposing his own personality upon them. The result is an intelligent, smooth-flowing production, in which the main action is always neatly but accurately focused, and the pace is controlled according to the dramatic tension.[16]*

Another characteristic tactic Hall now exhibited for the first time was the seizing upon and milking of a controversy. On 15 November *Varsity* carried a front-page story headlined EMPTY HOUSE:

'We're going to lose a lot of money on this production' said Peter Hall, the producer of Saint's Day *at the ADC this week. Bookings have been abnormally low. Only 14 tickets had been sold for the whole run by the opening day. Later in the week the situation improved, although only 40 seats were booked for the Thursday evening performance.*

Making a special announcement after the first night, Peter Hall told the audience: 'There is a remarkable absence of enthusiasm in Cambridge for new experimental plays, although there is a safe, solid box office for Shakespeare.' Such an attitude was all the more surprising in a university city. In an interview he deplored the ADC's 'lack of a consistent policy'.[17]

This interview was the work of a budding impresario, and was intended to produce a free advertisement for the Saturday evening performance. *Granta* explored the meaning of *Saint's Day* across two pages, and the *Daily Telegraph* critic, W.A. Darlington, gave Hall his first national notice: 'Excellently handled by Peter Hall, they play together like a team.'[18]

The controversy over *Saint's Day* provided another glimpse of the mature Hall – as propagandist. In an article on the leader page of *Varsity*, Hall made a case for an experimental theatre in Cambridge that would do for modern plays what the Marlowe Society did for Shakespeare: 'An experimental theatre must be avant-garde and intellectual, and to many people it must seem pretentious. It cannot itself hope for lasting achievements for its business is to be untraditional and unestablishment.'[19] In his article Hall argued for a new theatre group, similar to the Maddermarket Theatre run by Nugent Monck in Norwich in the 1930s: he proposed a company of thirty to forty amateur actors led by a full-time director, with a small professional and technical staff. There is no mystery about the sub-text: if offered such a job, Hall would take it.

In the mean time, he was directing *Uncle Vanya* and getting top billing. The advertisement read: 'The University Players present Peter Hall's production of *Uncle Vanya*' – an early example of the director taking precedence over the actors. Hall thought he had cracked Chekhov: he made the characters anarchic, cruel and funny: monuments of egocentricity. The audiences liked it; opening on 17 January 1953, *Uncle Vanya* did such good business that the run was extended for three days. Hall had a swift reaction ready for *Varsity*'s reporter: 'This shows how unpredictable Cambridge audiences can be.'[20]

W.A. Darlington was so enthusiastic in the *Daily Telegraph* that Grace Hall cut his review out and kept it:

> *If a stranger who knew nothing of what was going forward had happened to
> stroll into the ADC Theatre to-night during the performance of Chekhov's
> 'Uncle Vanya' by the University Actors I do not think he would have guessed
> that he was seeing a cast of undergraduates under an undergraduate producer.
> There was a maturity of style both in Peter Hall's direction and in the acting
> of most of the company which is not often found under such circumstances
> . . . Generally one expects to find the more obvious emotions conveyed by
> young actors in a hearty bellow and the subtler ones in an inaudible whisper.
> Under such treatment a Chekhov play would inevitably sink with all hands.
> Instead it was firmly and lightly guided into port.*[21]

Having become an undergraduate star in only four months, Hall
was already a suitable target for abuse, and *Varsity*'s review by
Ben Driver of his next production, a play by John Barton entitled
Winterlude, was a stinker:

> *Both* Winterlude *and* Saint's Day *failed because the producer either did not
> understand, or did not bother to make clear, the hidden emotional interplay of
> his characters. The unsatisfactory feature of university drama – its inability to
> affect its audience either mentally or emotionally – is due to the emphasis on
> technique rather than feeling.*[22]

By the second term of his last year, Hall's tutors began to warn him
that, since he was doing so little work, he might get no better than
a third-class degree. He needed their permission to direct plays,
and Hall was lucky to be supervised by Tom Henn and Douglas
Brown, his mentor from the Perse. Brown, wonderfuly permissive,
finally said that if the theatre was what Hall was determined to
do, he would not be too punctilious about essays.

Hall now wrote to Rylands to ask about his prospects in the
professional theatre. Dadie Rylands was always proud of his reply:
'My advice to those wanting to enter the theatre is the same as the
advice Mr Punch gave to those contemplating matrimony: Don't.'
But Hall persisted, so Rylands wondered whether he should ask
Binkie Beaumont whether there were vacancies for stage managers
in the West End. Hall replied that that was not what he had in mind;
he did not want to find himself in the same boat as Peter Wood, who
was contractually committed by Beaumont to stage-manage with
a Whitehall farce called *Seagulls over Sorrento* for the duration of
its run – and that was years, not months. Recalling his arrogance
years later, Hall said that it took his breath away.[23]

Hall was now involved in anything staged in Cambridge, even

in Rylands's triennial Greek play, despite the fact that he didn't
speak a work of Greek. 'He couldn't bear not to be in it,' says
Rylands. *The Agamemnon* was performed in February, and Hall
understudied the Captain of the Guard, who had exactly one line.
In case of emergency, should he have to appear, Hall's single line
was written out phonetically on the back of his shield.

Advertisements for the ADC's May Week production of *Love's
Labour's Lost* (early in June 1953) announced Hall's name in bold
capital letters. The cast contained all the best Cambridge actors.
Tony White, who had come to the notice of J. Arthur Rank's casting
directors, was Berowne; John Barton was the King of Navarre, and
Michael Birkett played Marcade in an enormous dressing gown
that Harry Andrews had worn on the Stratford stage. Toppet Moore
played the Princess of France. There were children too; they were
to become a feature of Hall's professional productions.

The sets and the costumes, designed by Freddie Nicolle, who
had worked with Hall in *Point of Departure*, were pretty to look at.
Most of the costumes had been specially made for the production
at a cost of £120, and the cyclorama was painted in the rich shade of
blue used in miniatures by Nicholas Hilliard; there was a gazebo,
and the actors wore Elizabethan ruffs. The music was selected by
Raymond Leppard, and played live on the harpsichord by Leppard
or by Peter Hall.

But the single thing Hall cared most about was the verse-
speaking. Having rejected the romantic style of declamation that
Gielgud had made standard, Hall and John Barton wanted the text
spoken with the naturalism they had admired in Richard Burton's
Prince Hal in the Stratford *Henry IV*. Having sat at Rylands's
feet, they decided to teach verse-speaking differently. 'They were
Aarons to his Moses,' says Michael Birkett. 'They did it better than
Rylands did.' They had learned about breathing and the forms of
the verse from Rylands, and, having discussed it endlessly at the
ADC, their new trick was to have Shakespearian verse spoken in
lines rather than words or clauses. The lines were spoken briskly
and clearly. In addition, they applied Leavis's tests of meaning and
clarity through rigorous textual analysis. Here was the origin of the
Cambridge style of theatre directing.

Stanley Price, Hall's Perse contemporary, was enchanted: 'It is a
young person's play . . . about sexual frustration; it struck a deep
chord.' A review in *The Times*, having praised the set, commented
that Hall had 'gone admirably to work in all things except the

lighting, which is true "producer's lighting" and does not always illuminate the actors' faces'. Visitors from London included a young theatre administrator named Yolande Bird who has since seen most of Hall's professional work: she claims he has never done anything better than his Cambridge *Love's Labour's Lost*.[24]

Rehearsals for *Love's Labour's Lost* were rudely interrupted by final exams. Hall crammed hard and just got by, but after the exams he suffered a recurring nightmare: it begins with him in a panic on the day before the exam and merges into the examination room where he is unable to answer any of the questions. In fact, Hall got a 2:2, an average degree. But the class of the degree matters only to teachers or professors. More important was the quality of the education Hall had received at Cambridge: 'Although I wouldn't pretend that I am a Shakespearian scholar . . . I don't feel at a loss confronting a Shakespeare play. I know the background, and I know where to look.'[25]

He had had a theatrical apprenticeship alongside people who intended to work professionally: Tony Church, Toby Robertson, John Barton – if he cared to leave King's. Michael Birkett already had a job in the film industry. Peter Wood and Timothy O'Brien were already at work. Tony White was confidently expected to become a star. (White preferred instead to fish for lobster in the west of Ireland, and translate from the French; he died, aged forty-five, from an injury received playing football in Battersea Park.)

This was a new breed. Earlier generations of directors had learned their craft in the theatre itself, in stage management, or, like Gielgud and Olivier, by acting. There were exceptions, such as Tyrone Guthrie, the electrifying Russian, Komisarjevski, and the young Peter Brook. Guthrie and Brook had both been to Oxford, and their conceptions and conceits had caused actors to start muttering about 'producer's theatre'. But this new crowd of university-educated directors from Cambridge were different again: directing plays had been part of their education. While claiming that they had much to learn, they already suspected that they knew best, and they were in a hurry. ('I've always been in a hurry,' Hall said shortly before his sixtieth birthday.)[26]

The reviews of his productions in national newspapers gave Hall a foot in the stage door. Having rejected Rylands's offer of assistance, he wrote letters to every repertory company in the country. He says he wrote either sixty-eight letters or seventy-three (depending on whether he was recalling this period in 1993 or 1983) and received either three or five replies; each of these was a rejection. 'Memory is dangerously creative and sometimes bewilderingly inconsistent,' he observes. Though John Whiting, the author of *Saint's Day*, had become a friend and had given him some introductions, no one responded.

Like most students, Hall would have been run down and mentally exhausted when his exams and *Love's Labour's Lost* were finished, and he was vulnerable to a severe attack of Pamment glooms. In his autobiography Hall says that, at the age of twenty-two, he contemplated suicide, for the second time.

> *I had put my parents through a deeply anxious time; I was in debt and worried about money; I was always in top gear, overworked, overstretched, overenthusiastic . . . I was an unfulfilled, unsuccessful scholar, an unfinished musician, an untrained administrator and an appalling linguist. I knew how to act, but I had no talent for it. I knew I could talk to amateur actors and help them develop, but could I talk to professionals? I was also aware that I was a cliché: the working-class boy who had turned himself into a phony member of the middle classes. I didn't belong with my parents or relations, but I didn't quite belong with my new friends.*[27]

There was to be only one cure for this morbidity and that was plenty of work in the theatre.

When he got over his depression, Hall admitted that Cambridge had given him some assurance. He was already conscious of the rich spectrum of his moods:

> *When I'm feeling strong and healthy, I quite like the sense of never having belonged anywhere. I was the elementary schoolboy at the grammar school and not really part of it. The scholarship boy at Cambridge and not part of the scene in the conventional sense. I have always felt like an outsider in everything, and when I'm feeling strong I don't mind that. When I'm weak, I just feel as if I don't really want to belong.*[28]

He once said of Cambridge that it had helped him make his mask.[29] He was referring to his theatre director's mask, but there were others: of charm (worn regularly), and of ambition (not often seen, but others were aware of its existence). Most contemporaries were sure he would succeed. Michael Mayne, whom he had directed in two plays, says: 'Under the gentle exterior there was a steeliness. He knew what he wanted and he got it in the nicest possible way. I had every confidence that he would make a name. What surprised me was that he did it quite so fast and in so dramatic a manner.'[30] (A theology student, Dr Mayne eventually became the Dean of Westminster.)

A footnote to Hall's Cambridge period is to be found in the minutes of the first ADC committee after he had gone down. The secretary drew attention to the finances of *Love's Labour's Lost*, which looked like making a slight loss. 'Considerable surprise was registered by all members of the committee, with the exception of the Treasurer, who signified his disapproval of the budgeting of the play being based on grim complacency.'[31] Even after the sale of the specially made costumes, there was still a loss. University provided the first evidence of yet another characteristic of Hall's work: his habitual extravagance meant that it was unusual for any company to be in profit when he left it.

One thing Hall left behind in Cambridge was an uncashed cheque for £54 0s. 6d., which was discovered the following October in an old file. The secretary contacted him, and the ADC committee's minute book reports: 'Mr Hall had been very surprised but quite willing to believe the situation as he had not examined his bank business in detail during the past year. However, he promised to investigate the matter, and, if it was as it appeared, he would try to raise the sum so that the cheque could be cashed as soon as possible.' It does seem strange that neither party should have noticed what happened to £54 0s. 6d., the equivalent of £745 forty years later. The minute book gives no clue about the purpose of the cheque: in fact, it was his bar and restaurant bill. 'I lived there in my last year,' Hall says.

Hall's single-mindedness already excited envy and anger as well as respect and affection, and a reaction set in fast at the ADC. Its new president, Gordon Gould, announced an immediate change of style: 'For one thing productions will no longer be advertised mainly on a star basis.'[32]

5

At Home at the Arts

'There was something about the boy'

Peter Hall directed three more plays in Cambridge in the summer of 1953, while living with his parents at Wittlesford. The Cambridge Arts Theatre Trust's summer season was like a short anthology of avant-garde taste: Anouilh's *Antigone*, John Whiting's *Marching Song*, and Luigi Pirandello's *Henry IV*. Having seen Hall's production of *Henry IV*, Alec Clunes, the director of the Arts Theatre in London, asked him to take it to London to fill a two-week gap there. It opened on 25 August, and, while he occasionally succumbed to depression in the years ahead, from that day on Hall was never unemployed in the theatre.

The Arts occupied a warehouse-like building a short distance from Leicester Square, and once Clunes had established a reputation for new work and classical revivals, its publicists seized on the phrase 'our mini-National Theatre'. Christopher Fry's new plays opened there, linking the Arts with the revival of poetic drama in the early 1950s. It was a club theatre, and although it regularly submitted scripts to the Lord Chamberlain, it was not required to do so. It was a proper club, too, with a bar and a restaurant. The actors' pay was not generous (£10 a week for the leading actors; £8 for the rest), but the exposure they had there was as good as in the West End. Hall's direction of *Henry IV* was 'straightforward' enough (said *Theatre World*)[1] to persuade John

Counsell, the director of the Windsor Rep, to ask him to direct
The Letter by Somerset Maugham a couple of weeks later. 'John
thought there was something about the boy,' his widow, Mary,
remembers.[2]

To socialists like Hall, radicalism meant changing institutions.
Hall was not a dialectician, but he did believe that institutions
like the theatre would improve if they had the right structure. That
meant, where necessary, state control and state subsidy. In 1953
even moderate Labour voters did not question nationalisation. The
Halls, father and son, never doubted that the railways ought to be
in public ownership. Hall believed the commercial theatre in the
West End was feeble; managements depended on the star system,
and produced an unadventurous repertory. He assumed this
would end with the establishment of state-subsidised companies,
like a National Theatre; but this view was not widely held in
the theatrical profession, even in a non-commercial theatre like
the Shakespeare Memorial Theatre in Stratford-upon-Avon. In his
autobiography, *A Time to Speak*, Anthony Quayle describes how
actor-managers who ran companies thought about government
subsidy:

> *Occasionally the Arts Council gave its great cough and asked if perhaps
> we would like a little money from them. I would go and consult Fordie
> [Fordham Flower], and we would both agree that it was wiser to decline
> the offer courteously. The moment we started to depend on outside help,
> our bloodstream would become vitiated, and if ever support were withdrawn
> we would collapse. While we could exist on our own box office, we must
> continue to do so.[3]*

Subsidies to theatres were still rare. The Bristol Old Vic, the
Birmingham Rep and the Belgrade Theatre in Coventry received
some public money, but not much.

Hall was inspired by the subsidised companies whose work he
had seen in Germany, and by books like Edward Gordon Craig's
On the Art of the Theatre. Craig believed that theatres should be run
by directors like Konstantin Stanislavsky, the legendary director
of the Moscow Art Theatre, and his message was that a passionate
love for the theatre could not co-exist with the requirement to
make an immediate return on money invested. (All Craig asked
for – in 1910 – was a standing company of 100, two theatres, a
school for theatre workers, and £5,000 a year for five years.)

Hall was critical of the West End, but he did not think its intellectual poverty meant that the theatre was necessarily dead, or dying. Three interviews he gave in the eighteen months after he left Cambridge form a loose manifesto of his views. The fundamental problem, as he saw it, was the absence of new writing. Staple West End playwrights like Rattigan and Charles Morgan were reluctant to push an argument as far as it would go.[4] Hall could name eight French playwrights who were producing good plays, but the only new English writer he admired was John Whiting, 'our most important new dramatist'.[5]

> For the most part the British theatre does not take into account the fact that we have had a World War since 1939, and that everything in the world has changed – values, ways of living, ideals, hopes and fears. As I see it, our theatre is far too often pre-war, safe and easy-going in what it offers, and lacking in the stimulation that will attract fresh audiences. In any audience today you'll find that the majority are middle-aged and elderly people.[6]

He was speaking of 'Aunt Edna', the legendary theatregoer who wanted a good evening's entertainment, with a tray of coffee and biscuits in the interval. English audiences were not as willing to listen to argument as the French, he said, and he wanted new writers who would attract a new audience. Hall had his eye on people in their twenties who were more inclined to go and see a foreign film than a play. His objective was 'to attract the younger generation who enjoy an evening's entertainment that also provides a discussion topic for the coffee bar on the way home'.[7]

He longed for a more rigorous acting style and thought that, 'Our acting has become too small. There are plenty of excellent actors and actresses and they could soon learn to come out of their corners and act with vigour and colour.'[8] 'Today the emphasis is on gorgeous sets, and verse is on the whole badly spoken.'[9]

Hall's last requirement comes as no surprise:

> I think it is essential to have a permanent company when the classics are being presented. One of the troubles with the Old Vic is that the company changes every season. There is still no company in this country where definite styles of acting can be seen, and where our classics can be played as they ought to be.[10]

The man most responsible for this dismal state of affairs was never mentioned by name, but Hall was criticising the power of Binkie Beaumont, the managing director of H.M. Tennent. Beaumont's taste was reflected in a majority of the plays that appeared, and his favourite actors could rely on regular employment. Beaumont was a homosexual, and he tended to advance homosexuals – an early example of positive discrimination. He was at the centre of a magic circle in the London theatre of which Noël Coward and Ivor Novello were the trustees. Beaumont's influence was shared with his partner, John Perry, who ran the Company of Four. John Gielgud was a member, along with stalwarts like Harry Andrews. Peter Wood was up for membership, but he was to have a foot in both camps. Dadie Rylands was a distinguished country member.

Some actors were also disenchanted with the state of things. In spring 1955 Eric Porter, a promising young Shakespearian actor, was identified by *Theatre World* as the spokesman for discontented, serious-thinking actors: 'The iron grip of management is ruining the serious drama, according to Mr Porter, because any producer that diverges too far from the norm stands no chance of being seen. In France an actor's theatre exists which is better than having a manager in supreme control.'[11] Here Porter uses 'producer' to mean director; in the 1950s the words were interchangeable.

By his rejection of Rylands's offer of help and his coded public criticism of H.M. Tennent, Hall was making the case for a new style and trying to form a new circle. His circle would tend to be heterosexual, though not exclusively so; and it would be led by directors, though there would be no rule against their being managers too. It would provide him with a power base of his own.

In the next two years Hall had a remarkable number of opportunities to form this circle. The first was with a company which illustrated Hall's belief that the best way to become a director is to join a new company and to direct it. But, while the idea was sound in theory, Hall found that in practice it was rather unsavoury. The original company had been founded by a pair of Oxford graduates, Colin George and Gordon Gostelow, and when John Barton and Toby Robertson agreed to join them they became known as the Oxford and Cambridge Players. Like William Poel and Granville-Barker, these young idealists intended to sweep away scenic dross and rely on a simple, permanent set; the emphasis was to be on well-spoken verse. The company intended to tour and would be non-profit-making. Their ambition was not, however, modest: they proposed to replace the Old Vic as the country's best-known company for classic drama.

Hall says in his autobiography that he was one of the company's founders, but in fact by the time he came along, it had already been formed. Its patron was Thane Parker, who ran the London Mask Theatre and gave the company office space and the use of a telephone at the Westminster Theatre. Barton convinced Parker that Hall should join them, asking him to take a look at Hall's *Love's Labour's Lost*. Parker was captivated, and Hall was co-opted while he was still an undergraduate. But when the offer came, Hall was committed to seeing *Henry IV* into the Arts Theatre, and by then he had also had Counsell's offer to work at Windsor.

Hall had been frightened of directing professionals for the first time, but at Windsor he discovered how much he had learned at Cambridge. His problem was more one of confidence than technique. Shortly afterwards, the job of director of productions at the Windsor Rep came up, but when Hall was offered it by John Counsell, he turned it down. Counsell, who thought he had done Hall a favour, wrote angrily to him, saying that such arrogance would guarantee that he never got anywhere in the theatre.[12]

Among the people who helped Hall decide to turn down a job in repertory was Felicity Douglas, who argued that Windsor was too small a canvas for him. She was Toby Robertson's mother, and Hall was living in a room in her house in Brunswick Gardens off Kensington Church Street. A scriptwriter by occupation, she took a keen interest in her son's contemporaries, feeding them and giving them advice.

Hall took advice more easily from the parents of his friends than he did from his own, who were still nervous at the prospect of his spending a life in the theatre, and who were unable to judge the comparative merit of Windsor Rep and directing Shakespeare for an unknown touring company (although they would probably have said that the Windsor Rep sounded more like a proper job). Hall's devoted mother did, however, continue to provide the domestic services that working-class boys then took for granted. For instance, she still did his laundry. He would take the underground to Liverpool Street; she would take the train from Wittlesford, and they would exchange clean for dirty shirts, socks and underpants on the station forecourt.[13]

Hall was already finding repertory work unrewarding. Having directed an American thriller at Worthing, he said that he had learned nothing, except compassion for the actors. So, instead of taking steady work at Windsor, he decided to throw in his lot with John Barton and Thane Parker.

Parker had offered the Oxford and Cambridge Players a season at the Westminster Theatre in the summer of 1953. Once in London, the company was renamed; since it was Coronation year, it became the Elizabethan Theatre Company (ETC). Although Toby Robertson wrote invitations to the critics in verse, few took them up.[14] One who did was Kenneth Tynan of the *Evening Standard*, but he patronised their *Julius Caesar*, writing: 'The young company speaks clearly enough, but acts hardly at all.'[15] Despite a capable *Henry V* by John Barton, the season was a box-office disaster. None the less, because the ETC was committed to tour, the Arts Council gave them a £2,000 grant and Dartington Hall agreed to build the permanent set. That was the point at which Hall joined them.

Touring defined the ETC as a mixture of showbusiness and adult education. Yolande Bird, the company's general factotum, recalls that some dates were in old and uncomfortable Number Two rated touring theatres; other bookings were for church or school halls and the repertory was heavily influenced by the school exam syllabus. Some theatrical digs were comfortable; others were perfectly awful.

According to Yolande Bird, as well as directing, Hall agreed to become company manager; the ETC could afford to pay him £10 a week only if he took on both jobs. Bird believes he did the job for a fortnight or so, until the company reached Basingstoke. He then confessed to Bird that he simply could not manage the company as well as directing a play, and she says that she took on the extra chores while Hall worked on *Twelfth Night*.[16] Hall, however, has no memory of being company manager. The production was memorable for the melancholy of the background music, Vaughan Williams's *London Symphony*.

Twelfth Night was part of a presentable repertory. Peter Wood had now joined his Cambridge colleagues, taking time away from Whitehall farce to direct *Romeo and Juliet* and *Hamlet*. John Barton's successful *Henry V* was included, and Toby Robertson contributed *The Taming of the Shrew*. *Theatre World*'s critic commented that seldom had it been his pleasure to hear so many good voices in one company making such excellent good sense. The company at the time included such promising actors as Frank Windsor, Peter Jeffrey and Emrys James.

There is confusion about the moment at which Hall quit the ETC. Hall's second commitment there was to direct *The Merchant of Venice*, and he says he did it. Yolande Bird says he didn't; she recalls an argument on a train, in which Hall said he couldn't do the *Merchant* because they didn't have a Shylock. Bird's recollection is that Tony Church proved to be an admirable Shylock in a production directed by Hugh Golding. Hall's recollection is that Church was an admirable Shylock in his production. Since Hall's memory for plays and actors is so clear, it is hard not to take his word, but Bird was making a more general point: 'Peter's trouble was deciding what job he wanted to do. In those days, he didn't try to do two things at once. I thought he was behaving abominably and he knew it, but he just ploughed on regardless. If I hadn't known before, I knew then that he was going places very quickly.'

Criticisms of Hall which were later to become familiar were now heard for the first time. For instance, Toppet Robertson, who was part of the ETC and played in Hall's *Merchant*, remembers thinking that Hall, as director, should have been around more often: 'We felt slightly abandoned and a bit miffed.' None the less, his strengths remained in the memory longer than the failings. Yolande Bird was impressed by his charm, his gift of the gab, and his charisma. 'He could just as easily have gone into politics. Even when he was letting you down he wanted to be loved. He wasn't looking at his watch all the time,' says Bird. Hall's memories of his brief time with the ETC are indistinct: a church hall in Reading and some beastly digs. He thought touring dismal, and he was, contrary to Yolande Bird's recollection, already managing to do two things at once.

Alec Clunes sold the Arts Theatre in December 1953 to Campbell Williams, who had run Keith Prowse, the ticket agency. Williams did not know much about running a theatre, but his wife had money and he was willing to learn. Clunes suggested that Williams might employ Hall to read plays for him; in fact Hall was paid £7 a week to assist John Fernald. Fernald, who had run the Playhouse in Liverpool when Hall was stationed at West Kirby four years earlier, was an unselfish teacher, and he immediately asked Hall to name the play he would like to direct himself.

Federico García Lorca's *Blood Wedding* was an inspired choice for Hall's London début: rare enough to attract a full house of highbrow critics, and continental enough to attract the young avant-garde. Hall cast the play particularly well, with Beatrix Lehmann and Lionel Jeffries, and an Australian actor called Trader Faulkner who was expert at Spanish dancing; the musical accompaniment was Andalusian music for the guitar and the bandurria. Faulkner recalls Hall's disciplined mind, precision ('He knew what he didn't want'), and sense of humour. 'He gave me a feeling of safety,' he says.[17] 'Imaginative' was the adjective most commonly used to describe the production after it opened on 30 March 1954. To Anthony Hartley of the *Spectator*, *Blood Wedding* was one of the most exciting things he had ever seen on the stage.[18]

Hall had now begun to turn work down. Moran Caplat, the general manager at Glyndebourne, hearing news of Hall's talent, asked Peter Ebert, the son of Carl, Glyndebourne's artistic director, to look Hall over. Ebert suggested that Hall join them as an assistant director, but Hall replied to Caplat on 1 March 1954 saying that his commitment to the Arts ruled that out: 'Any compromise is impossible.'[19] He did ask, however, if he could spend a week at Glyndebourne in June studying Carl Ebert's work.

But by the summer of 1954 he was already running the Oxford Playhouse, where Thane Parker had taken a lease. Parker had great faith in Hall, having detected that he was a political animal as well as an artist. For the rest of that year Hall travelled between London and Oxford, double-booking only once, when Fernald had to take over a production of a play by Pirandello in London because Hall was doing Giraudoux in Oxford. The Playhouse soon courted controversy with a production of André Rosenthal's *Third Person* in which two men kissed on the English stage for the first time. One of them, Trader Faulkner, insists that Hall was only being faithful to the text.

His first real flop was Goldoni's *The Impresario of Smyrna* at the Arts in May 1954. Hall thought the translation by Clifford Bax facetious and silly, and the cast wrong; it included old professionals like Cyril Luckham and Hugh Paddick, and promising newcomers like Prunella Scales and Donald Pleasance. Harold Hobson declared the direction 'heavy-handed', and Hall wondered if he would ever work again.[20]

But no one else seemed to notice this failure, or care, and his next production at the Arts caused him to be the subject of the Limelight profile in the *Stage*.[21] The accompanying photograph shows him as clean-shaven and smoking a pipe; the beard came much later. The Arts Theatre play was an adaptation of André Gide's *The Immoralist*, an item on the Lord Chamberlain's banned list because it dealt with homosexuality. Perhaps Beaumont's 'magic circle' did not wish to draw attention to itself by producing overtly homosexual plays – homosexuality between consenting adults was still a criminal offence – or maybe Beaumont thought there was no audience for them. But for Hall, who represented the new heterosexual wing of the English theatre, the issue was not sexuality but intolerance and censorship. Although the Arts preferred to get a Lord Chamberlain's licence to put on plays, it admitted members only when it was clear that no licence would be forthcoming, and with both of these plays admission was for members only. Yvonne Mitchell and Michael Gough led the cast, but the most memorable thing about *The Immoralist* was the controversy, and the name Hall was already making for himself in the profession.

The Oxford Playhouse looked promising, but Hall's restless ambition made it unlikely that he would stay there long. In the summer of 1954 Hall wrote to David Webster, the general administrator of the Royal Opera House: 'Thane Parker had suggested it might be a good idea for me to write to you in the hope of furthering in some small way my chief ambition in life – producing opera.'[22] Webster talked to Hall on 23 July 1954, but, for the time being at least, there was nothing on offer that was better than the Oxford Playhouse.

A Playhouse production of Gogol's *The Government Inspector* had toured successfully, and the Arts Council had been persuaded to add £500 to a £2,000 subsidy agreed by the Oxford City Council. (Part was used to reduce the best stalls from 7s. 6d. to 6s. 6d. – or from 37.5p to 32.5p.) Plans were announced for a repertory season that refused any compromise with Aunt Edna: Hall's model repertory was Giraudoux, Sheridan, Shaw, Pinero, Ibsen, T.S. Eliot and John Whiting. A permanent company of ten was put on contract. There was some promising talent too. Ronald Barker, who had been making a local reputation as a light comedian, was afraid that the new man from London might not appreciate him. 'Hall was fresh, full of ideas, energy, enthusiasm, and luckily for me, we took to each other,' Barker wrote.[23] A local girl called Margaret

Smith, known as Maggie, was playing small parts; though she and
Hall did not get on so well. 'There was nothing humble about her,
and he was just beginning to feel his power,' says Faulkner. When
Hall played the piano at an old-time music hall, the pages were
turned by an assistant stage manager called Eileen Atkins.

The Oxford Playhouse Christmas production of a new play
by Angela Jeans, *Listen to the Wind* (with music conducted by
Raymond Leppard), was good enough to transfer to London the
following Christmas, when Ronnie Barker persuaded Hall to let
him play in two productions simultaneously. He was already
appearing in a Hall production of Ugo Betti's *Summertime*, but
only in the last act. Barker invented a composite make-up and
proved to Hall that it was possible for him to begin the evening
in *Listen to the Wind* and to end it in *Summertime*: 'The clincher
for Peter Hall, when he was uncertain whether to let me try, was
my pointing out that it *had* been done before, by a certain D.A.
Clarke-Smith in 1935.'[24]

Then Hall received an offer he could not refuse. This can be
dated accurately, because on 12 January 1955 Moran Caplat in
Glyndebourne wrote to Hall at the Oxford Playhouse saying that
he had followed Hall's recent success with much interest and
wondered if he would like to join the producer's staff for the
forthcoming season. Hall replied two days later: he could not
go to Glyndebourne because during the past week he had been
appointed director of productions at the Arts. 'Needless to say,
this is the chance of a lifetime, and I have accepted with much
gratitude,' he explained. Hall added that he hoped none the less
that Caplat would consider him for the 1956 season.[25]

The vacancy at the Arts occurred because John Fernald had
now been appointed principal of the Royal Academy of Dramatic
Arts (RADA). Fernald had not been RADA's first choice: they had
originally offered the job to George Devine, who had turned it
down to become the first artistic director of the English Stage
Company. If Devine had taken the post, and Fernald had stayed
at the Arts, he might well have directed the play that made Hall
famous.

When Hall took over the Arts Theatre, he was twenty-four years
and two months old. He was not quite as young as Peter Brook
had been when he became director of productions at the Royal
Opera House in 1947 (Brook was twenty-two), but there was no
one else to rival them in precocity. The designer Timothy O'Brien,

who went down from Cambridge a year earlier than Peter Wood, met Hall at the Arts and remembers how far behind his university contemporaries then seemed.[26]

At the Oxford Playhouse, Hall's new company were glad for him, but sorry for themselves. 'We were left up there like carriages that had been shunted into a railway siding,' says Faulkner. Peter Wood took over the Playhouse, and the Elizabethan Theatre Company made guest appearances there. The Arts Council had offered the ETC a grant of £2,000 if it would continue touring, but that was not enough and the company folded. Peter Hall had stepped off this theatrical vehicle when it was still moving; when it stopped, Robertson left for Stratford, and Barton returned to academic life in Cambridge. Barton observes that when a company is not strong enough to support its stars, they are drawn to other work and the company inevitably folds. The significance of the Elizabethan Theatre Company was that its stars had not been clever young actors, but young directors just down from university.

In 1954 and 1955, the once impregnable bastion of the West End London theatre was crumbling. No one saw this sooner or exploited it more ruthlessly than Kenneth Tynan, who had replaced Ivor Brown as the *Observer*'s dramatic critic in the summer of 1954. Tynan was not much less precocious than Hall or Brook. He had reviewed Brook's *Love's Labour's Lost* at Stratford when he was nineteen, and his first volume of collected criticism was published in 1950 when he was twenty-three. So he had come to the job of critic of a posh Sunday paper rather late, aged twenty-seven, but he was still known sarcastically in the profession as 'The Boy Wonder', and he was a sworn enemy of the 'glibly codified fairy tale world' of the West End. Tynan calculated that during the 1953–4 season, 22 of 26 straight plays were about life in the upper or upper middle classes: 'The setting is in a country house in what used to be called Loamshire, but now, as a heroic tribute to realism, is sometimes called Berkshire.'[27] His admiration for the theatre abroad extended beyond its playwrights; he thought it was necessary to bring foreign directors to London to revive English acting. Among actors, Tynan inspired fear: John Gielgud called his criticism 'It's-wonderful-when-it-isn't-you'.[28]

Tynan was respectful of Hall's production, the first in English, of *The Lesson* by Eugène Ionesco at the Arts in March 1955. When he returned to the Arts in April to see another play

with a homosexual theme, Julien Green's *South*, Tynan wrote
flamboyantly: 'My faith in English directors was suddenly
restored by *South*, from which Mr Peter Hall extracted many
more subtleties than did his opposite number in Paris a year
ago.'[29] The play opened during a national newspaper strike,
but word of mouth attracted actors and directors to see Hall's
direction and Denholm Elliott's central performance for themselves. After watching *South*, Peter Brook telephoned Hall to
invite him for a drink.

The summer of 1955's ambitious project at the Arts was Eugene
O'Neill's *Mourning Becomes Electra* – its first production in London
since 1937. It is a monumental piece: 'runs four hours, feels like
eight,' said one critic. On Saturdays when there was a matinée,
the audience for the evening performance scheduled to begin at
6.30 p.m. often had to wait for the matinée to finish. Tynan called
it 'the greatest unwritten play of the century'. It was a bold choice,
and had a respectful if somewhat low-key reception. Much more
vivid emotions were to be aroused by Hall's next production at the
Arts, 'the most talked-about piece of theatre to be seen in London
for a long time'.[30]

Peter Hall was a lucky young director, and the best example of
his luck is the story of how he came to direct *Waiting for Godot*.
Samuel Beckett had written the play in French and it had opened
at the Théâtre de Babylone in Paris on 5 January 1953. Beckett had
done his own English translation of his uncompromising farce in
which nothing happens between long pauses while two men called
Vladimir and Estragon wait for a Mr Godot on a country road.
He was anxious that it should be performed in London. 'Beckett
knew that he needed a London success if he were to be known as
something more than the curious Irishman who wrote in French.
American appreciation was welcome for the dollars it brought,
but English acceptance had deep meaning for him.'[31]

The first person to bid for the English rights of *Waiting for Godot*
was the director Peter Glenville, who had received the script from
a French agent. Having directed a number of French plays for the
Company of Four, Glenville saw himself as the proper director for
the London production, but Beckett's London agent, Kitty Black,
suggested that a deal should be done with a management as well
as a director. Consequently, in March 1953 Glenville bought a
share of the option with Donald Albery, the son of the theatre

manager Bronson Albery, who was making his own way as a manager.[32]

Glenville and Albery liked avant-garde plays, but they had conventional views about the West End. They wanted stars for their production, and they showed *Godot* first to Ralph Richardson and Alec Guinness. Each turned it down; so did Michael Hordern. Readings were held in the circle bar of the New Theatre (now the Albery), and Kitty Black remembers that the best performance she heard was by an Irish actor named Denis Carey; she realised then, she says, that *Godot* was written in Irish English.

The Lord Chamberlain was a separate problem. His office was profoundly suspicious of French plays, and had refused a licence for Jean-Paul Sartre's *Vicious Circle* even if it was played in French. After painstaking negotiations in 1954, some cuts in *Godot* were agreed with Beckett, but there were other changes which he refused to make – for example, the dialogue in which Vladimir and Estragon discuss the possibility of getting an erection if they hang themselves. Beckett also insisted on Estragon's dropping his trousers in the final tableau.

By the spring of 1955 Glenville had decamped to the United States, leaving the option with Albery. Since he knew Campbell Williams, and admired Hall's production of *South*, Albery sent the play to the Arts to see if they were interested in the option. Campbell Williams asked Toby Rowland, a shrewd commercial producer whose judgement he trusted, to read it; Rowland reported that the Arts ought to do the play, and Hall should direct it.[33] Hall read it during technical rehearsals for *Mourning Becomes Electra* and during a train journey to Cambridge, where he met Yolande Bird. She recalls his telling her about an extraordinary play: 'He said he had no idea what was going on, but he thought he was going to do it.'

Casting proved troublesome. For Vladimir, the older of the two men, Hall hoped to persuade Cyril Cusack, who had been in self-imposed exile from the West End, to make his comeback at the Arts. When Cusack turned the part down, Hall cast Paul Daneman, a talented young actor who was having a second good season at the Old Vic and was available for *Godot* between engagements. To Daneman, Hall described it as an odd play. 'He said it would run for four weeks and he didn't think it would transfer.' Hall cast a Cambridge undergraduate called Peter Woodthorpe. 'Not an amateur?' Daneman asked. Hall replied that

Woodthorpe had been a wonderful Lear at university; that was that.[34] The second pair of characters in the play – Pozzo, the master, and Lucky, his slave – were played by Peter Bull and Timothy Bateson.

Hall had hoped for Beckett's help during rehearsals, but the constant delays and uncertainties made Beckett doubt whether the production would ever take place, and he declined to come to London. Although they did not meet, Hall did speak to him on the telephone. Hall told Daneman that he had asked Beckett what *Godot* meant, and had been told: 'It means what you want it to mean.' (To the same question put by the American director, Alan Schneider, Beckett replied: 'If I knew, I would have said so in the play.')[35]

At the first rehearsal Hall announced that Vladimir and Estragon were clowns in a circus. 'We're going to have fun with it,' he said. Rehearsals took place on the top floor of the Arts during a hot summer. The actors found the repetitive lines particularly difficult to learn; they hadn't yet had Pinter to practise on. Pauses and silences presented an unusual problem, since the actors feared that the audience would assume they had forgotten their lines. But Hall told them that when the script said pause, they should wait for as long as possible. 'Until they start to giggle?' they asked. Hall said yes. 'And shift with embarrassment?' Hall said yes: 'It's a bizarre play and we might as well play it bizarrely.'

Daneman recalls that in rehearsal the humanity of the characters began to emerge. They had been played in the Paris production as clowns, but now the cast began to think of Vladimir and Estragon as tramps. It was partly because of their costumes; they were dressed out of second-hand shops. 'By the first night we had a fairly good idea of the play, but no sense of the weight of it. We knew there were laughs at the beginning, and that it became rather moving,' says Daneman. But when he asked Hall about signing a contract for his next play, Hall told him to go ahead: he did not think *Godot* would go any further.

Waiting for Godot opened for a four-week run on Wednesday, 3 August 1955, and Peter Bull wrote later about 'waves of hostility whirling over the footlights'. Daneman heard a few people leaving during the first act, and more followed them at the interval. 'The curtain fell to mild applause, we took a scant three calls and a depressing sense of anti-climax descended on us all. Very few people came round,' said Peter Bull.[36] 'For the rest of the week, the audience sat on their hands. It was hot and airless, and we were wearing dirty clothes from a second-hand shop, a wig and a nose. I wondered why I'd ever agreed to do this bloody thing.' Daneman remembers Hall telling the cast that it was a good try, but it hadn't worked; he warned them that it might not last the full four weeks of the run.

Since *Waiting for Godot* is one of the twentieth century's most influential plays, it has inevitably attracted myth and legend. One myth is that the early reviews were disastrously bad. Hall himself says that on the morning after the first night, Campbell Williams called him into his office and announced that the play would have to come off immediately. Hall's account suggests that Williams agreed to wait until the Sunday notices, 'after a lot of persuasion'.[37] But the Arts Theatre was so small that even if only a hundred people turned up, it was half full. The actors were being paid a mere £10 a week; and the reviews on the morning of 4 August were certainly good enough to have persuaded the management that at least a hundred people in a population of eight million would be interested in the play.

In his autobiography, Hall writes: '*The Guardian* reflected that this was just the sort of thing that could be seen in smoky basements in Berlin in the Twenties, but that we did not really need it now.' Writing in what was still the *Manchester Guardian*, what Philip Hope-Wallace actually said was:

> The play bored some people acutely. Others found it a witty and poetic conundrum. There was general agreement that Peter Hall's production did fairly by a work which has won much applause in many parts of the world already . . . There was only one audible retirement from the audience, though the ranks had thinned after the interval. It is good to find that plays once dubbed 'incomprehensible and pretentious' can still get a staging. Where better than the Arts Theatre?

Hope-Wallace's review was condescending, but it was not a bad one. Nor was that of *The Times*, whose anonymous critic (Arthur Cookman) took the play very seriously indeed:

> The dramatic instinct reveals itself in a flow of unexpected, absorbing happenings upon the stage. But a play is something more – it is the flow gradually emerging as some significant image of life. Mr Samuel Beckett's Waiting for Godot, now to be seen at the Arts Theatre in a brilliant production by Mr Peter Hall, insists that these truisms shall be restated.

That Mr Beckett . . . possesses the dramatic instinct in a most original sense one cannot doubt. His work in two acts holds the stage most wittily, but is it a play? The significance -- and how, one feels, Mr Beckett must abjure the word – would seem to be that nothing finally is significant . . . His patently elemental personages are figments in whom we cannot ultimately believe since they lack universality . . . They are, though, remarkably well played in this production.

The *Times* review cross-referred to a picture of Bateson, Daneman and Bull on the back page. W.A. Darlington in the *Daily Telegraph* was bemused, identifying Beckett as 'head boy of the school of dramatists whose pupils love obscurity for obscurity's sake', and in the *Daily Express*, David Lewin said that he too became weary of waiting for Godot.

A second myth about the reviews is that it was Harold Hobson's that single-handedly saved *Waiting for Godot*. Hall is partly responsible for this, claiming in addition that Hobson was influenced by reading a copy of Beckett's novel *Watt* which Hall had sent him after the first night. In fact, Hobson's review in the *Sunday Times* on 7 August made no reference to *Watt*, and Hobson had his doubts about the play. He detected a meaning in it which he thought false. 'The objections to Mr Samuel Beckett's play as a theatrical entertainment are many and obvious,' he began; but his enthusiasm grew as he wrote. Of the dialogue between Vladimir and Estragon, he said:

Their conversation has the simplicity, in this case the delusive simplicity, of music hall cross-talk, now and again pierced with a shaft that seems for a second or so to touch the edge of truth's garment. It is bewildering. It is exasperating. It is insidiously exciting . . . Go and see Waiting for Godot. *At the worst you will discover a curiosity, a four-leaf clover, a black tulip; at the best, something that will lodge in a corner of your mind for as long as you live.*

Hall remembers Kenneth Tynan as liking *Waiting for Godot*, but taking time to work up to full enthusiasm. But Tynan was, if anything, more enthusiastic than Hobson. *Waiting for Godot*, he wrote,

frankly jettisons everything by which we recognise theatre . . . It does this, I believe, by appealing to a definition of drama much more fundamental than any in the books. A play, it asserts and proves, is basically a means of spending two hours in the dark without being bored . . . It forced me to examine the rules which have hitherto governed the drama; and, having done so, to pronouce them not elastic enough. It is validly new: and hence I declare myself, as the Spanish would say, Godotista.

Of the two reviews on 7 August, Tynan's is the *tour de force*, and, at a time when the circulations of the two papers were much the same, Tynan's would have been at least as influential as Hobson's. Perhaps Hall's memory unconsciously reflects the dislike he later came to feel for Tynan.

On that Sunday, when Daneman tried to get through to the box office to book seats for friends, the telephone was constantly engaged. Hobson and Tynan between them had transformed *Waiting for Godot* into a hit. Hall now told Daneman that the run might even be extended for a couple of weeks. His optimism was confirmed by a second excited piece from Hobson the following week, in which he did refer to Beckett's *Watt*. After the Sunday papers had pronounced, the only dissenting voices were those of W.A. Darlington and Bernard Levin, the twenty-six-year-old critic, in the weekly magazine *Truth*, who declared the play the funniest literary hoax since the poems of Ern Malley. Levin also described Hall's direction as brilliant, and had praise for the cast. 'After the second week we were the toast of the town,' says Daneman. Donald Albery arranged a transfer to the Criterion Theatre in September. Poor Daneman went into the *Punch Review*, and it closed in weeks; *Waiting for Godot* ran for months.

After the transfer, even W.A. Darlington was converted. The only person central to the whole affair who did not much like what he saw seems to have been Samuel Beckett. When he watched the production with Alan Schneider early in December, he kept finding fault with it. He criticised the background music; he thought the stage too cluttered and the pauses too short. 'He wanted harsher simplicity,' according to Schneider. 'Samuel Beckett thought perhaps the rudimentary qualities of the primitive Babylone production were better suited to the Théâtre de Babylone than the charm and comfort of the Arts Theatre Club. The production reminded him of the plush, overstuffed quality of English life that seemed to permeate the theatre with all that he considered worst in English society.'[38]

Hall seems not to have known how hard Beckett was to please, although the actors sensed it when the author gave them a party. Bull says that they were all rather rude to him, and that Beckett left for France telling them that the pauses were not long enough. 'We told him that if they were any longer, not a customer would be left in the building.'[39]

The Arts Theatre production of *Waiting for Godot* became a theatrical legend, and it made Peter Hall famous. He appeared on BBC's *Panorama* with Malcolm Muggeridge, and became a champion of his unknown contemporaries in the theatre. Harold Pinter, for example, loved *Godot*: 'I was very much for the play. It was a great thrill,' he says.[40] Pinter had yet to write a play, but when he did, he wanted it to be directed by Hall.

Toby Rowland asked Hall to direct a film star (Dirk Bogarde) in the West End, and by the end of 1955, aged twenty-five, he had three plays running simultaneously. The revolution in the London theatre had begun, and he was playing a leading role in it. The theatre of anonymous and powerful managers like Binkie Beaumont was slowly being discredited, but its place was not being taken by the actors' theatre that Eric Porter aspired to. In 1955, Samuel Beckett's success showed there was an audience for new writing. Peter Hall's success showed that it was not necessary to be an actor to become a star.

6

To Stratford, via Leningrad

'He was nervous, but it was a terrific opportunity'

Peter Hall first saw Leslie Caron when he was a sixteen-year-old schoolboy and she was the fifteen-year-old star of Roland Petit's celebrated Ballet des Champs-Elysées on a visit to London shortly after the war. Born in Paris, where her father was a well-to-do pharmacist, she was the daughter of an American dancer. Caron was slim, with large brown eyes, a snub nose, big mouth and a captivating smile; she was neither beautiful nor *jolie laide*, but once seen she was not forgotten. Hall went to the cinema to see her when she was nineteen, dancing with Gene Kelly in *An American in Paris*; and, five years later, to see her as Fred Astaire's co-star in *Daddy Long Legs*. At twenty-five, Caron had already married and divorced a millionaire named George Hormel, the heir to the Spam fortune. Not long afterwards, she married Peter Hall. It was one of a number of things that happened to Hall which can be directly attributed to the success of *Waiting for Godot*.

In 1955, Hollywood regarded Caron as a desirable and costly property. MGM had proposed that she should star in a film of Anita Loos's adaptation of Colette's *Gigi*, but before she made the film she wanted to work in the straight theatre, and had taken a part in a play called *Orvet*, written and directed by her friend Jean Renoir. Hearing of this, Donald Albery, the West End impresario who had passed *Godot* on to the Arts, decided to bring Caron to London. He thought of casting her as Max Beerbohm's bewitching Zuleika Dobson, but when he met her in Paris he dropped the idea: Caron recalls his saying she was not English enough.[1] Albery asked if there was anything else she would like to play, and she said *Gigi*, on stage. When he asked who should direct, Caron telephoned her New York agent, Audrey Wood, for advice. 'She said that Tennessee Williams was her best author and he swore by Peter Hall. "He's the brightest young thing in England," she said. "Why don't you ask for him?"' Caron did, and Hall seized the opportunity. He was half in love with her before they met. Ever since he had fallen for a little blonde girl called Emma at the Morley Memorial School in Cambridge, Hall had loved falling in love. But, apart from Jill Mortimer, his ardour had usually gone unrequited. By 1955 Hall was primed for an affair, and he was now in a position to make it a grand one.

Hall had been busy during the previous winter, working in the West End for the first time with Toby Rowland, the American producer who preferred London to Broadway, whom he had met at the Arts. They had discovered a light romance by the Italian Ugo Betti, called *Summertime*, and Rowland had persuaded Dirk Bogarde to play the lead. It was shrewd box-office because Bogarde, the handsome young doctor from *Doctor in the House*, was the British cinema's leading juvenile. On tour, before opening in London, there was a mob outside the stage door in Glasgow and full houses wherever they went.

Hall, who was drawn to motor showrooms the way other people cannot resist a bookshop, was smitten in Manchester by a bright blue Ford coupé, costing £390. (The sum was recalled exactly by Toby Rowland.) That was beyond Hall's means, though what he could afford was about to be radically redefined. Rowland told Hall that, since he was set to earn much more than £390 from *Summertime*, he would buy him the car, deducting the money from his royalties.[3]

When it opened on Shaftesbury Avenue in November 1955, *Summertime* was poorly reviewed. Although Tynan praised with faint damns (complimenting Hall on soft-pedalling the platitudes and speeding over the *longueurs*), Harold Hobson declared it Hall's first major defeat – because of 'the poverty of vocal emotion' in the two leading performers, Bogarde and Geraldine McEwan. But this was a star vehicle and the critics hardly mattered. Business was brisk until Bogarde became ill, when it faded; it did not recover even after he had.

Jean Anouilh's *Waltz of the Toreadors* at the Arts, which opened in February 1956, was a more substantial piece; it transferred from the Arts to the Criterion and ran there for seventeen months. Anouilh had directed the play in Paris and, when it flopped, had banned further performances, but Hall wrote a provocative note to Anouilh saying the fault lay in the production, not the play. Moreover, he had Hugh Griffith, the feisty Welsh actor, to play the lead. Sufficiently flattered as an author, Anouilh lifted his ban; he came to see the production at the Arts, and liked what he saw.[4]

At the same time, Hall was casting his first production at Stratford – *Love's Labour's Lost*, the melancholy comedy with which he had had such success at Cambridge. He asked James Bailey, who had designed *Summertime*, to work with him again, and persuaded Geraldine McEwan to join him too. Casting a play at Stratford was easy. Instead of a puny £8 a week in a club theatre, he could now offer actors better-paid work in a high-profile theatre. But first there was *Gigi*.

Leslie Caron believes that something happened between them almost immediately. Holding her hands wide apart, she says: 'His brain was so big.' She was impressed by Hall's erudition, and his sense of drama. His background was right, too; after her first marriage, Caron had developed an aversion to heirs to American business fortunes and had decided that she preferred self-made, working-class men. 'I think he was the answer to everything I was longing for,' she says. In rehearsals, however, both kept their distance. For Caron: 'It shuffles all the cards wrongly to be in love with the director while you're rehearsing. When you become involved with something other than the play, you lose your independence and sense of judgement.'

When *Gigi* was on tour, Hall's Cambridge friend, Toppet Moore, went to see it in Brighton, and he told her that he was going to marry Caron. Toppet thought he had taken leave of his senses. By the time *Gigi* reached Oxford, Caron, content with her performance, was ready to surrender; in the Randolph Hotel, as a matter of fact. They married in May, during the run of *Gigi*.

He was only twenty-five, she was seven months younger.

On 8 May 1956 *Look Back in Anger* opened at the Royal Court, directed by Tony Richardson; on 24 May, Brendan Behan's *The Quare Fellow* opened at the Theatre Royal, Stratford, directed by Joan Littlewood. Albert Finney had made his début the month before at the Birmingham Rep, as had Robert Stephens at the Royal Court. *Gigi*, which opened at the New Theatre on 23 May, was more glamorous but less memorable than any of these. *The Times* critic reported: 'There is a charming performance by Miss Leslie Caron of a tomboy turning into a marriageable girl. Where the acting wants more in the way of sheer technical accomplishment, the deficiency is partly made good by miming so certain in touch as to appear instinctive, and the actress's altogether pleasing personality does the rest.' Hall's direction fared less well. In July's *Theatre World*, it was described as the most disappointing thing about the production: 'It is perhaps too much to expect a truly Parisian atmosphere from an English company, but in this company there isn't even a whiff of Paris, 1900, and the whole production lacks overall style.'

 Gigi did nothing for Hall's reputation as a director, but it did wonders for his public image. Leslie's celebrity rubbed off on him, and immediately they became the property of the gossip columns and the monthly magazines. Their wedding photographs were taken by his Cambridge contemporary, Tony Armstrong Jones.

Accounts differ about Hall's introduction to the Shakespeare Memorial Theatre, but they usually involve lunch. Hall himself gives two versions of that significant event. In one he is taken to L'Escargot in Soho shortly after the opening of *South* in March 1955, and is asked by Anthony Quayle and Glen Byam Shaw, two of the triumvirate who ran the Shakespeare Memorial Theatre (the third was George Devine), whether he would consider leaving the Arts to direct modern plays for their company at its new London venue, the Royal Court. According to Hall he said yes, shook hands on it, and never heard another word. In a second version, Hall is taken to lunch by the two of them after *Waiting for Godot* and asked whether he would direct the occasional Shakespeare production at Stratford. Hall describes this as 'a very satisfying moment'. Later, Quayle was to say that his enthusiasm for Hall was qualified by a niggling feeling that he was still an apprentice, and that his approach was too academic; but Glen Byam Shaw's recollection is that as they walked away from the lunch, Quayle turned to him, and, echoing his own thoughts, said: 'That's the next director of the Stratford theatre.'[5]

Quayle's version is told in his autobiography without dates, or meals; in it he makes clear his conviction that, because the Old Vic was probably destined to become the National Theatre, the Stratford company must have a London outlet for its work. His own success at Stratford made expansion inevitable. Quayle had been chosen for the job by the chairman of the governors, Fordham Flower, who shared his wartime background as a bluff and brave officer and gentleman. Quayle's take-over from Barry Jackson had happened at a moment when audiences had grown weary of the drab, post-war years. Quayle had fed the thirst for glamour; his Shakespeare was colourful, and his casts were led by stars, many of whom took parts because their West End patron, Binkie Beaumont, a governor of the Shakespeare Memorial Theatre himself, encouraged them to do so. Under Fordham Flower's benign patronage, Quayle made Stratford fashionable, and tickets were hard to come by. Even the local townspeople thought well of the Memorial Theatre.

Quayle, as the leader of a managing triumvirate, also saw it as his duty to protect the theatre's reputation and its independence. His determination to do so marked the start of a tricky relationship between the Shakespeare Memorial Theatre and the proposed National Theatre, which was to top the political agenda in the English theatre for the next two decades. Quayle explained his thinking as follows:

> [The National Theatre] would be well subsidised: actors could live at home in London; they were not confined to a diet of Shakespeare; they could range through the centuries; they could pick their plays from any foreign country they wanted, while we were stuck in Warwickshire like rabbits, growing fur all over us. We had to find a London theatre where we could present every sort of play, then change round and bring our own productions to London. It was too early to know how this would be financed, but it had got to be done or our premier position would very soon be lost.[6]

There was no shortage of good will in Stratford for Hall's début with *Love's Labour's Lost*; but he seems to have felt burdened by a keen desire to impress, and by the vivid memory of Peter Brook's production only a decade earlier. James Bailey's designs aroused mixed opinions. Harold Matthews in *Theatre World* was impressed by the 'slender and graceful architectural setting', but John Barton thought the design camp and sugar-like, and his view mattered more to Hall. He did not work with Bailey again. Matthews described this *Love's Labour's Lost* as 'competent . . . a mechanical exercise performed in a beautiful setting'.[7] The production was neither the great success Hall had hoped for, nor a critical and artistic disaster. But Hall and Barton, schooled in the Cambridge tradition of candid criticism, each declared that it had been nothing less than a disgrace.[8] Before Byam Shaw offered him *Cymbeline* for the following year, Hall's capacity for self-dramatisation led him to wonder whether he would ever be asked back.

His morale was not improved by his next job. After *Gigi*, he had signed a two-year contract to direct for Donald Albery, and their first play together sounded promising: John Whiting's *The Gates of Summer*, with Paul Scofield, who was working with Hall for the first time. But Albery did not like what he saw, and while the play was on tour, he went to Brighton and, without consulting Hall, altered the lighting.[9] Outraged and humiliated, Hall terminated their brief partnership. At the end of 1956 he was still heavily publicised as London's brightest young director, but after the marvellous run in 1955 he was finding failure hard to live with. Three of his four productions in 1956 had been disappointing, and, although he had a wife to console him, Hall was inconsolable.

Hall insists that he cares only about the future, and that he has never kept scrapbooks, designs, photographs or reviews. But in 1956 he did start to keep letters, and he did so for more than a decade. He later believed these letters had been destroyed in a fire at his parents' house in Wallingford, when it was lying empty after their deaths, but in fact the letters had been stored in a garden shed, not in the house; and when Jacky Hall, his second wife, moved to London after their divorce she took them with her.[10] As a record of Hall's life, they are patchy, but because they are written in the private language of theatre people speaking to each other, they are absorbing and revealing.

The first letter in the collection is from Tennessee Williams, and if anything could arouse Hall from his melancholy, this should have been it. Williams wrote in December 1956:

*As I told you at lunch at Claridge's, I think you are the best living
director in Europe, but you mustn't quote me! Nevertheless I think you
are, and possibly in America, too. Let's say one of the two greatest living
directors! – on the two continents. So naturally I'm just longing for you
to stage one of my plays. You may take your pick. At any time, any
place. Just write and tell me which one, where and when and I will come
over to see it.*

(After telling Hall he mustn't quote him, Williams added a
footnote: 'I don't tell this to *all* the boys!')[11]

H.M. Tennent had postponed a production of Williams's *Cat
on a Hot Tin Roof* that Hall was hoping to direct in the coming
spring, and Williams wondered whether it was a result of Anglo-
American political misunderstandings after the humiliating climax
of the Suez affair a few weeks earlier: 'I mean have they created
some anti-American feeling that would prejudice the English
public against American plays at this time?'

Williams offered Hall *Orpheus Descending*, which was about
to be produced in the United States; 'as for *Sweet Bird of
Youth*, I doubt very much that it would ever get by your Lord
Chamberlain'. Finally he suggested: 'Why not do *Camino Real*?
Nobody could do it better than you, and there is nothing in it
to trouble the Lord Chamberlain – I don't think. Of course it
was an expensive flop in the States and might be the same in
London, but you have such wonderful actors and audiences that
I have a feeling that if you did it, it would have a very exciting
reception.'

Such letters made no difference; Hall sank into deep gloom.
Leslie Caron dates the first of the breakdowns that were to
recur throughout Hall's career to the winter of 1956 and 1957:
'He worked much too hard and couldn't sleep properly. He
cracked.' To try to revive his spirits, Caron suggested a visit
to New York. He had never been there; Audrey Wood was
now his agent as well as hers, and he could visit Tennessee
Williams in Key West, Florida and talk about *Camino Real*.
They spent two weeks in Florida and, although Williams had
little to say about the play, the journey cured Hall of his
depression. By the time they sailed back across on the SS
America, he was sufficiently himself again to fret at the enforced
idleness.

Leslie Caron soon became pregnant. She was happy about
that; otherwise, the adjustment to her new life was proving

troublesome. She and Hall had moved into the small bachelor flat north of Marble Arch in Montagu Place which he had shared with John Barton. It was on the wrong side of the park, the maid was a dresser at the New Theatre who would not do what Caron asked, and, by her standards, they were hard up. (She says she only had $30,000 to her name when they married; to Hall that 'only' was riches.) 'I found the English brittle; impeccably behaved and very forbidding. They intimidated me abominably. I dreaded having to use the telephone. I was very timid,' she recalls. Being a film star was no help: she sensed the hostility of other actors, who behaved to her as though she was slumming. Shyness made her appear aloof: 'I would get fits of such shyness that I was catatonic. I couldn't speak because I was frozen.'[12]

To Paul Daneman, who had been in *Godot* at the Arts, Caron was a tough Parisian bourgeois who was vetting Hall's friends in the profession and judging them not big enough.[13] She thought the same harsh judgements were being made about her. Socially smart dinner parties were no better. Caron found it unappealing that women retired to another room to discuss the servant situation while the men stayed at table, smoking cigars and drinking port. She felt that, because of her reputation as a film star, people expected to meet a glamorous woman, whereas what they got was quite different: 'An unsophisticated little girl who'd done nothing but work very hard. I didn't know how to make speeches, or how to behave in public. I was totally inexperienced in the social graces.'

Caron's decision to break her contract with MGM so that she could have the baby had made her feel even less secure. In fact, it did her career no harm. MGM, deciding *Gigi* needed gingering up, had asked Lerner and Loewe to set it to music, and while that was happening, MGM was content to wait for Caron until after the birth of her baby. She was glad of that; Hall less so. Differences about work were the origin of the rift that eventually broke their marriage, and the first crack appeared within weeks of their wedding.

Leslie Caron is quite specific about the timing. As they were driving to Stratford, where Hall was rehearsing *Love's Labour's Lost*, he made it clear that, as far as he was concerned, there was room for only one ambitious person in any happy family.

He asked why I was so ambitious, and I replied that I wasn't, but that I did want to work. I was trained for it; I didn't know what else to do. To him, that was something he could not comprehend. He felt women should be in the kitchen, the nursery or the garden and that, as soon as we married and had a child, I should stop work. That was even before Christopher was born. It sent a chill through me.

Hall felt the uncertainty too; in his autobiography he says he thought it stemmed from the conflict that arose inevitably between two people leading diverse and demanding careers. He was conscious of that reason, but seems less aware of the influence of his own upbringing. Although he had been critical of his parents, Hall's unconscious assumption was that his children would be brought up in the same way that he had been brought up. His mother gave up work when she married Reg, and Hall's behaviour suggested that he expected his wife to do the same.

They returned from New York to a new house in Hyde Park Square, which Caron had bought to make enough room for the child. Their son, Christopher, was born on 30 March 1957, between the technical and dress rehearsals for *Camino Real*. After his unhappy experience with Donald Albery, Hall had resumed his partnership with Toby Rowland. Though anxious to direct in the West End, he still felt compelled to make the work sound intellectually respectable, as if to prove that he was not in it just for the money. Hall's venture with Rowland and a Swedish producer called Lars Schmidt was called the International Playwrights Theatre. The launch, which coincided with the opening of *Camino Real*, sounded remarkably high-minded: '[Its] policy is based on the conviction that there is a wide audience for out-of-the-ordinary plays, and that plays that enlarge the frontier of the theatre have a great contemporary importance.'[14]

Tennessee Williams was heartened by Hall's casting report for *Camino Real* ('I've always been crazy about Diana Wynyard'). After a fraught experience with *Orpheus Descending* on tour in the United States (the leading lady drank even more than he did), he spent two weeks in London publicising the production. Williams was still a controversial playwright, and commercial managements like H.M. Tennent were wary of him. In a fan letter to Hall, Hermione Baddeley recalled that Williams had asked her to play the lead in *The Rose Tattoo*, and that Tennent decided not to do it 'because it was too dangerous in some way or another'. *Camino Real* had some good reviews, but the cast numbered forty and the run lasted only three months: it would have needed six months to repay the investment. It was a prestigious but uneconomic start for the International Playwrights Theatre.

Cymbeline at Stratford-upon-Avon was the most significant event in Hall's 1957, but before starting rehearsals there he made an interesting detour to Sadler's Wells, where he directed his first opera. This was the story of the life of Gauguin by John Gardner, based on Somerset Maugham's novel *The Moon and Sixpence*. Without understanding that singers normally gave acting a low priority, Hall made them act; for example, he insisted that they look at each other rather than constantly at the conductor when they were singing. Without ever fully appreciating that conductors normally swaggered in late in the production process, Hall assumed that Alexander Gibson would be involved from the beginning, in the set designs and all the rehearsals. As Hall explained some time later:

> If [the conductor] comes in and plays the music only when the audience appears, he will normally ruin all the work we've done in rehearsals. If you have decided that a phrase has a particular psychological or emotional meaning, and the conductor then comes along and plays the music faster, even half a second faster – the singer can't feel it, and the drama's gone.[15]

The Moon and Sixpence was not good enough to enter the operatic repertory, but it was important to Hall: by doing it, he had proved to himself that he was able to combine his knowledge of music with his experience of directing. He was sure he would return to opera one day.

Hall was apprehensive about *Cymbeline*. Peggy Ashcroft was to play Imogen, and he had never worked with one of the heroes of his youth. Ashcroft, on the other hand, was eager to try him out. She was a dominant figure in his earliest memories of the theatre, in *The Duchess of Malfi* in 1944; and he was one of the new generation of directors who seemed to share her radicalism.

They clicked. Ashcroft, who became the only person to call Hall Pete, had a profound effect on his method of work. Before starting rehearsals on *Cymbeline*, Hall had scrupulously blocked the actors' moves, as though they were toy soldiers. At the end of the first week of rehearsal, during a particularly difficult scene, Hall instructed Ashcroft to move from one side of the stage to the other. Having done so, she announced: 'Pete, that move's wrong. I can't do it.' This was a dramatic moment. Hall could either assert his authority or he could trust the actor by leaving her free to move in the way that best suited her. He chose freedom.

> *She was right. It was arbitrary. It was a pattern. When I now say I never block a play, I have to know what the physical life of a scene will be; I have to know that the exits and entrances are right, and the furniture, but I never give moves any more. I suggest, or say what I like and what I don't. But the actors must always feel they've invented it. She taught me to have the confidence to use their responses. It started a whole new method for me.*[16]

Caron watched each draw a performance out of the other. 'Peggy was full of fun, full of wonderful passion for the theatre, with great talent and generosity, but domineering; and she loved having this handsome young man, learned and respectful. She was very fond of boys like Peter. But she was very finely strung, like a racehorse. You needed to take care of her if she was to come to the opening night in good shape.'

Hall also worked with Lila de Nobili for the first time. She had come as part of Caron's dowry to Hall, for she and Leslie had known each other in Paris, where de Nobili had worked as a painter. Her work was dominated by rich brown, russet, red and gold – Rembrandt's colours. Having designed the scenery, she painted it herself and hung it behind gauzes. The effect was often magical; for *Cymbeline* it made a fairy-tale world of trees and turrets, half-hidden staircases and grottoes. She was a great discovery; her romanticism suited Hall's artistic temperament, and she had, in her way, as decisive an effect on his work as Peggy Ashcroft. John Barton says that, once Hall and de Nobili began to work together, Hall became the most romantic director in England.

The reviews of *Cymbeline* concentrated on Ashcroft's performance, which was extravagantly praised ('She moves with the moon's soft pace' – Alan Dent), rather at the expense of Hall's direction. The exception was Tynan's. He wrote that Hall had 'created an ambiance in which the ludicrous anomalies of the plot are believable, even lovable . . . my admiration for Mr Hall's production is boundless'.[17] The Stratford audience was admiring, and Glen Byam Shaw wrote to Hall after the opening night: 'I realise you have suffered some agonies with this production, but I sincerely believe the best work is often the outcome of such tortures. I think *Cymbeline* is a most skilful and beautiful production full of imagination, sensitivity and true romantic feeling.'[18] Hall had clearly established himself as a director of Shakespeare.

The timing was excellent. Tony Quayle had resigned, exhausted by the job and fearful that he was sacrificing his acting career. Within a few weeks of the end of the 1956 season he was gone, leaving Glen Byam Shaw in sole charge. Byam Shaw, at fifty-two, was liked and respected. He had been an actor himself until his early thirties, and was married to Angela Baddeley, Hermione's sister, herself a good actress. There was never any doubt about his loyalty to the acting profession. In his office in Stratford he collected photographs of all the Stratford stars, but all showed them as children – before they put on disguises, he said.

Having worked as Quayle's partner in a series of successful seasons, Byam Shaw's credentials as director at Stratford were excellent but, unlike Quayle, he was neither ambitious nor physically strong. He found the regime hard. The director's responsibilities were not confined to choosing the repertory and directing a couple of plays in the summer. It was a full-time occupation involving casting and contracts, finding directors and designers, keeping an eye on the budgets and the box-office. Walking with Byam Shaw in her garden, from which the Memorial Theatre could be seen in the distance, Lady Flower remembers him shaking his fist at it, saying that he'd given his life-blood to it and it wasn't enough. When Fordham Flower had offered him the job, Byam Shaw accepted it only for a three-year term. During his first season, in 1957, the director and the chairman of the governors were already considering the succession. By the end of 1957 Byam Shaw had begun to prepare the ground for Hall: 'I have been trying to think ahead . . . I owe it to you and your theatre,' he wrote to Fordham Flower on 10 December 1957.[19] He was talking about it to Hall, too.

That winter, Hall made his New York début with a play called *The Rope Dancers* by Morton Wishengrad, learning about lighting from the American designer Boris Aronson, who, says Hall, 'encouraged me to be confident about colour, shape, and shadow'.[20] In London, Binkie Beaumont, who had finally nerved himself to produce *Cat on a Hot Tin Roof*, hired Hall to direct it. (To evade the Lord Chamberlain's censorship, Beaumont turned the Comedy Theatre into a club for the occasion.) Toby Rowland and the International Playwrights Theatre surfaced again with a play for Hall by George Tabori, *Brouhaha*. With Peter Sellers, the star of *The Goon Show*, it was scheduled to open in July 1958, but before that Hall was to direct *Twelfth Night* in Stratford, and Rowland sensed that his heart was there already.

Hall cast young actors in *Twelfth Night*: Richard Johnson, Ian Holm, Geraldine McEwan as Olivia and Dorothy Tutin as Viola; they played them as a pair of mischievous and vivacious young women. Tutin admired Hall's knowledge of Shakespeare and the fact that 'he left one alone a bit'.[21] The last scene was stubbornly refusing to take shape until Hall announced, late in rehearsals, that they were going to play it without a break. 'We just played the text with the rhythm that Shakespeare had given it. Because of Peter's musicality, he could orchestrate it,' recalls Tutin. John Barton thought the result was wonderful; thirty-five years later he said that this was Hall's greatest ever production. Glen Byam Shaw wrote in a note to Hall: 'It seems to me that the company under your direction has developed as a whole, and there are a number of most interesting and delightful performances which I know are entirely due to you.'[22]

Ivor Brown, Tynan's predecessor at the *Observer*, who wrote the critical introduction to the three-year photographic records of Stratford productions, added a marker for the future to his praise for *Twelfth Night*: 'Peter Hall's production was a happy one and not marred by any determination to impose strikingly new notions on a masterpiece which can be left to run its own course.'[23] Not all the daily and Sunday newspaper critics were so generous, and the mixed reviews disappointed Hall. On 30 April 1958 he wrote to Flower: 'On the whole, I am pleased with the reception of the play. Some of the critics were asinine but then they always are, one can't expect too much of them. I did enjoy working on the production very much; partly because of the play but mainly because I adore working at Stratford.'[24]

Hall already knew that Byam Shaw was advising Flower that he should be his successor. It was an informal business; there were no public advertisements or executive searches. 'The torch passed on in an amiably pre-arranged way. The Board of Governors didn't have much to do with it, and Fordie was all for Peter,' says Flower's widow, Hersey Flower.[25] And on 9 July 1958 Flower wrote to Hall:

Glen has kept me informed of the confidential talks that he has had with you recently. I can't tell you how pleased I was to learn from him that you would be willing to take his place when he leaves us.

Well, the [Executive] Council met today and was unanimous in asking me to write to you, on behalf of the Governing Body, to invite you to come to Stratford as Director of the Theatre in succession to Glen. This I do with all my heart, and with my sincere assurance that you can count on the utmost support, not only from me but also from all the Governors.[26]

Hall replied three days later on both sides of a sheet of blue notepaper in a boyish hand:

I was delighted to receive your letter. My happiest experiences in the theatre have been working in Stratford and with Glen. I am therefore very honoured that he should have suggested me as his successor . . . At this moment I think Stratford is the most important theatre in the country, and it has been made so by the work of Glen and Tony during the last 10 years. It is a marvellous heritage and a great responsibility.

Ever since Glen spoke to me about the possibility, I have been very excited. I would want to be, as Glen knows, not a revolutionary, but someone who wants to carry on a fine tradition by developing it in his own terms.

Naturally, half of me wonders whether I can do the job at all – but your letter makes me feel happy and secure . . . So I accept wholeheartedly; my only qualms are personal and I think they are healthy.[27]

The affectionate tone of those letters was not forced. Flower and Hall liked and trusted each other from the start, and Hall's relationship with Lieutenant-Colonel Sir Fordham Flower – Fordie – was one of the most influential of his life. When Hersey Flower says Hall was closer to Fordie than to his own father, she is neither exaggerating nor sentimentalising the relationship.

The Shakespeare Memorial Theatre was a family business, like the Flower's Brewery in Stratford, of which Fordham Flower was also chairman. Their beer had a reputation well beyond Warwickshire (it was a favourite in rugby clubs around London), and the successful brewery was a secure base from which to run the theatre. The Memorial Theatre had been founded by Flower's great-uncle, Charles, a remarkable figure who was inspired not by the trade a new theatre might bring, but by the example of the Duke of Meiningen in Germany, who subsidised a permanent company of skilled actors. Charles Flower found another model for Stratford in Bayreuth, where Richard Wagner had opened his Festspielhaus in 1876 just as Charles Flower was raising funds for a new theatre on two acres of Bancroft meadow by the Avon. (He provided more than half the £11,000 himself.) Sadly, Charles Flower's great expectations of a brilliant permanent company were not fulfilled by the actors of his day.[28]

The chairmanship remained in family hands, passing first to Charles's brother Edgar, and then to Edgar's son Archibald, Fordham's father, who ran the theatre from 1903 until 23 April 1944. It was then handed over to Fordham, who had been granted special leave from his regiment for the occasion. Flower was a soldier. He went to Sandhurst and served with the 9th Queen's Royal Lancers in the Middle East and India for eight years, resigning his commission in 1932 to learn the beer business and become a prospective Parliamentary candidate, in the Conservative interest. He dropped his political ambitions when he married Hersey Balfour in 1934, which meant that the Shakespeare Memorial Theatre became a distant relation by marriage of the future National Theatre. Hersey was a niece of Dame Edith Lyttelton, who had been campaigning for a National Theatre since 1910.

Dame Edith remarked of Hersey's husband: 'Fordie's too easily lit.' She was speaking of his lively enthusiasms. Flower responded to new ideas and liked change, but his military experience – he was recalled to his regiment in 1939, was twice mentioned in dispatches, and was promoted to Lieutenant-Colonel in 1944 – meant that he was also a clear-headed administrator. 'You could tip a basinful of facts at his feet and he'd sort it,' says Hersey Flower.

Unlike his father, Flower did not believe he knew best how to run a theatre. In 1946 he persuaded Barry Jackson to come to Stratford from the Birmingham Rep. Though Jackson introduced Peter Brook and Paul Scofield to Stratford, Flower did not warm to him. Quayle became director in 1948, and Flower grew to admire and understand artists. One reason why Quayle, Byam Shaw and Hall were so fond of Flower was that he hardly ever said no to them. But none of his directors asked him for half as much as Peter Hall did.

Although Hall's letter of appointment said that the announcement of his appointment should be delayed until January 1959, it was much too good a story to keep secret, and by the end of the Stratford season it was so widely known that the announcement was brought forward to 15 November 1958, a week before Hall's twenty-eighth birthday. As director of the Shakespeare Memorial

Theatre he was to be paid a salary of £5,000 a year; his accom-
modation was taken care of, 'including lighting, heating, and the
wages of all necessary cleaning staff'; the car allowance was £150
a year and sixpence a mile. The contract was satisfactory to Hall,
who asked that it should be made with Fontped Securities Ltd,
'a company who own my exclusive services'.[29]

After the announcement, Flower wrote: 'I'm sorry you have
been pestered by the press. I dare say that Glen's hope that the
news could be kept quiet until January was over-optimistic, the
world being what it is.'[30] Hall never minded being pestered by
the press. Journalists found his availability a refreshing change
and his views were normally treated with unusual sympathy.
But in the interviews he gave after his appointment he was
guarded about his plans, suggesting only that some Stratford
productions were over-decorative, that verse-speaking techniques
needed examination, and that a permanent company would be a
good idea.

At that time, John Barton was able to assess Hall's mood as
accurately as anyone. 'He was excited and nervous,' he says, 'but
I remember his enthusiasm and ideals, coupled with an awareness
of the difficulties. It was a terrific opportunity. If he was going to
do it, he was going to shake everything up. He wasn't going to
do it under existing conditions. He might come a cropper, but he
was going to have a go.' Anthony Quayle seemed to understand
this too. In his letter of congratulation, he said: 'I know you – and
no-one but you – can start a new phase and bring fresh life to a
great theatre.'[31]

Though Hall had told Flower that he did not intend to be a
revolutionary, he was already working feverishly to get Flower
to agree to a totally new, not to say revolutionary, agenda for
the Shakespeare Memorial Theatre. They had talked regularly
through the summer of 1958, but Flower had said little in response.
When the company left for Leningrad in December, Hall was still
uncertain where he stood.

The month-long Russian tour was the first by an English
company playing a full repertoire since 1917, and since Hall's
production of *Twelfth Night* was one of the three – along with
Michael Redgrave's *Hamlet*, and *Romeo and Juliet* – Hall was
in the party. Leningrad was cold and forbidding. Though the
company did not know it at the time, the British ambassador
to Moscow, Sir Patrick Reilly, later told Flower the company was

not treated as well as it ought to have been because the Soviet government thought the Moscow Art Theatre had not been treated handsomely enough on its visit to London.[32] Commissars accompanied the company wherever they went, making frank and interesting conversation impossible. The food was awful, and drink was scarce: Dorothy Tutin made many friends by sharing the eggs and Guinness flown in by the RAF to coddle her delicate digestion. The actors were frustrated by the lack of free communication with Russians off-stage, but once they were in the theatre the audiences were a revelation. Warmly appreciative and, considering they were listening to an English text, remarkably knowing, they laughed at some of the jokes in *Twelfth Night* that had been met with silence in Stratford.

Hall was curious about the organisation of companies like the Gorky Theatre in Leningrad. For a man who found the West End free-market system wanting, the state-sponsored and subsidised companies in Communist countries had strong theoretical attractions. Disenchantment set in fast: Hall saw that in practice they were stultified vehicles for state propaganda. Talking to Fordham and Hersey Flower, who had accompanied the company to Leningrad, he was inspired by his discontent, and for the first time he outlined to Flower the complete range of his ambitions.

The Flowers had a suite in the Astoria Hotel. There was no plug in the bath, and the furniture had been covered with dust sheets to cloak the pre-revolutionary red plush and gilt. 'Edwardian grandeur, scuffed at the edges,' says Hersey Flower, who remembers the evening vividly. Fordham had found something for them to drink. Hall began by describing what he had discovered in the Soviet Union. You could smell the mould, he said; things were set in concrete, so much so that actors played the same roles into old age; in Leningrad they even had an official Puck. On the other hand, the Stratford system was profligate. Actors and directors who had done marvellous work simply dropped out of sight from one season to the next. The answer, Hall said, was a permanent company, not just so as to create a unified style, but to stop the wastage. He proposed a company of actors on three-year contracts who would develop a style of ensemble playing that was unknown in England.

Flower was interested; it reminded him of the original ambition of his Great-uncle Charles. He was familiar with the next strand of Hall's argument – that a permanent company could not confine

the repertory to Shakespeare nor its performances to Stratford. He
had heard it before from Quayle, who had already convinced him
in principle that Stratford needed a London theatre where actors
could extend their range and experience by performing new plays
and exploring other parts of the classical repertory. Besides that,
the best of the Shakespearian productions at Stratford would
extend their life-span by transferring to London.

There was another factor to consider. Hall reminded Flower
that a National Theatre under Sir Laurence Olivier would be
established, probably within five years. Flower had also heard
about this from Quayle: how Stratford would be unable to compete
with a National Theatre in London for actors and directors. Hall
pressed the point: the National Theatre might be a death blow
to Stratford if Stratford remained as it was. To compete, the
Shakespeare Memorial Theatre would have to become a national
institution, like the National Theatre itself.

In the small hours, Hall started to talk about money – the part
of his scheme that would test Flower's loyalty most severely.
Flower and his predecessors had never relied on grants from
the government. Like the opera festival at Glyndebourne, the
Memorial Theatre had been self-financing, and the hard-nosed
businessmen who ran it had been proud of its independence.
Hall believed that his plans not only required a government
subsidy, but deserved one, as of right. He had never doubted
the rightness of government subsidy for the arts; indeed, he took
it for granted as a fundamental element in a civilised society. The
obstacle, however, was the theatre's reserve fund of £175,000,
accumulated by the prudent businessmen. 'I knew we would
never get any form of state grant whilst the fund existed,' Hall
writes. 'I suggested to Fordie that the money could be well spent
on launching us in London.'[33]

Hall reports that Flower blinked. Since Hall was proposing to
ditch a policy that had been maintained in Stratford for eighty
years, this was a modest reaction. Sally Beauman's history of
the Royal Shakespeare Company calculates the scale of Hall's
audacity. 'That Fordham would accept the proposal was, as Hall
must have known, totally unlikely.'[34] Hall knew he was taking
a risk. Flower's outright rejection would force him to consider
resigning from the job he had always wanted, without even
having begun it. He appreciated that he was forcing Flower to
make an agonising decision; no one had ever proposed a policy of

deliberately running down the theatre's accumulated reserves, and there would be strong opposition from members of the governing body, who would also hate the shift of the company's centre of gravity from Stratford to London.

None the less, in the early hours of a December morning in Leningrad, Flower agreed to back Hall, and without reservation. Fordie had been lit. Although she understood that this would cause turmoil, Hersey Flower shared his new enthusiasm. She, more than anyone, knew how courageous he had been. 'That he did accept it was both a testimony to his own daring and to Hall's now legendary powers of persuasion,' says Beauman.

Bold though it was, Flower never regretted the commitment he made in Leningrad. And there were other factors that assisted Hall's case. As chairman, Flower knew Stratford was no longer quite as fashionable as it had been when Quayle was in his prime. Television was a new market for actors, and the effort of persuading stars to work for comparatively poor wages with scratch companies in repertory in Stratford had exhausted Byam Shaw. Flower feared that the glamour was fading, and knew he needed to allow Hall the resources to restore it.

From Leningrad, Hall went on to Moscow, from which his departure was delayed by the Russians for a nerve-racking two days. Hall, deciding that the commissars must have been displeased by a mildly critical article for the *Observer* that he had telephoned to London from his hotel room, enlisted the help of the British Embassy, and eventually returned to London via Stockholm, Oslo and Stavanger. 'I was very relieved to see the decadent West again,' he wrote to Flower on 30 December 1958.[35]

The main purpose of the letter was to let Flower know that he was anxious to press ahead. 'I believe this is the time we start to move in on Prince Littler,' he wrote. Littler was the lessee of the Aldwych Theatre, which Hall had discovered the previous summer when he was directing *Brouhaha*. Peter Sellers, starring in it, had been trouble (his understudy, John Wood, held a party to celebrate his fiftieth appearance in the Sellers part), but *Brouhaha* had done good business, and Hall had liked the Aldwych. It would, he thought, do nicely for his London theatre.

7

A Company is Born

'We became hot and fashionable'

The 1950s were star-struck years at the Shakespeare Memorial Theatre. By 1959 – Byam Shaw's last year as director as well as the hundredth season of plays at the Memorial Theatre – the policy of hiring stars seemed extravagant; even to have gone over the top. Laurence Olivier was Coriolanus; Charles Laughton, a prince from across the water, was to play King Lear and Bottom; Paul Robeson, the great American bass, was Othello; Edith Evans, the greatest old lady of the English theatre, who had not been seen in Stratford since 1913, was Volumnia in *Coriolanus* and the Countess of Roussillon in *All's Well That Ends Well*, which was directed by the fabled figure of Tony Guthrie. Hall himself was directing *A Midsummer Night's Dream* and *Coriolanus*, two productions he thought of as Byam Shaw's parting gift to him. By now, of course, Hall was a star himself; and when the elite were photographed together that summer, he was always in the shot.

Leslie Caron made sure he looked the part: she took him to have his suits made by Cecil Beaton's tailor in Savile Row. Hall was slim and clean-shaven, and his wardrobe was the only thing that made him look any more than twenty-one: the pipe helped hardly at all. His lifestyle, however, was grown-up. He was living beyond his own wildest dreams but still within his wife's means. In 1958 Caron had prepared for the birth of their second child, a daughter named Jennifer, by buying a house at 31 Montpelier Square, between Harrods and Hyde Park, in an expensive part of Knightsbridge – though in the late 1950s it was, Caron says, still an unpolished gem awaiting gentrification.[1] She played an enthusiastic part, redecorating the house from top to bottom in matching curtains and wallpaper. There were always vases of flowers on the side-tables. Hall used the house for staff meetings when he was in London, but some of his old chums like John Barton felt mildly intimidated by the grandeur of the surroundings. A few friends came round – Cecil Beaton, the Tynans, Peggy Ashcroft and her barrister husband Jeremy Hutchinson, Harry Andrews – but the Halls were not socialites. 'We didn't really have friends as such because he worked so hard and I wasn't very comfortable as a hostess,' says Caron. It did not matter greatly; for much of the time, they were not at home in Montpelier Square to entertain.

As director-designate at Stratford, Hall's role in the 1959 season was subordinate to Glen Byam Shaw's, but the plans he had outlined in Leningrad were being fleshed out and brought to life. He had a few outside distractions and obligations: in January he directed two short plays by Anouilh at the Arts Theatre, the last work he did there himself. (The production credits mention Toby Rowland and a newly established company named Peter Hall Ltd.) Towards the end of the year, he directed *The Wrong Side of the Park* by John Mortimer with Margaret Leighton. It was his last job in the commercial West End theatre for almost twenty years. But his mind was on Stratford, even when he was travelling, and he did more of that in 1959 than he had previously had time for.

At the end of January, Caron went to Hollywood to make a film with Henry Fonda called *The Man Who Understood Women*. She was not looking forward to it: she often felt lonely there, and she suspected that, after her success in *Gigi* in 1958, MGM did not quite know what to do with her. But she was contracted to them to make a film a year for three years. This time, since he had the pretext he required for his journey, Hall spent a couple of weeks with her in Los Angeles. Charles Laughton and Laurence Olivier were both there, filming *Spartacus*, and he wanted to talk to them about their roles that summer.

Hall had absorbing conversations with Laughton, who had left the stage, committed himself to films and become an international star, but who still venerated Shakespeare. An exiled autodidact, Laughton had developed some odd ideas about the texts. He believed, for example, that the random appearance of capital letters in the Folio and Quarto editions was Shakespeare's own clandestine method of emphasising words; he went on believing this even when Hall and Byam Shaw, who was directing Laughton in *King Lear* in 1959, told him he was rupturing the rhythm and dismantling the meaning of the verse.[2]

Olivier was less interested in speculative analysis. When he and Hall met, Olivier announced that Coriolanus himself should be played with no hint of modesty, and that the play's text should be cut accordingly. They argued for hours before Olivier began to back off, and they continued the discussion by letter. The first of Olivier's letters to Hall was sent from Los Angeles in May. In it he immediately adopts the intimate, chatty tone and the vigorous vernacular language that infuse all his letters and make them the most rewarding of the letters that Hall kept; they are also the longest. Writing from Los Angeles, Olivier is concerned about how he will look:

> *I like the 'Golden Boy' idea very much, except as far as the hair goes, as I feel rather fixedly that he's one of the raven-haired tribe. I don't know quite why, possibly because it makes me feel so much more definitive . . . I think it is quite right that he should always look military minded about his clothes, but there could, I think, be a sort of undress version in case the breast plate is a little tough to act in all the time . . . Tony Curtis has now torn an Achilles tendon, so it will be even more difficult for them to finish with me by the stop-date . . . But WORRY NOT, I will be in the rehearsal room if not fresh, then smiling and punctual on Monday morn, 8th.*[3]

While in Los Angeles, Hall sought out Aldous Huxley to ask permission to dramatise his book *The Devils of Loudun*. Hall wanted his friend John Whiting to adapt *The Devils* for the company's new London theatre when it opened and, after some hesitation, Huxley agreed. Hall had already sent the book to Dorothy Tutin, hoping to persuade her to play the leading role. 'Fascinating – alarming too, no idea such macabre things really happened. How, how will John write it as a play – long to know about it,' she wrote in reply.[4]

In Hollywood, as the husband of a film star, Hall met a number of celebrities: Fred Astaire, Gene Kelly and Buster Keaton. He, Leslie and the children stayed in a Gothic creation in Beverly Hills called the Chateau Marmont. But Hall never really warmed to Hollywood: not only was he an outsider, he was also mildly anti-American, in the way of left-wing English intellectuals in the 1950s. His irritation was triggered by the accent, and exacerbated by the intellectual vacuum he found in the film industry. Since Hollywood provided Caron with an income that helped to service Hall's developing tastes in housing and transport, Hall's anti-Americanism annoyed her, and she felt it was aimed partly at her too.

Back in Stratford in the spring Hall had cast promising young actors to appear with Charles Laughton in *A Midsummer Night's Dream*: Ian Holm, Albert Finney and Vanessa Redgrave – names that only five years later an impresario would die for. (One of the bit parts was played by an Australian actor called Michael Blakemore, who incorporated some of his experiences that summer and the next into an intriguing theatrical *roman-à-clef* entitled *Next Season*.) The set, costumes and music were provided by familiar faces: Lila de Nobili and Raymond Leppard.

Byam Shaw, in a note to Hall, spoke of real magic: 'Your conception and the way you have carried it out is brilliantly and perfectly true to the author.'[5] The disappointing press notices had colleagues rushing to reassure Hall, who, despite his new eminence, still needed such reassurance. Enid Bagnold wrote: 'I was swept away by the beauty, the intelligence, the subtle ideas behind it all . . . an eighteenth-century homosexuality (or ambidextrous sexuality) in the conception of the men-fairies Oberon and Puck, which is of course absolutely right.'[6] Dorothy Tutin commiserated: 'I don't really care awfully for critics – o, how reticent can you get – but anyway they made your production sound "interesting" – poor Peter, they are rotten and I've heard from so many people and members of the cast that it's *lovely*.'[7] Later in the summer Lila de Nobili also urged him to ignore the bad notices: 'In the distance, even more, I can tell you how much I *trust* and believe in the way you have done it. Every year, more and more, it become [*sic*] a certain feeling.'

Sally Beauman's history of the Royal Shakespeare Company (RSC) declared the *Dream* the most interesting production of the season: 'It came closest to overall coherence and evenness of style in playing.'[8] Without anyone's being conscious of it, this production, like *Twelfth Night* the year before, was part of a gentle transition from the Quayle/Byam Shaw star-driven regime to Hall's ensemble style; and there were more hints of the future in the second of Hall's productions in 1959.

Two distinguished generations of actors came together in

Coriolanus: the establishment, represented by Laurence Olivier, Edith Evans and Harry Andrews, and the opposition, who played Roman citizens (Albert Finney, Julian Glover, Roy Dotrice, Ian Holm) and Volumnia's daughters (Vanessa Redgrave and Mary Ure). Hall's designer and composer were fresh faces at Stratford. The score was by Roberto Gerhard, a Spanish *émigré* composer of music whose modernity contrasted strongly with Leppard's well-mannered classicism. The designer was Boris Aronson, Hall's friend with whom he had made his directorial début in New York, who before accepting the work had to overcome his incredulity at the paltry fee: £250 plus £50 for the model, and a *one-way* fare from New York to England. This *Coriolanus* is the first of Hall's productions to be described and dissected in depth for, besides Olivier whose career is extensively chronicled, Aronson wrote about it in his autobiography, and Stanley Wells, from the Shakespeare Institute in Stratford, subjected the production to academic scrutiny.

Hall's letters to Aronson display a confident young director's eclectic taste, intellectual conviction and theatrical common sense. They reveal strongly held views on a variety of theatrical matters:

On abstract theatre: *Of course, I don't want to make the production archeologically correct, but I do want to give it some overall period flavour – a sort of barbaric reality. Because I can't bear abstract theatre, particularly for Shakespeare, who is warm, human, even dirty and smelly.*

On modern dress: *Obviously the play has enormous contemporary signifi-cance. For that reason I had thought for some time of doing it in a sort of modern dress. I still haven't quite given up the idea, except that I usually find modern dress Shakespeare to be disturbing, in that some aspects of the play may come out clearer, but an awful lot gets lost and confused. I imagine that the parallels one would draw in the play are strong enough to take care of themselves.*

On the Stratford stage: *The one thing essential [about the stage] is to keep the action right on the forestage. It is practically impossible to play a scene at Stratford behind the setting line. This means the set must be only a background.*

On visual sources: *It is vital to have a heroical, stark, hard romantic set. All this could be Etruscan, but it's the dark greens and umbers of this period, rather than the light blues . . . I've been looking at the Skira volume of Roman painting, and there are things there which seem enormously apt for*

Coriolanus . . . This is B.C. Rome, not Cinemascope and Julius Caesar . . .
The play is not all barbaric. Things like the Valeria scene and the character
of Menenius have renaissance elements and belong to the world of Veronese
and Mantegna.[9]

Aronson designed a permanent set – placed forward on the
stage, as instructed – with a variety of steps, gates, porches
and platforms on a rock-like structure. The only flat playing
area was small, which, says Wells, may have helped to disguise
the fact that the crowds were also rather small. Tynan, who liked
the set's mountainous quality, did not like the steps, and quoted
Alec Guinness's remark about Shakespearian productions: that he
himself had very few conversations on the stairs of his own house.
The architecture of the set meant that there could be no ceremonial
entrances, no dense mobs or marching columns, and Aronson was
blamed for this in mostly unfavourable reviews. The experience
made one thing clear to Hall: the stage at Stratford would have
to be altered.

In his score, Roberto Gerhard used gongs and tam-tams that
combined music with sound effects on a pre-recorded *musique*
concrète score. Stanley Wells, the professor, found this striking
and sometimes shattering, and commented on the way Hall used
a musical score to enhance the mood created by the actors:

Sound effects were used to reinforce the noise made by comparatively small
stage armies. But Peter Hall also used musical and lighting effects as a
means of articulating the scenes and effecting transitions of mood. He was
careful to create a theatrical structure which would relax as well as create
tension, so that the audience would not be excessively stretched. In the first
act there was an episode of domestic repose in the scene with Volumnia and
her ladies, introduced by soothing music. The battle scenes that followed
were undoubtedly noisy, but there was some effectively peaceful and eerie
music for the return to Rome at the beginning of the second act.[10]

The text was heavily cut: almost 800 lines out of 3,325 – almost a
quarter. Stanley Wells declared that the cuts were judicious, on
the whole. In a lecture given in 1976 he described it as a measure
of the shift from the commercial Stratford of 1959 to the subsidised
theatre of the 1960s and 1970s. While Hall's 1959 *Coriolanus* ran for
two hours and thirty minutes (with one interval), Trevor Nunn's
of 1972 ran for three hours and ten minutes (one interval, plus a
three-minute break).

The best notices went to the young performers, especially Ian Holm and Roy Dotrice, who were playing Aufidius's servants in Welsh accents, in contrast to Finney's Lancashire-accented First Citizen. Accents were the most obvious distinction between the generations. Indeed, the vocal mannerisms and nuances of expression for which Edith Evans was famous made it difficult for her to cope with Volumnia's stridency: 'It seemed a bit like asking a born Susanna to play Brünnhilde,' comments Wells.

Hall was more deferential towards Olivier than any other actor: in rehearsal, Olivier's suggestions were usually incorporated, and Hall then concentrated on the rest of the cast. Olivier's son, Tarquin, reports: 'Larry did not really *like* taking direction from Peter Hall, but he admired his intelligence.'[11] Olivier's was a charismatic performance that typified the 1950s, but it was judged, in part, by standards that would become common in the 1960s. Leslie Caron was shocked by the disrespect the younger critics showed for Olivier, but it was a clue to changing attitudes to reputation and to new fashions in acting. Tynan thought Olivier 'terrific' (he usually did); and *The Times* said that Olivier played Coriolanus 'just as well as it can be played'. But the new brusqueness was expressed by Alan Brien in the *Spectator*: 'I would ask for less consciousness on Olivier's part that every word is putty and can be moulded to his whim. I would ask for less technique – instead I would like to feel that the lines are mastering him occasionally . . . I would ask for less decoration, less personality, less expertise.'[12] The smart thing to say that autumn was that after Olivier retired for a while with a cartilage injury, his understudy, Albert Finney, was the better Coriolanus. Again the profession rallied. Gwen Ffrangcon Davies said she thought Olivier's performance was the most completely satisfying she had ever seen at Stratford, and Joyce Cary wrote to Hall: 'It was crystal clear and quite alarmingly modern, n'est ce pas. *Darling* old Shakespeare!'[13]

The performance is best remembered for the athleticism of the fifty-two-year-old Olivier's dying fall. Tarquin Olivier was staggered by it:

> *Coriolanus stood backstage on a platform 12 feet high, bleeding from his many stab wounds and determined on one final dying plunge to drive his sword through Aufidius. To reach him, he had to leap upward, far out*

across, to stand a chance. So he seemed to fly up towards the dress circle – we thought he was going to land in our laps – only to be snatched back by strong men grabbing his ankles, gripping him and letting him swing down. But that on its own would have ended with his rump towards us, so he had to spin round in mid air, with the retainers changing hands and ankles so that when he was dangling upside down, it would be his face we saw, arms swinging in utter defeat. It was difficult and dangerous – a crowning reminder of the physical risks of his career.[14]

During that summer in Stratford, Olivier sought out Hall to tell him that he was going to have a go at making the National Theatre. He asked Hall to join him as his number two. This was not simply an opportunistic move to undermine the opposition: despite the wariness between then, Olivier and Hall had a good deal in common. They both liked running things; both were very ambitious; both were wily and liked attention; both were conscious of their star status. That was part of the problem: they had too much in common. Hall gave the offer hardly any thought at all. He told Olivier that he was flattered, but that he was going to make his own theatre – 'as number one'.[15]

Having agreed to Hall's new agenda, Fordham Flower loyally set about persuading the governing body that Hall was doing the right thing. First he let them hear about the plans from Hall himself. Fordham's cousin, Dennis Flower, also a governor, recalls other members saying to him before the meeting that they had heard this new man wanted to ruin them by opening a theatre in London.[16] Listening to Hall, they fell victim to his charm and intelligence. Many still had reservations, but he won their collective blessing.

There was much to do, and two ways of going about it. If Hall had done it Peter Brook's way, he would have begun by re-examining the company's objectives and working methods, and arrived at a measured assessment of what he hoped to achieve before acting on it.[17] But Hall was temperamentally incapable of thinking like that. He was impatient to get on, and that meant doing at least three things at once. His first season, 1960, had to be planned, the permanent company had to be chosen and contracted, and a suitable London theatre had to be found. In doing all this while directing two plays in Stratford, Hall displayed two characteristics that he and his colleagues would learn to live with during the next twenty-five years.

One of these was a manic appetite for work. When workaholic became a word, Hall colonised it. He said later that a medical examination had revealed a tendency for his body to manufacture too much adrenalin; his colleagues thought the fault lay in his brain rather than his bloodstream. He and Caron went to Italy for a month in March, a holiday she remembered fondly, because Hall had taught her about Renaissance art and architecture, and because long holidays were to be a rarity in the next four years.

The other characteristic exposed in 1959 was the exhilaration Hall felt when he took risks. Because he was not a gambler, these risks were always calculated, but Hall knew that if his experiment was to work, it would have to be done boldly and quickly. The name was something Hall wanted to change for a start, to de-emphasise the 'Memorial' aspect. He also wanted the Stratford stage redesigned so that it would thrust out in front of the proscenium arch. But the very first task he set himself was to persuade Peggy Ashcroft to lead the permanent acting company. They had worked together for a second time in October 1958 in the last of the International Playwrights Theatre's productions: a documentary drama called *Shadow of Heroes* by an American writer, Robert Ardrey, about the events leading to the Hungarian uprising in 1956. Ashcroft had been emotionally engaged by the part of the wife of one of the victims of the revolution, and the critical response had been gratifying. Tynan, for example, was uncommonly kind: 'On a stage naked except for a rostrum and a collection of dun, portable screens, it flows as atmospherically as lightning. A masterly controlling tact is everywhere perceptible.'[18] A cast of fifty and the play's proximity to the actual event were fatal to its commercial prospects, but Ashcroft had been excited by the idea of political documentary and by the hints of Brechtian influences that critics detected in the writing and the direction.

Early in 1959 Hall took Ashcroft out to dinner, and explained what he hoped to do in Stratford. But he was too nervous to pop the question until they were driving home through Trafalgar Square. If she would be the first three-year contract artist, he said, the scheme would work. Ashcroft's biographer, Michael Billington, writes: 'No proposal from any nervous suitor was more welcome to a willing bride. Her whole professional life – from reading about the Moscow Art Theatre to working with Gielgud at the New, the Queens and the Haymarket – had been one long quest for a permanent company.'[19]

Hall was fashionable now, and actors would have wanted to work with him anyway. Offering them financial security and guaranteeing continuous work made any proposal from him even more attractive. The three-year contract was a revolutionary idea in the theatre, and among the first to sign on were Ian Holm, Dorothy Tutin, Patrick Wymark, Harry Andrews and Roy Dotrice. Promising youngsters were Diana Rigg and Ian Richardson; old hands were Max Adrian, Denholm Elliott, Eric Porter and Jack MacGowran.

All were included automatically in the plans for the 1960 season of Shakespearian comedy, tracing its development from the simple early verse of *The Two Gentlemen of Verona* through to the sinewy late work in *Troilus and Cressida* and *The Winter's Tale*. Hall's commitment to the concept of an ensemble did not prevent him seeking also to bolster the company with some box-office stars. In March 1959 he wrote to Flower with the news that Rex Harrison and Kay Kendall had said yes to the last two plays of the season: presumably, Kendall would have played Bianca in *The Taming of the Shrew* and Harrison would have appeared in *Troilus and Cressida*. 'So 1960, temporarily at least, looks in very good shape.'[20] Paul Scofield seemed to have agreed to play Shylock opposite Dorothy Tutin (*Merchant of Venice*), as well as Petruchio with Peggy Ashcroft (*Taming of the Shrew*) and Thersites in *Troilus*.

For his directors, Hall was loyal to his Cambridge contemporaries. He proposed directing *Two Gentlemen* and *Troilus* himself, along with a revival of *Twelfth Night*. Peter Wood was to direct *The Winter's Tale*. Tyrone Guthrie had said he was too busy to direct *The Taming of the Shrew*, so John Barton, besides helping with *Troilus*, would take charge of that. The only outsider was Michael Langham, directing *The Merchant*.

Among the names that were missing was that of Tony Richardson, Devine's assistant at the Royal Court, who seemed set to become a fixture at Stratford, directing *Pericles* there in 1958 and *Othello* in 1959, but Hall had made up his mind that Richardson was not a director of classics. Commenting on that decision long afterwards, Hall said: 'What I was trying to do in the early years was to find a team of people with the same assumptions . . . [and] there is no point in having a Shakespeare Company in which one director tells actors not to take any notice of the verse, and the next tells them that the verse will reveal the play.'[21] Since it was Richardson who had told actors not to bother with the verse, Richardson was never asked back.

Six years out of university, Hall still trusted John Barton's judgement more than anyone's. They enjoyed each other's company, playing competitive memory games: name the titles of Shakespeare's plays in the order in which they are printed in the First Folio; name them in the order in which it is understood they were written; give the first line of each play; the last line; give the first line spoken by each principal character. Barton was intimately involved in all the plans for Stratford. He now had a grand title at Cambridge – Dean of King's – but immediately he had the security of a fellowship he became unhappy and he developed writer's block. So when Hall asked him to come to Stratford as assistant director, Barton was delighted.

The title did not mean assistant to a director, but *the* assistant to *the* director, with particular responsibility for improving the quality of verse-speaking in the company. Barton attended some of the *Coriolanus* rehearsals before he formally went on the payroll on 1 September 1959 – at the very decent wage of £2,000 a year. He was confident that he had plenty to contribute, and evidence of the central role he was expected to play in the future was Hall's note to Flower in April 1960 requesting that Barton should be allowed to attend all meetings with the governors. Flower agreed.[22]

Together Hall and Barton now knew how they wanted the actors to sound. Hall explained this clearly in an interview years later with the critic Irving Wardle:

> When I was first at Stratford in 1956, actors did not understand what a blank-verse line was. They were either taught that if you got the sense right, the verse would take care of itself. Or they were taught that if you elongate the vowels to make it musical, the verse would support itself. It doesn't. The worst excess of the 19th century was declamation.
>
> English as a language is full of consonants. Rhythm is made by consonants, and the real Shakespeare rhythm comes much more out of consonants than out of the vowels. To a certain extent, the vowels take care of themselves. Where you breathe is the most important thing in Shakespeare. Larry [Olivier] always says you have to be able to say at least four lines in one breath. I'm sure you do. But it is far better for an actor not to take a breath in places where it is convenient for his own idiosyncratic sense of himself. You can only take a breath in Shakespeare on the end of a line or a caesura. Otherwise you fracture the line.[23]

Two generations of English actors were duly taught to speak verse by breathing at the end of a line.

Hall's efforts to find a London theatre continued through the summer of 1959, unimpeded by open opposition from the governors – except one. Binkie Beaumont was commendably frank about his views. If the Stratford company successfully ran a year-round repertory in London, Hall would attract the best actors and mop up the best new plays. That would ruin the West End. And, Beaumont thought, if Stratford came to London unsuccessfully, that failure would ruin the Shakespeare Memorial Theatre. It is Hall's belief that Beaumont tried to prevent the move by persuading his colleagues not to grant him a lease on any West End theatre.

Beaumont appears to have influenced Prince Littler, who had the lease to the Aldwych Theatre, which was the theatre Hall wanted most. Turned down by Prince Littler, Hall tried his brother, Emile, who leased the Cambridge Theatre. Emile and Prince were not on friendly terms and Emile was a member of Stratford's executive council. Whatever his motive, Emile's response was positively enthusiastic. He was keen to show Hall the Cambridge: 'every seat is tip-up and it has a large number of comfortable cheap seats'. He saw possibilities in visits by foreign companies under Stratford's auspices: 'Instead of Leon Hepner and Peter Daubeny taking the profits, it should be possible for us to deal directly with them.'[24] He wrote, in June 1959: 'If the Cambridge doesn't suit you, then we will have to think of another theatre.'[25]

The Cambridge was unfashionable, a little out of the way and not what Hall had in mind; but Emile Littler's enthusiasm breached the united front Beaumont had hoped for, and it gave Hall a pretext for having another try at the Aldwych. He had quietly deployed his former partner, Toby Rowland, to see if Prince Littler might not change his mind, and eventually Littler did so. The Aldwych was taken on a three-year lease from the end of 1960; the rent was low, but Littler was guaranteed 25 per cent of the gross, which virtually ruled out the idea of any profit for the Stratford company. The terms were presented by Flower and agreed by the executive council on 11 November 1960. The contract – for the Aldwych or 'if not the Aldwych, an alternative West Theatre of approximately equal size' – was formally confirmed on 3 March 1960.

Beaumont resigned as a governor on 15 March 1960, citing potential conflicts of interest and assuring Flower that it had nothing to do with the new directorship: 'Peter Hall and I are close friends,' he wrote.[26] Toby Rowland was aggrieved to discover that all he got for his pains in helping Hall was the resignation of his capable and experienced general manager, John Roberts, whom Hall poached to manage the Aldwych. The other aggrieved party was Emile Littler: he may have felt used, and was certainly disappointed. Hall had made a serious enemy.

Fixing the Aldwych contract was an exhilarating start to Hall's first summer as director. The geography of the Memorial Theatre suited the new mood at Stratford. Rehearsals took place in the conference hall, where the Swan Theatre now stands, so that actors and administration were cheek by jowl. Unlike the Quayle and Byam Shaw regimes, there was little sense of hierarchy in Hall's first year. Dorothy Tutin remembers a happy, exciting and eccentric company in which individual talents were respected. 'You were paid enough to live, no more, but you didn't do it for the money. You did it for the experience and the pleasure.'[27]

A new recruit to the administrative staff shared the actors' enthusiasm. A stage-struck young woman named Jacqueline Taylor had joined the press office as an assistant, and was smitten by Hall's charm. 'He was so full of enthusiasm, and youth, and ambition. He always smiled, and laughed, and talked. He was so thrilled to have the job he desperately wanted; he had tremendous power, and glamour, with his film-star wife. He was a very exciting person. Everybody thought so.'[28]

John Barton was a good judge of Hall's skills in casting and directing plays, but he was amazed by how well Hall ran the company because he had never been an administrator before, and was not a committee man at Cambridge. 'The rest of us had run things there. But he had a natural administrative ability; much greater than I had thought – and I'd done more of it than he had. That was the greatest mystery of all: he was immediately spot on the ball.'[29] The summer of 1960 was the origin of Hall's reputation as a skilled committee man. The powers of persuasion, or manipulation, the ruthlessness and the silky diplomatic skill that were now fully exposed for the first time made Leslie Caron think of him in terms of a notable fellow countryman of hers, Cardinal Richelieu.

Hall's skill in casting had been thoroughly put to the test

already. Since March 1959, when he had told Flower that the 1960 season looked in good shape, there had been a string of disappointments. Not long after Easter 1959 he had received a sharp lesson in how difficult it is to please star actors. Rex Harrison wrote a hurried, muddled letter from Portofino:

> *I received your letter this morning and do feel deeply disappointed that you find yourself so completely embroiled in the 'Shrew', as it was after all going away from your pattern of the comedies with dark characters, and only, I felt, found as 'an inducement' rather than part of the scheme. I should still be most interested to play in 'Troilus' if we could put our heads together and find perhaps one to put in before and less dark, but on the darkish side. It is more likely that Kate [Kay Kendall, his wife] will be absolutely at full bore by next year as her health is enormously improving but she has always been completely adamant that she only wanted to do [the Shrew] with somebody who had never done a Shakespearian production before i.e. Peter Glenville, so that we all started from scratch and got something new in the right sense, in other words something new but which suited us, rather than just an idea for a production.*
>
> *I also fully realise that you cannot get into the 'War play' or out of pattern but perhaps it is worth working over 'Measure for Measure' or 'As You Like It', but I don't really want to prance about in gold earrings at the advanced age of 51 – that is why I am very anxious to play 'The General' – so if you really have seriously settled for the 'Shrew' at any cost, which I find hard to believe, don't bother to answer this as believe me we both completely understand.[30]*

Harrison was over-optimistic about Kay Kendall's health. She died of cancer later in 1959. And Hall was indeed determined to press ahead with *The Taming of the Shrew*. But even more dismal news came from Paul Scofield. Hall's flirtation with him had begun late in 1958, when he had suggested Shylock, Malvolio and Pandarus. 'I'm not sure of Pandarus. I'm wondering if I have enough variety – but I will read it again,' Scofield wrote on 25 November 1958. On 2 January Scofield still appeared to assume he would be in Stratford in the summer of 1960, saying that he thought he preferred Thersites to Jaques but that could be settled when they met. He had a suggestion to put to Hall – that Joy (his wife), could, if Hall thought it an idea, play Julia, one of the ladies in *Two Gentlemen*. Scofield also thought his wife would be a splendid Cressida, and wanted to know what Hall thought.[31] Not much, was the answer to that.

Then, in the following winter, Scofield wrote a strange letter

Grandparents: George Hall, ratcatcher to Queen Victoria, and his second wife, Edith.

Father and son: Reg and Peter on the beach at Kessingland.

Three generations: Grace Hall, with her mother and son.

Peter Hall as a baby with the family dog; in the company of his father's animals; and in school uniform at Barnham.

A promising
young man:
Peter Hall as
head boy and
as Hamlet at
the Perse
School in
Cambridge.

Sergeant Instructor (Acting) Hall, P.R.F.: 20 years younger than his colleagues in the mess.

An undergraduate worth knowing: Hall performs for an audience that includes John Barton, sitting on the floor looking faintly amused.

Waiting for Godot: irreversibly changing the face of the British theatre, with Timothy Bates, Peter Bull and the tramps, Paul Daneman and Peter Woodthorpe.

Hall takes over at Stratford, aged twenty-nine: the youngest impresario.

A memorable marriage: Leslie Caron was a glamorous wife, a fashionable interior decorator and a dutiful daughter-in-law to Reg and Grace Hall.

Stratford legends: *The Wars of the Roses* in 1964 — (above left) David Warner, as Henry VI, with Peggy Ashcroft; and (below) with Donald Sinden (Duke of York), and Brewster Mason (Earl of Warwick); (above right) Warner as a student Hamlet in 1965.

Father-figure: Sir Fordham (Fordie) Flower, Chairman of the RSC.

Company leader: Peggy Ashcroft and Hall on the terrace at the Memorial Theatre in Stratford in 1962.

A second wife: Hall marries Jacky Taylor, attended by his two children, in 1965.

to Flower asking for an advance on his whole salary for 1960. This was refused. Subsequently Scofield wrote to Hall saying that he felt he could not play Shylock, Petruchio and Thersites – a shattering blow, since they were the star male parts of the summer. Hall wanted a star to play them, but since his star had refused to start, he took a risk and played a hunch.

When Glen Byam Shaw had heard talk of Peter O'Toole, the twenty-six-year-old Hamlet at the Bristol Old Vic, he asked Kate Flanagan, his personal assistant, to take a look at him. She was enthusiastic. O'Toole auditioned for Byam Shaw, who found the scruffy figure in an overcoat with a newspaper hanging out of his pocket exceedingly distasteful.[32] Hall, who had also admired the Hamlet, was less fastidious. O'Toole had done well in London, taking Albert Finney's role in *The Long, the Short, and the Tall*, which had been something of a finishing school for promising young actors. Hall now boldly offered him Scofield's complete line of parts.

Since Peggy Ashcroft, at fifty-three, was almost twice O'Toole's age, she informed Hall that it was silly to cast them together as Katharine and Petruchio; and when Hall disputed this, she insisted on being auditioned for the part. It was a memorable occasion. Late one night, after the show, Hall and Barton met in a West End theatre to audition the pair of them. Riffling through the canon, O'Toole and Ashcroft discovered that the only scene from Shakespeare they both knew was the quarrel scene between Brutus and Cassius in *Julius Caesar*. Both are male parts, of course, but Ashcroft had played Cassius at school (opposite Diana Wynyard's Brutus) and could still remember every line. Barton thought they were staggeringly good together that night. Hall told Ashcroft that she had got the part.

O'Toole was inspired casting. Both *The Merchant* and *The Taming of the Shrew* were successes with the critics and the audiences. Eric Porter established himself in the company as Leontes in *The Winter's Tale*. Hall's own efforts were mixed. *The Two Gentlemen* that opened the season was, by his own admission, 'dim'. *Twelfth Night* was successfully revived, though Hall still complained that the critics had misunderstood his intentions. But *Troilus* was another matter entirely. Hall had chosen Leslie Hurry, a painterly designer, and had persistently described scenery that lay beyond Hurry's imagination. He asked for a set with a hexagonal shape in the middle of the stage that strongly suggested the texture of sand. After a number of his suggestions had been rejected, Hurry lost his temper: 'Why don't you just try some fucking sand?' he said.[33] That, said Hall, was exactly what he was looking for. It took Hurry time to adjust to the idea, but the sand ('a symbol of barrenness and shiftiness', according to Alan Brien), a blood-red cyclorama, and liberal use of dry ice provided a dramatic setting for the fights, which were John Barton's speciality. Inspired by the set, the cast – led by Denholm Elliott, Max Adrian, Eric Porter, Peter O'Toole and Dorothy Tutin – produced the only original work of the summer.

But the routine nature of the repertory hardly mattered. The company's enthusiasm communicated itself to the press and the audience. Stratford became a popular subject for newspaper and magazine feature writers, and the box-office figures reflected the attention. 'We became hot and fashionable,' says Hall.[34]

The drama off-stage, however, was profoundly unsettling. John Barton had looked forward to confirming his role as Hall's deputy with *The Taming of the Shrew*, his first production with a first-class cast of professionals. He had conceived a clever notion of keeping Christopher Sly on stage throughout the play, and had added a few lines at the end, as Sly staggers away to put Petruchio's lesson into practice on his own wife. The cast was excellent: Ashcroft and O'Toole, supported by Patrick Wymark, Elizabeth Sellars and Peter Jeffrey. Set and costumes were good. When it opened on 21 June, the programme named the director as John Barton. But that was not the case: his place had in fact been taken by Peter Hall. More than thirty years later, most of the participants still felt agitated by John Barton's purging.

One of Barton's problems was that many professional actors still mistrusted or, perhaps, feared the analytical and historical approach of academics. Not Peggy Ashcroft – she had worked with Dadie Rylands in Cambridge. But she was highly strung and needed careful handling in the last weeks before an opening night. When Hall looked in on rehearsals, he could sense the nerves; Barton, he thought, had not realised the difference between admonishing a student and guiding Peggy Ashcroft. So he was not surprised when a delegation comprising Ashcroft, O'Toole and Wymark came to his office to say they could not work with Barton any longer, and asked him to take over. 'Peg said he was so obsessed by detail that they couldn't get hold of the play,' Hall recalls.[35]

This was a bad moment. Barton was a friend; Hall had brought him to Stratford from a secure position at Cambridge to take the number two job in the organisation. Barton thought the rehearsals were going well, but Ashcroft was saying that if he was not replaced, the *Shrew* would be a catastrophe.

The news of his replacement came to Barton as a surprise – 'a complete, horrific surprise'. He pleaded with Hall, saying the decision was wrong and unjust. While he appreciated that Hall was in a difficult position, he did not understand why it had happened, and he did not want to go. Probing for an explanation, he thought the problem might be Peter O'Toole, with whom he had had an embarrassing public row one night in the Dirty Duck, the actors' pub across the road from the theatre. If that was the reason, the sacking was unfair.[36] Hall says it was not: 'O'Toole turned against everybody from time to time. I did not take him seriously. But I took Peg seriously. It was Peg who did it.'

Hall expected Barton to leave Stratford altogether. Although Hall no longer remembers the details, Barton says that Hall suggested that Barton leave and come back in two or three years' time. Dorothy Tutin, who was a chum of Barton's, drove with him to London, and was amazed to learn that he proposed to stay on. Barton told her that the one thing he knew was Shakespeare, and he was still confident that he could direct his plays.

Hall's reaction would have been quite different. He would have stormed out amid a flurry of accusations and a fuss in the newspapers. When he arrived at the theatre for rehearsals for the *Shrew* he was now running himself, he would say to Jacky Taylor, who was helping out in his office: 'Has he gone yet?' Hersey Flower remembers Hall spending hours discussing the crisis with her husband. 'It baffled Peter that John took it this way. He didn't understand why there was no outraged response. He and Fordie really didn't admire John for it.'[37]

Barton's solution was to continue to work on the company's verse-speaking, teaching actors to breathe at the end of a line, and to learn by watching other directors work. Hall eventually accepted this, but he remained loyal to Barton only in the sense that he did not actually fire him. Instead, he told Barton that he should not expect to direct a new production for three years; he would no longer be his deputy; and there would be no meetings with the governors. Barton doggedly stayed put, and, for the future reputation of Hall and the company, this was just as well. When *The Taming of the Shrew* opened, incidentally, it was a hit, and Ashcroft's and O'Toole's performances were especially praised.

The story did not leak to the newspapers, and it was years before it was spoken of at all freely, but its impact on the theatre is clear from a letter Byam Shaw wrote to Flower in October 1960: 'Peter is doing a splendid job. He has had real difficulties to contend with – particularly the Barton trouble – and it is really remarkable what he has achieved in his first season as director.'[38]

The Halls had moved into Avoncliffe, the Stratford director's house, in 1960. The house came with the job and Hall's contract had stipulated that it would be redecorated to suit his taste, or hers. Avoncliffe was a long, low house built of white Bath stone, with a galleried hall, fine plasterwork, and a lawn sloping down to the Avon. Hall could travel to work by boat from his mooring at the bottom of the garden. It was a Regency house, built by a family that had prospered in India. The stables had been converted into flats for staff from the theatre. John Goodwin, the publicist, had one; Kate Flanagan occupied another. A Spanish couple lived in, and there was a daily cleaner.

Leslie Caron loved Avoncliffe. 'It was heavenly, a lovely house. The plasterwork was of museum quality, although when I arrived there it was washed in white. I thought that was a shame, and I brought it all out in blue, pink and green.' Kate Flanagan remembers the delight Caron took in painting the nipples on the cherubs. Caron also replanted the garden with roses, and lined the paths with bay trees in tubs. She liked Stratford, which she found much more interesting than Hollywood, and she would slip into the theatre to watch rehearsals.

There were some memorable occasions at Avoncliffe. One summer night the whole company danced on the lawn in the headlights of their cars, which had been drawn up in a circle. But, much as she liked her surroundings, Caron was not happy. As the boss's wife, she found it difficult to make friends, and she felt that the actors were frightened or suspicious of her. Apart from overnight guests who came for first nights, and the annual visit from Hall's parents and her own, she did not entertain regularly. Fordham and Hersey Flower, for example, were seldom to be seen at Avoncliffe. Hall's talks with Flower took place in Flower's house on the hill overlooking the town. Hersey Flower observed Caron's difficulties: 'Leslie was like an elegant bird, always interested and inquisitive. In a way, things had been hard for her. She had become the property of the film machine, and she was accustomed to being packaged. Consequently, as a hostess, she never introduced anybody or handed round the drinks.' This was the result of inexperience rather than unkindness or lack of interest. When Kate Flanagan fell ill, Caron brought her meals on a tray, with a single rose in a small vase and a glass of wine. Caron now thinks she was too young to entertain properly.

But their marriage was the real problem. Hall was working unusually hard, even for him. When either set of parents was staying, he was hardly to be seen at all. The days were long; Caron was lonely. She was a theatrical animal herself, and had looked forward to sharing in the backstage jokes and dramas of the day. What she got instead over dinner was a litany of Pamment complaint. 'He took things very much to heart. After rehearsals he'd say "We'll never get there", and after a good first night he'd still fear that the notices might be bad.'

Caron had hoped they would work together on stage again, but Hall failed to warm to that idea – or, indeed, to the idea of her performing Shakespeare elsewhere. The Canadian Shakespeare Festival at Stratford, Ontario, had asked her if she would be interested in playing Cleopatra, and perhaps Juliet, in Tyrone Guthrie productions. Hall persuaded Caron to decline; he may have thought the parts were beyond the reach of her English, but she remembers his saying that it would look bad for him if his wife were to appear at the other Stratford. Hall believes she, and not he, was the problem: 'Leslie, like many actors, was very insecure. Only sporadically did she believe in herself, and was repeatedly torn, wondering whether her career lay in the movies or the theatre. Or whether the happiest kind of life for her was being a wife and mother.'[39]

Hall thought Caron's French accent was a real difficulty. When she particularly asked to play Titania in a revival of his production of *A Midsummer Night's Dream*, he would not agree ('perhaps mistakenly,' he said thirty years later).[40] But there was one piece they could do together: Giraudoux's play about a few nymph called *Ondine*. They worked together on the translation, and *Ondine* was fitted into the repertory at the Aldwych. It was scheduled to open in early January 1961 as the third production in the momentous first Stratford season in London.

Rehearsals took place through the winter in London amid the

chaos created by a new company moving into an old West End theatre. Staff from the management, the production and the press offices were crammed into a room with just one telephone. There was too much to be done, and an SOS went out to Stratford for another body to soak up the work. Jacky Taylor was asked whether she would like to go to London. She was herself rehearsing for the local amateur pantomime (playing the Fairy Queen), but she dropped that without a second thought. She had been to London only once in her life, when she was eleven, and had fainted in the Chamber of Horrors; she was not going to ruin this chance. It all happened so quickly that she arrived at the Aldwych with nowhere to live. So she moved into the attic at 31 Montpelier Square.

8

High Stakes,
Imperfect Victory

'Do you act, Mr Hall?'

Leslie Caron's romantic image of Hall's public personality was indestructible. To her, he was a leader in the war against the philistines, struggling against an entrenched and determined opposition: 'He wanted to change life in Britain . . . to raise the role of the state, to get rid of the class system and raise the level of literacy. He wanted to bring England into the twentieth century.'

Hall was more enthusiastic about this agenda than the electorate was. Harold Macmillan's Conservatives had thrashed Labour in 1959, and Macmillan's political priorities were foreign affairs and defence. At home, the emphasis was on attempts to find the elusive secret of steady economic growth. Social reform was at the bottom of the political agenda. Two decades later, right-wingers would see the permissive Sixties as being the origin of the social problems of the 1980s and 1990s. But the Sixties they were talking about did not begin until 1967 or 1968. In the early 1960s, the Labour Party still cared more about nationalisation than individual liberties. The Lord Chamberlain was the theatre censor. The Metropolitan Police entrapped better people than themselves, including John Gielgud in Chelsea in 1963. Sex before marriage was a bit of luck; the licensing laws were repressive; the food was uninviting; and the last train always left long before midnight.

In this frustrating period, the new generation of university-educated theatre people were, unlike their predecessors on the stage, fairly uniformly left-wing, and if they could not reform anything else, at least they would change the theatre. In the mid-1950s there was an anxious debate about whether the theatre was dead or not. It was not. The first six months of 1961 saw productions of new plays by Harold Pinter, Arnold Wesker, John Mortimer, Keith Waterhouse and Willis Hall, N.F. Simpson, Alun Owen, J.P. Donleavy and Henry Livings. John Osborne's *Luther* opened in July. And that was just the work of British writers: new plays by Eugène Ionesco, Jean-Paul Sartre, Jean Anouilh, Jean Genet and Jack Gelber were also produced. Jeremy Brett played Hamlet in the West End; John Stride played Prince Hal at the Old Vic. There were revivals of Ibsen at the Mermaid and the Queen's; and of Middleton's *The Changeling* and Webster's *The White Devil* at the Royal Court. On 10 May a revue that had first been seen at the previous summer's Edinburgh Festival opened in the West End to marvellous reviews; that was *Beyond the Fringe*.

The arrival of the Stratford company at the Aldwych contributed to the theatrical excitement. The Aldwych repertory opened on 15 December 1960 with Peggy Ashcroft in *The Duchess of Malfi*, the same part that she had played when Hall first saw her in 1944. This was followed by a revival of Hall's *Twelfth Night* and plays by three popular middlebrow playwrights' – Giraudoux (*Ondine*), Anouilh (*Becket*), and Christopher Fry (*Curtmantle*). All were well received, but none made the blood race. The only significant new play was *The Devils*, John Whiting's adaptation of Aldous Huxley's novel. Directed by Peter Wood and starring Dorothy Tutin, Richard Johnson and Ian Holm, *The Devils* was declared a masterpiece by T.C. Worsley, the eminent critic of the *Financial Times*. 'The play justifies the whole of Mr Hall's venture,' he wrote.[2]

In Stratford, however, hardly anything went right. Hall's concept of three-year contracts was upset by Peter O'Toole, who intended to become a film star rather than playing Henry II (in *Becket*) and Richard III. Christopher Plummer made a very capable replacement, but O'Toole's cavalier behaviour undermined the principle. Although the company now numbered a hundred, the Stratford contingent was weakened by calls upon it from London.

The company's strength was bolstered by imported stars, but most did not fit in well with ensemble playing.

When Lindsay Anderson turned down the chance to direct Ian Bannen as Hamlet, Peter Wood was drafted in to replace him. Anderson was never asked to direct again; and Wood himself returned to Stratford only rarely after a production that made Tynan grow testy with the new regime: 'As paltry and undercast as any I recall from the days before Sir Barry Jackson took over.'³ Zia Mohyeddin, whom Hall had cast as Romeo, did not even make it to the play's first night. The ruthlessness with which Hall dispatched him ten days before the play opened surprised admirers of his, like Dorothy Tutin (playing Juliet), who would have preferred him to be more patient. But the greatest disaster of the season was the production that had sounded more promising than any other – John Gielgud's first *Othello*, with Peggy Ashcroft, directed by Franco Zeffirelli, who had just done a famous *Romeo and Juliet* at the Old Vic. A series of letters written to Hall by Gielgud in the months before the first night provide an unusual insight into the turmoil of an artistic director's life and the making of a catastrophe.

Gielgud was high on the list of actors Hall had asked to work in Stratford. The perpetual calendar confirms that a letter dated only '11 April, Monday' was written in 1960; in it, Gielgud is turning down Hall's offer of work with the company: 'I feel I have done my share of pioneer work both at the Vic and Stratford and my own main problem is to decide what I really want to do – am able to do – to contribute some sort of decent work, for which – with luck – I have another ten or twelve years or so to accomplish.' The door was not completely closed, however. Gielgud added: 'Should a particular play to be directed or part to be acted come along for which you might feel I was indispensable, we could always meet and discuss the possibilities of fitting it into your general scheme.'⁴

Reluctant to let such a big fish slip away, Hall made Gielgud an offer. In a letter dated 27 June 1960, Gielgud refers to Hall's suggestion that he play Gayev in *The Cherry Orchard* with Peggy Ashcroft; Michel Saint-Denis would direct. Gielgud says that he has an option to direct a play by Enid Bagnold in September 1961, but does not turn Hall down.

Gaev [sic] is not wildly exciting to me, and I have seen it played quite

*perfectly by Esme Percy in the production I did myself some years ago.
But I adore the play, and would, of course, love working with Peg and
Michel again. If I was free at the time I would naturally be very willing
to undertake it, and that is about all I can say for the moment. I am sorry
to seem so elusive, and to refuse to tie myself down each time you write
to me. One is terrified of committing oneself ahead of time and then having
to recant and put everyone to great inconvenience.*

Hall persisted, despite another equivocal letter in August, and by
October 1960 Gielgud was discussing the possibility of combining
Gayev and Othello:

*I have been pondering a bit. The only Shakespeare part I want to try is
Othello – you may think this madness – and I shall not be hurt if you
think so. But supposing I do a Gayev for Peggy and there was a chance
of O'Toole playing Iago, do you think Peg would consider playing Emilia
– and perhaps Peter Brook to direct? That would be a wonderful contrast
in parts for me, and it would mean that one could alternate. I'm sure
Othello is impossible to play eight times a week and I think O'Toole –
who is so young and wild – would be marvellous against me . . . I have
always feared I would be too cold for the part, but, in studying it lately,
I believe I could have a shot at it . . . Othello should, it seems to me, be
an innocent, simple, romantic – only roused to real fury in the third act.
The last two are in a kind of removed demonic sacrificial mood, and the
end of the play is surely deeply simple and tragic in the noblest possible
simplicity.*

Gielgud was hooked; moreover, Ashcroft did agree to play Emilia,
and both *Othello* and *The Cherry Orchard* were written into the
schedules for Stratford and London. Unfortunately, Peter Brook
was unavailable, and so, it turned out, was O'Toole. But the
director was no problem. It appears from Gielgud's next letter,
on 25 October 1960, that Zeffirelli was his idea:

*I lunched today with Zeffirelli – he was more congenial I thought than ever
– and seemed very thrilled that I should have approached him – very modest
about R and J which he says he realises is only a first experiment which is
overpraised – took my criticisms in lively but delightful part . . . I asked him
to cable me if he would, as soon as he has thought the idea over carefully,
and then I would get you to get in touch with him if he was anxious to
undertake the work. We exchanged some exciting and infectious ideas about
the play.*

Zeffirelli consented, leaving only the casting of Iago unresolved, and Gielgud interested himself in this as if he were directing the play. On 10 April 1961, he writes:

> *I hope we can all three meet again and discuss the question of Iago further. Are you prepared to engage somebody from outside? Alan Badel, Edward Judd, Robert Shaw?? if we should decide neither [Ian] Bannen nor [Christopher] Plummer seem to be right. I gather Richard Burton would like to have done it, and I would have liked that too, but I also gather he does not leave Camelot until November. I also have a sneaking desire to approach Rex Harrison, but do not think there is any possibility he might be available, though I think he might be fascinating casting. Of course I have not really discovered how Zeffirelli sees the character.*

In a postscript Gielgud adds: 'Peter Finch? Not likely I imagine. He played it with Orson [Welles], but I don't think he had much chance. He is a fine actor, I think.'

Ten days later, casting Iago was still a problem, and Gielgud began to sound agitated:

> *I think Franco and I were neither of us too keen on Badel, skilful though he is – but a bit obvious . . . Freddie [Judd?] evidently out and I suppose Peter Finch also . . . I do rather like the idea of [Robert] Stephens. I too admire and like him, but he makes awful faces when he is acting and has he really the wit and power? I think we should audition him – and perhaps Shaw too. Is Finney out of the question? Franco thought he looked too boyish – but he could make up a bit older. Is there any chance of his being available? . . . Feel pretty certain Rex would not consider it. I think he is tied to Binkie [Beaumont] for Terry [Rattigan's] new play – but have refrained from asking – why not investigate –*

Another postscript reads: 'We mustn't delay too long, or everyone will be booked up.'

Two days later, Gielgud makes more bizarre suggestions. John Mills suddenly springs into his mind. 'The more I think of it,' he writes, 'I am sure with Peggy and myself, we *must* have an Iago of some equal status in experience and style – and who speaks very well.' He mentions John Clements, who was then fifty-three, and Jack Hawkins, who, like Mills, was fifty-one. The name of Maurice Evans, who had emigrated to the United States in the mid-1930s to become a famous Hamlet, also occurred to him. 'I find to my surprise that he is actually 60 – I thought he was younger than that – indeed he tried once to get me to do it with him in [19]36 when I was playing Hamlet in NY . . . The only one

of the younger men I think we should consider is Robert Shaw . . .
I still [*word missing*] Bannen would be best for Roderigo.'

On 3 June, still with no Iago, Gielgud was becoming disenchanted. He wrote to Hall:

> To reconsider the final position . . .
> 1. [*Ian*] Bannen
> 2. [*Alan*] Webb
> 3. [*Harry*] Corbett
>   I talked at some length to Gwen [*Ffrangcon-Davies*], Edith [*Evans*] and
> Peggy. All of them seemed to be in favour of Ian – and it seems to me that if
> disaster should fall on us – either through his fault or mine – we should not
> bring Othello to London (or conceivably find a new Iago) . . . I don't want
> to stress such a possibility but I do think one should keep it as a sort of air
> raid shelter in case of a desperate emergency in the back of our minds.

Bannen, who was also playing Hamlet in 1961, eventually got
the part.

All Gielgud's premonitions of 'disaster' were justified. Bannen
could not remember his lines on the first night. Gielgud lost his
beard half-way through a crucial scene; moreover, his brown
make-up was indistinguishable from the colour of the huge sets
that Zeffirelli had designed himself, and which took so long to
change that the first-night intervals seemed to last an hour. In
his autobiography, Zeffirelli says that the opening night must
have been the most disastrous and ill-fated in the history of
the English and possibly the world stage.[5] Tynan was merciless.
Bannen was 'all warts and no face', Gielgud 'simply overparted'.
Gielgud took refuge in his metaphorical air-raid shelter, and
Othello never transferred to London. *The Cherry Orchard* did,
however, where it was one of the biggest hits of the early
1960s.

Hall took responsibility for Gielgud's failure: 'After all, I had
listened when he and Franco had said they wanted to do the play
. . . But he was never the soldier: the poetry was extraordinary and
the naivete was honest, but the animal wasn't there.'[6] Gielgud took
his failure to heart, and never returned to Stratford. The disaster,
however, added to the Peter Hall legend. He tells the story himself
of a conversation with Zeffirelli about Iago's character: 'I see him
as very young, with a baby face, always smiling,' Zeffirelli said.
'But behind the young, round, smiling face is a heart of steel. Do
you act, Mr Hall?'

The 1961 Stratford season was rescued, almost single-handedly, by Vanessa Redgrave, whose Rosalind in *As You Like It* inspired Bernard Levin, then the critic for the *Daily Express,* to rococo extravagance: 'her voice a golden gate opening on lapis lazuli hinges, her body a slender supple reed rippling in the breeze of her love'. Levin's enchantment echoes that of many men who found Vanessa Redgrave irresistible. Hall was one of them. He was also a close enough friend of hers for Vanessa's mother, Rachel Kempson, to write to him confidentially asking him if he could persuade Vanessa to spend less time demonstrating outside the Russian and American Embassies on behalf of the Committee of 100, and to take better care of her voice: 'Dear Peter please have a shot at making her *limit* her political work . . . I love her with all my heart and I sympathise with her views as I know you do, but she can't do the two jobs.'[7] In this case, Hall was powerless.

Hall's opinion was that the 'Shakespeare Memorial Theatre' sounded provincial. He wanted a name that de-emphasised the memorial aspect and added the lustre of royal endorsement. Buckingham Palace was willing, and agreed to the 'Royal Shakespeare Theatre' but in February 1961 Hall told Flower: 'It's too Stratford.'[8] He chose the Royal Shakespeare Company, and in March the Palace acquiesced to this. It was a euphonious title, either spelled out or abbreviated, but what mattered most was the impression it gave that this was a national company, capable, were the powers that be ever to deem it necessary, of becoming a National Theatre.

For the most part, Hall's audience forgave the failings of a single summer, although there was considerable ill-feeling in Stratford itself. The townspeople were not targeted in Hall's public relations strategy. Hersey Flower remembers complaints that Hall was a communist because he had referred to Marx in a programme note ('I think your remarks about Marxist influence are a bit far-fetched,' Flower wrote to Sir Gyles Isham, one of the Midlands industrialist governors).[9] But the biggest controversy was caused by Hall's decision to drop the playing of the National Anthem at the end of each performance. A new arrangement of the anthem on wind instruments was played in the presence of royalty and at the beginning and end of each season. Flower's correspondence files show that protests about the anthem never dried up; it was a continuing affront to a vocal minority.

Hall was more concerned by the reactions of Harold Hobson

of the *Sunday Times*: his reviews affected business. A year earlier, Hall had taken Hobson to task for his unsympathetic attitude to the Aldwych expansion. Since complaining directly to critics risked retaliation, this had seemed a bold thing to do. (Hall also complained to the *Manchester Guardian* about Gareth Lloyd Evans's reviews, and threatened to ban him from the Stratford theatre.)[10] Hobson had tempered his criticism of the Aldwych; but now at the end of the 1961 season he was concerned about the absence of a coherent style at Stratford:

> *The unfortunate players are blown about in gales of contrary doctrine. Sometimes they have a curtain, sometimes not; sometimes they imitate the previous performances of greater players than themselves, sometimes they are built on novelty . . . often they match ducal costumes to dustbin voices . . . as a preparation for a National Theatre this is no good at all. We need a style, and Stratford ought to be able to find it for us.*

In this, Hobson was echoing the views of Peter Brook, who thought that in the early 1960s Stratford, like the BBC, had no artistic policy, by which he meant no cultural or political attitude. Brook told Sally Beauman that its ideal 'was to do good things very well, the traditional target of liberal England'.[11] From 1962, Stratford had a new directorate of three. Hall had persuaded Brook to join the company as associate director; the third member was Michel Saint-Denis, who was to teach in the new studio, and to direct. Unlike John Barton, and Peter Wood whose reputation had been tarnished by his unsuccessful *Hamlet*, these were older men. Jacky Taylor observed that Hall, at the age of thirty-one, seemed to find it easier to listen to them than to his contemporaries.[12] Michael Kustow, who worked with both Hall and Brook, notes that Hall always knew that, in the event of a power struggle, he could not conquer Brook; so he never bothered to try.[13] Saint-Denis, who had been an important but irregular presence in the English theatre for thirty years, wrote a delightful letter acknowledging Hall's offer: 'You are young and I am old – how wonderful if we can be friends at work and confident – completely in each other – and if we could be certain friendship and collaboration will lead to a fidelity so simple and evident that it has radiance and influence.'[14] Hall did not feel threatened by either of his new collaborators. Although Saint-Denis was no longer physically well, the new directorate was an experienced, cosmopolitan and powerful team.

A new name, a new leadership – and, if Hall had his way, they would have a new theatre too. The designer for *The Devils* was Sean Kenny, a young Irish architect who had worked in Frank Lloyd Wright's studio. Kenny had submitted a plan to rebuild the Memorial Theatre, which, so far, Hall had only tinkered with by thrusting the stage out beyond the proscenium arch into the auditorium. Hall wrote to Flower on 20 January 1961 saying that Kenny's scheme would make Stratford the most exciting theatre building in the world. The trouble was the cost – 'a cool half million'. What did Flower think they should do? Hall asked. 'Drop the idea, petition the Treasury, or what?'[15]

Flower's reply shows how he buoyed Hall up while lightly letting him down. He pointed out that, in the absence of help from the government, Stratford would have to borrow the cool half-million. The interest on the loan would be more than £25,000 a year, which would have to be paid out of profits. 'Now if our economic situation in the future is going to need a subsidy, in order to cope with an anticipated annual deficit, there are not going to be any profits. Having said that, I think this is a wildly exciting idea, and if it is at all possible, we should try to do it.'[16] Because Hall believed a subsidy was essential, Flower's reply meant that Hall himself must admit Kenny's scheme was impossible. No more was heard about it. Profit, loss and subsidy, on the other hand, were never absent from their conversations. The propects for the future were fraught until the principle of a subsidy had been established; and that was always in doubt as long as the relationship between the Shakespeare Company and the National Theatre remained undecided.

Discussions on this topic were influenced by a number of conflicting relationships. 'Some people within our family circle were on the other side,' says Hersey Flower, whose aunt was Didi Lyttelton, the mother of Oliver Lyttelton, Lord Chandos, the chairman of the Joint Council for the National Theatre. They talked about the National Theatre together and Chandos told Flower that Stratford's attitude would be vital: 'Frankly my idea is that we should make a tripod of Stratford, the Old Vic and the National Theatre,' Chandos wrote late in 1959. Flower was asked to join the Joint Council in 1960, though Chandos assured him: 'Collaboration does not mean amalgamation of any kind. It only means that when the National Theatre comes into being, we should work out how we can most usefully scratch each other's backs.'[17] Chandos felt the Joint Council met a political imperative because the government would insist on the three companies working together, but both Fordham and Hersey were suspicious of Laurence Olivier, who had been Chandos's candidate for the directorship of the National Theatre since 1957. They were convinced he wanted to prevent Stratford opening in London.

Fordham Flower was Stratford's leading man in the relations with the Joint Council and with the Arts Council. These had been perfunctory as long as the Shakespeare Memorial Theatre was self-financing, but once the decision to run down the financial reserves had been taken in principle in Leningrad, Flower's job was to negotiate with the authorities. On the Joint Council, Flower made his own membership conditional on Hall's being asked to join as well, and the two of them were a team.

Behind their masks, Hall's relationship with Olivier was less good-natured than it appeared. Both claimed that they were on the same side; both felt they ought to be allies; but instinctively they were competitors. Olivier's discussions with Hall during rehearsals for *Coriolanus* in 1959, when Hall refused to join him at the National Theatre, coloured their subsequent relationship. In 1960, for example, when Hall asked Olivier to consider working again at Stratford, it provoked one of Olivier's urgent but discursive handwritten letters.

Dated 3 July 1960, it begins:

> It doesn't seem easy to meet, so I'm going to try to put my thoughts down on paper to you.
>
> I feel the central duty of my career should be towards the establishment and creation of a National Theatre.
>
> Until the combined forces of the Vic and Stratford have expressed themselves in entire unity in the Nat. Theatre movement by your company playing at the Vic it would not be to the main interest for me to work for either party.
>
> Any desire I might have to do this I find hampered by two considerations
>
> a. one is that the Vic and Stratford alone are not enough to form the schools of acting necessary to make the foundation of a company large enough to fill the needs of a National Theatre company, which should be able to draw on about 150 people in three years time. (Sh's birthday in 1964 – 400th anniv – is the selling date of the opening to the Treasury and the public).

> *b. And the other is my own desire to have one more independent fling at it before incarcerating myself in the service of the state.*

Olivier goes on to explain that he is involved with Sidney Bernstein of Granada Television, and the independent producer Oscar Lewenstein in plans to establish a company at the Metropolitan Theatre, Edgware Road, a fine old music hall.

> *I remember telling you of these sort of ambitions in the restaurant at Strat during Corio rehearsals at which time you confided that you had similar ambitions for your Strat co. It did not at that time seem at all productive to me to plunge on in rivalry to you . . . but now that the idea seems to have some usefulness to our common aim I find myself back with it.*

Olivier cannily kept his options open:

> *I think now (not sure for how long, of course), that I should always want to feel that I had one leg free to shake in another camp if I wanted to do that, and this would apply to any Nat. Th. contract should I ultimately have one. I realise that everybody couldn't expect that sort of freedom but I have served the business for 35 years now, and it's possible that sort of privilege could be extended to a very few of a certain record . . . I have put these thoughts very bluntly so they will be clear to you without saying 'do you see what I mean' or 'if you'll pardon my saying so'. I hope you accept them in this spirit which you know is very close to your own in comradeship and friendship.[18]*

In the twelve months after Olivier wrote this letter to Hall, he had every reason to feel confident of Hall's comradeship. In a number of meetings of the Joint Council designed to produce a National Theatre plan for the Chancellor of the Exchequer's consideration, Hall seemed to support wholeheartedly Chandos's three-legged scheme. The minutes record this: 'Mr Hall said that it must be understood that upon the completion of the NT both Stratford and the Old Vic would be entirely absorbed in the overall NT organisation.'[19] A later minute reads: '[Hall's] governors were prepared for the fact that while Stratford would continue to exist geographically, it would be a National Theatre company that was playing there.'[20]

During this period, Olivier was writing cordially to Hall from the United States where he was appearing in Anouilh's *Becket* (playing first a run of Becket and then of Henry II), which Hall was scheduled to direct at the Aldwych in 1961. Olivier was generous with advice:

> The requirements for the part of Becket are very obvious ones, but the least obvious is the most important, and it is this. This man who plays it simply must have glamour. Cast it for the first act and the second act will follow on quite easily if the man has any imagination at all. Spiritual quality upon the stage is so closely related to star quality that it is quite easily grasped by any possessing such.[21]

Although the Joint Council's minutes do not mention the Aldwych, Olivier wrote from New York on 10 November 1960 – a month before the opening of the first Aldwych season: 'It does seem to be clearing up about the Old Vic. I shall be writing to Kenneth [Rae] as soon as I can get down to it, about concertina-ing with the Aldwych enterprise and the Old Vic theatre.'[22]

But it was Olivier who got squeeezed. To the astonishment of all the participants, Selwyn Lloyd – Macmillan's Chancellor of the Exchequer – announced on 21 March 1961 that the government had decided against a National Theatre. Lloyd's announcement contained wonderful news for Stratford. Instead of paying for a National Theatre, he said, the government proposed spending £400,000 a year to subsidise the Old Vic, regional repertory theatres, and Stratford. Quite suddenly, the principle of subsidy seemed to have been accepted, and in the absence of competition from Olivier's as yet unformed company, Hall would be running what was effectively a National Theatre.

Olivier wrote to Hall from Boston on 31 March: 'I am absolutely distraught about the news of the National Theatre, and because I have been so concentrated upon the present work, have not allowed myself to dwell on it as the gorge rises about the Old Vic in a really throttling way. It's a poor return for Stratford's immaculate behaviour.'[23] The Old Vic believed, correctly, that it would not survive the establishement of the National Theatre, and never showed much enthusiasm for the idea.

Hall and Flower could not have engineered a better outcome if they had sold their souls for it. Although good manners prevented them from crowing, Flower said later that Lloyd's announcement completely satisfied the RSC. Their euphoria was, however, very short-lived. Lord Chandos was not likely to take no for an answer, and he deployed all his considerable political clout with Tory ministers, making a charge that establishment figures use only *in extremis* – that the Chancellor had insulted the Queen Mother, who had laid the foundation stone of the National Theatre in 1951. Three months later, Lloyd announced a U-turn: the National Theatre would happen after all. The London County Council (LCC) had offered to put up more than £1 million itself, and Lloyd asked the Joint Council to come up with a new scheme that would spend an annual subsidy of £400,000 on the opera and ballet as well as on the theatre; and the South Bank site was to have an opera house as well as the National Theatre. Lloyd's message suggested that, having changed its mind, the government was determined to crush any mavericks. 'If any one of the three organisations concerned should not participate in the scheme, any annual subventions would have to be reconsidered, and the Government would be under no obligation to contribute monies for the improvement of their existing premises.'

This was not what Stratford wanted at all. In May 1961, when the Arts Council had asked how much Hall wanted as a subsidy, he said £124,000. That, he added, would only cover the deficit for the current year. Since the deficit turned out to be closer to £30,000, this was an extravagant claim, but the budgets for the rest of 1961 and the whole of 1962 had been drawn up on the assumption that the company would get some money from the government. When Flower asked Lord Cottesloe, the new chairman of the Arts Council, how much Stratford might expect to get, the reply was shocking: while the National Theatre project was being considered in detail, nothing at all was to be budgeted for Stratford. The clear inference was that unless Stratford agreed to the new plans that were being concocted for a National Theatre, there never would be any money.[24] Perhaps Cottesloe did not intend it as such, but to Flower and Hall this was a declaration of war. They seemed to relish the challenge. While they had been willing to contribute to a partnership of equals, this new concept made Stratford an appendage in what looked like an arts conglomerate; one, moreover, that would be ruled by Laurence Olivier.

The first skirmish occurred during a visit by Arnold Goodman, as Chandos's emissary, to Stratford in August 1961. Goodman had intended to see a performance of *Hamlet* and to explain the constitution he had written for the National Theatre in which the National Theatre would embrace the Old Vic and Sadler's Wells as well as Stratford. But he had a rotten weekend. His companion, Jane Samuel, slipped and fell on some steps, and his meeting with

Flower and Hall was embarrassing. He tells his version of the story
in his memoirs.

> *[I met] Sir Fordham Flower, the chairman, much beloved, simple and nice.*
> *Peter Hall, much beloved, effective and complicated . . . to whom I explained*
> *the document in the naive belief that the principle had been agreed . . .*
> *Who, they said, is to be the head of the organisation? I coughed slightly*
> *since no-one had then told me, but I opined that it was likely to be Sir*
> *Laurence Olivier. There was an exchange of glances, and faces which had*
> *never been wholly welcoming became rather distant. It was clear to me*
> *within seconds that, on the basis of the leadership of Laurence Olivier, to*
> *whose qualities they paid tribute of unstinting eloquence, there would be*
> *no Stratford included in the new entity . . . I withdrew fairly convinced we*
> *had seen the last of them, at least while Sir Laurence dominated the scene.*
> *I was right. Stratford withdrew at great speed for reasons which were not*
> *the real ones.*[25]

In the months since they had accepted the principle of amalgamation, Flower and Hall had grown much prouder and very
cross. They believed that the Treasury had welshed on a promise
to provide Stratford with a subsidy, and that let-down was
transformed into an insult by the suggestion that any subsidy
at all was conditional on Flower's agreeing to Chandos's plans for
amalgamation. Flower spoke of coercion and blackmail: it was like
'a shot-gun marriage', he wrote to Cottesloe. Flower later refined
to three the reasons why Stratford backed away from the idea
of amalgamation. One was the fear that Stratford would quickly
become the poor relation in the partnership; another was that, 'to
put it very bluntly, we didn't like the set-up'; the third was his
belief that public opinion was opposed to the idea.[26]

In his autobiography, Hall admits that he switched his own position completely, remarking that it seemed almost unbelievable to
him that they had agreed in the first place that the amalgamation
was a wise decision.[27] In the autumn of 1961 the change of mood
was signalled by Flower's new uncompromising attitude towards
his fellow Joint Council members. A mood of self-righteous
paranoia was developing in Stratford, and it surfaced in Flower's
confidential minute to Hall about a meeting of the committee on
20 September 1961.

Chandos had hoped the meeting would adopt the 'complete
amalgamation' plan, despite Stratford's 'cooling off'. Chandos
had played the political card: amalgamation was the only solution

that the moneybags in the Treasury and the LCC would accept, he said. Olivier tried the artistic argument: 'a big, centralised company is the only way to do it'. But Flower was unapologetic about Stratford's second thoughts. 'I surmise that the caucus, and Larry in particular, wants to eliminate Stratford as a competitor. If Larry takes on the job of the Big Panjandrum his reputation is at stake.' Flower imputed four motives to Olivier: that he wanted to eliminate Stratford as a competitor, commercially and for actors; that he wanted to have Peter Hall working for him instead of against him; that he wanted Stratford's technical know-how and managerial experience; and that he wanted 'to get his mitts on Stratford revenues'.[28]

During the winter, tension between the two camps rose steadily, and a coldness developed between Hall and Olivier. The pretext for the first skirmish between them was Olivier's approach to some Stratford actors whom he wanted to cast in the first Chichester Festival season. (Instead of starting a company at the Metropolitan, Edgware Road, Olivier had become the first director of the Chichester Festival Theatre in March 1961, and it was due to open in the summer of 1962.) In his letters to Hall Olivier's language is jocular throughout, though not without an undercurrent of hostility. On 10 October Olivier addresses Hall as 'My dear Peterkin', and begins by asking his pardon if he has been discourteous.

> *I am so slow and time goes so quick that I have not thought that perhaps I should have approached you before doing so to any of your players . . . I feel you have noticed my approaches to your stars. I only hope you have noticed that I have not approached Scofield, because I realise that he is sac(h)rosanct [sic]. For all kinds of reasons. Thank you. I would rather have him than have you have him, and I think the poor sod would rather do it for 10 weeks than 10 months – who wouldn't – but this only offers to show how thoroughly decent I am at bottom (as they will say in our sort of plays).*
>
> *The Nat. Th. seems to be at a complete impasse, tout laisse, tout casse and fuck me all dandy. I am in a bad way. I can't get a National Theatre. I can't get a cast or repertoire for Chichester. I can't get into my home, and Joannie's baby is bursting out. I can't wake up in the morning or go to sleep at night. I'm absolutely fucked.*
>
> *How are you, cock!*[29]

Scofield was 'sacrosanct' because Hall had persuaded him to play King Lear in a Peter Brook production at Stratford the following summer. (And, incidentally, Olivier did move into his house in Brighton in December, a week after Joan Plowright gave birth to their son, Richard.) But Olivier's cheery prose did not improve relations between them.

Chandos was annoyed too. When Flower complained that the National would be using its grant to outbid the RSC for actors, he replied that 'your energetic Mr Hall' had signed up as many artists as he could lay his hands on, so the National Theatre needed some latitude over salaries if it was to build up a company. Relations continued to deteriorate through the winter and reached a low point in the New Year.[30] Olivier's anguished handwritten answer to Hall's questions about Stratford's place in his plans was twelve pages long. Written in January or February 1962 from Dublin, where Olivier was making a film called *Term of Trial*, it is a bitter and impassioned document. Perhaps for the first time, Hall is accused of empire building, and the letter confirms Olivier's profound suspicion and mistrust of the RSC's motives, an attitude that eventually permeated the National Theatre and undermined Hall's own authority when he succeeded Olivier. Marked *Private* and *Confidential*, the undated latter begins:

> *My dear Peter,*
>   You're *worried!?*
>
>   *love Larry*
>   is about all I thought I could manage in the way of an answer to your
>   letter when it arrived, but the thing I realise is too serious for jokes.

Olivier goes on to complain that he has so much on his mind that he would prefer not to have to think about the National Theatre:

> *The Nat[ional] Theatre and all its considerations is a horribly formidable
> spectre to me, but one which I can and must put aside if I am going to
> know my words and give a decent show in this film, all the other time
> I must devote to Chich[ester] or I am going to make a botch of that. So
> up to now I have managed to live with the Nat Th as a safely locked
> away black cloud. This is how I would like to continue if I could – but
> I am stopped from doing so by the thought that such would naturally be
> regarded as prevarication by you with overtones of hedging and duplicity.*

Olivier, his dander rising fast, says how important it is that friends should be open and frank with each other, and that he will deal with Hall's worries item by item, beginning with Hall's assertion that people are thinking the two of them are not in perfect agreement:

I don't know who these people are or what they are saying. Whatever it is, they cannot be quoting me as I have said nothing to anyone. It is possible that some of your statements to the press have given the impression of grievance and dissension. I always consider the press as a thoroughly unreliable means of expressing oneself, and my present determination to resist the use of it is principally to avoid misunderstandings and also to avoid looking like a cunt. It is their nature to see that the results of communication through their columns are always angled to ensure one of these two alternatives. I have explained that any statements you make about the Nat Th are bound to be embarrassing to me, and have indeed advised you never to talk to the buggers on any subject for your own sake, but you seem determined to enthrone yourself among the decoy ducks.

Olivier then proceeds to deal with Hall's assertion that the Stratford governors withdrew from the amalgamation talks because they were trying to be constructive and clear the way for the National Theatre: 'Forgive me dear boy but that is absolutely rubbish. They withdrew entirely for their own reasons, entirely to do with their own amour propre, and when at the meeting with Fordie when you were not present, it was pointed out that this attitude, as it seemed at the time, was the complete finish of all our proposals, there was nothing more constructive offered than an apologetic shrug.'

Olivier next targets Hall's statement that he wants the National Theatre as much as Olivier, and that, although his first loyalty is obviously to Stratford and the governors, he has worked for it to happen.

You have caused Stratford to do a great deal towards following your ambitions both from a professional point of view and from their point of view. They have stuck (as they would be bound to do at something sooner or later) at being part of the National Theatre. This at the moment must be a matter between you and them rather than between you and me.

The trouble as I see it (and have from the beginnings of your schemes) is that you have really set out to be the Nat Th yourself, or if you prefer it, for Stratford to develop a position for itself as heir to the throne, or else to make such a throne unnecessary. If this is not so (as I know you genuinely want a Nat Th) it looks like it (to observers I mean, not to me). The trouble is that there has been for many years organisation and machinery (no, not empowered) but recognised and dedicated to the construction of the thing. And you can't kick them out. These boys have been working at it for years,

*long before Stratford ever thought of it. So Stratford must now (we think)
join in to survive . . .*

*Now this question of Federation. I do promise I shall study and think
about it but I can't see it yet. God almighty I haven't even begun yet.
You know very well that I do not want and never would allow anything
to 'kill' Stratford, except over my dead body; and you really mustn't throw
up words like 'Empire' to me, not you with Stratford, Aldwych and now the
Arts, because here again you seem to be assuming N.T. responsibilities, and
it could be argued that Stratford's present monopoly . . . has contributed to
the decline of the Old Vic. You can offer better facilities, better terms and
better conditions etc, so it would appear that you are not against monopoly,
unless it is held by the N.T. instead of Stratford! Is it reasonable to expect the
N.T. to give financial encouragement to competition quite as formidable as
Stratford's 'Empire' when it is only in the earliest stages of conception?*

*Your letter carries to me a slightly hysterical (if I may say so without
meaning to be the tiniest bit offensive) – note once or twice which worries
me and makes me feel you are not in a good state – or else you are pulling
the wool over my eyes, which I don't like much better(!) (Never shit on
a shitter.)*

Hall's own letter to Olivier had said that they must work in
harness somehow, and this thought led to the grand climax of
Olivier's attack:

*Finally, the statement which, to me, represents the kernel of your feelings:
– 'otherwise the foundations I have fumblingly laid at Strat[ford] during
the last two years might just as well not have happened'! That's it, isn't
it? And, my God, I understand it completely and I have apprehended it
throughout. I realised all these implications when we first talked during
Coriolanus rehearsals, naturally. The work you have done and the schemes
you envisage belong in a N.T. set up. But the sad thing, as things have
worked out, is that it is your Governors not the N.T. who are responsible
for your present impasse.*

Olivier finishes with a caustic job description of his role at the
National Theatre: 'At the moment it looks like the most tiresome,
awkward, embarrassing, forever-compromise, never-right, thank-
less fucking post that anyone could possibly be fool enough to take
on and the idea fills me with dread.'[31] But Olivier was influenced
more by his sense of destiny than his sense of dread.

Finally convinced that Hall would only be happy running his
own national company, Olivier and Chandos made their own
plans. Flower had formally withdrawn from the Joint Council in
January 1962. This was not the mortal blow that Chandos and

Olivier feared: their plan satisfied the LCC and the Treasury, and in July 1962 Selwyn Lloyd announced that the money for the new South Bank theatre would be handed over. In August Olivier was formally appointed the first director. The inevitability of the choice is borne out in a note to Hall from Peggy Ashcroft. 'Darling Pete,' she writes, 'Your telegram *much* enjoyed as it took a great deal of elucidation – *prevent* having been written as *present*! I *do* agree – it seemed to me that Larry could really be the *ONLY* choice. Oh well.'[32] Their enthusiasm was well under control.

While plans for the birth of the National Theatre were being made, the RSC appeared to be fighting for its life. Flower had revealed the precarious nature of the company's finances to Lord Cottesloe at the Arts Council on 15 January 1962: anticipated losses for 1961–2 were £30,000; in the following year the deficit would rise to £40,700, or £58,000 if the actors got the 17 per cent pay increase they deserved. (Top rates were £60 a week.) Cottesloe promised to consider Flower's case carefully and sympathetically, and spoke of hopes for giving a grant in 1962–3, but of no more than £10,000. So Flower was astonished to be informed by an Arts Council official in Stratford in May that the RSC was hardly likely to get a grant, since it had not asked for one. Nonsense, Flower wrote to Cottesloe, adding a formal request for £50,000.[33] This produced the best news yet from Cottesloe, who told Flower on 11 May 1962 that, while any more than £10,000 was unlikely in 1962–3, he had every hope that the Arts Council might be able to get £50,000 for the following year. That offered a real hope of victory in the struggle to establish the principle of a subsidy for the RSC. But Hall, who had decided to embark on a public campaign for public money in February, was not going to concede that the game might be won. Flower described the campaign as Hall's 'virile policy'. What he meant was that Hall had got involved in a scrap.

Few people were more adept than Hall at orchestrating a public campaign. He had prepared the way in February 1962 in a private and confidential letter to Flower saying it was time for some softening up in the press and asking his permission to talk to one of his friends in Fleet Street: 'In fact, I want to give him a discreet leak.'[34] With the assistance of John Goodwin, the RSC's astute chief publicist, whose speciality was timing and method, Hall leaked the news, in March 1962, that without a government grant the Aldwych would close. ('He knew how to tell a sad tale,' says Caron.) Both appreciated that this story would have most impact if it was given to a news reporter, and the chosen recipient was a theatre correspondent, Ronald Hastings. The sad tale was launched with a splash in the *Daily Telegraph*. That was just softening up, said Hall, for the big campaign starting in April, when they were likely to be told formally they were to get no money.

The fact that the RSC was told in May that it would get a government subsidy made no difference to Hall's virile campaign. Early in July he wrote a remarkably frank memo to Flower about the campaign in the press:

> *Nearly all the press is strongly on our side, and while retaining an official silence for the moment, this campaign obviously must be fostered in every possible way during the next three or four weeks. All this is preparing the ground very well for our announcement of our definite withdrawal from the Arts [Theatre season of experimental work] which we plan to make in a month's time, and which should be shown as the first stage in our shrinking future. This will make very good news after what has happened already. Various critics have offered to take up our cause. Findlater is trying to organise something in the* Observer, *and Worsley is trying to organise a letter to* The Times *signed by all the major critics. All this will be fostered.*[35]

In his theatre, Hall was an impresario; when fighting those who would close it, he was a general, so determined to win that the end always justified the means. Hall's reputation for ruthlessness stems from Machiavellian memos like this.

The critics, having been fostered, did as expected. On 8 July the three posh Sundays printed articles by Harold Hobson, Kenneth Tynan, and the *Sunday Telegraph*'s Alan Brien, deploring the lack of a subsidy for the RSC. The following day they were joined by eight more daily and weekly critics, who signed a letter (to the *Daily Telegraph* rather than *The Times*), affirming their belief in the vital importance of the RSC to the life of the London theatre. The critics were Felix Barker, W.A. Darlington, Bamber Gascoigne, Philip Hope-Wallace, Bernard Levin, Robert Muller, Milton Shulman and T.C. Worsley. Richard Findlater had organised a leading article in the *Observer* which concluded: 'It is hard to believe that the Arts Council can stand by and see such a remarkable and successful venture being extinguished for the lack of State alms which are now freely given to all kinds of unsuccessful, unexciting and uncreative establishments.' Hall and Goodwin could not have done better if they had written it themselves.

The campaign's climax came at the end of July with an attack on the National Theatre. T.C. Worsley, writing in the *Financial Times*, said:

> *Perhaps it is time to be blunt. There are ugly rumours about that some of those who have negotiated the National Theatre scheme would not be sorry (to put it no lower) to see Peter Hall's RSC out of London. They are said to fear competition, and so far from wielding such influence as they have to get a grant for the RSC, they are carefully avoiding using it.*[36]

In fact, the campaign was so pervasive and opinion so unanimous that Whitehall began to smell a conspiracy. John Profumo, Stratford's MP and a promising junior minister, told Flower that the new Chancellor, Reginald Maudling, thought the publicity for the RSC was not entirely spontaneous; the Treasury suspected it was all got up by Hall and Flower, and was reluctant to believe Profumo's denial.

The Arts Council itself became a target in the campaign when Flower replied to Profumo. Since by now the Council had already informed him that the RSC would be receiving a grant, Flower had to deploy a fresh case. He told the MP that his guess was that the secretariat at the Arts Council intended to provide only an inadequate subsidy so that the RSC was always stretched and ever getting weaker: 'A situation would thus be created in which no artistic director would work here and then the Arts Council would force us into the NT set up on the latter's terms.'[37]

When Olivier travelled to Stratford on 20 October 1962, he thought he was bearing an olive branch. Of two proposals he wished to discuss, the first was flattering and uncontroversial: he wanted the three members of the directorate to sit on the National Theatre Building Committee. The second proposal was that the RSC should perform for three months each year in the new building which they would help design for the South Bank. Instead of treating this proposal as a peace offering, Flower and Hall reacted as though it were a cup of hemlock. Flower wrote immediately to Olivier, accusing him of insisting that, in return for a season at the National Theatre, the RSC should leave the Aldwych: 'This is an unreasonable condition to make and an impossible one to accept.' He raised the emotional stakes further by suggesting that Olivier saw the presence of the RSC at the Aldwych as a threat to his National Theatre: 'Isn't this precisely what you meant when you told me that the one thing which sticks in the gizzards of the powers that be is the Aldwych?'[38]

Olivier's sorrowful reply came the next day. His proposal would come into play only if the government decided there was not enough money to go round, and the RSC were forced to withdraw from the Aldwych:

> There is no point in beating about the bush, so let us accept the fact that we are all aware of the impossibility of asking the government to support two national theatres when they are still arguing as to whether they will meet the required sum for supporting only one such project. This is what was meant by my intimation that your lodger in the gizzards is the Aldwych.[39]

Flower had indicated that Olivier should support his plan for a federation embracing both the National and the RSC, each with equal status (and each, presumably, with equal access to the government's cash). But that would have gone against the NT's interest, and neither Chandos nor Olivier showed any desire to do that.

To persuade the government that this should be the policy, the RSC deployed its most potent weapon. Lord Avon, once Sir Anthony Eden, the Prime Minister from 1955 to 1957, who had been MP for Stratford and was chairman of the RSC governors, spoke to his successor as Prime Minister, Harold Macmillan, about the plight of the RSC. But neither he nor Profumo appears to have had much impact. Towards the end of October, Cottesloe wrote to Flower confirming his letter of the previous May; he added that the grant to the RSC should be considered as recognition by the government of the need for the RSC to continue its activities in London.[40] Shortly afterwards, the secretary-general of the Arts Council, Sir Emrys Williams, informed Flower that the RSC would get £47,000 in 1963–4. What this meant was that the vigorous press campaign had had no effect on the size of the grant. The only hint of better things to come was a note from Sir Emrys to Flower to say that now the RSC was on the Arts Council's books, there might be 'brighter prospects' in succeeding years.[41]

This was a victory of sorts, though not a resounding one. On 29 November 1962, in a letter to Hall, Sir Emrys admitted that the grant fell far short of his expectations: 'but this place has taught me the necessity (if not the virtue) of patience . . . There is plenty of good will for Stratford here, but unfortunately, we are seldom able to translate such good will in the proper terms of arithmetic.'[42]

The truth was that the Arts Council's freedom for manoeuvre had already been circumscribed by the Treasury, which had instructed the Arts Council to pass a message to the RSC about its relationship with the National Theatre:

> *There are references in the papers which we have seen on this subject of Stratford assuming in the future that 'it will be necessary for them to operate on a National Theatre level'. If this statement means no more than that their productions will in due course have to compete with the National Theatre, there can be no quarrel with it. I am bound to put formally on record, however, and to ask you to tell the RST [sic] authorities, that the Treasury will not be able to accept any wider implications which might be held to flow from any such assumptions.[43]*

Flower's immediate reaction was to say that he could not make head or tail of this. Unfortunately, the meaning was clear: despite Hall's and the press's concerted efforts, as far as the British establishment was concerned the RSC was to take second place to the National Theatre.

Hall and Flower had achieved in principle the objective they had set themselves in Leningrad in 1958: Stratford had been recognised as a national institution deserving a government subsidy. This was good news for theatre audiences, and for actors and technicians: once the government started to fund the National Theatre as well, there would be two British companies of the highest calibre performing a complete repertory of plays. But the RSC was cast in the role of poor relation, depending for its continued existence on last-minute handouts from a hard-pressed Arts Council. The chronic underfunding that was a persistent problem at Stratford was partly the result of Hall's campaign, which had made it impossible for the Whitehall establishment to close down his London theatre, but which made them determined not to give him an easy ride. They had long memories.

The grant did not end hostilities with the National Theatre, either. Throughout the RSC's publicity barrage in 1962, Chandos and the NT caucus remained quiet in public, and behaved well in private. For instance, after the London County Council agreed to a grant of £100,000, Chandos, hoping to help the RSC in Whitehall, voluntarily renounced £100,000 of the £230,000 promised to the National Theatre by the Chancellor. But such was the ill-feeling in Stratford that Flower and Hall were slow to acknowledge the NT's support, and this rankled. As Chandos told Flower, he had received no thanks for the NT's self-denial.[44]

Hall's vigorous campaign had begun to make him some influential enemies. His high public profile also made him vulnerable to the young satirists who were popping up in London. In a piece of inspired lunacy in the sixth issue of *Private Eye*, in March 1962, John Wells wrote an imaginary interview in which Hall, who has gobbled up the job of director of the National Theatre, is asked about his plans:

> 'Well, we have plans to build a new theatre on the South Bank, which will probably be called Peter Hall.'
> 'On the lines of the Albert . . .'
> 'Yes, only obviously rather larger.'[45]

Hall deliberately cultivated his image as a young and powerful impresario, and John Goodwin, his publicist, had no qualms at all about that: 'A public figure has power to get things done because politicians and the media will listen when he speaks out.'[46] Hall was a founder member of the new school which got its way with the establishment by behaving badly; he would have questioned his behaviour only if it were not working. And while he did not always get all that he wanted, he was certainly getting things done.

Unlike 1961, the RSC's 1962 season at Stratford and London was full of excitement. There were a number of successful revivals: *As You Like It* moved from Stratford to the Aldwych, as did Hall's *Troilus and Cressida*. His 1959 production of *A Midsummer Night's Dream* was revived at Stratford with a new cast led by the promising young actors Ian Richardson and Judi Dench. Ralph Richardson had rejected Hall's approach to appear in Brecht's *Caucasian Chalk Circle* at the Aldwych ('I am sorry that I cannot see what you perceive in the Brecht play – it is no doubt blindness in me,' he wrote).[47] But Hugh Griffith took the part, in a production that proved to have troubles echoing those of Barton's *Shrew*. It was the first large-scale production of Brecht in England, and the director was William Gaskill from the Royal Court, but Hall took over from him in the final stages of rehearsal. 'I used a lot of improvisation,' says Gaskill, 'and the actors panicked, but I was devastated when he said he'd have to take it over. It wasn't as though he radically re-thought it. I was very bitter. I never really forgave him.'[48] As with Barton's *Shrew*, the eventual product was particularly well regarded.

Vanessa Redgrave went to Stratford to play Peggy Ashcroft's parts – Katharine and Imogen. The *Shrew* was redirected by Maurice Daniels from the ill-fated 1960 production, but John Barton's personal recovery from the debacle of the *Shrew* in 1960, begun a year earlier with an anthology of kingship called *The Hollow Crown*, continued with an adaptation of *Les Liaisons Dangereuses*.

One reason why Olivier had alluded to a Stratford 'empire' was the RSC's seven-play season, mainly of new plays, at the Arts Theatre in the spring and summer of 1962 (the season for whose cancellation Hall 'prepared the ground' in July). The tone of the Arts season was set by David Rudkin's *Afore Night Come* in which a tramp was ritually sacrificed on a rubbish dump. ('Shouts of quiet from the audience almost drowned the noise of a fainted spectator being slapped back into consciousness,' reported Alan Brien.) Other new plays were by Henry Livings and Giles Cooper. Anthony Page, David Jones and Clifford Williams showed their paces as directors; Nicol Williamson, John Thaw, Timothy West, Ian McShane, Peter McEnery, Edward Fox and John Normington all made early appearances on the stage. West End theatre managers, fearing a loss of business, muttered about the RSC over-reaching itself, and the small seating capacity of the Arts meant that there was no money to be made out of the season.

Perhaps because he was so busy fighting for the subsidy, Hall directed only one new production himself in 1962, the least he did in any year before, or after, at the RSC. It was a short play by Harold Pinter called *The Collection* which was part of a double bill at the Aldwych. Pinter's full-length play *The Birthday Party* had been sent by the producer Michael Codron to Hall in 1958; he liked the play but he had other commitments, and Peter Wood directed the production at the Lyric, Hammersmith, where it closed after five nights. Hall had put money into Pinter's next play, *The Caretaker*, at the Duchess, and had made money back.

He and Leslie Caron had then put £1,000 each into the film of *The Caretaker*.

By 1961 Hall was anxious to have a Pinter play in the Aldwych repertory. Pinter wrote to him on 11 January 1962: 'I'd like to meet, though I'm not sure I can come up with anything positive.'[49] Between them, they came up with a television play called *The Collection*, which had been transmitted the previous May with Olivier in the lead. Part of the attraction for Hall was that he only had time to do a short play; for Pinter, it was that they would direct the play together. It was a familiar kind of Pinter piece: an enigma about a sexual incident in Leeds which might, or might not, have happened.

Each learned from the other, Hall said, in directing it. 'We got on very well,' says Pinter. 'I've never co-directed anything with anybody else, but I liked the way it happened. His attitude has never changed: he was absolutely scrupulous about nuances, about the text. He doesn't go in for decoration or theatrical effects. I think he is a very honest director.'[50] Hall's finished technique for directing Pinter plays was to be perfected later, but the relationship had begun well. Hall next asked Pinter to direct a revival of *The Birthday Party* for the RSC, and it seemed likely they would get Pinter's next full-length play.

The other drama of 1962 was Paul Scofield. Peter Brook was scheduled to direct *King Lear* late in the Stratford summer season, and, after toying with the idea of having Scofield and Hugh Griffith alternating in the part, Brook and Hall settled on Scofield. To have Brook at Stratford producing his first *Lear* was a great box-office catch for Hall, and it was particularly pleasing to have Scofield too, after the let-down in 1960. Then, shortly before rehearsals were due to begin, Scofield sent a sick-note from his doctor, and cancelled. For Hall, this was one blow too many. He got in touch with the doctor and asked him to say when Scofield would be sufficiently recovered to work again. Having obtained a date, Hall rescheduled the rehearsals, and postponed the opening night. Scofield played Lear.

When the production finally opened, on 6 November 1962, it was immediately clear that this was a remarkable *Lear*. Alec McCowen was a brilliant Fool; Diana Rigg a memorable Cordelia; but Scofield, with a grey crew-cut, great energy and an unsentimental approach to the verse, was unforgettable. Tynan declared Brook's production incomparable: 'brings me closer to Lear than I have ever been'. The production won innumerable awards at home and abroad, and the offer of a knighthood for Scofield, which he turned down. (The only victim of Brook's *Lear* was Cyril Keegan Smith, the kindly wardrobe director who had lent costumes to Hall and his friends when they were undergraduates. Keegan Smith fell out with Brook's design team and was summarily sacked by Hall. Not even a personal appeal from Scofield could save him.)

Delaying the opening night of *King Lear* meant finding a new production to fill the gap, and Hall, impressed by what he had seen of his work in *Afore Night Come*, asked Clifford Williams to direct *The Comedy of Errors*. Unlike most of the young directors at Stratford, Williams was not a Cambridge graduate, or, indeed, a graduate of any kind, except of the mime theatre he had founded and of the repertory movement. He had joined Stratford as a dogsbody among the assistant producers and was understandably nervous about his conversion into a director on the big stage at the Memorial Theatre. He chose his cast from the actors who had been engaged for *Lear*, like McCowen and Rigg, and from others in the company who could fit in the rehearsals, like Ian Richardson. (A walk-on part was played by the novelist Margaret Drabble, then married to Clive Swift.) The Sunday after the opening night, Tynan's review in the *Observer* said:

> *The* Comedy of Errors *is unmistakably a Royal Shakespeare Company production. The statement is momentous: it means that Peter Hall's troupe has developed, uniquely in Britain, a classical style of its own. How is it to be recognised? By solid Brechtian settings that emphasise wood and metal instead of paint and canvas; and by cogent, deliberate verse-speaking that discards melodic cadenzas in favour of meaning and motivation.*[51]

Such praise – and a government grant as well. It had been a remarkable year. And Hall was still only thirty-two.

9

Break Up, Breakdown

'I just wandered away one day'

It is not true that Peter Hall never took holidays: he took them, but he did not enjoy them. In September 1962, he wrote to Flower from the Hotel Formentor in Majorca: 'Leslie and I are assiduously doing nothing. I think we will be able to stick it out. I'm already looking forward to being back in harness. I'm very bad at holidays.'[1]

Hall and Caron personified success. The Aston Martin was joined by the Rolls-Royce she had bought for him from the proceeds of a lucrative commercial he had helped to arrange for her. A row of decorative orange trees had taken root at Avoncliffe; there was a large shaggy dog named Simpkin and two pretty and prettily turned-out children. Leslie Caron was consistently generous with her money. When Hall's father was due to retire from British Railways, for example, she bought him a shop. Reg Hall had made desultory moves up and down the line from London to Cambridge after leaving Shelford. He had been disappointed not to get the stationmaster's job at Wolferton: as the station for the Queen's house at Sandringham, it paid well and there were perks. Reg was told that he got the job, and then that he hadn't; he always wondered whether his politics had been the obstacle. His superiors suggested he should apply for a senior position at Liverpool Street, but Reg declined. Suburban stations like Stamford Hill and Seven Sisters were as close as he got to central London.

Thoughts of retirement perturbed Grace Hall. Caron recalls her agonising about growing old, and wondering what she and Reg would do with the rest of their lives.[2] Knowing of Reg's commercial skill, Caron asked why they didn't run a shop. When Grace replied that they were not rich enough, Caron said that she was; so she bought one for them. They chose a general store on the high street of a seaside resort in Suffolk called Kessingland where they had gone for holidays when Peter was a child. It was not far from Lowestoft; Reg's eldest sister lived nearby in Beccles.

But Spanish holidays, glamorous cars, and Leslie's good heart could not make the marriage a success. She blamed Hall's Pamment genes for his insecurity about possessions – his fear that all would be lost – and about Leslie herself, because he worried that she would leave him. On the other hand, Hall continued his opposition to her international film career, and persuaded her to give up her Hollywood agent. He disliked her speaking French to the nanny or to Lila de Nobili. For her part, she was angered by his affectionate relationship with pretty Jacky Taylor, who had become his personal assistant. 'He had started to do things so harmful to me, by bringing his secretary above me. First she came to live in our house. He drove up and down to Stratford with her and if I was on the trip, I'd be in the back seat and he would be working with her. Then she would phone and tell me Peter would rather that I wasn't at lunch today.' As early as 1962, Hall claims, there was not much left of the marriage except resentment.[3] By this time each had been unfaithful to the other. Caron had had what she calls 'a little fling . . . somebody I'd met on a film, nothing serious. I was so cooped up.' Hall had also had an affair that he had not concealed from very close friends. Everyone was in love with the tall and beautiful Vanessa Redgrave, and he was no exception.

In May 1962, Suzanne Goodwin, John Goodwin's wife, took their eight-year-old son Tim to play with the Hall children at Avoncliffe. After the visit, she wrote in her diary: 'In the Avoncliffe garden at eight in the morning Tim was joined by Leslie's miniature children, Jenny in olive green and Christopher disguised as a sailor. They spent one of those mysterious children's mornings, busy and armed with sticks, attended by their sheepdog, the huge Simpkin. Later I talked to Leslie, whose face is like a pansy, her eyes painted a wonderful pale mauve. She is so pretty, small and delicate, and there's a tone in her voice which is rather as heartbreak might sound if you could hear it.' At least Caron had work in 1962: she was making the film version of a successful novel, *The L-Shaped Room* by Lynne Reid Banks, in London. She was clearly unhappy during shooting; because they thought she was behaving too self-consciously like a film star, the crew made cruel jokes behind her back. But Caron's performance was her best for years, and after *The L-Shaped Room*, she went to make another movie in Hollywood.

Hall's own work was going well. In the spring of 1963 he re-rehearsed the 1959 production of *A Midsummer Night's Dream* for its London opening in June. This was to end his six-year collaboration with Lila de Nobili. Caron thought the partnership had worked as well as it did because de Nobili's richly painted sets, gauzes, and her use of old materials for costumes had combined perfectly with Hall's mellow, melancholy style. But fashions were changing, and he had discovered John Bury.

Bury had come from the other Stratford, in the East End of London where Joan Littlewood ran the Theatre Workshop in the Theatre Royal. Hall had tried to persuade her to work in Stratford-upon-Avon too, and had tentatively scheduled the two parts of *Henry IV* for her to direct in 1962. Charles Laughton was interested in playing Falstaff but had had to rule himself out. 'I know how sick this is going to make you,' Laughton wrote: 'It will be no consolation to you but I feel an almighty sick fellow myself. I wish to heaven my four-letter word tax situation in England had not set such a ransom on my continuing this year.'[4] Peter Ustinov was next on the list, but he was not available either: 'I really think I am too bound up in the fortunes of [the] Nottingham [Playhouse] to betray that new threat to the artistic conscience of the nation.'[5]

Joan Littlewood actually made an appearance at the Aldwych, where her scruffy appearance caused a stir among the cleaners, but the reason she eventually withdrew was more to do with authority than appearance. Since she ran her own company, Littlewood was not accustomed to anyone else planning rehearsal schedules or dealing directly with casting and design, as Hall routinely did at the RSC. In her autobiography, *Joan's Book*, Littlewood says she wanted the brilliant American actor Zero Mostel to play Falstaff, and that Hall had insulted Mostel and her by asking him to audition.[6] While Hall and Brook waited to watch the auditions in the theatre, Littlewood was holding them in a nearby pub. The relationship deteriorated, and she withdrew, saying Hall should run his company and she would run hers. (An unforgiving person, Littlewood wrote that whatever administrative ability Hall possessed, he was the very worst director in the country.) John Bury was Littlewood's legacy to Hall; although it was an unintentional one.

Bury was five years older than Hall. The son of a chemist, he had served in the Navy where he learned about electronics. Left-wing politics drew him towards Littlewood's first company in Manchester. (The Theatre Workshop was left-wing but not Marxist: 'It was a people's theatre not a [Communist] Party theatre,' Bury explains.)[7] Bury became the man who made the sets, and among the first productions he designed was the *Mother Courage* which marked the British début of Bertolt Brecht. This took place in the town hall in Barnstaple in Devon, and the reviews were so bad that it closed after three nights. When the Theatre Workshop moved to London, Bury made a virtue of their poverty, constructing sets from wood picked up in Epping Forest, sand from the local railway goods yard, and bricks that fell off the back of a lorry. Some of the first lighting spots were scavenged from a crashed US Air Force plane.

Bury's politics made him welcome in East Berlin where he watched the Berliner Ensemble rehearsing. He was impressed by what he described as a combination of total clarity and selective reality: by furniture and windows that looked utterly real, lit by an unreal bright white light and placed on a white floor with white surrounds. When the Berliner Ensemble visited London in 1956, the style towards which Bury had been working since the early 1950s was becoming more familiar. Tynan, who had already extravagantly declared that Brecht's work had converted him to Marxism, promoted his work hard, but the English theatre was slow to respond.

Hall had been aware of the impact of the Berliner Ensemble, although the company concept at Jean Vilar's Théâtre National Populaire in Paris was more influential on his early work at Stratford. Brecht and the Berliner Ensemble did not begin to make an impact on the Stratford company until the end of the decade, when it had already undergone revision. 'We used the Brecht model in a totally English way,' Hall told Irving Wardle.

'Influenced by Leavis, we were not asking whether something nice was dialectically honest, but whether something nice was necessary. Cambridge rigour. We were taking away scenery, costumes, plumminess, music from the text, and crowns from the princes.'[8] Hall, like many others, was sceptical about the hero-worship of Brecht, but he had started to look for something a 'little rougher' than the romanticism of Leslie Hurry and Lila de Nobili.

When Bury turned up at the RSC in 1962 to work on *Measure for Measure* and *Afore Night Come*, Hall invited him to help with Pinter's *The Collection* at the Aldwych as well. He liked the way Bury used light. Technical advances had made stage lighting more powerful, and, while it exposed the unreality of painted sets, it also revealed the texture of real materials. 'We got more focused light, more architectural light and John [Bury] became a designer from being a lighting designer,' says Hall, who decided in 1962 that Bury, not de Nobili, would design the ambitious project he had planned for Stratford's 1963 season based on the three parts of *Henry VI* and *Richard III*.[9]

These plays had been on Hall's mind since he was an undergraduate. He had discussed them with John Barton, of course, and Barton had already identified the themes of political power and corruption that would infuse any production he was involved in. But Barton was one of the few who saw anything in the *Henry VIs*, which had been produced only three times in the twentieth century, most recently at the Birmingham Rep in the early 1950s. The generations of scholars and directors who had ploughed their way through them thought that, on the whole, they had been justly neglected.

Hall was not especially keen to do the plays himself, and Barton was not on his list of candidates to direct them. His first choice was the director of the celebrated history cycle at Stratford in 1950, Tony Quayle, who, so rumour later wrongly had it, was never invited back to Stratford once Hall took over. Quayle wrote to Hall on 17 June 1960:

I am very touched that you should ask me to tackle such a vast undertaking. It is wonderful of you. The first thing to do is to sit down to study these plays, for I barely know them, and then to get on to you again when I have reflected . . . I have seen some parts of Henry VI when they did them at Birmingham, and I found them patchy; but that is not a conclusive opinion. Of course I have mixed feelings about your suggestion: half of me leaps at it, and the other half draws back. So I won't waste your time with my half-cooked

thoughts now, but let it simmer for a week . . . Whatever the result I want
you to know how pleased I am that you should ask me. I very much want
to direct in the theatre again; the problem is what *and* when.[10]

The half of Quayle that drew back won. Peter Brook would have
understood: Hall twice asked him to direct the plays, and twice
Brook said no, saying it would take three years and he could not
spare the time. Rejecting Hall for a second time, Brook told Hall
that the simplest solution was for him to direct them himself.
Hall was now receptive to the idea. He felt he finally understood
Shakespeare's strict interpretation of the natural order in which
men can be beasts and kings ought to be kings and any attack
on that order leads to destructive anarchy. For Hall, that was the
theme of the *Henry VI* plays. His own observation of contemporary
politics led him to believe that they were not so different from those
of medieval England, and he wanted to illustrate the connection on
the stage.[11]

By the end of 1962 the basic decisions had been taken. Because
Hall and Barton thought the three plays too long to sustain
sufficient box-office interest, John Barton was asked to prepare a
script which edited the three *Henry VI*s into two plays, the second
of which was to be called *Edward IV*. The story was to be taken to
its conclusion in *Richard III*. Strung together, the three plays were
to be called *The Wars of the Roses*. Captivated by the swords and
armour they saw on a tour of Warwick Castle, John Bury and
Hall decided that colour, sound and fabric should be inspired by
steel. Margaret of Anjou, who ages from a twenty-seven-year-old
princess to an eighty-year-old crone during the span of the plays,
was to be played by Peggy Ashcroft. Henry VI was to be played
by an unknown twenty-two-year-old named David Warner, who
had impressed Clifford Williams playing a small part in *Afore Night
Come* at the Arts. Brook had cast him as Trinculo in an early-season
Tempest at Stratford, and suggested Hall take a look at him. When
Donald Sinden first set eyes on Warner he saw 'a tall spotty youth
who had not woken up', but Hall liked the sweetness he saw in
Warner's character. Rehearsals were scheduled to start on 25 April
1963 and to last for twelve weeks.

It is an inflexible rule of the theatre that, no matter how much
rehearsal time there is, it is always chaos at the end. *The Wars
of the Roses* was chaos at the beginning and the middle as well.
Barton's new edition was the first big problem. He was looking

forward to reducing three plays to two: it gave him something to get his teeth into again, and, because the undertaking seemed too huge for one director, he sensed a chance to direct on the main stage again himself. He and Hall had agreed to a unifying conception and proposed to emphasise the politics by making the King's Council the central feature of the series, the rise and fall of the barons in power being indicated by their place at the council table. Hall asked Barton 'to pare down the inessentials, clarify the plot line and have fewer scenes'. The three parts of *Henry VI* comprise 12,350 lines: if that was to be reduced to a manageable length, Barton realised he would have to write linking passages himself.

Ideally, Barton would have concentrated on editing his text throughout the winter. Instead, he went on a three-month tour of the United States with *The Hollow Crown*. He hated the travelling; even more so when he got bronchitis. By the time he was back in London early in March 1963 there was so much to do that a labour of love had become torture, and he needed help from Hall. Because Hall was rehearsing *A Midsummer Night's Dream*, he and Barton met first thing every morning and again in the evening at Montpelier Square, to go through Barton's work.

Paring down had meant the disappearance of sixty characters, and the gaping ends left by the cuts were smoothed by juggling with the texts or writing linking passages based on material from Holinshed's and Edward Hall's chronicles, or even from Shakespeare himself. 'It was much more drastic than had been envisaged at first, certainly by Peter, but I discovered an instinct in me as an adaptor. I was in my element,' says Barton.[12] Hall was nervous, and would cut back Barton's most exuberant additions, but once, when he accused Barton of having gone too far, Barton could not in fact remember having written the passage. They checked, and found that Shakespeare had. They were not the only ones who were confused. Peggy Ashcroft made the same mistake, as did a Shakespeare scholar who was critical of Barton's rewriting.

The actors got their scripts only just before rehearsals began, and these were subject to constant revision. One of the enduring images from the rehearsals of *The Wars of the Roses* is of Barton lying on his side on the stage rewriting the text as the rehearsal proceeds around him. When the version was complete, 12,350 lines had been reduced to 7,450 – of which Shakespeare had contributed a little more than 6,000; 1,444 were authentic first folio Barton, some of which had, in turn, been rewritten by Hall. This epic achievement drew on desperation, exuberance and arrogance. The arrogance was expressed, quite innocently, by Hall: 'At any given moment . . . there is one way only of expressing the intentions of that play. And those intentions must be expressed in contemporary terms. At any given moment it may mean that there is a slight refocusing of the dramatist's original intentions.'[13] In practice, this meant that Barton deleted Shakespeare's references to Parliament, to emphasise the struggle for power between the noblemen. Later, when he became a devotee of unadulterated Shakespearian texts, Hall regretted the liberties they had taken. If he did it again, he said, he would insist on performing all three parts of *Henry VI* as they were written. At the time, however, his priorities were different. In 1963 he felt he could drum up an audience for two *Henry VIs*, but not three.

On 25 April 1963, Hall's Aston Martin would not start, so he took the train from London to Stratford and was late for his introductory talk to the cast. On the journey he read a proof copy of a book by a Polish professor Jan Kott, called *Shakespeare Our Contemporary*. Kott's theme was that Shakespeare is a mirror to every age, including our own. Thirty years later the argument sounds trite, but Kott's originality lay in relating the power politics of the history plays like *Henry VI* to the totalitarian Communism practised behind the Iron Curtain. This confirmed all Hall's theories, and when he finally spoke to the cast he cautioned them against theoretical bias. To take either a Christian or a Brechtian view would be to oversimplify. 'The stuff of these plays,' he said, 'is our lives today.' He summoned up images from newspapers and television of the Soviet Praesidium, the purges, Suez, de Gaulle, Kennedy and Khrushchev. These were relevant, he said, because the plays, 'first and last, are a study of power, the need for power, and the abuse of power.'

Hall insisted that the ruthlessness of power would be revealed only if the characters were humanised. He wanted his power brokers to appear absolutely sincere, truthful, candid and honest: 'I'm not saying that they are lying all the time, but they are certainly wearing a mask all the time, and charm and candour and straightforwardness are parts of the role that a politician has to play.'

Hall had a cast capable of meeting this challenge, drawn mainly from a company accustomed to ensemble playing. Ashcroft was joined by Ian Holm, who was to play Richard III, Roy Dotrice, Brewster Mason, Michael Craig, John Normington, Charles Kay and Janet Suzman. All of them were familiar with the company's speaking style, which had become flexible, light, unsentimental and quick. 'It appealed more to the head than to the heart, and made people think about what it meant; in that sense it was highly political,' says Richard Pearson, who played a small part in the production and was so absorbed by it that he wrote a valuable book about it, entitled *A Band of Arrogant and United Heroes*. Donald Sinden, an established film star who was so keen to return to the classical stage that he auditioned for Hall, was to be the Duke of York. David Warner, in the leading role, was Hall's calculated risk.

John Bury had found a scrapyard on the Birmingham Road in Stratford where he could buy thin metal sheets, but his problem was that, from a distance, the surface of a thin steel sheet looks no more metallic than a piece of hardboard. Bury achieved the right look by treating steel with acid and covering it with tarnished copper. The plates were attached to two side walls which, when moved, dictated the size of the playing area. The main floor of expanded steel had exactly the right cold ring when actors crossed it wearing steel heels. The 13-foot-long pentagonal council table was centre stage. The effect was simple, monumental and timeless. It was not, however, universally admired. Leslie Hurry, the designer of *Troilus and Cressida*, who was always impeccably dressed, watched Bury walk up to the theatre dressed in a filthy, acid-stained boiler suit and shouted, 'Go home, you fucking cement-mixer.'[14] But Hurry was the one on the way out. Stratford was now home to Bury; Hall had tied him down with a contract.

Shakespeare's histories were always a gamble, but now the stakes were rising fast. The capital built up by the success of *King Lear* at the end of the previous season was dissipated by the first two plays of the new Stratford season. Both *The Tempest* and *Julius Caesar* were critical disasters. Despite the Arts Council grant, the company's deficit was still rising, and its reserves were falling fast. Flower understood the pressure: 'These productions were Peter's last chance; he sank or swam by them, and the fortunes of the company depended on them.'[15] Hall knew it too. Moreover, he was not well. Jacky Taylor observed the symptoms: 'He became withdrawn, tired, and looked very white. Then he turned grey. He looked terribly ill.'[16] The first reading of the script went well; Sinden found it one of the most exciting things he had ever experienced. But, four days after rehearsals began, Hall collapsed. Within days a severe nervous breakdown had been diagnosed. The doctors insisted on at least six months' rest, but Jacky Taylor was so distressed by Hall's condition that she thought to herself that he might never come back.

Hall retired, exhausted, to a darkened room in Avoncliffe, where he suffered a variety of physical ailments – in his stomach, head and sinuses – and mental turmoil. He fell into one of his periodic fits of weeping, and, he says, thought about suicide again. To occupy his mind he built a battleship out of matchsticks. William Sargant, a fashionable Harley Street psychiatrist who advocated shock therapy in severe cases of depression, thought Hall a suitable case for the treatment. That made Hall determined to get well without it.

Peter Brook, backed by Peggy Ashcroft and Caron, administered a more effective form of shock treatment: Brook told him that the only cure was to get back to work; if he did not, he might lose his nerve and never work again. According to Hall's own diagnosis, they were right: his nerve was his problem.

> *I felt as frightened as a child, sometimes to the point of panic. Our Stratford season had been rather shaky, especially at the start. Money worries were threatening the future of the company. The disintegration of our marriage was wrenching me apart . . . I was not ready to meet the greatest challenge of my professional life. Like a child who doesn't want to take an exam because he fears he will fail, I collapsed.*[17]

Paddy Donnell, the RSC's general manager, had hoped that a week or ten days' rest would see Hall well enough to continue. After three weeks' absence, Donnell postponed the opening night for a fortnight, to give Hall more time to recover. Brook's medicine had begun the cure, and on 27 May, four weeks after his collapse, Hall returned to rehearsals, propped up with cushions and wearing dark glasses.

While he was away John Barton had taken charge, with Frank Evans as assistant director, and they had devised a scheme for rehearsals. The first two parts of the epic would be worked on seven hours a day, seven days a week, for twelve weeks, as if it were a production line with different components of the performance being rehearsed simultaneously by all three directors. The two parts of *Henry VI* were divided into thirty blocks, three of which could be worked on simultaneously so that actors were not left hanging about. Once Hall returned, he would begin by going through the text and basic moves. Then the group of actors would move on to Barton to discuss the verse and the meaning of the text. Finally, Evans would fit the parts together.

Sinden describes Hall asking each of the barons round the council table about his attitude to the last line that had been spoken. Was it news? Did he approve? Who was he looking at? One lunchtime Hall took Sinden aside and complimented him on the ease with which he could manage extrovert heroics on stage, especially in a scene where York returns triumphantly from Ireland. Sinden, Hall observed, had no problems with the scene. 'None at all,' Sinden replied. 'I thought not,' said Hall. 'Why not try it the hard way?'[18] The hard way meant ignoring the obvious, and Sinden admired Hall for saying so.

The fights were choreographed by John Barton, as always. Bury's colleague, Ann Curtis, designed the costumes out of unbleached calico, floor cloth and leatherised suede cloth; chainmail was butcher's string covered with silver lacquer and beaten flat; the sound of cannon was made by recording bursting chip packets. Sinden weighed his complete costume; it came to 56 pounds. Guy Woolfenden's music was scored for harsh brass and percussion.

By 16 July Hall was sufficiently recovered to tell an exhausted cast that a lousy dress rehearsal had been perfect, and that if the audience failed to realise this, it was all his fault. The next day, when both plays were given their first performances, the actors' energy revived and all the components came together. The audience yelled its approval and the applause thundered on after the actors had got back to their dressing rooms. Critics were divided only in the degree of extravagance of their praise. Bernard Levin, in the *Daily Mail*, wrote: 'A production of epic, majestic grandeur, a landmark and beacon in the post-War English theatre, a triumphant vindication of Mr Hall's policy, as well as his power, as a producer.'

Richard III was still to be rehearsed, and when it opened on 20 August, the volume of praise grew even greater. Ashcroft, David Warner, Ian Holm, Donald Sinden, Brewster Mason and Charles Kay were singled out; but many of the reviews emphasised that it was a triumph for the company. Peggy Ashcroft declared that *The*

Wars of the Roses could not have been possible unless it emerged from a solidly based company accustomed to ensemble work, by directors as well as actors. Hall thought the plays had established the style and purpose of the RSC: scrutinising texts fiercely, speaking them well, and making them relevant to the times.

It had been a near-run thing, and was expensive in terms of emotional and physical energy as well as the company's financial resources. Hall has said that he learned from this experience that he didn't have to be happy or to feel well to do his best work. Hall's illness had been no secret, and the award of the CBE in June enabled friends and relations to express their concern as well as their congratulations. The CBE was the subject of one of the two surviving letters written by Grace Hall to Peter:

> *I must just write to say how proud of you we are on your Honours Award. I find it difficult to say how I feel – but I know you will understand our love and thoughts are with you now, as always, and I am praying that God will give you good health and spirits so you may reach that target you have set yourself. As you know my English is never very good. I only know I feel too full up to put any more on paper. God bless you dear – your dear wife, our Leslie and the children. You both deserve the best the world and God can give you.*[19]

Besides the love of his mother and his family, Hall also received some heartfelt advice from one of the RSC's governors, Lord Avon (Anthony Eden), whose resignation as Prime Minister in 1956 was caused by ill-health. After congratulating Hall, Avon added:

> *You have had a very thin time with so much work on your hands during the last year. If I may give you one word of advice, from my own experience, do not over-drive yourself. It is tempting to do, especially if one has a strong constitution, but believe me one pays for it in the end and you ought to have at least another forty years of leadership in the theatre for the enjoyment of us all.*[20]

Hall spent the autumn recovering from the shock of his breakdown and the rigours of three months' rehearsal; while he was away, Michel Saint-Denis took over the role of company director, assisted from time to time by Peter Brook. Saint-Denis was able to reassure Clifford Williams, who was directing a controversial play about the Pope's failure to combat Nazism, *The Representative* by Rolf

Hochhuth. And Saint-Denis wrote to Hall on 3 October 1963, saying that everyone was looking forward to his return, but that he should not rush it.

Not all comments were so sympathetic. One of Fordham Flower's cronies on the executive council was Tom Boase, the Master of Magdalen College, Oxford, who was not as enchanted by Hall's managerial performance or by his ambitions as Flower was, and who never hesitated to express his reservations. On 7 June 1963, Boase wrote to Flower that Hall's health had become almost as great a problem as finance, and that he ought to cut down his commitments. 'This can only be satisfactorily done by reducing the size of his empire rather than by multiplying assistants . . . Peter has shown a steady tendency to increase his demands and to underestimate their costs.'[21] Boase returned to the subject of costs in November 1963, telling Flower that it was possible to plan a company policy that fitted the budget, but that overspending had produced another financial crisis. 'Peter, I am sure, consciously or unconsciously, has always been influenced by his theory that we must run down all our resources . . . and his creation must either be made viable or abandoned.'[22]

Flower knew that Boase was not exaggerating. In June 1963 he had written to the Arts Council to announce an estimated loss of between £50,000 and £60,000 in 1963–4. At that rate, the RSC's reserves would be virtually exhausted by the spring of 1965. Flower calculated that a grant of anything less than £100,000 a year over the next three years would be insufficient to sustain the RSC's work, especially at the Aldwych, where an interesting but fairly thin repertory was haemorrhaging cash.

Lord Cottesloe, the Arts Council's chairman, informed Flower on 30 January 1964 that the Treasury had made a non-recurring addition to the grant for 1964–5 of £20,000, bringing it to £80,000 in all; and that for the following year – 1965–6 – they would manage £90,000. While this was insufficient by Flower's reckoning, Cottesloe clearly thought the Arts Council had been generous: the extra money, he said, was a result of the Council's belief in the importance and value of the RSC's work, and its recognition that a bigger grant was required. However, Cottesloe finished his letter with a word of advice: 'The pressure that it has been sought to apply to the Council through the medium of the Press has not helped, and I hope it may now cease.'[23] In other words, they wished to hear less from Peter Hall.

Some hope: within days of this news, Hall wrote to Flower noting that there had been grumbles in the press that the RSC had not been given enough, and they must use this to negotiate from strength: 'I doubt if we should agree to £90,000 the year after next.'[24] Both Hall and John Goodwin were sure that the only reason for their increased grant was that they were noisy, and that the public was on their side.

The Arts Council was not alone in being upset by this permanent offensive. Because Hall – or, perhaps, his colleagues – could not resist the opportunity of a crack at the opposition, hostilities were now revived between Hall and Olivier. Two letters from Joan Plowright to Hall, written just two months apart during that winter, show that the rivalry between the two companies had not lessened with the birth of the National Theatre.

This had opened at last, on 20 November 1963, with Olivier's production of Peter O'Toole's Hamlet. It was not an artistic success, but it was a start, and Hall had written an encouraging note to Plowright. Her reply was sympathetic – 'Having experienced [management] at second-hand from the other side, I am more deeply aware of the miracle you have performed in keeping going over the last three years' – and generous: 'I saw Michel [Saint-Denis] the other day and he told me how desperate the situation has become; I don't know what sort of negotiations are in progress but if there is anything we can do to help you must say.'[25]

But hostilities erupted on 16 February 1964 when Atticus in the *Sunday Times* reported 'sharp and fundamental' rivalry between the two companies. Atticus was written by Nicholas Tomalin, a Cambridge contemporary of Hall's, who reported that Hall – who already knew the news – was in purdah waiting to hear about the Treasury grant. Whether it was a device or not, Tomalin quoted a remark attributed to 'one member of the Stratford company' which sounded remarkably like Hall himself: 'It was only because Peter Hall went to Larry Olivier and told him quite straight that we were determined to stay in London, and would make the private fight a public one if he didn't make some gesture of support that [any] statement was made at all.' This fighting remark was balanced by an emollient statement from Lord Chandos, and Atticus concluded that the rivalry between the two companies seemed to be diminishing.

Not so; in a sorrowful note, handwritten on the Sunday evening, Plowright described the charge that Hall had had to threaten

Olivier as ridiculous, misleading and rather dangerous. She continued:

> The feelings of the ordinary members of the two companies are being roused against each other. I know from past experience of press items how the kids at the N.T. will react – and it isn't healthy for the profession. Actors want to work for both companies . . . There should be sympathy, empathy, whatever you like between us . . .[26]

Because he was in bed with a temperature, Olivier had not seen the offending article, but when he did he wrote another of his explosive letters to Hall, who had evidently dashed off an apologetic explanation. Olivier replied from Brighton on 19 February 1964:

> The National has taken it pretty heftily on the chin on account of Stratford for the last two years and more and I don't think that either its attitude or its efforts for Stratford should be rewarded in quite such an ungallant way.
>
> I know you are averse to engaging yourself with the Press by letter, as I remember when I asked you to join with me in writing one to Levin some two years ago, you refused to do so, but I really think the time has come when a gesture from you is what it takes.
>
> I think Lord Chandos is extremely generous the way he refers (though wrongfully alluding to you by name) to Stratford's opting out at the time it did. You remember and I remember very well that when it did so it was a death blow to the existence of the National Theatre and Stratford knew it. I am only bringing this up again as a reminder that quid pro quo the National owes Stratford no consideration whatsoever.
>
> In light of this, I feel that the constant maintenance of our good relations, Chandos's mission to the Treasury, my own private missions to the Chairman of the Arts Council, our patient endurance of a falsely-drawn image in relation to Stratford, our timely announcement of support in the hour of need and finally, when you do get your bloody dough it is due almost entirely to the clever talking of Lord Chandos, all of which history seems to me to be pretty bloody immaculate, and I think it is now time somebody said so and I think that somebody is you . . .
>
> That's what I think ought to happen. Sorry cock, over to you.[27]

But the next time Olivier wrote to Hall, only two months later, his tone was full of sympathy. So was his wife's. On 4 April 1964 a joint statement had been released announcing the separation of Peter Hall and Leslie Caron. It said: 'We have found that the demands made on us by our very different careers, often in different parts of the world, make it no longer possible for us to remain together.' Their careers, which had brought them together, had driven them apart. The newspapers were full of the news: 'My heart turned over 50 times when I saw you with your ravishing children this morning,' wrote Plowright to Hall.[28]

Hall had been warning close friends like Peggy Ashcroft and her husband Jeremy, and Michel Saint-Denis in March, that the bad news was about to break. In the end, says Caron, she just wandered away one day, and she met Warren Beatty, Hollywood's demon lover, who had already had well-publicised affairs with stars like Joan Collins and Natalie Wood. Caron met him in Hollywood at a party designed to boost her chances for an Oscar for her performance in *The L-Shaped Room*, which had been well received. She arrived at the Oscar ceremony on 13 April 1964 on Beatty's arm.

Caron says now that she never fell out of love with Hall, but did fall out of sympathy with him. 'I would not accept the sort of life he made me lead . . . I just refused to be only a housewife. My liberty, my self-expression was more important.' In an interview in the *Sunday Express* shortly after she left Stratford, Caron said the reason she preferred living in Hollywood was that Hall's friends were solely concerned with the theatre and did not care for films. When she went on location to Jamaica to make *Father Goose* with Cary Grant, Warren Beatty went along too. So did a private detective hired by Hall to photograph Caron and Beatty together to provide evidence of adultery. Whatever hope Caron may have had of obtaining custody of the children was subsequently dashed when a court gave an interim order banning her from taking Christopher and Jenny out of the country. Hall was adamant that they should stay in England, and used all the resources of the legal system to make sure they did. The divorce was time-consuming, costly, and occasionally farcical. (Hall once received by mistake a report prepared for Caron's solicitors by a private detective who had followed him to a rehearsal in the theatre and had mistaken it for a wild party.)

The divorce was more painful than the participants realised. Years later, Jenny Hall vividly recollected hearing the news: 'I stood behind my brother Christopher's shoulder as I heard Papa say: "Your mother and I going to be divorced, but we want you to be happy and you'll see both of us. We won't do it unless you agree. What do you say?" . . . I heard my brother saying okay, and then I nodded my head in agreement. When I look back, I am amazed now that I never actually asked what the word "divorce" actually meant. I think my father knew as little about what it was going to be like as I did.'[30]

At the divorce hearing in February 1965, Caron's adultery with Beatty was formally acknowledged, while the court only exercised discretion over Hall's admitted adultery with an unidentified woman. He appeared to be the winner, being awarded custody of the children. But Caron was granted care and control, and she called it a draw. Despite his instinctive fear that Caron would leave him, Hall understood why she went, and the children over whom they had fought eventually brought them together again. Hall credited Caron with having softened his English snobbery and his East Anglian puritanism: 'Leslie tempered that, and I became a little better at living.' His friend Peter Wood commented that what Hall had actually learned from Leslie Caron was how to live beyond his means, and that he would do so for the rest of his days.[31]

Hall received letters of condolence from friends, none of whom was so heartbroken as Peggy Ashcroft. She said she had known it might happen, but always hoped it wouldn't.

> *Why do I write? Just to tell you I'm thinking about you would be too sentimental a reason. It's really because I know how exhausting and straining the last weeks of production are and that under these circumstances they must seem sometimes too promethean to support . . . but you will have your loyal company to lead to the big push; and your very loving friend wishes she was there to push with the rest.*[32]

Ashcroft's good wishes were no help. Only three weeks before the opening of the Stratford season, Hall collapsed again.

To celebrate the 400th anniversary of Shakespeare's birth the RSC mounted the whole series of history plays in Stratford in the summer of 1964, beginning with *Richard II*, and tracing the story through the reigns of Henry IV, Henry V and Henry VI to the death of Richard III on Bosworth Field. The opening months of the season were devoted to the four new productions. Hall was flanked by Barton, whose reputation was now fully recovered from the unhappiness of 1960, and by Clifford Williams, whose own reputation was already looking formidable. David Warner added Richard II to his Henry VI; Ian Holm was Henry V as well as Richard III; and the rumbustious Welsh actor, Hugh Griffith, joined the company to play Falstaff. *The Wars of the Roses* returned to Stratford, with veterans like Peggy Ashcroft and Donald Sinden, to complete the great Shakespearian panorama of English history. Sinden reports that Hall had told him at the end of 1963 that his York was the linchpin of *The Wars of the Roses* and that if he did not repeat it, the whole of the 1964 season was at risk. Boasting idly of this in the green-room, Sinden learned that Hall had said the same thing to no less than five other actors round the same table. 'This is one reason why Peter is such a great administrator,' Sinden concluded.[33]

Hall was confident about his interpretation now. He wrote in the programme note for *Henry VI*: 'Over the years I have become more and more fascinated by the contortions of politicians and by the corrupting seductions experienced by anyone who wields power . . . I realised that the mechanism of power had not changed in centuries.' *The Wars of the Roses* was now taken for granted as a comment on contemporary European politics: there were photographs of Hitler, Stalin and Mussolini in the programme for *Richard III*. Hall's confidence was justified by the reviews, which grew ever more extravagant. Harold Hobson in the *Sunday Times*, for example, doubted whether anything as valuable had ever been done for Shakespeare *'in the whole previous history of the world's stage'* (my italics). When *The Wars of the Roses* was televised at the end of the season, it was, apart from the Coronation and the World Cup, one of the most ambitious enterprises ever undertaken by the BBC, and when the plays were transmitted over three nights they were watched by more people than had seen them since they were written.

Hall's second collapse was even more dramatic than the first. Having muttered to Barton that he felt a bit groggy, he fell to the ground unconscious and had to be wheeled out of the theatre on a handy piece of stage property – the royal bier. Peter Wood was drafted in to help Barton and Williams with the direction, and Jacky Taylor was instructed to take Hall away for a few days to give him a complete rest from the theatre. They took separate rooms in the comfortable Sharrow Bay Hotel in the Lake District, where Hall, between bouts of tears, expressed the melodramatic view that the theatre was all he cared about and it looked as though it was going to kill him. Shortly after their arrival, he began to insist that Taylor should take him back to Stratford: 'He didn't want them buggering it up,' she recalls.[34] Even if it proved fatal.

Despite an unprecedented workload, the *Richard II*, and the *Henry IV, Parts One and Two* opened in two days, and *Henry V* a week later – and the directors Hall left in Stratford did not bugger them up. They had developed a new method of directing plays, which had not been dictated by Hall's illnesses so much as by the extraordinary volume of work. It was beyond the capabilities of any one man, and so delegation became inevitable. Although the critics tended to concentrate on Hall (the others were resigned to that), the programme gave them all equal billing – except for Wood, who had told the management not to bother with his credit, and left regretting it. This was a collective of directors with Hall in the position of chairman, or conductor. The last word was always his, and he inspired much of the work, but the company had become robust enough to survive his absences. It was a singular compliment to him, though there were, of course, some difficulties. The one role that could never be delegated successfully was dealing with stars, who always needed Hall's individual attention, especially when they turned truculent. Like Hugh Griffith.

Griffith had starred in Hall's production of *The Waltz of the Toreadors* in 1956; each admired the other and at the beginning of this short, sad correspondence they were the best of friends. Griffith, who was born in Anglesey, was a distinguished character actor with a potent cocktail of qualities: he was funny, mischievous, scandalous and bloody-minded, with a natural liking for the drink. He wrote to Hall on 16 April, addressing him as 'My dear, sweet, Peter' and thanking him for a lovely letter: 'First, let me tell you – you have not failed anyone – so forgiveness is out of the question . . . You are big and great and because of that you will weather any storm whether it is physical, mental or domestic . . . The plays are going great guns and you can rely on me to see that today's marathon will float and swim as if it had always afloat [*sic*].'[35]

Hall evidently considered Griffith a good enough friend to consult him about his divorce, because Griffith's next letter, of 18 May, implores Hall not to allow Leslie Caron to visit Avoncliffe. 'Domestically, if I may say so, *you* are apt to be weak (not so strong as in many other spheres) – (Goodness knows I am worse, in many spheres) – but there is always a basis of reason – and I beg you to realise your greatness as a man of the theatre – and not to allow domesticity to interfere with your inevitable and eventual achievement.' Griffith was also anxious about his own future: 'There please be more confident and open with me – regardless *of any difficulties* . . . I don't wish to be buggered about. I must know so that I can plan my future.'

Griffith's next letter was written a few days later, after Hall had sat in on one of his performances. Hall had high hopes of this Falstaff, but felt that Griffith was concentrating too much on the dark side of the character at the expense of the clown, and had evidently written him a severe note about his performance. In his letter, Griffith refers to Hall's, which said that he could hardly watch it; that Griffith was worrying the company; and that he (Hall) had been dismayed, embarrassed and alarmed. Griffith conceded that Hall had seen a performance which was not as good as he himself would like it to be. He was unwell, and, unwisely, he had taken pills; besides which, he felt depressed 'and to set about clowning in those circumstances is like meeting a worse hurdle than the Grand National has to offer'. Apparently, a man in the front row of the dress circle had complained that Griffith was inaudible. Griffith wrote that he had asked the house manager to get an address so that he could apologise and ask them to come again at his expense: 'Jesus Christ!' he wrote:

> Do you think, for a moment, Peter, that actors of any great consequence, about 200 years and more or less ago, would think of spending their lives, as I do, for next to nothing. Hell! They were paid £50 per performance in those days – which must be £1,000 at least today. Do you think if I was paid £500 (say) for a performance I would make a mistake?!!
>
> The whole system is gone to cock (you must face it and put it right . . . Here, at S[tratford] one has a mass of some, perhaps, nonentities; perhaps scholars and professors etc; but there never is to one's knowledge one *person for whom one acts*. This should be corrected.

The reference was, presumably, to John Barton who had been one of the directors of the two *Henry IV*s; what this reflected was the frustration caused by Hall's absences from Stratford.

Griffith's next letter, started on 16 July and finished on 22 July, was fifteen pages long and so full of pain and anger that it might have been written in blood. Indeed, in a PPPS Griffith says that he has hesitated a great deal before sending it, but has concluded that he should.

Griffith's trouble was a tax problem which would be helped if he could appear in the film of *Moll Flanders*, which was being shot while he was appearing as Falstaff. Griffith claims that every attempt he has made to discuss this has failed. He confesses to having been abrupt and possibly rude when the two of them bumped into each other in Stratford. Hall appeared to be under the misconception that the film company might buy Griffith out of his Stratford contract. Shown this red flag, the old Welsh bull lost his temper:

> As I told you, I never thought of leaving such a theatre as ours, especially in its 400th what not, whether its playing to 100% business or not. It would be unfair to everyone, including myself, to do so. It never entered my head that anyone anywhere could consider me capable of being unfair to anyone, on any scale . . .
>
> You came here [to Griffith's home] to talk to me about this auspicious season, long before it started, and I agreed to play Falstaff for you, and to be directed by you. Let's leave it at that. But it is to you surely that I should talk about it, and not to be 'fobbed off' on to people that I have no reason to respect . . .
>
> P.S. I never thought, Peter, that I would have need to write to you like this, and I hate having to do so . . . But you've brought it upon me, and I have no option . . . Your remoteness has bothered me, and has naturally made me think that you have fallen into a kind of megalomaniacal trap, whereas you could, with humility and common sense, fullfil all the great promises that are inherent in you. A great number of people trust you and look to you for their livelihood and well-being; but if you become remote to them, and create a kind of aura of untouchableness to them, they are bound to suspect your purposes. I suspect that this aura is created not by you but by your surroundings and it would be wise if you cut into them.

In the last letter of the series, dated 29 August, Griffith deals technically with a change in the cast, but he is unhappy that the actor playing Lord Chief Justice Shallow was unable to continue with the role, and there is a coldness in his tone for the first time that summer: 'It is a pity, so far as the audiences at Stratford are concerned, that this cannot carry on and that you can't arrange *your* dates to suit our mutual purposes better.'

Next season Falstaff was played by Paul Rogers; Hugh Griffith did not return to the RSC. He was difficult, no doubt, but his case exemplifies a number of Hall's problems as director. His nervous breakdowns could not be helped, but running a large company in two centres seemed to mean that he was always in the wrong place: he could not reassure actors when he was not there. Even when he was in the right place at the proper time, he was also busy planning the repertory, casting actors and directors. He chose never to rest from the politics of being the RSC's impresario, and was always willing to talk to any journalist who might help him. No one doubted that it was too much for one man, and a circuit-breaker in Hall's internal constitution had called a halt twice in two years. Despite the acclaim for *The Wars of the Roses*, there was no time to relax and enjoy his successes. On the contrary, the pressure on him was intensifying.

10

Abdication at Stratford

*'The most exciting time in my life is entirely
due to you'*

It was hard to be neutral about Peter Hall any longer. His bold and
committed work for the RSC had contributed to the company's
sharp political profile. 'A radical identity could be seen in every
aspect of its existence,' says Sally Beauman.[1] Hall relished an
anti-establishment role, and, because he believed that the public's
support offered him good protection, he never worried about
making enemies in the Arts Council and the Lord Chamberlain's
department.

The campaign against theatre censorship, a leading item on
the RSC's agenda, was conducted with hardly any less energy
than the struggle to get a government subsidy. By the 1960s the
concept of the Lord Chamberlain as theatre censor was absurd.
The Theatres Act had been passed in 1737 to protect Sir Robert
Walpole's venal administration from criticism in the theatres.
Since any play written before 1737 was exempt, the filthiest and
most ungodly Elizabethan and Restoration dramatists could be
performed uncut. Scripts written after 1737 had to be submitted
to the Lord Chamberlain's examiners, who, for a fee of two
guineas, would license them for performance or refer them to
a Comptroller – normally a middle-aged army or navy officer.
The final arbiter was the Lord Chamberlain himself. From 1963

this was Lord Cobbold, a former governor of the Bank of England. His department was united in its distaste for four-letter words like crap, balls, fart, arse and piss – never mind the worst of all beginning with f – which were never uttered on the English stage; nor, because of unquestioned deference towards organised religion, were the words Jesus or Christ. Homosexuality was viewed with the gravest suspicion, and the institutions of the state had to be treated with profound respect. The Lord Chamberlain, as the true inheritor of Walpole's tradition, believed it was his job to prevent fun being made of the Prime Minister – by representing his voice, for instance; and he disapproved of criticism of Britain's close allies, such as the United States. The only way to evade censorship was to perform in a licensed club. This was done at the Arts and the Royal Court; the drawback was that, since the audience had first to pay to become club members, the box-office always suffered.

Hall's early skirmishes with the censor had been over the homosexuality that infused Tennessee Williams's plays: a censor with a naval background wanted to ban the phrase 'up periscopes' because, he explained, everyone knew that it referred to buggery. There had been trouble at the Aldwych over *The Devils* in 1961, and *The Representative* in 1963, but 1964 was the year in which battle was finally joined. Before *Afore Night Come* opened, the Lord Chamberlain demanded thirty-four cuts in the text (including bloody, hell, Jesus and Christ), and Hall announced that in future every cut ordered by the Lord Chamberlain would be reprinted in the programme. When seven lines from a poem by e.e. cummings were deleted from a poetry reading called *The Rebel*, the house lights were raised at that point in the script so the audience was able to read the poem in full. Hall wrote in the programme for *Afore Night Come*: 'We are not deliberately setting out to bait [the Lord Chamberlain], but it is no accident that the plays we are going to present will bring the issue to the front and keep it there.' In the production of a surrealist 1920s piece by Roger Vitrac called *Victor*, one of the characters was required to break wind at regular intervals. The stage direction suggested that a bass trombone make the effect from the wings. But that was too imprecise for the Lord Chamberlain who demanded that the trombonist play the destiny theme from Beethoven's Fifth Symphony. Besides that, he cut four pages of text from the guts of the play. Hall said he would cancel the show at a cost of £10,000 unless the Lord Chamberlain relented. In this case, Lord Cobbold did so.

Peter Brook was the mischief-maker-in-chief. The pace at which new productions entered the Stratford and Aldwych repertory was beginning to remind Brook of a production line, and he wanted to spend more time with his actors. Michael Kustow, a cosmopolitan figure who had joined the press office of the RSC, observed the differences between his two chiefs: 'Brook was a more fundamental person than Peter Hall. He was pursuing the improvement of his soul, and trod a path where he wasn't afraid to be naked. Peter Hall followed the path of accumulation. He didn't have the distance from the surface phenomena of the Sixties that Brook did.'[2]

Hall's respect for Brook was unconditional. Despite vigorous internal opposition, he told Brook he could select a dozen actors and work on an experimental programme which would explore techniques like improvisation, mime, acrobatics and vocal exercise. Tom Boase, Flower's Oxford friend, said that Brook's experiment ought to be ruled out on grounds of the labour it would involve as well as expense; 'If this means Peter [Brook] goes, it cannot be helped,' he wrote. This would have come as no surprise to Flower: Boase had already written sharply to him that the RSC's deficit might force the company to a retreat from the Aldwych to Stratford and to end touring: 'Whether this would be sufficient to retain the services of the triumvirate is doubtful, but there may come a point at which we cannot continue to be harnessed to their ambition.'[3] But given a choice between the views of Boase or Hall, Flower always supported Hall.

The early work of Brook's company went on show in a club theatre. Since one of the items was a reading of a letter from the Lord Chamberlain's department listing objections to Jean Genet's *The Screens*, this was prudent. (Another item was performed by a twenty-six-year-old actress called Glenda Jackson who undressed and bathed while representing simultaneously Christine Keeler and Jacqueline Kennedy.) Brook's season at the LAMDA theatre was entitled *The Theatre of Cruelty*. This phrase was open to misinterpretation, but Brook had taken it from the French dramatic theorist Antonin Artaud, who put uncomfortable and disturbing images on stage to make the theatre more provocative.

Brook's experimental work joined the RSC's Aldwych repertory in August 1964 with the production of Peter Weiss's *The*

Persecution and Assassination of Marat as Performed by Inmates of the Asylum at Charentin under the Direction of the Marquis de Sade – known, for short, as the *Marat/Sade*. One of the characters in the play, a spectator of the play within the play, says: 'I always thought plays were meant to entertain, but how can entertainment deal in sarcasm and violence? I always thought poets strove to achieve pure beauty, but what is beautiful about whipping and corpses?'

Plenty of people were just as puzzled, including Emile Littler, who, as a member of the RSC's executive council, was in a position to make real trouble. In an interview in the London *Evening News* on 24 August 1964, Littler said that plays like *Afore Night Come* and the *Marat/Sade* were entirely out of keeping with the public image of the RSC, and with having the Queen as patron: 'They are dirty plays. They do not belong, or should not, to the Royal Shakespeare Company.' The Dirty Plays row had opened, and it ran and ran, but it had been in rehearsal, as it were, for some time. The enemy within had found a voice, and Hall's regime was now under serious pressure.

Not all the members of the RSC's executive council thought the company's home in the Aldwych was a good idea. Besides Littler, who had often found something to complain about since Hall refused his offer of the Cambridge Theatre as the company's London base, another dissenter was Sir Denys Lowson, a former Lord Mayor of London and a fund manager who was eventually disgraced for enriching himself at the expense of his clients. Lowson, who had inherited his governorship, wrote to Fordham Flower as early as 30 July 1962, saying that the company should stop asking the government for money and stick to playing in Stratford. Another governor, Maurice Colbourne, took exception to the fun that had been poked at the Lord Chamberlain in Brook's experimental work and wrote to Emile Littler expressing his distaste. Littler sent the letter on to Flower, adding that a company operating under a royal charter had no right to be rude about the Lord Chamberlain, who was a member of the royal household. (Lord Cobbold himself had mixed feelings. He wrote to Flower that summer: 'As a personal admirer of your company, I am very much in favour of this confrontation being carried on, if it has to be carried on, as amicably and reasonably as possible.')[4] On 21 June 1964 Sir Denys Lowson wrote again to Flower saying that there would have to be changes in the direction and management of the company. So the opposition was aroused even before the Dirty Plays row began.[5]

Hall and his colleagues were conscious of the criticism, and did not like it. John Roberts, the general manager of the Aldwych since 1960, took the opportunity of his retirement in June 1964 to give Flower a piece of his mind:

> *The achievements of the last four years have been considerable, but, yourself excepted, the part played by the governors has been minimal. Our policies have been pursued with the grudging permission of the executive council and the finance committee, who, I feel, would have blocked them altogether if they could . . . The fact that Peter, Paddy [Donnell] and I, with the background of . . . a public of 750,000, have had to play the role of naughty and irresponsible children at finance committee meetings has been extraordinary.[6]*

When the Dirty Plays row started it was not merely an opportunity for retaliation by the philistines, it was a pretext for an attack on Hall's artistic and managerial style. Although he later denied ever having sent it, Sir Denys Lowson's name appeared on a letter fully supporting Littler in the *Evening News*. Peter Cadbury, who ran Keith Prowse, the ticket agency, stated that it was about time the West End was cleaned up, bolstering suspicions at the Aldwych that what really bothered West End managers was that the RSC was doing good business while they were having a poor summer.

Fordham Flower treated the accusations with disdain. When a delegation of RSC actors, led by Peggy Ashcroft and Tony Church, asked to see him, he reassured them of his complete support for Hall and his policy. Flower later confessed to Douglas Fairbanks Junior that he was much more worried than he had appeared. He genuinely feared that, from Hall downwards, the company might just walk out: 'They damn near did.' He added that, while he had never liked Littler, he now detested and distrusted him.[7]

Flower was a conscientious chairman of the board. He wrote to all the governors explaining why he was supporting Hall, and stating that he would be forced to resign if his policy were rejected. Replies were unanimous about one thing: he should not resign, in any circumstances. But the governors were divided about the policy. Lord Radcliffe, one of Whitehall's great post-war panjandrums, replied that since the direction – Hall, Brook and Saint-Denis – valued things he considered unimportant, he was a lukewarm supporter. Sir Alexander Maxwell, a Midlands manufacturer, told Flower he was staggered that the executive council did not vet RSC scripts. Only a few months later, the National Theatre board refused Olivier permission to produce *Spring Awakening* by Frank Wedekind because of a suggestion of group masturbation. That could not have happened at the RSC.

Flower must have been perturbed, however, by letters from governors who knew and loved the theatre and who disapproved of Hall's artistic style. Nevill Coghill, who was to theatre at Oxford what Dadie Rylands was at Cambridge, said that the RSC was not doing its job if it was not faithful to Shakespeare's text and intentions: the inference was that *The Wars of the Roses* had been unfaithful. But the harshest words came from Ivor Brown, an old ally of Stratford:

> *If, as I surmise, Peter Brook is a big influence on Stratford and Aldwych policy, I think this is a pity since he appears to have so strong and marked a proclivity for horrors. His craftsmanship is not in dispute, his taste is (incidentally, his favourites Artaud and Sade were both insane). I hope therefore the council will take a firm line and let Peter Hall know that he does not direct them, but for them.[8]*

Hall, who was licensed by Fordham Flower not Lord Cobbold, was not prepared to budge even an inch.

The approval of Hall's colleagues was compensation for the abuse of the philistines. Harold Pinter, impressed by the *Marat/Sade*, told Hall that 'the RSC bestrides the world – I must say it – like a colossus'.[9] Pinter had directed a revival of his own first play *The Birthday Party* at the Aldwych in June 1964, and he was becoming a presence at the RSC, writing notes to actors that were memorably critical and encouraging at the same time. For instance: Saturday night's 'performance was flat, colourless, uneasy, constipated, introverted . . . Bring the play up, please . . . Courage, boldness, clarity, vigour, precision, relish is what is needed. Play!'[10] But Pinter decided that, in fact, the fault was basically his; since he was the author, the actors took his advice literally and this inhibited them. Although he gave a number of capable performances in his plays, this was the last time Pinter directed his own work.

Pinter's commitment to Hall was significant because it meant that the RSC finally had an established house playwright as the Royal Court had had John Osborne and the National Theatre had

Peter Shaffer. All Pinter's first nights, directed by Hall, designed by John Bury, with strong casts led, at first, by Vivien Merchant, were at the Aldwych – until Hall took Pinter away with him to the National Theatre.

Impresarios like Michael Codron were keen to produce Pinter's new work, but he stubbornly chose the RSC because, as he says, he hated the West End. 'Everything depends on one night, while in the subsidised theatre you can get a play on and, however it is received, people get the opportunity to go and see it.'[11] When he had finished his next play, *The Homecoming*, Pinter sent it to Hall, who immediately said that he wanted to do it. He did not tell Pinter until years afterwards that not all his colleagues shared his enthusiasm. A vote among Hall's inner circle went against doing *The Homecoming* at the RSC. Hall, behaving as the first among equals, simply overruled them.

Although Hall alone was billed as director of the Pinter plays, their relationship hardly changed from their first collaboration with *The Collection*. Pinter attended all the rehearsals and there was absolute candour between them. If Hall wanted an actor to make a move, he would ask Pinter what he thought and if Pinter thought it might be more effective a bit later, they would try it later. 'That came from real assurance,' says Pinter.

The Homecoming was cast partly from the company (Ian Holm, Michael Bryant, John Normington) and partly from outside (Pinter's wife Vivien Merchant, Paul Rogers). During the six-week tour before the production opened at the Aldwych, Pinter and Hall watched a tired, edgy performance together in Brighton. As they walked to the theatre together the following morning, Pinter told Hall he thought the actors were exhausted. 'May I suggest you don't give them any notes, just say hello and let them get on with it and we'll both go back to London?' Hall agreed. Meeting the actors, he told them they needed a break: he'd just give them one or two notes, and call it a day. Three hours later, the one or two notes were finally finished. 'Once he'd started,' says Pinter, 'he could not stop.'

The opening of *The Homecoming* in June 1965 was part of a burst of work by Hall in which he seemed incapable of failure. He responded to Pinter's piece with relish, clarity, vigour and precision, and the production established the style of menacing and precise playing, full of repressed emotion, which remained the conventional way of performing Pinter for more than twenty years.

Ronald Bryden, a Cambridge contemporary who had succeeded Tynan as the *Observer*'s drama critic, used a phrase that could be applied to any one of the four major Pinter first performances: it was 'razor-sharp'. It was a technique Hall had never fully realised when he and Pinter were doing *The Collection* in 1962; he cracked it half-way through the rehearsals for *The Homecoming*, when the actors began to trust the words they had been given. When Hall asked Pinter what a line meant, Pinter, in turn, would ask what it said or what it didn't say. By concentrating on the text, they got it near perfect.

The walls of John Bury's set were bare as chalk, with a blackened, broken-backed three-piece suite and dresser. Pinter even changed a line in the text to accommodate Bury's set: a record, Bury believes. But Pinter was in an accommodating mood. 'I loved Hall's touch, his understanding and the discipline. I loved his productions of my plays, and *The Homecoming* was, without question, one of the high points of my professional life.'

Hamlet was the last production at Stratford that summer and it confirmed the growth of a new, devoted, and young audience for Shakespeare. Although 703 lines, about one-fifth of the play, were cut from the text, Hall clearly did not wish to offend traditionalists like Nevill Coghill, who had complained about Hall and Barton rewriting Shakespeare. In a speech to the Shakespeare Institute that summer, Hall said: 'You should approach a classic with the maximum of scholarship you can muster – and then you honestly try to interpret what you think it means to a person living now.'[12] His view of the play was unconventional, however: he did not classify *Hamlet* as a tragedy; rather he thought it belonged with *Troilus and Cressida* and *Measure for Measure* as a clinical dissection of life. 'Brechtian' was the fashionable way of describing Hall's *Hamlet*, although his own description of the motivating idea put no trust in theory:

> For our decade I think the play will be about the disillusionment which produces an apathy of the will so deep that commitment to politics, to religion or to life is impossible . . . [Hamlet] is always on the brink of action, but something inside him, this disease of disillusionment, stops the final committed action.
>
> It is an emotion which you can encounter in the young today. To me it is extraordinary that in the last fifteen years the young in the West, and particularly the intellectuals, have by and large lost the ordinary, predictable radical impulses which the young in all generations have had. You might

march against the Bomb. But on the other hand, you might not. You might sleep with everyone you know, or you might not. You might take drugs, you might not. There is a sense of what-the-hell-anyway, over us looms the Mushroom Cloud. And politics are a game and a lie, whether in our own country or in the East/West dialogue which goes on interminably without anything very real being said. This negative response is deep and appalling.[13]

This is expressed with such clarity that it is likely that Hall was reflecting, in part at least, his own thoughts. It would not have been surprising. He was approaching thirty-five; his experience at the RSC gave him no confidence in the benevolence of the state towards the arts; and Harold Wilson's nimble opportunism was transforming the enthusiasm with which people like Hall had greeted his election in October 1964 into weary cynicism.

Hall had caught a mood, and in David Warner he had a Hamlet who could express it. At twenty-four, young enough to play Hamlet as a real student with a long scarf wound round his neck, he was gangling, spotty, his traces of a Midlands accent entirely lacked Gielgud's colour and elegance. He was modern and classless, like a disaffected existentialist drop-out. True to this character, Warner had nowhere to live that summer, and when Hall offered him a room in Avoncliffe for a few nights, Warner moved in for the season. Hall kept the only documentary record of their collaboration, a note scrawled on a torn piece of paper saying: 'Sorry didn't see you today. Thanks for all, love to all. See you when you get back. Luv David W.'[14]

Warner's technique was underdeveloped, and his verse-speaking tended towards monotony, but he converted Ronald Bryden:

It's hard to convey the excitement of seeing him make each discovery, seeing the play's machinery dismantled and fitted together before your eyes . . . This is a Hamlet desperately in need of counsel, help, experience, and he actually seeks it from the audience in his soliloquies. That is probably the greatest triumph of the production: using the Elizabethan convention with total literalness, Hamlet communes not with himself but with you.[15]

Warner was Bryden's 'unfinished hero'. Other memorable performances were Glenda Jackson's neurotic Ophelia, so abrasive that some critics thought she should have been playing Hamlet; and Tony Church's Polonius, a shrewd establishment figure modelled on the first ministers to successive Elizabeths – Lord Burleigh and

Harold Macmillan. John Bury's forbidding and simple set was made of shiny black Formica walls, separated by two large doors; the floor was in a striking geometric pattern of black and white.

The reviews were mixed, but the audience response was almost unanimously enthusiastic about Hall's conception, and business remained good for more than 150 performances over the next eighteen months. The only hint of serious criticism of the production did not appear until 1976, when Stanley Wells, of the Shakespeare Institute, scrutinised Hall's assertion that his Hamlet's actions were dictated by the disease of disillusionment. Wells argued that such a man would surely not justify the killing of the King as an active, moral action, as Hamlet does in the lines: 'And is't not to be damned/ To let this canker of our nature come/ In further evil?' Wells then exposed Hall's masterly solution to this tricky problem of interpretation. The line had been cut.[16]

For five years Hall had concentrated exclusively on the RSC. In the summer of 1965, he finally accepted an outside engagement, at the Royal Opera House. In the eleven years since Hall had written to David Webster, the general director at the Opera House, saying that his chief ambition in life was to produce opera, he had turned down plenty of opportunities to achieve it. He had refused Verdi's *Macbeth* in 1959, Benjamin Britten's *A Midsummer Night's Dream* in 1960 ('I realise it will only lead me into doing bad work if I try to fit it in. One shouldn't "fit in" masterpieces,' he wrote to Webster),[17] Verdi's *Forza del destino* in 1961; plans for Shostakovich's *Lady Macbeth of Mtzensk* fell through in 1963. But Webster wanted Peter Hall, was determined to get him, and finally tied him down to direct Arnold Schoenberg's difficult, unfinished work, *Moses and Aaron*, in 1965. Hall had not directed an opera since *The Moon and Sixpence* at Sadler's Wells in 1957, but his life had been been a training for opera. As an accomplished adolescent musician, Hall could read and understand a musical score; as an experienced theatre director, he had established an individual style based on his fidelity to the text of a work. Hall instinctively appreciated the relationship between the score and the libretto – the combination that can produce performances of unusual emotional depth.

As bright young men at the cutting edge of the English theatre, Hall and Bury were determined to show the opera world a thing or two. Hall did not like the translation of *Moses and Aaron*; David Rudkin was commissioned to write a new one. The chorus master worried that Hall was asking too much of his singers. The production manager, John Sullivan, never grew used to Bury's way of working. Bury asked him to make, for example, a dead cow as a prop: he did a quick sketch of it. When he saw the finished product, he remarked that it looked nothing like a dead cow. 'No, but it looks like your drawing,' retorted John Sullivan. Hall and Bury decided that Sullivan would have to go, and so he did.[18] 'Hall stretched the organisation, especially the electricians,' says John Tooley, who was then Webster's assistant.[19]

Schoenberg's libretto contained an orgy scene, and four months before the first night newspapers were already speculating about the extent of Hall's realism. Not wanting to direct the first Dirty Opera, Hall said, the orgy would be as tasteful as possible, 'but it's got to make its point.' The point was made by hiring some strippers from Soho, and after Tooley had alerted the Lord Chamberlain that they would appear on stage bare-breasted and that some of the men would wear phalluses, even the *News of the World* put the Royal Opera House on its front page. Having seen the first night, the Lord Chamberlain's man reported that the orgy scene was 'just all right'.[20] But the real innovation was the animals. The script called for two horses, one cow, two donkeys, six goats and a camel. Hall made a great point of the camel: if Schoenberg asked for one, he must have one. A camel by the name of Sheena was obtained from Chessington Zoo, although her keepers warned Covent Garden that camels go berserk in the presence of donkeys. Sheena behaved well until a rehearsal during which her hoof slipped and she lashed out. Extras scattered. Sheena mounted a rostrum, which collapsed under her weight, and crashed into the scenery. At this point, terrified, she relieved herself copiously. Hall turned wearily to his production assistant. 'Cut the camel,' he said.[22]

Failure would have been expensive in terms of reputation as well as of anxiety, emotion and the Opera House's production budget, but *Moses and Aaron* was a huge success. Although the score was unfamiliar, and atonal, all six performances were sold out. *The Times* announced that the production was a triumph for Solti and Hall. Andrew Porter, in the *Financial Times*, went even further: 'It is surely the greatest achievement in Covent Garden's history,' he said.[22] One of the few people who was not altogether satisfied was Schoenberg's widow, who thought the tameness of the orgy scene would have disappointed her husband.

That was a wonderful summer for Hall. He was well again.

Pinter at the Aldwych, Shakespeare at Stratford and Schoenberg at the Royal Opera House had consolidated his reputation as the most exciting and controversial young theatre director in Britain. But there was a worrying gap in his life. He had a home, although Leslie had dug up the roses and the yellow forsythia before she left. His lawyers made sure that the children remained in his custody and at school in England. The children were shunted between London and Stratford, sometimes in the care of a member of the company who happened to be on the same train. Hall assumed that they needed a mother, and the house needed a woman's presence. The children seemed happy enough, and Jenny Hall did not complain at the time, but when she finally did, she said that she did not think either of her parents knew what they were unleashing on their children.

When his marriage to Leslie Caron was deteriorating, Hall had found solace, as she had, in brief affairs with people with whom he had been working at the time. After Leslie left, Hall began an affair with his personal assistant, Jacky Taylor. She had been a constant presence since 1961, organising his working life. Now Jacky became part of his private life too. But there was no question of living together at Avoncliffe: that would have caused scandal in Stratford.

Peter Wood remembers Hall asking his colleagues, somewhat doubtfully, whether he ought to marry Jacky. She was slim and lively, dark-haired, with a fashionable fringe, and she had a quick smile. Hall liked her boldness; on holiday in the South of France that summer, she had imperiously ticked off French police who wanted her boat to change its course. But if the fun were to continue, they would have to make the relationship socially acceptable in Stratford. 'We just got married one day,' says Jacky Hall. It was in October 1965. Long after the marriage was over and her memory was framed by disenchantment, she alleged that, when they were working together, Hall had said she should not fall in love with him: 'I eat people,' he told her.[23]

Jacky Hall was in her late twenties when she married. (She is discreet about her age, but she was at King Edward VI School in Nuneaton with the film-maker Ken Loach, who was born in 1936, so let us say she was twenty-eight or twenty-nine.) Her father was a bank manager of the old school, who did not expect his daughter to work, except as a prelude to marriage, and so denied her the chance of higher education. But he dinned into her the importance of sound housekeeping. Throughout their marriage, Hall's domestic accounts were properly kept.

With marriage, Jacky Hall did as her father would have expected and her husband wanted: she gave up work. Having done so, she was at a loss. 'I do remember afternoons, thinking, what am I going to do?' The Spanish couple still kept the house tidy, and now when she wandered down to the theatre all her friends there were busy. First, she learned to cook properly; but, since that was not a full-time occupation, she applied for a place at teacher-training college. She was interviewed and accepted, but never took up the place. Her husband was no more liberal than her father about her further education. 'He said I was the root of the marriage and burst into tears,' says Jacky Hall. She gave in and concentrated on home and children, the first of which – a boy named Edward – was born thirteen months after their marriage, on 27 November 1966.

Once the divorce was settled, Christopher and Jenny moved freely between the Hall and Caron households, but different habits created frictions. Jenny later said that she remembered Jacky burning clothes that her mother had bought for her. Jacky Hall denies that any such thing occurred. The arguments about the children's clothes were about convenience, not loyalties. 'When our housekeeper kept clothes because they were suitable for the country, the London housekeeper would phone and ask what had happened to the red pullover,' says Jacky Hall.

However imperfectly she remembered these disagreements, they lodged in Jenny's memory, although they became dormant after 1967 when she and Christopher were sent to Bedales School in Hampshire. A liberal regime at the school suited both the children, and Bedales provided a stable environment throughout their adolescence. 'Whatever else was happening, we knew we would always be back at school in term-time,' says Jenny Hall.

Among the letters congratulating Hall on his marriage was one from Tony Quayle, wishing him happiness after his tumultuous divorce and illnesses. 'God knows, you deserve it after all you've been through.'[24] But November 1965, when Quayle's letter was written, was a time of more turmoil in the RSC. And it was the same old problem.

It had been supposed by optimists in the arts that the election of a Labour government would end their financial crises; and, if

confirmation were needed of the new administration's commitment, it came in the form of Jennie Lee, Aneurin Bevan's widow
and a favourite of Harold Wilson, who was made Minister for the
Arts. Hall reported to Fordham Flower that he had had a vague
but encouraging meeting with her. She had assured him that the
RSC should not worry – 'although the savings would have to go'.
Prospects appeared to improve even further in April 1965 when
Arnold Goodman became chairman of the Arts Council. 'I think
this may make a lot of difference to our future,' Hall wrote to
Flower.[25]

On Goodman's second day in his new office, Hall announced
that he wished to see him at 2 p.m., and marched in to say that
the Arts Council had been thoroughly unfair in its allocation of
money to the RSC, and that if the theatre were to survive it would
have to have more money at once.[26] But Goodman was immune
to Hall's pressure. He did, indeed, nearly make a lot of difference
to the future of the RSC, but not in the way Hall and Flower were
contemplating.

The RSC's balance sheet was a familiar sight. The Art Council's
£80,000 grant in 1964–5 had only been enough to reduce the
remaining deficit to £65,643. In 1965–6 the grant was up by
£10,000 and box-office receipts were at record levels; but so was
the deficit. Hall, whose way with figures was always to present the
worst case in its most dramatic form, told Jennie Lee that the RSC
was costing £170,000 more than it could earn; and in 1965 the last
of the reserves of the old Shakespeare Memorial Theatre would be
spent to cover that shortfall. What the company needed, he told the
Minister, was £247,000 a year for the next three years. At the Arts
Council, Goodman was thinking of a sizeable increase, but nothing
like that: in July 1965 he told Flower that the Arts Council ought
to be able to manage £150,000 for 1966–7, an offer he thought was
'munificent'. And, as if to let the RSC know that it had no secrets
from him, Goodman told Flower that individual governors of the
RSC had asked him to use his influence to shut the Aldwych.[27]
(No names were mentioned, but it was hard to imagine Emile
Littler resisting the opportunity to put the knife in.)

In fact, the split inside the RSC was even deeper than Goodman
knew: for the only time, Hall and Flower were at odds. When
formally telling Hall about the £150,000 offer, Flower wrote that
he did not see how the Arts Council could have gone any
further.[28] For that reason he thought they should not endanger

good relations with Jennie Lee and Goodman: 'I think it would be a mistake which we might all regret for ever if we were to refuse the Arts Council's latest offer on the grounds of inadequacy.' Flower appreciated that there would be artistic sacrifices, but asked for Hall's support. If the RSC, he said, 'were to retire now and give it all up, we shall have few sympathisers'.

Hall's response was to open a vigorous campaign for more than £150,000, and to complain to his close friends about lack of support from Flower. First, he let Jennie Lee know what the consequences of a grant of £150,000 would be: a six-month season in Stratford instead of eight months; only four and a half months' work at the Aldwych, sacking half the company, getting no new plays, and no touring, ever. Learning of this threat, the Arts Council sharply reminded the RSC that its first responsibility was to Shakespeare at Stratford, and the Council's reaction to any reduction of work there would be a reduction in the grant. Hall's second negotiating position was that the company could keep ticking over with a grant of £200,000; to appease Flower, however, Hall began to prepare contingency plans for a full Stratford season within the cash limits of the £150,000 grant.

What Hall and Flower did not know, in the summer of 1965, was that Goodman had decided on a radical solution to the RSC's financial problems. Although much new money was flowing into the Arts Council, there were so many applicants, and grants had started from such a low base, that there was still not enough to go round. Moreover, the National Theatre was now providing classic repertory in London. Goodman's solution, then, was that the RSC should close the Aldwych and concentrate on Stratford. His second-best strategy was to have the National Theatre take over the RSC's lease on the Aldwych for half the year, and to put on an expanded repertory there. The RSC, which thought it had won the argument about its London base, now found it had to be fought all over again.

Goodman's first move was to tell his plans to Hugh Willatt, chairman of the Arts Council advisory Drama Panel which brought together artists and administrators in the theatre. Willatt, a Nottingham solicitor, had been influential in building the Nottingham Playhouse before moving to work in London. He admired Hall and the risks he had taken in opening the RSC's London front, and, as chairman of the Ballet Rambert, he had held long, good-natured but fruitless talks with Flower and Hall about the Ballet Rambert and the RSC sharing a redeveloped Mercury Theatre in Notting Hill Gate. Willatt knew where he stood on Goodman's plan: he was against it, and he believed there would be no support for it on the panel. Willatt told Goodman that he should explain his proposal personally and judge the panel's reaction for himself. When he faced its unanimous opposition to his plans, Goodman knew he was defeated. 'As I watched him manoeuvring his way out of it, I finally understood what workers' solidarity meant,' says Willatt.[29]

The RSC's defences had held again; but Goodman, having lost the Battle of the Aldwych, refused to come up with a larger grant. It stayed at £150,000. Hall accepted it, and lost the Battle of the Better Grant. The price of this defeat was a Stratford season with only one new production; actors were let go; Michel Saint-Denis's studio was closed. There was also a considerable loss of spirit, especially in Stratford during a season consisting mainly of repeats. Hall defiantly refused to cut back at the Aldwych, where the year began with his directing Paul Scofield in a memorable performance in Gogol's *The Government Inspector*. It then tailed off with a run of new plays by continental playwrights that enhanced neither their reputation nor the company's. Sally Beauman asserts that Hall must have known these plays had virtually no chance of filling a theatre the size of the Aldwych.[30] He was stubborn as well as defiant.

In the autumn, however, Peter Brook mounted a controversial documentary drama about the Vietnam War titled *US*, which managed to generate both hype and hysteria. Knowing of its content, Lord Avon discreetly resigned as chairman of the governors before the row became public. The Lord Chamberlain, Lord Cobbold, called the script bestial, anti-American and pro-Communist, and said it should be banned. Brook and Hall, accompanied by George Farmer, the industrialist who was Flower's deputy, went to St James's Palace to defend *US* on the basis that it criticised the United Kingdom as much as it criticised the United States. The Lord Chamberlain was eventually persuaded that the play would not destroy the special relationship, but he still managed to excise a few adjectives. For Brook, the crisis with the Lord Chamberlain was an image of the war in Vietnam itself: 'Remember,' he told the cast, 'if this crisis had taken place in Vietnam, some of us would be dead by now.' But, for many in the audience, it was the play that died. At the end of the performance, as the cast stood silently and menacingly on stage, confronting the audience, Ken Tynan called out: 'Are we keeping you waiting or are you keeping us?'[31]

The only really good news that summer was a production of the black Jacobean melodrama *The Revenger's Tragedy* that had been hurriedly added to the repertory with a shoestring budget and a cast of little-known actors. In it, Alan Howard, John Kane, Patrick Stewart and Norman Rodway made their first appearances at Stratford, and the critical praise for the production was virtually unanimous. Ronald Bryden wrote in the *Observer*:

> *Lord Goodman may yet go down as a back-handed benefactor to the Royal Shakespeare Company. Every time the Arts Council tightens the screws on the company's subsidy, arguing that one National Theatre is enough, the RSC bounces back with some victory of sheer theatrical resource over economics, so brilliant as to suggest that it works best with its back to the wall. The new Stratford production of* The Revenger's Tragedy *is one of the finest things the Hall regime has accomplished.*[32]

It was also the Stratford début of the director Trevor Nunn.

Nunn had first been attracted to Hall in 1959 when he was an undergraduate at Cambridge and he chanced on a lecture Hall was giving about his idea of an ensemble company. The following year Nunn went to Stratford with the Marlowe Society's *Dr Faustus* and decided that was where he wanted to work as a director. He started at the Belgrade Theatre in Coventry, and in 1963, after Hall had seen his production of *The Caucasian Chalk Circle*, he was offered a job as an assistant in Stratford. Nunn, who thought he would learn more by directing plays in Coventry, turned it down. But Hall did not forget him, and a year later invited Nunn for a drink at Avoncliffe.

Nunn missed his bus and hitched a lift from a car mechanic. His smart white coat was covered with grease stains and he was late. Hall calmed him down on his arrival, and when they began to chat, Hall discovered that Nunn was from Suffolk, too. (Nunn grew up in Ipswich.) Nunn, who did a cabaret performance of Suffolk stories, did his act, and Hall loved it. He asked him to stay on for dinner, which they ate by the river. Although Nunn was the younger man by ten years, Hall confided in him about his problems at the RSC and at home now that Leslie had gone. 'It was like a fairy tale,' Nunn recalls.[33]

At midnight, Hall announced that he would drive Nunn home

to Coventry. Out came the Aston Martin, down came the roof, and Hall raced like a rally driver at 90 m.p.h. along the B-roads to Coventry: 'I was yelling with excitement and terror,' Nunn says. When they arrived at his home, Hall offered him a job. He would have to be an assistant for a few months, but he guaranteed that he would be an associate director before long. So he was. Hall's decision may sound impetuous, but he had found a kindred spirit, and the trust and affection between the two of them was instant. Nunn made such a poor start at the RSC that many of his colleagues thought he could not possibly last, but, despite some misgivings, Hall retained his faith in Nunn. 'He was absolutely unshakeable. He never spoke to me about anyone else's doubts, and he never revised my schedule.' *The Revenger's Tragedy* was Nunn's thank-you.

Hall returned to Covent Garden that summer to direct his first Mozart opera, *The Magic Flute*, with Solti conducting once again. John Bury went along too, in spite of David Webster's doubts ('We all know of his stern, masculine qualities, but does he have enough magic for the job?').[34] The libretto had been translated into English by the poet Adrian Mitchell, and Hall and Bury proposed to try to fulfil Schikaneder's elaborate stage directions. 'Carefully prepared and conscientious,' was the opera critic Andrew Porter's judgement.

During rehearsals for the *Flute*, Stratford's general manager, the much loved Paddy Donnell, began to find Hall increasingly elusive. Since the opening of the Aldwych, it had been a company rule that the director was always in the wrong place: when he was needed in Stratford, he would invariably be visiting the Aldwych, and vice versa. But now Hall was not in either place, and important company decisions were being delayed.

The worst news that summer concerned Fordham Flower. He had been ill the previous winter, telling Douglas Fairbanks Junior that he was convalescing 'from something akin to jaundice'.[35] At the end of May 1966, he was reflecting on retirement in a further five years' time. Less than two months later, on 9 July 1966, Fordie was gone. He died in St Mary's Hospital, Paddington, of cancer at the age of sixty-two. This was devastating for the RSC, and for Hall personally. The two had settled their tactical disagreement over Goodman's Arts Council grant, and one of Flower's last instructions, given though his wife, Hersey, was that just to revive old productions was a form of suicide and the company should get back into top gear. Hall's obituary in the *Guardian* masked the emotion he felt: 'His constant and imaginative work in public life was completely selfless . . . Because he never asked, he never received the great public recognition that was his due . . . He was a good man and a constant friend.'[36] Flower had loved Hall's energy and intelligence. Hall had loved Flower's tolerance and generosity. David Brierley, who worked closely with Hall and watched them both, thought there was a psychic link between them. Flower, he says, was the ingredient that released Hall's creative talent and energy: 'They had an acute sense of shared purpose that enabled them to persuade the governing body to do the most hair-raising things.'[37]

Hall was not always open to instruction from his mentor. Hersey Flower says: 'He gave such leadership, and yet I remember Fordie taking him aside one day to tell him what a good idea it would be if he sometimes noticed some of the front-of-house people. There was a curious lack of that kind of courtesy. I suppose it was his tunnel vision, but it doesn't matter. I loved the man, and because of his love for Fordie we saw his vulnerable side. There was no constraint in his love for Fordie.'[38] The loss of a father-figure who appreciated his work and his personality, and whom he could trust and rely on, left a chasm in his life. Hall mourned Fordham Flower for years.

The natural successor from within the family was Dennis Flower, Fordham's cousin, who was a co-director at the brewery and a fellow-governor of the theatre. As chairman of the local Conservative Association, Dennis Flower was a good-natured worthy, but Hall could not imagine him facing down Arnold Goodman in a negotiation over grants. Hall's candidate was George Farmer, the fifty-eight-year-old chairman of the Rover Car Company – despite the fact that he disapproved of the way the reserves had been run down.[39] An accountant by profession and by nature, Farmer once observed wryly to Flower that every single thing Hall wanted to do cost money. It was Farmer who got the job.

While the administration was in flux, Hall managed to move Paddy Donnell sideways, to co-ordinate the RSC's new relationship with the City of London's Barbican project. Donnell was of the *ancien régime*, a practical man who had grown used to authority during the war when he, like Flower, became a lieutenant-colonel. Donnell grew impatient at Hall's lack of appreciation of front-of-house problems, and his increasing inaccessibility. For his part,

Hall thought that an up-to-date theatre company should be run like an industry, by an industrialist. Derek Hornby, the man chosen to replace Donnell as general manager, came from Texas Instruments.

The Barbican, to which Donnell had been exiled, was to provide the RSC with its permanent London home. The RSC had been tempted by a brand-new theatre in the development of flats in the City of London: the City Corporation promised a preferential rent, and the idea seemed much more attractive than sharing a home with the Ballet Rambert in Notting Hill – especially as Hall and Bury were to act as design consultants at the Barbican. Towards the end of 1966 they revealed their plan: a proscenium theatre without a proscenium, in which no seat was more than 60 feet away from the stage, and with no gangways. The cost was given as £1.3 million, and the new theatre was scheduled to open in 1970, although, in 1967, the date was put back slightly, to 1972. It finally opened in 1982.

By 1967 the pace of Hall's life was changing. Running the RSC and directing plays had taught him how to do two things at once, and once he knew he could manage that, two were not enough. Having found opera, Hall next discovered films. A deal had been done with CBS in New York to film Shakespeare's plays, and the initial contract included two Hall productions. The first was his *Dream*; the second was the *Macbeth* he planned for the summer of 1967 in Stratford with Paul Scofield and Vivien Merchant. The idea of the film deal, he announced, was to bring in a large regular income: 'The future of our company is bound up with films.'[40]

In February shooting had started on Hall's first feature film, an adaptation of *Eh?* by Henry Livings, which Hall had directed at the Aldwych in 1964. The play was renamed *Work is a Four-Letter Word*, and the cast was drawn mainly from the RSC, topped up with Cilla Black, the Liverpudlian pop singer, whose presence brought plenty of publicity during shooting. While making this film Hall was the subject of an interview in the *Daily Mail* of a kind that was to become familiar in the next twenty-five years. Based on a breathless account of a working day beginning at 6.30 a.m. and finishing at 10.30 p.m., the article described an appetite for work that seemed greedy, almost inhuman.

David Lewin, the interviewer, asked Hall what was the point of it? 'Well, power, obviously,' Hall replied.

Everyone wants power, and it really is rather a puritan thing to say power of necessity is a bad thing. What is important is that there should be checks. The Royal Shakespeare Company is not a democracy, but there are people who come to me and say 'Eh – why are you doing that?' and I'll listen to them . . . But you don't go into a meeting asking 'What shall we do?', you go in saying 'This is what I'm going to do'. That is the way to get things done. I want to be an administrator, an impresario and a director of individual plays as well. I am not happy just doing one job and not the other.[41]

There was a high price for these furious bursts of work. His breakdowns of 1956, 1963 and 1964 were followed by one in 1967. This time it was entirely physical and threatened permanent damage. Hall had been helping out Christopher Morahan, a fellow-director at the Aldwych, who had caught chicken-pox from his daughter and was not allowed to get too close to the actors or technicians. Unfortunately, shingles, one of Hall's childhood diseases, belongs to the same family as chicken-pox. Hall was tense, run-down and vulnerable, and Morahan's chicken-pox became his shingles. This time the bitterly painful rash came out in his face. He retired to a darkened room to be nursed again by Jacky. She was at her wits' end: the diagnosis was desperately serious and there was nothing she could do. Doctors came and went; the eye specialist from Leamington informed them of the real possibility that Hall would lose the sight of one eye. He didn't, but the eye was permanently damaged.

The illness occurred when he was due in rehearsals for *Macbeth*, of which much was expected. A prestigious continental tour had been scheduled for it, as well as the film; Paul Scofield was anxious and distressed about the part; Vivien Merchant was finding it difficult to learn the lines; and the audience was keenly anticipating Hall's first Shakespeare production since *Hamlet*, two years earlier. The 13 July first night was put back, first to 26 July, then until August. When Hall did get back to work, he was listless, depressed, and out of luck. Scofield confessed he found the verse difficult, and never got it right. Vivien Merchant found acting Shakespeare difficult, and never got that right either. John Bury thought his own work was no better than fifty-fifty. The witches made a memorable entrance climbing out from under a carpet dyed purple-red, like heather; but the climax of the play got a big, unscheduled and humiliating laugh on the first night, which confirmed Hall's fear that the curse of the Scottish play

had struck again. In a last-minute improvisation, Bury decided
to substitute real leaves on real branches from real trees for the
branches of Birnam Wood provided by the props department. 'I
thought it would be a *coup de théâtre*, but the audience did not.
The leaves looked too real in this artificial world. Peter was very
cross, and we went back to the phony stuff,' Bury says.[42] *Macbeth*
was one of Hall's most disastrous productions. The scheduled tour
could not be cancelled, but Scofield refused to immortalise a poor
performance on film.

The failure of *Macbeth* put the vital CBS film deal, which was
already causing anxiety, at risk. *A Midsummer Night's Dream*, being
filmed at Compton Verney near Stratford, was being plagued by
early winter weather. The set was deep in mud, and between
takes Hall's colleagues were pestering him to finalise details for
the following season. Hall's post-production work was being done
in a caravan parked in the drive at Avoncliffe, and George Farmer
was fussing about the financial arrangements. Needless to say,
the film was badly over budget. Hersey Flower remembers Hall
telling her, after a gruelling cross-examination from Farmer, that
he could not bear another one. He was still dreadfully tired.

This time the financial crisis was profoundly serious. Despite
his experience of big business, Derek Hornby's appointment was
not a success. Extraordinary tales of administrative blunders were
circulating in the company: of an RSC production having been
scheduled to play in Zurich and the Aldwych on the same night;
of actors being committed to perform on cruise ships without their
consent, or knowledge even; and of an expensively misconceived
venture to publicise the company in the United States on a train
that travelled from coast to coast. Finally, the loss in 1968–9 was
£161,126, compared to £32,536 in the previous year, and one of
only £444 in the year of the belt-tightening, 1966–7. (Hornby, who
had been given the title of administrative director, left the RSC
in 1969.)

Jacky was encouraging Hall to leave the RSC. After the *Macbeth*
crisis, she felt that it was inhuman for Hall to go on working
so hard. And there were attractive alternatives: 'I think he was
seduced by the idea of becoming a film director, and he wanted
to do opera. But he couldn't do that and stay at Stratford; the
governors simply wouldn't have it.'

By December, Hall decided that he had had enough, and he
told his senior colleagues that he was about to quit. Hall's own

explanation was similar to his wife's: 'I just wanted to go and do something that was just for me, where I could look after myself.' One of the strongest motives was to improve on his basic salary of £5,000 a year from Stratford; from working in films, he knew that real money was to be made elsewhere.

Trevor Nunn was astonished to learn from Hall that he had designated him as his successor, and his colleagues were no less surprised. Nunn, who was twenty-eight (a year younger than Hall when he had taken the job), told Hall that the company was indivisible from his presence. Hall's reaction was to talk. Together they agreed that the RSC was a team, and to retain the spirit it was important that leadership be handed on to someone who already belonged to it. But who else was there? John Barton declined to involve himself in the drudgery of administration; David Jones at the Aldwych had a low profile. That seemed to leave only Nunn. ('He's one of the best politicians outside Parliament,' says Nunn.)

Nunn finally became a candidate on condition that, as Hall's loyal lieutenant, he would act as caretaker, until Hall's eventual return. Hall, talking the idea over with Hersey Flower, told her that he did not believe such arrangements could work. But Nunn did not agree: 'I seriously imagined he would return to take his place,' he says.

In fact, Hall may have chosen the right time to go. The magic that had clung to him in the first six years in Stratford was becoming a little tarnished. An influential article had appeared in August 1967 in the glossy magazine *Nova*, and the extended headline to the article by Peter Lewis was a useful summary of what was going wrong: 'PETER USES YOU – Diana Rigg/ HE'S POWER MAD – Roy Dotrice/ YES, I AM A DICTATOR – Peter Hall/ BUT THE ROYAL SHAKESPEARE COMPANY DOESN'T HAVE THAT LEAN AND HUNGRY LOOK NOWADAYS'. Lewis's article contained a quote from Glenda Jackson that dogged Hall for years: 'I do wish he'd stop pretending to be so bloody nice and simple and democratic when really he's very complicated and ambitious and a dictator. You have to have a boss. All right.'[43]

At the Royal Shakespeare Company, Hall had built his first great empire. He had created a vigorous permanent company; that company had forged an influential style of playing Shakespeare and speaking verse and had found a new audience for the theatre. When Hall took over, the classical theatre was considered moribund by many young people; now it was full of originality and excitement, and a whole generation of bright schoolchildren had learned to love Shakespeare at Stratford. A set of memorable productions bore his stamp. Of *The Wars of the Roses*, Irving Wardle wrote almost thirty years later that it was the greatest Shakespearian event in living memory. John Barton felt paralysed when asked to do *Twelfth Night* because he thought Hall's 1958 production could not be bettered. Hall had found the key to Harold Pinter's work. This had been accomplished with the help of actors and directors who surprised themselves by the quality of their work. He also had close relationships with colleagues like John Goodwin, the publicist, John Bury, the designer, and Michael Birkett, the factotum, whose greater loyalty was to Hall himself rather than the company. It was a brilliant achievement, unmatched by that of any theatrical impresario in the twentieth century – even Olivier's at the National Theatre.

But the permanent drain on Hall's energy was that there was never enough money for him to realise all his plans. The RSC always had to prove itself, which made the task of directing the company even more daunting and exhausting. Without Fordham Flower's loving encouragement, Hall might not have stuck it as long as he did, especially since there were distinguished governors who would not have been at all upset if he had left. With Flower gone, Hall was more exposed and more vulnerable.

Hall kept two of the letters he received after his resignation, both overflowing with emotion and affection. One was from Laurence Olivier, who began by congratulating him on the efficient way he had managed his departure. Olivier doubted whether he could do it as well himself. He mentioned that Tyrone Guthrie had been right – 'of course' – to say that no artistic director should stay more than three years because anything longer made life too hard for his successor.

I felt depressed, feeling that perhaps this lot of harness was bearable, but doubting if I had whatever it takes to break in a new lot. Perhaps my particular case, aye, and mission makes things a bit different. I hope so as I don't know what else to do. Dear, dear this letter is not intended to be about myself. I was not even supposed to be mentioned. It was only meant to bring you my joy for the joy that the change should bring you and my LAUD for the miracles you have worked, for the guts you have found to work them, and the dazzling brilliance with which you have coped with all. Our relationship has been one that others might have found difficult, but you have always made me believe that the great liking (somehow truer and more trustworthy than 'love' which is less precise and more fraught with impossible responsibilities, also somehow more treacherous, also too fucking hackney'd for words) was, together with the undoubtedly wholehearted admiration – somehow reciprocated. I did say, that is what you have made me believe. If it is not so, then don't tell me.

It was signed: 'Ever, Larry.'[44]

The second letter was from Peggy Ashcroft. 'I was deeply touched that you told me of your decision,' she wrote. 'As I think I said, it was partly a terrific shock but also a relief because I have long realised the strain you have been under – and finally Gordian knots *have* to be cut. You have achieved *so much* that both makes it harder to give up, but *should* also be some consolation and makes it *possible* to give it up. There is the RSC and *you* have made it. As you say, even if – which we pray won't happen – it has to disintegrate, it will never be a waste, for parts will flower. But I feel it *won't* and *shouldn't* come to an end. In whatever solution is found I think the operation should learn from your predicament (??) that should never be allowed to happen again, and that there should be some system of rotation and *not* resignation.'

Ashcroft, one of the stars who had inspired Hall's ambition to become a theatre director, added a postscript to this letter which runs around the margin of the last page: 'What I have never said is that 1960–1967 has been by far the most exciting time in *my* life in the theatre and that must go for many more – and that is entirely due to *YOU!*'[45] It is hard to conceive a greater compliment.

11

A Novice and Experimenter

'I have to admit to a great mistake'

Since he had forgotten to pack his razor when he went on holiday in 1966, Peter Hall started growing a beard. He almost stopped smoking a pipe, preferring Havana cigars instead. The boyish looks were fading; his beard hid a double chin – a hint of his addiction to Mars bars – and his hairline was beginning to recede. He had given up the Aston Martin and the Rolls-Royce and was driving, or being driven, rather, in a Range Rover. As he approached forty, Hall's reputation was established; his views were sought; he was confident enough not to dissemble about ambition and his taste for power. He had fought battles for state subsidies for the theatre and against state censorship of the theatre, and both had been won. Hall was a man of his time, a new time – the Sixties.

In London, Hall, his wife and children (there were now four, Lucy having been born in April 1969) lived in a glossy magazine world, which the dictates of fashion made black and white at the time. The floor of their flat at 18 Buckingham Street off the Strand was white vinyl, and it had white walls, a white ceiling, and white Saarinen dining-room chairs. The furnishing fabric was black leather. According to *Vogue*, Hall's stark modern phase began in 1964, when Leslie left Avoncliffe and bric-à-brac was banished. When the Halls bought a house in the country, it was not a period property, but a single-storey, flat-roofed brick house built in 1958 by the architect Lionel Brett (later Lord Esher). This was the family's principal residence: The Wall House, Mongewell Park, near Wallingford in Oxfordshire. Set in 18 acres, the house had six bedrooms; there was a heated swimming pool and a tennis court. The 38-foot drawing-room overlooked a four-acre lake.

Wallingford, situated between Stratford and London, and convenient for Heathrow, was intended as the office for Hall's movie business. Since it was in the country, a French couple was required to keep the house and do the driving. Jacky Hall, who acted as his secretary and provided the only service that did not cost Hall a lot of money, says they had nothing in the bank. But Hall did have prospects.

Work is a Four-Letter Word, Hall's début as a film director, was released in June 1968 to violently mixed notices. Alexander Walker in the *Evening Standard* declared the film 'a triumph' – the first underground film for mass audiences, in which David Warner 'acts with genius'. David Robinson in the *Financial Times* decided that Hall's début was 'disappointing'. Noting that experience in the theatre is often the least fitting background for a film director, Robinson damned the film with faint praise: 'It is at least likeable in [Hall] that he did not approach the new medium cautiously . . . but with the humility and reckless blindness to disaster of a novice and experimenter.'

Hall's second film was *Three into Two Won't Go* with a script by Edna O'Brien. This was a star vehicle, and Hall was not one of the stars. They were Rod Steiger, then forty-three, an Academy Award winner; Claire Bloom, who was his wife at the time; and Judy Geeson, who, at nineteen, played the third member of a ménage. Steiger took himself very seriously as an actor. As a former student of the Actors' Studio in New York, he liked to improvise, and Hall told visitors that his main duty as a director was to give Steiger plenty of rope: 'One must leave well alone,' he said. The fact was that he had no choice. Working with Steiger was a nightmare for Hall, and, although it paid well enough to make Wallingford feasible, the misery was not worth it in terms of his reputation as a film director. The distributors also decided that *Three into Two* wouldn't do; twenty-five years later Jacky Hall could still remember the disappointment of the phone call saying the film would not go on general release.

Hall cast someone he knew he could work with as the star of his third film. David Warner, with Ursula Andress to provide the looks and Stanley Baker and Patience Collier to do the character acting, appeared in *Perfect Friday*, the caper movie about a bank robbery. This time Hall's work was generally admired by the American critics. Only Vincent Canby in the *New York Times* wondered why he had bothered: 'Perhaps it has to do with the economics of moviemaking, with the type of movie that can be expected to make a profit on its investment, granted a certain minimum degree of quality . . . Within these very important limitations, Mr Hall has made an intelligent and quietly funny film.'

The film of *A Midsummer Night's Dream* had a cast that would have guaranteed success on the stage (Diana Rigg, Judi Dench, Helen Mirren, David Warner, Ian Holm), and when it was shown by CBS on its television network it received a nomination for an Emmy Award. But, as a film, it bombed. Hall commented later that he had been trying to discover whether Shakespeare was filmable: this film persuaded neither the actors nor the audience that he was. The actors had been overcome by the conditions and Hall had been too busy to concentrate properly on directing the film. 'Not a frightfully good film,' was David Brierley's view from inside the RSC.[1] Outside opinion was less generous: 'Frankly terrible on almost every conceivable level,' wrote John Russell Taylor in *The Times*. Since the plan to film *Macbeth* had not survived the stage performances, CBS cancelled the contract after the *Dream*. The RSC's future was not to be bound up with films, after all.

There were epic plans for a film of *Don Quixote*, with David Warner, to be made in Spain, and for a film of Aldous Huxley's *Brave New World*, but in the way of epic film projects, they died. While making *Perfect Friday*, Hall had struck up a friendship with the producer Dimitri de Grunwald, and together they set up Script Development Ltd, which was intended to give a group of English writers and directors more control over their work by providing packages for production companies. There was talk of a film written by Robert Bolt, with his wife Sarah Miles, to be directed by her brother Christopher, and with parts for Olivier and Richardson; but nothing came of that, nor of any other plans.

'We had many meetings, but we never achieved much. It just faded away,' says John Goodwin, who was its publicist.[2]

By 1971 Hall said that he had learned how to make films by making them.[3] He had not learned so well, however, as to become a bankable name in the film industry. Film directors judged that Hall was too wedded to a theatrical style of directing: rather than letting the camera tell the story, Hall always relied on the words. Christopher Morahan, who had worked for BBC television before joining Hall at the RSC, traced Hall's lack of visual taste back to the Cambridge humanist and poetical tradition; the development of character is regarded as more important than the presentation of spectacle, Morahan says.[4] But while failing to make a reputation as a film-maker, Hall was consolidating his standing in the opera world.

He had become a friend, in 1967, of the Earl of Drogheda, the chairman of the Board of the Royal Opera House (ROH), and, incidentally, of the *Financial Times*. Garrett Drogheda was intrigued by power and fascinated by Peter Hall. Drogheda and his wife had been invited to Avoncliffe for the opening of *Macbeth* (the shingles prevented that), and he and Jacky Hall were on recipe-swapping terms. The ROH had been anxious to arrange Hall's return to Covent Garden after *Moses and Aaron*, and *Aida* had been proposed, but Hall was not available. Now ambitious plans were afoot. In October 1967 Drogheda mentioned that Georg Solti was anxious to talk to Hall about a production of Richard Wagner's *Ring*. In March 1968 an inter-departmental memo specifies the dates for a Hall *Ring*. The first two parts, *Das Rheingold* and *Die Walküre*, would open in the autumn of 1970; the second two, *Siegfried* and *Götterdämmerung*, in June 1971; the whole cycle would be in the repertory by autumn 1971.[5] Planning was sufficiently detailed for it to be noted that Hall had refused to cast the two most important roles, Wotan and Brünnhilde, from Covent Garden's permanent company of British singers.

Solti, the music director, was due to leave in 1971, and when the young English conductor Colin Davis was chosen to succeed him, Drogheda arranged a meeting between Hall and Davis. They had dinner together at his house early in 1969: 'It was like love at first sight,' Drogheda said.[6] Davis had always wanted a theatre director at the Opera House, and here was one who understood the music as well. Hall found the conversation so stimulating that he compared this 'magical evening' to the night spent talking to Fordham Flower in Leningrad in 1958. Within days, Davis was making a partnership with Hall a condition of becoming music director. Hall's enthusiasm matched Davis's, and John Tooley, Webster's successor as general administrator, judged he was anxious to get a foot permanently in the Opera House. Hall's friends thought the idea of having an office and a secretary again was also a powerful incentive.

By March 1969, it was agreed that Hall would become artistic director in partnership with Davis, the music director. Hall committed himself to spending twenty-six weeks a year at the ROH when Davis took over, but he would be directing a number of productions before then. The first was intended to be a new opera by Sir Michael Tippett; then there were to be productions of Tchaikovsky, Wagner and Mozart. He quickly involved himself in repertory planning, and was invited to attend meetings of the Board's opera sub-committee.

By the end of 1969 Hall was talking confidently of bringing together Harold Pinter and Harrison Birtwistle for a new opera to be ready in 1972. In January 1970, Hall outlined the plans he had agreed with Davis and John Tooley. Besides Birtwistle, there would be work from a second contemporary British composer, Peter Maxwell Davies. Another idea was to engage the maverick television and film director Ken Russell to direct operas by Debussy and the Czech composer Martinu. Hall's note commented that the opera sub-committee would shortly be hearing from Davis about 'all these hair-raising ideas'. The note ended: 'Let battle commence.'[7] Hall was aware that this programme would upset the establishment members of the Covent Garden Board, and he clearly relished the idea.

In May 1970 Hall made his début at Glyndebourne, seventeen years after first discussing a job there with Carl Ebert. Glyndebourne had been founded by John Christie, who owned the house and built the theatre in 1934; the rural environment was not unlike Stratford's, and the happiness Hall found in the Sussex countryside was to affect his relationship with Covent Garden. Unlike London, there was no other business to be done there, and Glyndebourne encouraged and enabled artists to concentrate on the business at hand. Although he still tended to move restlessly from one place to another, Hall could have a room in the Christie house whenever he asked. Instead of turning lunchtime into a business meeting, Hall would slip away for a drink and a discussion about the morning's rehearsal with Moran Caplat, Glyndebourne's genial administrator, who, as John Christie grew older, and before George Christie felt ready to take over, was responsible for the working environment.[8]

Caplat's way of running an opera house suited Hall and John Bury, who came with Hall. He never set budgets for individual productions, believing that budgets were an irresistible temptation to spend all that there was in them, and probably more. Caplat put a cost on a whole season and then gave most money to the production that needed most. Since Hall already had a reputation for prodigality, this could have been a recipe for disaster. But Caplat's liberality was accompanied by an absolute rule: if scenery or props were ordered, they had to be used. This encouraged directors and designers to look at a model before spending real money. Caplat, a submariner during the war, was the captain of this ship and his rules were adhered to. One consequence of this was an absence of the extravagant waste of international opera houses like Covent Garden.

Raymond Leppard, a Cambridge contemporary who had been Hall's musical adviser at Stratford, was a missionary for early music long before it turned into a movement. He scoured Venetian libraries for the scores of seventeenth-century operas that had not been revived since their first performances. One of his most exciting rediscoveries was Pietro Francesco Cavalli, whose music had first been heard again in 1967 when Leppard conducted *L'Ormindo* at Glyndebourne. It was an intimate piece of the kind that worked well on Glyndebourne's stage, and when Leppard was asked to propose another Italian baroque opera, he came up with Cavalli's *La Calisto*, and suggested that Hall should direct it. Caplat hired Hall gladly.

Hall settled in at Glyndebourne comfortably and quickly. Wanting some 'animals' at the end of Act I, so that Calisto's transformation into a bear was not too arbitrary, he asked nicely, and got what he wanted. The cast was a good one, led by Ileana Cotrubas, to whom Hall had taken a great liking when they worked together on Covent Garden's *Magic Flute*, and by Janet Baker, with whom he established an instant bond. Glyndebourne's technical staff liked John Bury, and the designs were received as well as Hall's direction of the cast. Peter Heyworth in the *Observer* found *La Calisto* 'mercifully free of anachronistic camp';

John Warrack in the *Sunday Telegraph* described Hall's touch as deft and musical.

Noel Annan, who was a Provost of King's, Cambridge, when Hall was an undergraduate and who had become vice-chancellor of University College, London, wrote to Hall to say that the routs of satyrs and bevies of nymphs and swains that normally reminded him of dreadful masques they had seen together as undergraduates had been dazzling: 'Pastoral is the hardest thing in the world to do.'[9] Hall was delighted to have been understood; he told Annan that he had always believed that artificiality, done sincerely, could be remarkably full of meaning. But the most touching letter he received came from Janet Baker, whose role of Diana had been boldly extended to include the part normally sung by a castrato, of Jove disguised as Diana. She wrote to him: 'I emerged from Calisto a different person and a better performer . . . You give us such a wonderful sense of freedom; your sense of creating, moment by moment, is the most exciting way of working I have ever seen.'[10]

Anxious for more, Caplat signed Hall up for another baroque opera at the first available opportunity, but *The Return of Ulysses* by Monteverdi was two summers away. Hall's first commitment was still to the Royal Opera House, where he was due to direct two operas, *Eugene Onegin* and *Tristan und Isolde*. Hall established real rapport with Davis: 'There is enough common ground for us to fight like cats and dogs in total candour and honesty about what we're at.'[11] His relationships with the Board and the audience at Covent Garden were not so satisfying. Hall told them he was worried every time he went to Covent Garden because he always seemed to see the same people in the audience. Garrett Drogheda was still a friend, but he was also an irritatingly hands-on chairman of the Board, and the Board exercised real power. Hall's contract stated that final decisions rested with the opera sub-committee of the Board. Moreover, a clause in a non-contractual working agreement with Davis stated that any serious disagreement between them would be submitted to John Tooley for binding arbitration.[12] Hall was used to running his own show, and he had never before been asked to sign away artistic control. Tooley thought he seemed happy enough, but Jacky Hall knew how reluctant he had been to submit to another authority.

Hall and Davis had a number of precise ambitions. For example, they wanted to found a company of singers who would work together for three or four months a year. Hall, who was always in a hurry, grew anxious when nothing actually happened. But the only row was about opera in English. Hall was not dogmatic about it; whether an opera ought to be sung in English depended on the opera, but he thought it was 'potty' not to do *The Magic Flute* in English because of the quantity of spoken dialogue. He and Davis, supported by Tooley, thought the same was true of *The Marriage of Figaro* (in which they had cast an unknown New Zealander called Kiri Te Kanawa as the Countess). 'We thought we were not doing the right thing by the public, and, besides, we wanted to have the freedom of choice,' Hall said.[13]

Drogheda and his colleagues, already simmering about the prospect of Ken Russell and Martinu, began to boil. They felt that singing in English endangered Covent Garden's status as one of the world's top four opera houses. Lord Robbins, a good classical economist, wrote: 'Suppose your Figaro falls sick, where do you immediately find someone equally capable of performing in English rather than the original language?'[14] The argument was not daft, but it presented an administrative rather than an artistic problem. Hall and Davis doggedly fought their corner, and the Board gave way to *The Magic Flute* in English only after a long argument – on condition that all the singers agreed. Having won the battle with the Board, Hall and Davis then discovered, to their chagrin, that one of the singers – an Italian – refused to sing her part in English.

The Magic Flute was sung in Italian, but what Hall had resented most was the tone of the opposition. He scribbled a note to Drogheda before rehearsals one morning, saying that there had been no basic disagreement but 'Colin and I felt we were not wanted as policy-makers: – men, that is, whose convictions about such work are what the Board wants and supports.'[15] Throughout the winter, however, there was no suggestion that the breach was fatal. In March, Hall wrote to John Tooley suggesting that they should fix his and Colin Davis's dates for the next three or four years.

Eugene Onegin – which was sung in English, incidentally, with Cotrubas again in the leading role, and a vividly realistic set by Julia Trevelyan Oman – opened successfully in February; but the most controversial production in 1971 was Hall's *Tristan und Isolde*, which was also Solti's last production as music director. At the opera's climax, Hall ignored the libretto and reunited Tristan with

Isolde while he was still alive, instead of having her discover him when he had died. Moreover, the nearness of Tristan's death was dramatised by the gruesome way in which his guts spilled out after he tore the bandages off his wounds. This theatrical coup was heartily disliked, both inside and outside the Opera House. Drogheda lost his temper; Andrew Porter thought Hall's climax was 'cheap' and Hall got a taste of the vitriol from Harold Schonberg, who wrote in the *New York Times*: 'Peter Hall's ideas about opera are curious, fussy and ridiculous . . . the pip squeak posturings of a director determined to show his cleverness at the expense of music and action.'

What made Hall unhappiest, however, was the stage staff. He told Tooley that, technically, the first night of *Tristan* was the worst he had experienced in twenty years. One reason Tooley had been glad to have Hall at Covent Garden was because his colossal demands would stretch the stage staff, but they had not stretched far enough for Hall, who had begun to wonder whether they would ever get his work right, especially in revivals over which he would have only minimal control.

Tristan opened in the middle of June. Hall was due formally to take up his position at the Royal Opera in September; but by then he was gone. On 4 July Drogheda received what he described as the bitterest blow in sixteen years at the Opera House: a letter from Hall that began: 'I have to admit to a great mistake.'[16] The problem, Hall said, was that his two years in Covent Garden had shown him that a twenty-six-week commitment was not enough: it had to be all or nothing, and, since his discovery that he was not temperamentally suited to a repertory opera house, he had no heart for the future. 'The fault is mine and nobody else's.' He added that he was particularly sorry for the difficulties his resignation would cause Colin Davis, but still hoped they could do Wagner's *Ring* together.

Davis was sad and angry; Drogheda went berserk about an article in the *Sunday Times* in which criticisms of Covent Garden bore a remarkable resemblance to those Hall had expressed privately. The Arts Minister David Eccles, and Lord Goodman at the Arts Council, both tried to console Drogheda. Eccles wrote: '[Hall] never looked like a man to share a job, so I'm not surprised.'[17] Tooley had himself thought that Hall would pack his bags sooner or later, probably after a blazing row about production values. Since he had left sooner rather than later, their relations deteriorated fast, and Hall withdrew from *The Ring*. What irritated him most was the 'systematic dismantling' of his work, in revivals by other directors. Finally he wrote to Tooley that, while they should not behave like enemies in public, the partnership was, as far as he was concerned, ended.[18]

But the most interesting letter in the Covent Garden archive is Goodman's letter to Drogheda. He wrote on 14 July 1971:

> *I had sensed from a short conversation with Peter Hall that he was unhappy, but I think his own explanation is valid and truthful.*
>
> *I have a feeling that in the end it may be for the best that the release of Hall's remarkable talents for full theatrical employment is of no small advantage.*
>
> *You and I both know that opera is only in a very small degree theatre – but then we are both so wise that it is unreasonable to expect others to emulate us![19]*

Goodman gives no date for his 'short conversation' with Hall (it took place at Glyndebourne), but it was clearly before the resignation, and Goodman suggests that he told Hall of the coming vacancy at the National Theatre: 'I sounded him out; the response was immediate enthusiasm. In a sense we seduced him away from opera back to the theatre,' he wrote years later.[20] Soon after their Glyndebourne meeting, Goodman asked Hall to join him and his friend Sir Max Rayne for lunch. Rayne was due to take over the chairmanship of the National Theatre from Lord Chandos on 1 August, and felt he could not meet Hall until he had finally taken over, but it is clear from Goodman's letter to Drogheda that the fix was in: whether Hall knew it or not, and he has always vigorously denied that he did, Goodman already had Hall lined up as Olivier's successor. Tooley, who also remembers Hall saying to him that the National Theatre was boiling up again, was convinced that, before he left Covent Garden, Hall knew he was going to the National Theatre. Tooley assumed Hall had left them because he needed to be free to take the job.[21]

After Hall ceased to be director of the RSC he directed no Shakespeare at all and concentrated on new work by established playwrights. While at the RSC, he had shown an interest in Peter Shaffer's work, but Shaffer had preferred to see it done at the National Theatre. By the end of the 1970s, Shaffer was a successful commercial playwright who, like Pinter, normally remained loyal to the subsidised theatre, but there were exceptions and *The Battle of the Shrivings* was one of these. Hall directed this in 1970, at the Lyric Theatre in Shaftesbury Avenue. Had it been as successful as Shaffer's earlier work, like *The Royal Hunt of the Sun*, Hall would have earned a small fortune; that was one strong attraction of directing a Shaffer play in the West End. But *The Battle of the Shrivings* was the wrong Shaffer. The right Shaffer at that time was the artful thriller *Sleuth*, by Peter's brother Tony, which Hall had also been offered and turned down. The reviews were lukewarm, and *The Battle of the Shrivings* soon ended in defeat.

All Hall's other work in the straight theatre was done for the RSC – where he remained an associate director – and always in the Aldwych. There were two plays by Edward Albee (*A Delicate Balance* in 1969 and *All Over* in 1972), but neither was as successful or as good as *Who's Afraid of Virginia Woolf?* Harold Pinter, on the other hand, was on consistently good form. He and Hall wanted to follow their success together with *The Homecoming* with an evening of two short plays, *Landscape*, and *Silence*, but there was a problem. Pinter wrote to Hall early in 1968 to find out when they might be done: 'All things being equal, including that cunt the Lord Chamberlain, do I take it you still see December as a practical date?'[22]

The problem was the censor's refusal to license the complete text of the two plays: he objected to the use of 'bugger' and 'fuck all'. This was the Lord Chamberlain's last stand, and he was implacable. The plays were performed on the BBC Third Programme in 1968 uncut, but, unless changes were agreed they would not be seen on stage. Sir George Farmer, the RSC's chairman, intervened personally with Lord Cobbold, but permission was still withheld. 'It is clear that your conversation achieved a great deal, but I understand there remains one stumbling block,' Pinter wrote to Farmer in a vivid thank-you letter on 27 February 1968.

> As I believe you know, I am willing to cut the phrase 'fuck all' but I see no good reason to change the word 'bugger', as in the context in which it appears it is used as a noun not a verb. The phrase 'gloomy bugger' is, of course, very common and very mild (even affectionate) usage all over the country.
>
> As I hope you will agree, in LANDSCAPE, as in my previous work, I take care to choose my words pretty meticulously and, after further thought, I do remain of the view that there is no possible or proper alternative to the word 'bugger', as it is used in the play.

> *How childish the whole thing is, and what a pity one word is now*
> *between us and public performance.*[23]

The plays (including 'fuck all') were produced at the Aldwych
in July 1969 when the Lord Chamberlain's powers had finally
been dumped in history's dustbin as a result of the Theatres
Act, whose passage through the Commons was directed by
Roy Jenkins, the Home Secretary. *Landscape* was a two-hander
located securely in Pinter country: man and wife remembering,
and at cross purposes. Peggy Ashcroft made her début in a Pinter
play; Pinter himself liked the production's emphasis on simplicity,
economy and clarity. Indeed, a week after the plays opened Pinter
sent Hall a handwritten fan letter, which, like all Pinter's letters,
is full of flavour.

> *Dear Peter,*
> *It's about time I put it down on paper.*
> *What you've done for my two plays quite seals – if it needed sealing –*
> *which it didn't – our working relationship. It was sealed – now it is even*
> *more tightly sealed. When I think of the problems Silence presented on the*
> *page and the way you've surmounted them & given it full & proper life –*
> *I'm overwhelmed. I've watched you work with total admiration & have been*
> *& am deeply moved by your concern, scrupulousness and understanding.*
> *I've never known such a closeness of mind between myself and another*
> *director.*[24]

By the time Hall directed the next new play, *Old Times*, in the
summer of 1971, fewer people were afraid of Harold Pinter.
Audiences at Aldwych productions had stopped fretting about
what Pinter meant and had become more willing to sit back and
let the words pummel them. *Old Times*, with Pinter's wife Vivien
Merchant in the cast alongside Colin Blakely and Dorothy Tutin,
received very long and very respectful notices. When it opened
in New York three months later, the play caused more confusion,
which Pinter did nothing to dispel. He told the *New York Times*:
'For New York I did change a silence into a pause. It was a rewrite.
This silence was a pretty long silence. Now it's a short pause.' This
was not entirely a joke. Jacky Hall thought one of the reasons Hall
admired Pinter was his capacity for being certain he was right.

In 1972 money was finally found to film *The Homecoming*. They
made the movie at Shepperton Studios, and Hall later remembered
the party atmosphere created by re-encountering a great text.[25]

The film, released in the United States in November 1973, made modest money for Hall, but he could sense that, for him, the big-time in Hollywood was receding. MGM had turned down his latest project. His film work from now on was to be on a small scale.

Two of the projects that preoccupied Hall in the last year of his interlude as a freelance director reveal the tension between the desire to enjoy the glitter and the money of international showbusiness, and the wish to remain faithful to his own view of himself and his art. On the one hand, Hall was a theatrical mogul, directing the most expensive musical ever produced on Broadway. On the other, he was a producer/director floundering in a bid to raise less than a quarter of a million pounds to make a film about the characters and countryside of his boyhood.

Via Galactica was the musical chosen to open the most modern, up-to-date theatre in the world, the Leon Uris (named after a property developer). It is hard to say what *Via Galactica* was about, but it was by Gail MacDermot, who had written the music for *Hair*, the quintessential Sixties musical hit, and it did not suffer from any lack of commitment from Hall. To direct it, he spent three months in New York with his family, the longest consecutive period he had spent outside England since his national service. John Bury was at his side.

Bury was pleased by the early stages of rehearsal. So was MacDermot, who thought the show would run and run. Hall's *Via Galactica* depended on complicated stage machinery powered by hydraulics, and its many visual images were produced by two super-projectors. As rehearsals went on, though, and more mechanics went into it, the heart went out of it. 'As it got more complicated, it fell apart. I should have said "just leave it", but I wasn't strong enough,' says Bury, who can recall no more spectacular failure during their long collaboration.[26] *Via Galactica* closed after five days. Since it was the most expensive musical ever produced, it was also the costliest flop. Hall said that if you can't have a monumental success, you may as well have a monumental failure, but he did not mean it.[27] He had failed to become a bankable film director; now he seemed to have lost the chance of becoming a fashionable director of lucrative Broadway musicals.

Money was also the problem with Hall's plan to film *Akenfield*, Ronald Blythe's book about a Suffolk village. Blythe had been excited to get a letter from Hall in the summer of 1969, shortly after the book's publication.[28] Since their backgrounds were similar, he was flattered that Hall should recognise his Suffolk in *Akenfield*. Hall told him, when they met, that at his parents' fortieth wedding anniversary that summer he had heard the clamour of Suffolk voices, and had realised that he no longer belonged to his close family. It made him wonder who he was, and when he read *Akenfield* he had heard the voice of his grandfather, and had wept. That experience inspired him to make a film about a passion for rural Suffolk, and about the need to escape from it.

Blythe started work on a story outline while Hall looked for the money. Rex Pyke, a film editor, joined them as co-producer, and they established a company called Angle Films. Together they gambled on being able to get local Suffolk people to improvise from a rough script. Unfortunately, this was a risk that the film business did not wish to share, and the only substantial investor was London Weekend Television, which put up £40,000. When the sum they raised still fell short of the budget, the crew took wage cuts in return for a share of the profits.

Good ideas – like getting Benjamin Britten, another Suffolk man, to write the score – fell through; he was writing *Death in Venice* at the time. As he prepared to cast the film, Hall worried that there would not be enough time to do the filming in the spring and summer of 1973, and thought of saying no. But saying no to work was no longer part of his vocabulary.

He found his leading female character at a flower show. Blythe remembers the scene vividly. She was called Peggy Cole and her husband worked on the roads. They had been talking about gardening in the churchyard, and when Hall asked if she would help them, she first thought he was talking about making the tea. Blythe played the vicar, and Reg Hall was thought to be well cast as the local policeman. A field was purchased and a crop of corn grown according to traditional methods. Blythe says that Hall seemed quite at home; he loved the landscape. But he never tried to be matey: 'He was not like us at all.' When they first met, Blythe had not realised that Hall saw *Akenfield* as autobiography, but during the filming Blythe watched him turning it slightly towards the personal experience of his own sense of loss at being forced to leave Suffolk. Hall himself said *Akenfield* was the most autobiographical work he had ever done.

*   *   *

Goodman arranged the promised lunch with Hall and Max Rayne in August 1971, and they duly asked Hall if he would succeed Laurence Olivier as director of the National Theatre. Hall remembers his doubts ('The idea horrified yet also attracted me').[29] Jacky Hall remembers his anticipation and sense of relief. 'When he first came back from that lunch I hadn't seen him so ebullient since the early days at Stratford. They overwhelmingly wanted him, and said he could have *carte blanche*. It was a tremendous relief that they had wooed him, and he was thrilled. He couldn't wait to get there. The light of battle in his eyes was lit again. The flame was burning.'[30]

Goodman and Rayne took so long to confirm their offer that Hall had to nudge them. One of their problems, of course, was that they had not informed Olivier of their decision to ask Hall to succeed him. Olivier had always known he would find it difficult to appoint a successor: no one had told him he would not even be consulted.

But that was a problem for the future. For the present, Hall was re-establishing himself in style in London. While still at Stratford, the Halls' name had gone down on the waiting list for the City of London's new skyscraper apartments at the Barbican, but because of legendary building delays, these were not finally allocated until 1972. Though the Halls' flat was not as high as he had wanted, they furnished it, and were about to move in when a vacancy occurred in a three-storey penthouse flat on the thirty-ninth floor. Hall insisted they should take that. At £4,800 a year, the rent was not cheap, and there was another £700 for the roof garden, plus service charges, but Edward and Lucy were enrolled at Prior Weston, the fashionable local state primary school. The Barbican penthouse flat gave him enormous pleasure. Jacky Hall recalls Hall saying that it represented his escape from his working-class childhood.

Not quite; there was Wallingford as well. In fact, Hall had many of the appurtenances of an English gentleman – homes in London and the country, a wife, four children, a dog, a Range Rover, and a position of some substance in the establishment. He was forty-three, and while the confident way in which he exercised authority had made enemies, he had many devoted and loyal friends in the theatre. He was respected by artists, and held in affection by theatre- and opera-goers because of all that he had made available to them. Peter Hall was a success.

12

Début at the National

'You may well find him an empire-builder'

From 1963 the National Theatre's offices had been located in a long hut behind a dour row of council houses on Aquinas Street, lying between the Old Vic and the site of the new South Bank theatre. The executive offices opened on to a single corridor at the end of which there was a rehearsal room; the roof leaked and the hut was intolerably hot in the summer. But Jonathan Miller thought it was just the right size, and remembers it fondly: 'The theatre is a companionable institution, and Aquinas Street encouraged playfulness and conviviality,' says Miller.[1]

During Olivier's decade at the National Theatre, Aquinas Street had been the seat of his court. At the heart of it were his wife, Joan Plowright, and Kenneth Tynan, the former critic, now literary manager, who enjoyed a role as *éminence grise*. The director John Dexter, recruited from the Royal Court, joined the court, then quit, and then came back. By the early 1970s Miller and his fellow-director, Michael Blakemore, had also joined the group, and the intimate environment bred fierce loyalties and strong feelings. To some of its members, Peter Hall seemed a shameless usurper.

The succession had become an issue in 1970, after Olivier suffered a bad bout of illness. His solution was to promote Joan Plowright to associate director so that he might groom

her as his successor. Lord Chandos treated this idea with such
contempt that Olivier refused to speak to him, and the feud
between the chairman and the director was resolved only by
the enforced retirement of the chairman.[2] Chandos's successor
was a protégé of Lord Goodman's, Sir Max Rayne, whose interest
in the arts (he collected paintings) had secured him a place on
the National Theatre Board in 1970. Goodman – still chairman of
the Arts Council – identified this rich, dapper, well-mannered,
well-connected-by-marriage property developer as the right man
to ease the company into its new building – especially as its
construction was already presenting problems.

When Rayne took over, Olivier formally offered him his resignation, which Rayne regarded as a courtesy, telling Olivier that it
was everyone's desire that he should lead the company into the
new building. That was scheduled for 1974, if everything went
to plan. At the same time, Rayne decided that Olivier was in no
physical condition to carry on for long, and that he must find
a successor. Hearing of Olivier's plan to promote his wife, he
decided to do without Olivier's help in finding one. In the letter
he wrote to Hall when he left the RSC in 1968, Olivier wondered
whether he would be able to handle his succession as skilfully
as Hall had handed over to Nunn. He never had the chance to
find out.

The one place Rayne did not bother to look for a successor was
in the National Theatre itself: 'I made a lot of inquiries personally
and it was very clear that the only serious candidate was Peter
Hall,' he said after he had retired as chairman.[3] Goodman had
pointed Rayne in Hall's direction, and as soon as Rayne took over
the chairmanship, on 1 August 1971, he lunched with the pair of
them. Rayne's recollection is that at the lunch he asked Hall if he
might be available. Hall's is that he was, in fact, offered the job,
and that he told Rayne his acceptance was conditional on Olivier's
approval. Rayne asked Hall not to mention the proposal to Olivier
until he had spoken to Olivier himself. Hall agreed, unaware that
this conversation would not take place for seven months.

Meanwhile, Rayne consulted his fellow board members. Though
it was true that Hall was the only serious candidate for the
job, Binkie Beaumont had reservations. John Mortimer remembers Beaumont's saying that Hall's trouble was he thought he
could direct three plays on the motorway between Stratford
and London.[4] Victor Mishcon, the solicitor and local London

politician who was already a fixture on the Board, vividly recalled Beaumont's assessment of Hall more than twenty years later: 'He is imaginative and immensely energetic, but you may well find him an empire-builder,' Beaumont had said.[5]

During the winter of 1971–2, Olivier was also thinking about his successor. He mentioned the subject to Richard Attenborough and to Richard Burton, before finally deciding that Michael Blakemore was his man. Blakemore says now that he never knew that he was Olivier's choice, but during that winter he had directed one of the finest performances of Olivier's career, as James Tyrone, the bitter old actor in Eugene O'Neill's *Long Day's Journey into Night*.[6] With his performance, Olivier heroically revived the reputation of the National Theatre after a dismal run of failures, which had resulted in a bad loss for the year. This loss had further convinced Rayne that the company was being badly run, and only he could be trusted to find the successor. When Rayne failed to respond to the idea of Blakemore, whom he knew hardly at all, Olivier proposed that a triumvirate should be formed, consisting of Blakemore, Tynan and Plowright. Rayne dismissed the idea with no less contempt than Chandos had done: 'It was totally unrealistic,' he said twenty years later.

Hall did not keep the news of Rayne's invitation to himself. Trevor Nunn was among the first to find out, during a long session at Wallingford.[7] He was shocked. He had never ceased to nurture the idea that Hall would return to the RSC as director; even when Hall became artistic director of the Royal Opera House, Nunn saw no reason in principle why Hall should not do both jobs. He and Hall discussed Rayne's offer on a number of occasions. There are two accounts and two dates for one of these discussions, when the two of them met with David Brierley in his office in Stratford. In Hall's diaries, it takes place on 15 April 1972; in Nunn's memory it happened in the late autumn of 1971. He remembers that, even after dusk, no one switched on the light; the three of them saw each other in silhouette, and they were all crying. In Nunn's account, they were crying because Hall had just outlined the reasons why he would take the directorship of the National Theatre rather than returning to Stratford. Hall believed they understood his decision. Nunn says their reactions were clouded – his by disappointment and a sense of betrayal; Hall's because it was the end of an epoch for him, and by a sense of guilt.

Hall also told Peggy Ashcroft, because if he was going to the

National Theatre, he wanted her to go with him. 'Poor Peg was caught in the middle,' says Nunn. Her first reaction was that Hall was betraying the 'Co' – her name for the RSC – though she eventually relented. But the conversations remained theoretical until Hall heard again from Rayne, and throughout the winter there was no more news.

The first hint of trouble ahead came when Hall told his agent, Laurence Evans of International Creative Management, about Rayne's offer. Evans, who was also Olivier's agent, was outraged by Rayne's secretive behaviour, and announced that if Olivier was not told what was happening behind his back when he returned in ten days' time from filming in Rome, Evans would tell Olivier himself.

Rayne's explanation was that he had thought it right to delay until Olivier had finished the run of *Long Day's Journey*, and that Olivier had then left for Rome before a date could be fixed. He and Olivier finally met on 24 March 1972, when Rayne announced that he had consulted the Board, and that their choice as successor was Hall. But only, Rayne added diplomatically, if Olivier were completely happy with the idea. Rayne recalls that Olivier expressed mixed feelings about leaving the job, but that he immediately telephoned Hall to welcome his appointment. Olivier's recollection is that Rayne gave him six months' formal notice, and that two things shocked him: the lack of consultation, and Hall's willingness to take the job. 'I had always thought Stratford would be his Ultima Thule, as the National Theatre was mine. I felt flattered.'[8]

Hall's meeting with Olivier on 27 March is the subject of the first entry in Hall's published diaries, the sign of the start of a new, and remarkably well documented, era for him. He noted that Olivier was upset, that his feelings were ambiguous, and he foresaw that the interregnum would be 'very difficult'.[9] Olivier was also afraid that the press would reveal the news before the official announcement, and he was quite right. The story leaked to the *Observer*, which published it as the lead item in its gossip column on 9 April.

First reactions were calm. Nicholas de Jongh in the *Guardian* wrote: '[Hall] is a pleasant man and it has been all wine and roses, with little bloodletting. He is at his finest as administrator and begetter of schemes: in this field he is without equal.' Within two days, however, the headline on the *Evening Standard*'s front page read: ASTONISHING TURMOIL AT THE NATIONAL. The emotional temperature was rising fast. Privately, Olivier had complained bitterly to Rayne about his secrecy, and accused him of bad manners. He had been treated shoddily, he said. Publicly, Kenneth Tynan stated that he and his colleagues felt that for the Board to take a decision of this magnitude without consulting the artistic executive was 'rather reckless behaviour'. When he adressed the company on 10 April, Olivier announced that Hall's appointment was not fixed and that he himself would be staying on until the move into the South Bank. By suggesting that the succession was not a foregone conclusion, these remarks gave his senior colleagues the impression that they might still impose their own conditions on Hall's appointment.

Dispassionate accounts of the turbulence created by Hall's appointment are hard to come by. The minutes of the National Theatre Board (written by Hall's old acquaintance, Yolande Bird) offer as cool an account as can be found, and even that dry record of the meeting of 18 April cannot disguise the indignation of Olivier and his close colleagues.

This meeting was specially called in response to fevered reports in the newspapers. They had, Olivier said, alarmed the company and the whole organisation. Rayne replied that it was most unfortunate that the press had become involved at all. It is clear from the minute that he felt on the defensive: he had, he said, maintained the closest liaison with members of the Board about his conversations with Peter Hall, and he had informed Olivier at the earliest opportunity prior to embarking on any detailed negotiations with Hall. (Both statements are strictly true and still somewhat misleading.) A definitive decision had been delayed until Olivier had finished *Long Day's Journey*, he added, and it was his clear impression that Olivier was 'entirely happy regarding the choice'.[10]

Olivier did not deny this, but he commented sharply that he felt he had been presented with a *fait accompli*. Rayne's style of chairmanship was to defuse any controversy before it surfaced at a board meeting, but it failed him on this occasion. He had agreed that Olivier's senior colleagues should make their case to the Board, and at this point Michael Blakemore, Kenneth Tynan and Frank Dunlop, the director of the Young Vic, joined the meeting.

Tynan, as spokesman, declared that the Board had been precipitate in its actions, and that its failure to consult the executive had given the public the impression that the National Theatre was moribund. In consequence, members of the company were cynical and demoralised. Tynan said that, for instance, he knew his views were shared by John Dexter. The minutes do not include what Tynan said about the RSC, but in his biography, his wife, Kathleen Tynan records – from the notes he took to the meeting – his saying: 'We are the Cavaliers, Stratford the Roundheads – with the emphasis on analytical intelligence and textual clarity. Under Peter Hall the country would have two Roundhead theatres.'[11] (This makes sense of an intervention by Olivier later in the meeting that was recorded in the minutes: '[Lord Olivier] said his personal fears had been considerably allayed when Mr Hall had assured him that, in his opinion, the National Theatre and the Royal Shakespeare Company should have completely different characters.')

Finally, Tynan made a series of proposals designed to alter the balance of power between the Board and the artistic excecutive. These were as follows:

1. Associate directors and the head of the literary department should attend Board meetings.
2. Assurances should be given that Mr Hall's connections with the RSC would be severed.
3. The present artistic policy would be continued and senior executives should be offered three-year contracts.
4. The executive should be consulted about the press release announcing Hall's appointment.

Tynan also proposed that a deputy director should be appointed to take charge when the director was away, and recommended Blakemore for the job. Tynan's colleagues concentrated on attacking the method by which Hall been appointed rather than the selection itself. Blakemore deplored the undignified haste and secrecy. Dunlop, who was also perturbed by the way the appointment had been made, did add that he saw no alternative candidate to Hall.

After the trio left the meeting, the minute records Olivier's opposition to the idea of associate directors' attending board meetings: 'It was very embarrassing if artistic decisions should be taken at a meeting of which he could not be present.' Finally, Rayne reiterated that his previous discussions with Hall had been directed to ascertaining his availability, a statement that would have come as news to Peter Hall. His appointment was ratified at that meeting, eight months after he had first learned that the National Theatre job was his for the taking.

Hall's 'detailed' negotiations with Rayne went well. His salary was set at £20,000 a year, with annual increases related to the retail price index, plus a generous contribution to the rent of his Barbican flat, and a £500-a-year car allowance. This was for Hall's 'full-time, but not exclusive' services. Hall also won some concessions that eroded the Board's power and increased his own. Chandos's Board had the power to appoint associate directors without the approval of the director. Rayne's Board surrendered that right. Chandos's Board had unilaterally banned productions such as *Spring Awakening*; Rayne's Board was to give the director as much freedom as possible, except in cases where blasphemy, obscenity and *lèse-majesté* were concerned. Hall added his own coda to this: if the Board stopped him doing a play once, he would stay; twice, and he would resign.

Tynan, who called the choice of Olivier's successor 'the most important decision in the history of the English theatre', never looked like being reconciled to the new regime.[12] Hall told the Board late in 1972 that his literary manager should have power plus responsibility, the implication being that Tynan had the former but not the latter. But the two had already agreed that they would not get on, 'both being so good at politicking; both with such strong ideas,' Tynan's diary reports Hall as saying. Before he left the National Theatre, Tynan learned that on 10 July the Board had rejected all the proposals he had put to them. Even John Dexter dissociated himself from them, writing personally to the Board to say that Hall was the ideal man for the job.

Hall and Olivier had agreed to work in partnership to begin with, and Olivier said this went 'easily and happily'. But under his compliant veneer, Olivier was convinced that he had been betrayed by Sir Max Rayne, just as he had been by Lord Esher who sacked him and Ralph Richardson from the artistic directorship of the Old Vic in 1948. After Hall formally took over, on 1 November 1973, Olivier's apearances in the National Theatre grew rare. He did turn up for the royal opening of the South Bank, and, years later, for his eightieth-birthday celebration, but he gave up the honorary title of president in 1975 because, he said, it gave the impression that he knew what was happening at the National, when, in fact, he was in the dark. Before long, the language being used by Olivier's admirers to describe Hall's appointment had become extravagant and emotional. Robert Bolt described the transfer of power as 'a moral outrage', and Jonathan Miller talked of a 'putsch'. This was the justification for regarding Hall as a usurper.

The choosing of Olivier's successor had been mishandled, but that was Rayne's doing, not Hall's; Hall had behaved properly throughout. None the less, he was about to get his share of the opprobrium for another matter, and this time it was entirely deserved. Three days before Olivier reported to the Board that he had Hall's assurance that the National Theatre and the RSC should be entirely different in character, Hall reported that he had secretly begun to talk about a merger between the two.

Whenever it was that the tearful meeting with Nunn and David Brierley took place, it seems certain that the idea of amalgamation was first discussed on 15 April 1972. The idea was that, with limited government money available to subsidise two companies, there were economies to be had by rationalising their activities. Since the costs of transferring productions from Stratford to the Aldwych were high, Nunn could see the advantage of a six-month RSC season in the Lyttelton, with some of Stratford's small-house shows transferring to the studio theatre in the new National Theatre. 'Once I realised Peter was serious, I did quite a lot of work,' says Nunn. Both assumed that Hall would be the supremo; Nunn had no objections to that. 'We were driven back to the idea for emotional and artistic reasons,' Hall said twenty years later.

On 21 July 1972, over lunch, Hall spoke of the plan to Arnold Goodman, who was overjoyed at the prospect. In October, Hall heard from David Brierley that Stratford's executive council was not keen on the idea; they thought Hall was empire-building. At the National, however, Olivier's first reaction to the proposals was unaccountably sympathetic, and he added his name to a draft paper on the NT/RSC merger plan in February 1973. By the end of March, though, Hall was wondering whether Nunn would push the plan hard enough.

The first person to get cold feet, as it turned out, was Goodman, who had sensed opposition among his establishment cronies: they suspected Hall of empire-building too. Goodman's advice was that Hall should forget the idea for three years, which caused him to doubt the plan himself. According to his diaries, he and John Goodwin decided to leak news of the merger discussions; Hall confessed that he rather hoped that public opposition would put an end to them.[13] The story appeared in the *Daily Telegraph*. (Peter Brook identified Hall as the source of the leak immediately.)

Only as a result of the leak did Hall's associate directors at the National Theatre finally learn of the merger talks, and none of them was in favour. 'He was shame-faced when he confessed it to us, like a naughty boy,' says Michael Blakemore, who did not look forward to being gazumped by Trevor Nunn. 'It was playing with our futures; it was disgraceful,' Blakemore said years later. It soon became clear that Hall's Board was unenthusiastic too. When the merger was first discussed openly on 14 May 1973, over a year after it had been conceived, the minutes record Hall's saying that instead of the the National and the RSC having distinctive policies, as in the early 1960s: 'Images and issues were becoming blurred'.[14] The RSC, Hall actually said, was prepared for a closer association than he was himself, but the talks should continue, and the RSC could and should be given house-room in the new Lyttelton Theatre when it opened on the South Bank.

Hall's diary for 15 May records that Olivier then tried to torpedo the plan, but that Rayne saved the day by smoothing the passage of a proposal that the talks should continue. The minutes reveal a less positive outcome, however: 'The Board agreed that, while a merger between the RSC and the National Theatre was undesirable, talks should continue along the lines indicated by Mr Hall.' This sounds as if the Board were humouring their new director; they were clearly offering him no encouragement.

Reaction elsewhere was less tolerant. Meeting the Arts Council's Drama Panel in July, Hall was shocked by the cold reception they gave him. He reported to the Board the panel's grave reservations about the merger, and added that he had found the general mood in the profession remarkably unsympathetic to the National Theatre. Many panel members worked in the provinces and feared that the National would steal their best people and bid up the price of skilled labour. (The concern was not confined to the provinces; the Nottingham Playhouse cried foul when Hall hired Peter Stevens, its general administrator, but the RSC was not much better pleased when Hall persuaded his old friend and publicist, John Goodwin, to transfer his allegiance to the National.)

At the end of September, Hall and Nunn wrote to the Arts Council to confirm that their merger was a non-runner; they added that they hoped the Arts Council would conjure up enough subsidy to enable the companies to operate independently. There the episode ended, but it had raised questions about Hall's judgement which had not existed before. Hugh Willatt, the secretary-general of the Arts Council, reminded him that together they had sweated blood to create two national companies, and said he for one did not propose to stand idly by while two were reduced to one.[15] Hall rested his case on the improbability of the government's providing enough money to run the RSC in the Barbican and the National Theatre on the South Bank; yet he himself had once been the author of the bold policy of standing firm and shaming the government into providing the money for a National Theatre and an RSC. But it is hard to resist the conclusion that the lure, for Hall, had been the theatrical empire he would have controlled, just as Binkie Beaumont had forecast. Whatever the reason, his friends were no more sympathetic to the idea than his enemies, and it had made him more of the latter. The abortive merger plan was not a good start to his term at the National, and Hall knew it. By August 1973, he had already decided that the merger was 'one of the silliest ideas I have ever been seduced by'.[16] (Nunn never recanted and, long after the event, commented: 'The idea was not as daft as all that.')

Although Hall was paid more than his counterparts at the RSC and the Royal Opera House, he was constantly short of money. Living beyond his means in London and Wallingford, he never really had enough time to enjoy his expensive possessions. But money was not merely a nagging worry. Because it eventually led to rebellion and rout, Hall's habitual need for it had a profound effect on his standing at the National Theatre.

Akenfield was an anxiety for two solid years. Through Angle Films, Hall and the producer Rex Pyke had borrowed just enough money to complete the filming in Suffolk and the editing in London, and the outlook looked promising. *Akenfield* was chosen to open the London Film Festival in November 1974, though it could not be screened generally because London Weekend Television's investment in the film gave it the right to show it first to the general public. When *Akenfield* was televised the following January, the *TV Times* ingeniously printed a ticket on its cover: 'Take your seat for a world première in your own home,' it said. The television ratings delighted LWT, but when the film opened, first at a small cinema in London and then at eleven provincial cinemas, the audience stayed at home. The reviews were good on the whole ('a masterpiece' – Valerie Jenkins, *Evening Standard*) – but not good enough to bring out the cinema audience. There was no money to publicise the film when it went out of London, and the finances were in ruins. When financial disaster threatened, LWT took over responsibility for distribution. Hall had gambled, lost, and been bailed out. Not everyone escaped scot-free, however. The annual report for Angle Films at 31 July 1976 showed that, while *Akenfield* had cost £145,932 to produce, net liabilities amounted to £167,180, and that was after some of the creditors had accepted a settlement of 50p in the pound. The company was bankrupt, and *Akenfield* was a small cloud hanging over Hall's head for years. (The Department of Social Security finally took the company to bankruptcy court, where Angle Films was formally wound up on 24 May 1989.)[17]

Before *Akenfield* was completed, Hall took the part of a newspaper editor in a film entitled *The Pedestrian* made by Maximilian Schell in Munich in 1973. Hall had not acted for twenty-one years, and rediscovered the agony of learning lines. It taught him humility, he said, and the £5,000 fee came in handy too. His performance so impressed the great Italian director Michelangelo Antonioni that he offered Hall a leading part in his next film in 1974, but that was a job too far, even for Hall. His thirst for income, did, however, lead him to accept a commission that dogged him for years. Sandersons, the wallpaper manufacturer, planned an advertising campaign in which they associated their expensive product with the good taste of well-known figures from the arts, like Kingsley Amis and Peter Hall. The catchline was always the same: 'Very Peter Hall, Very Sandersons' (or whoever the case might be). Hall sensed that he was selling himself to the wrong buyer when the photograph was being taken in Wallingford, but he accepted partly because Jacky Hall was keen to get new curtains for the long picture-window at Wallingford, which would come on top of the fee. A net curtain across the window looked pretty and preserved her privacy during the day, but the family budget would not stretch to the kind of curtains Jacky wanted to stop passers-by looking in after dark, which were heavy, plain raw silk. 'I begged him to do it so I wouldn't be frightened at night when I was on my own,' she now says.[18]

When the advertisement appeared in October 1975 it turned Hall into a figure of ridicule. John Dexter describes a night spent drinking with Olivier in New York 'moaning about Mr Sanderson Hall',[19] and Clive James, the *Observer*'s television critic, found the joke irresistible when he reviewed Hall's début as a television presenter:

> The new Aquarius (LWT) is very Peter Hall, very Sanderson. With a distinctly royal air (very Peter Hall, very Sandringham) the show's new moderator hands down instruction to the natives (very Peter Hall, very Sanders of the River) concerning the contents of his sack of cultural goodies (very Peter Hall, very Santa Claus), revealing himself the while as perhaps deficient in humour (very Peter Hall, very sanctimonious) yet tireless in plugging the National Theatre (very Peter Hall, very sandwich man).

In time, Jacky Hall, seeing how the opposition seized on the Sandersons advertisement as an example of Hall's venality, regretted that she had pressed him in the first place. As a bank manager's daughter, she realised that they had not been living sensibly, and she knew that he had taken on the Sanderson advertisement to meet the bills.

Hall had chosen a bad time to maximise his income. In the mid-1970s, Britain and the rest of the West were staggering from one economic crisis to the next. Inflation, which had begun to rise in the early years of the decade, took off when the oil price quadrupled after the Yom Kippur War in 1973. Amid the chaos, Labour was re-elected in 1974, and Harold Wilson reoccupied Downing Street without having any clear idea of what he wanted to do there. Labour was no better at controlling the economy than the Tories had been; expensive wage settlements with the miners and the railwaymen led to a pattern of wage bargaining in which any claim below 20 per cent looked wimpish. The success of militant action caused a sharp turn to the left in the trade unions, and unofficial strikes called by left-wing shop stewards became part of the British way of life. Accompanying this militancy was a tide of envy tinged with puritanism that sought out, spotlit and disparaged any evidence of greed, especially in organisations like the National Theatre that relied on state subsidy.

Turmoil and uncertainty began to fuel significant shifts in social attitudes, and, as often happens, early indications of this could be spotted in the arts. Because the old political system had failed to provide long-term stability, its institutions were becoming suspect, and the NT was one of them. Hall first noticed this in the summer of 1973 when he was mauled by the Arts Council's Drama Panel. Opposition to the National Theatre was based partly on its size. At the moment when small was becoming beautiful, a concrete building with three auditoriums, a long river frontage and a big subsidy was a soft target.

The *Aquarius* programme mocked by Clive James was LWT's arts magazine, and Hall had been asked to present it by Cyril Bennett, LWT's programme controller, who had been the angel of *Akenfield*. There would be twenty-two episodes annually, and the idea was that it would involve Hall in one day's work a week. When he told the Board of his intention to take the job, Hall reassured them that the time given to television would not make inroads into his NT activities.[20] During the summer of 1975, when Hall was in Greece for LWT making a film about Epidaurus with Denys Lasdun, the architect of the National Theatre, or in Paris interviewing Peter Brook, this grew hard to believe. After Hall became director at Stratford in 1960, he had done no freelance work until 1965. His doing *Aquarius* within a couple of years of becoming director of the National Theatre made some of his closest associates suspect his commitment. When canvassed, Michael Blakemore, Jonathan Miller, Michael Birkett and John Schlesinger, among the associate directors, expressed misgivings. But Hall needed the money – an extra £10,000 to £12,000 a year, according to his accountant.[21]

About the work itself on *Aquarius*, Peter Forster, who was hard to please, wrote in the *Evening Standard* that Hall 'is a brilliant natural teacher, a fluent man of great charm and wide knowledge. LWT could hardly have chosen better.' But Hall was not comfortable on television, and was mildly disdainful of the exuberant showbiz contributions of Russell Harty. Hall appeared earnest, in the manner of an adult-education lecturer who had learned his trade in the RAF, when what *Aquarius* really required was a silky front-man like Humphrey Burton, who came before him, or Melvyn Bragg, who came after. But it was not the way Hall did *Aquarius* that provoked criticism, it was the money he earned from it, and the time it took.

Hall asked Harold Pinter to become an associate director of the

National Theatre in a taxi on the way back from a day's filming
of *The Homecoming* in January 1973. In 1972 Hall and Olivier were
co-directors, and although this position remained unchanged for
most of 1973, he had started to select his own team. John Bury
was the associate director in charge of design; John Goodwin was
brought in as publicist from the RSC at the end of 1973, though
not without misgivings: he feared the National was going to be –
had to be – an organisation run by committees. Michael Kustow,
another Stratford veteran, also joined in 1973, as the man who
brought foreign companies to the National, and eventually as
the organiser of the pre-performance talks known as platform
performances. Hall's old university chum Michael Birkett joined
later, in 1975, with the title of deputy director and the role of
fixer and picker-up of pieces.

When John Dexter left the NT for New York (to be director
of productions at the Metropolitan Opera), his place was taken
by John Schlesinger, who had worked with Hall at Stratford
before becoming a Hollywood film director (he made *Midnight
Cowboy*). Olivier's attendances fell off sharply after he ceased to
be co-director in November 1973. Paddy Donnell was replaced as
general administrator by Peter Stevens, a talented administrator
from the Haymarket Theatre, Leicester, who had written to Hall
asking if there was a job for him at the NT.

Accounts vary about the style of Hall's early years at the
National. Pinter thought they were exciting. After April 1974,
the associate directors met once a fortnight in Hall's flat in the
Barbican. 'There was lots of food and drink, and we really talked
about what we were going to do. We used to have a wonderful
time,' Pinter recollected later.[22] But John Dexter, writing to Doris
Lessing in October 1975, said: 'Whatever the faults of the previous
establishment, at least it was run on fairly humane lines. Now it is
a kind of laughter and tears factory with not much regard for the
people working in it. I don't think the new director has yet learnt
the names of the stage staff and in some cases not even bothered
to learn the names of the company below the title.'[23]

The first public outbreak of serious disenchantment with Hall's
National Theatre was on 15 October 1974, when *The Times* printed
a letter from Oscar Lewenstein from the Royal Court and thir-
teen other theatre directors, including luminaries like Lindsay
Anderson and Joan Littlewood, and promising young men like
Richard Eyre from the Nottingham Playhouse. Toby Robertson

was a signatory, as was Frank Dunlop of the Young Vic. The complaint was that, by virtue of its size, the NT would absorb so much of the subsidy available to drama that other theatres – their theatres – would be starved; and, worse, that the NT would make offers to their best staff that they could not refuse. Years later, Richard Eyre, who succeeded Hall, was unrepentant about the letter. 'The National and the RSC at the Barbican did suck talent and resources towards the centre; the trouble with the letter was that it was 15 years too late to influence the argument.'[24]

Hall was enraged by Lewenstein's letter, seeing it as an attack on the idea of a National Theatre by those who should be its natural allies. In the past, Hall had been skilled at controlling his feelings in public, but now his legendary cool deserted him. When he bumped into Lewenstein on the day the letter appeared, he lost his temper. But he was not alone in being angry: Eyre remembers his own anger at the thought that he could put on a whole show in Nottingham for the price of a single frock at the National Theatre. The letter lent credence to the criticism that the National was more like a dead monument than a live theatre.

Jonathan Miller subscribed to this proposition. Miller had originally been told by Hall that, among the directors, he was to be the workhorse, and he liked the idea. But his first two productions in Hall's regime were Beaumarchais' *Marriage of Figaro* and a new play by Peter Nichols called *The Freeway*, and both were battered by the critics. After that Miller felt he got no encouragement from Hall: 'He didn't like them, and he turned his back.'[25] Miller's confidence was bruised by the reviews and by the weekly meetings of the associates, which he came to dread. Early in 1974 Miller had been upset when Pinter derided his idea of directing Oscar Wilde's *The Importance of Being Earnest* with an all-male cast. (Pinter, the playwright, argued that if Wilde had wanted the women to be played by men, he would have said so.) When his next three scheduled productions became victims of budget cuts, Miller decided he was not wanted. He resigned in February 1975.

Having left, Miller became one of the National Theatre's, and Hall's, most persistent and articulate critics. Twenty years later, the mention of Hall's name could still precipitate a torrent of disenchantment and abuse. He left, he said, because he did not like Hall very much, finding him crude, vulgar and ambitious. Miller, a doctor's son educated at St Paul's School and Cambridge, further charged that Hall's socialism was fake and his taste was middlebrow.

Miller was also upset by the change in the character of the National Theatre. He had liked the cosy atmosphere of the Old Vic, and had no sympathy with the changes in policy Hall was intending to make once the move into three theatres on the South Bank was completed. After he left, the adjectives he launched at Hall were 'uncultivated' and 'uncivilised'. While there was no doubt about the sincerity of Miller's commitment to the NT, his way with words made it hard to take him seriously.

Miller was only a skirmish on the way to the showdown – the last stand of Michael Blakemore, the only survivor from Olivier's reign. Apart from Hall, Blakemore was the most experienced director on the staff, a veteran with the *Long Day's Journey into Night* and a memorable production of Hecht and MacArthur's *The Front Page* to his credit. Hall considered both those the work of a great, as opposed to merely a good, director.[26] Blakemore, an Australian, had studied medicine before training at RADA, playing small parts with the Birmingham Rep and Stratford, and doing a director's apprenticeship at the Citizens Theatre in Glasgow. He is a fastidious man of the liberal left, suspicious of power and the powerful. The relationship between him and Hall was bound to be wary.

Hall knew Blakemore would judge him by the standards of the old regime, but when they first talked after Hall's arrival in 1973, Hall pressed him ardently to stay on because of his interest in the acting company. (As he turned to leave Hall's office, Hall mentioned *Next Season*, Blakemore's theatrical novel loosely based on Stratford which seemed to draw on Hall for the portrait of an inexperienced Oxbridge whiz-kid director. 'You should write more,' Hall said. Blakemore was flattered: 'He could make you feel wonderful.')

In the three years since Hall's arrival, however, Blakemore had become disenchanted. His own successes had been followed by a dismal failure, *Grand Manoeuvres* by A.E. Ellis, which had its run curtailed; and Hall had not admired his production of Ben Travers's Aldwych farce, *Plunder*, although it was a popular hit. Blakemore was not happy with Hall's way of running the theatre, either. He wrote a paper, had copies made of it, and handed them round at the associates' meeting on 17 March 1976. He then read out his paper. Hall was furious, shaken, and very upset.

We know what Blakemore's paper said because he eventually gave a copy of it to John Elsom, who was writing a history of the National Theatre. The associates' committee, he charged, was a charade, designed to rubber-stamp decisions already taken by the people who really ran the place: Hall, Birkett and Stevens. He deplored the higher salaries being paid to stars – the basic top rate was £550 a week for actor-knights and dames like Ashcroft, Gielgud and Richardson, compared to £100 for young leads, and a minimum wage of £45 a week. Blakemore believed these differentials sabotaged the company concept. If it was a sacrifice to work for the National Theatre, there was nothing wrong with that, he said.[27]

The most damaging charge, however, was that Hall had exploited his position to make money for himself when Harold Pinter's play, *No Man's Land*, transferred to the West End. This accusation, which was to recur throughout Hall's directorship, is too complex to settle easily, involving, as it does, unwritten rules about the relationship between the commercial and the subsidised theatre. Blakemore had not objected when Hall originally proposed that, when a play transferred to the commercial theatre, the National Theatre artists involved should be entitled to their full commercial reward. This was not a new policy: Olivier, for example, had received £100,000 on top of his salary when his performance of James Tyrone was filmed for television. And when NT productions transferred to the commercial theatre, their directors routinely received 4 per cent of the gross, as John Dexter had when his National Theatre production of *Equus* moved to the West End.

But Blakemore preferred to recall Olivier's belief that the National Theatre was a public service, and that staff directors should behave accordingly – by taking, say, 1 per cent of the gross from a transfer to the West End. They had, after all, already received a salary for their work. Hall took his right to 4 per cent for granted, even though it could create embarrassment. In the case of *No Man's Land*, for instance, the National Theatre had decided to dispense with professional advisers and negotiate the transfer itself, so Hall could have been accused of negotiating his fee with himself.

When Blakemore finished reading it, his paper was picked to pieces by the associates. Various errors were seized upon, and these Blakemore freely confessed to, but he stuck to the points of principle. The meeting ended at about midnight with what amounted to a referendum on Hall's leadership: Michael Kustow proposed that those who did not agree with Blakemore should return their copies of his paper to him. Though everyone present did so, Pinter later regretted it, feeling that Blakemore's argument deserved more careful study. Hall regretted having done so too, but only because he thought the paper had defamed him, and he had surrendered the only evidence.

What concerned Hall most was not libel, but what he saw as an attempted coup. Hall had convinced himself that Blakemore wanted power to be devolved to the associates, and he was determined to prevent that. At another associates' meeting three days later, Hall described the constitutional relationship between the director and the associates as follows: he chose them; he wanted them to check and criticise him; but final decisions would be his.

That was only the beginning of the Blakemore Affair. Soon after Blakemore had read his paper, an article critical of the National Theatre appeared in the *Evening Standard*, written by a friend of his called Gaia Servadio. It was the first of a number of newspaper articles which advanced the Blakemore line. He confessed that he had seen Servadio's article in typescript and checked the facts, but he denied being the source of the information. Hall did not believe him. When Blakemore's next production – Granville-Barker's *The Madras House* – was discussed at an associates' meeting, Blakemore's contract was made conditional on there being no further leaks from the National. Blakemore, who was also at the time involved in a bureaucratic dispute about his wages, reacted fiercely to the implication that the leaks were his doing, and he quit, not even bothering to point out that, as leakers go, few are as skilled as Hall himself.

Perhaps the clash of personalities ruled out any possibility of a dignified ending, but the only link with Olivier's team had been severed in circumstances that left some of Hall's team feeling despondent. Pinter's loyalty was unshaken at that time, and yet he felt that Hall had been too emotional about Blakemore: 'If he hadn't become so upset, I think it could have been more reasonably discussed. I don't think it was well handled.'

At the end of his term as director, Hall still believed that the opposition of Blakemore and Miller had been very damaging, Miller's most of all: 'He's only a pseudo-intellectual, but the media think he's terribly intelligent, and he makes good copy,' he said.[28]

Blakemore, on the other hand, was the most moderate of this new cast of enemies, always capable of seeing good qualities in Hall ('an impresario of genius') and of regretting his confrontational strategy ('the silliest thing I've ever done').

Hall thought that not getting rid of the pair of them straight away had been 'one of my biggest mistakes'. But a complete clear-out of Olivier's associates would have been politically impossible at the start of Hall's regime, even if he had wanted it at the time. What Hall's hindsight shows is how badly hurt he felt. By the autumn of 1976 he had made enemies of Kenneth Tynan, Jonathan Miller and John Osborne – because he felt Hall had prematurely removed a play of his from the repertory. All were immensely skilled at stylish vituperation, and each influenced London's chattering classes. In three years as director, Hall's public reputation was transformed from golden boy to hatchet man, and he had become susceptible to dizzying bouts of paranoia. But he had good reason to feel persecuted: his enemies were out to get him.

Among the wounded vanities and endangered reputations an interesting argument about how to run a National Theatre had got lost. Olivier's way had been to create an ensemble of actors who would work together and evolve a recognisable style. Even a great hit would stay in the repertory – as Peter Shaffer's *The Royal Hunt of the Sun* had done – because the actors would be committed to other plays in the repertory. Many believers in this approach thought of a National Theatre as a museum constantly playing classical drama; new plays were off the agenda. Like a museum, this was a public service heavily subsidised by the state. The model was theatres on the continent of Europe, both west and east.

Hall's National Theatre was intended to be a centre of excellence, a showcase for the best plays, new as well as old, and the biggest stars; audiences would attend because they wanted to, not because they felt they ought. It would have been that way even if the move from the Old Vic had never taken place, because Hall liked mixing and matching plays, actors and authors. His tradition was more Anglo-Saxon than continental, conscious of the market-place, and taking risks.

But the move to the South Bank limited Hall's options. There were three theatres instead of one, and 2,500 seats to fill to 75 per cent of capacity each night instead of 900. Since he was determined to make the new building succeed at any price, Hall had no problem in jettisoning the ensemble concept and luring star actors like Gielgud and Richardson, and famous writers like Pinter, even if they did expect their work later to transfer from the subsidised to the commercial theatre. Hall was not apologetic about his method, but the move to the South Bank gave him hardly any choice. To make it work, he would have to be the consummate showbusiness impresario.

13

A Concorde of Culture

'We can't go on for very long without shows'

On the announcement of Peter Hall's appointment as director of the National Theatre in April 1972, the *Times*'s Diary asked him how long he intended to stay. He replied: 'The natural cycle of a theatre's history lasts from five to seven years. One should not stay in a theatre beyond that time, as the risk of it becoming institutionalised is too great.'

By April 1976, Hall had already agreed to take that risk: his contract was extended by three years to run past the seven-year point of no return, until the end of 1980. The move to the South Bank was still incomplete – more than two years overdue – and the Board unanimously agreed that Hall ought to be given enough time to show what he could do in the new building.

When work began on the site in 1969, the builders, Sir Robert McAlpine and Son, had hoped to finish in the spring of 1973. When Hall signed on, the assumption was that he and Olivier would be co-directors until early 1974. Olivier, having led the company into the South Bank, would then exit gloriously. Hall was present when Olivier spoke at the topping-out ceremony, which celebrates the completion of the framework of a new building; but that did not happen until 2 May 1973, the original completion date.

Shortly after that, Olivier decided not to stay. Organising the migration from the Old Vic into the South Bank would be Hall's job; and, as it turned out, it was more of a burden than an honour. Everything that could go wrong did so. The new theatre, the consequence of a compromise between the RSC and the National Theatre factions on the building committee, was by far the biggest theatre ever built in Britain, costing £16 million.

Hall, Peter Brook and Michel Saint-Denis had favoured an arena stage thrusting out into the audience, not unlike an ancient Greek amphitheatre; Olivier had wanted a conventional West End theatre with a proscenium arch dividing the performers from the audience. The dispute was resolved the easy way, by opting for one of each, together with a studio theatre for small-scale and experimental work. The arena stage was called the Olivier; the conventional stage was the Lyttelton, after Lord Chandos (who was born Oliver Lyttelton), and the studio was called the Cottesloe, after the amiable figure who had been a famous rowing blue and then captain of the national rifle-shooting team before becoming chairman of the Arts Council and then the South Bank Theatre Board.

Denys Lasdun, the architect, belonged to the modern move-ment: he liked clean lines and concrete. His concept of decoration was to leave imprinted on the concrete walls the wooden planks that held the concrete in place when it was being poured. This is known as planked concrete and, as decoration goes, it is minimal. When the outline of the building was first to be seen, Hall pro-nounced it one of London's few post-war architectural beauties. Once the building became part of the skyline, the doubters began to speak out too – in, for instance, the *New Statesman*, whose readers would traditionally have been core supporters of an idea like the National Theatre. On 25 October 1974, a leading article began: 'The National Theatre is nearly finished, and already it seems as cumbersome as a Dreadnought; expensive to build and maintain; demanding a crew of hundreds; dubiously relevant to the later 20th century.' The leader concluded: 'The mania for grand brass and concrete, unchallenged in the early 1960s, has begun to look naive, if not, actually damaging to the cause of good theatre. It is time we cured ourselves of it.' But it was too late to effect a cure; unless, of course, the theatre were mothballed, like a Dreadnought.

Although Lasdun had designed the prestigious Royal College of Surgeons building in Regent's Park, his practice had never won a contract as big as this one. Despite this, he was reluctant to increase the size of his office to cope with the volume of work. 'Denys is very brilliant, but he is a very fastidious architect,' says Rayne.[1] What this meant, says Rayne, was that the architectural drawings were late. Lasdun soon fell out with McAlpines, who felt they were taking the heat for delays that were not their fault. But the builders had problems too; because of a boom in the building industry in the early 1970s, skilled labour was always in short supply. Over-ambitious designs for the stage machinery worsened the delays. By 1973, as a building site, the National Theatre was a disaster.

As delays became endemic, costs mounted. In 1972 Max Rayne discovered that no one on the South Bank Theatre Board knew how much the building would eventually cost, or when it might be finished. One of his first moves as chairman was to form a sub-committee of the Theatre Board and to put the questions about cost and timing that no one had asked before. The answers, when he found them, were depressing. By autumn 1973, Rayne had to tell the Board that, because the cost of operating the building would be so high and money would be so short, it might be necessary to close one of the two main theatres before it had opened. By July 1974, the opening ceremony had been delayed until April 1975. In October 1974, the Board learned that the best that could be hoped for was completion by May 1975, but that April 1976 was the more likely opening date. Hall's repertory plans were in ruins. While promising to salvage what he could, he told the Board that the latest delay was 'a most serious setback to the National Theatre'.[2]

Hall now went on the offensive, exposing the failings of the contractors (finding, for example, that there were only two electricians on the site when there should have been twelve). McAlpines replied with a solicitor's letter, hoping to shut Hall up. Max Rayne, a property developer, appreciated that disputes like this could cost money, and counselled caution, but Hall was in no mood for it. His diary records that when he went to a McAlpines lunch in February 1975, Alistair McAlpine looked at him rather as if he were a bomb that might go off.[3]

Hall's public behaviour was based on private fears and frustrations that went so deep he occasionally wondered whether the job was worth the anxiety. ('I begin to think what is the point of working at this pressure and putting up with all the shit about the National Theatre.')[4] An ambitious repertory plan, which had a

new production every three weeks between July 1975 and August
1976, had to be scrapped: it was based on the assumption that 23
April 1975 would be the South Bank's first night. The three acting
companies that had been formed to supply the Olivier and the
Lyttelton with a constantly changing diet had been dismantled.
The result was turmoil. These cuts were the pretext for Jonathan
Miller's resignation; many of the actors just faded away. Some
had to be retained on contract, however, to make sure of their
availability when the building did eventually open; this meant
that the deep cuts in the programme of plays did not lead to
matching cuts in costs.

In September 1973, the Board discussed an estimated deficit of
£215,000 for 1974–5. A year later that estimate had increased to
£585,000. In April 1975, when the Board heard the deficit might
be up to three-quarters of a million pounds, John Mortimer's
patience ran out. Mortimer, the lawyer and playwright, had
made himself the spokesman on the Board for the artists and
their standards, and he feared that so much of the available
money would have to be spent on the building that there would
not be enough left to perform the plays properly.[5] The cost of
running the building was only just sinking in: 'I think there is
going to be surprise in some quarters now to find they've built
a beautiful, great theatre that is actually going to cost a fortune
to heat, to light, to run, to insure and to pay the rates on,' Hall
said at the time.[6]

Mortimer told the Board that if high operating costs were
going to mean lower artistic standards, it would be better for
the National Theatre to remain in the Old Vic and forgo the move
to the South Bank for the time being. The minutes record that both
Rayne and Hall agreed with Mortimer's proposition. But Hall did
not hesitate when McAlpines told him, only a couple of months
later, that the only way to get the subcontractors to complete the
building was to force their hand by moving into any part of it
that was ready.

The management offices were the first part of the building to be
completed, and at the beginning of September 1975 Sue Higginson,
Hall's personal assistant, and other members of his staff moved
into their corner suite with fine views across flowing water to
Somerset House and down the Thames towards St Paul's. Hall's
striking desk – a large, single sheet of glass resting on moulded
concrete supports – was moved in, and he joined them three weeks

later. On 22 September he worked on *Hamlet* in the South Bank's light and airy rehearsal rooms.

A week later Hall announced that the building would open to the public step by step, starting with the Lyttelton in March 1976. Hall estimated that the cost of *not* opening the Olivier theatre was £50,000 a month: and yet he seemed powerless to do anything about it. The centrepiece of the Olivier's extravagant technical system was a drum revolve, 35 feet in diameter, which sank 60 feet below the stage. Divided into two parts, it had scenery lifts in each half, so that sets could be raised and lowered at the touch of a button. The contract had been given to a British company named Mole Richardson, which had never built anything like it before, and when the drum revolve was finally fitted into the Olivier stage, the machinery was too complicated and did not work.

Not opening the theatres was costing the National the cash it needed, but opening them would cost money the National did not have. Hall believed that if the company did not move in as scheduled the building might never be finished, but even in the Lyttelton the technical facilities were not yet as good as those at the Old Vic. Because of this, extra stagehands had to be hired, and large overtime payments swelled the budget deficit.

Given his track record, there was never any doubt that Hall would choose to spend money he did not have. His decision to do so again raised the National Theatre's deficit to £1,009,272 for the year 1976–7; of this £691,860 was attributed directly to the delays, and the other £317,412 to lost revenue. Hall's decision to spend his way into the South Bank led to a financial crisis in 1977 that forced the Board to consider collective resignation as an alternative to bankruptcy, but his preference for pugnacity over prudence won the day.[7]

The very first performance in the National Theatre, on 8 March 1976, was a matinée in the Lyttelton of Samuel Beckett's *Happy Days*, a monologue performed by Peggy Ashcroft. This was followed by semi-private press previews of productions that were transferring from the Old Vic: *Plunder* (director, Michael Blakemore); Hall's productions of Ibsen's *John Gabriel Borkman* (with Ralph Richardson), and *Hamlet* (with Albert Finney); and John Osborne's *Watch It Come Down*.

Reviews were naturally preoccupied with the building, and they were remarkably good. Simon Jenkins in the *Evening Standard* did not share Hall's well-publicised scorn for gilded cherubs and red plush, but he declared Lasdun's building a masterpiece of British architecture; it was, he wrote, 'a Concorde of culture'. Others noted the absence of decoration, and Robert Cushman in the *Observer* said the Lyttelton reminded him of a lecture hall rather than a theatre. But Michael Billington reassured *Guardian* readers that the building was neither a white elephant nor a cultural mausoleum. The bars and the bookshop were applauded as evidence of Hall's policy of making everyone welcome, whether they wore dinner jackets or jeans, and not just for half an hour before performance began but for twelve hours a day. To show he meant business, Hall applied for a street-trading licence so that stalls could be opened along the riverside, like the bookshops along the bank of the Seine in Paris. A poster had been designed by Tom Phillips with the slogan 'The National Theatre is Yours'. Billington especially admired the implication of classless, communal warmth. Compared to West End theatres, with their crowded foyers, bad-tempered bar staff and contemptible programmes, going to the National Theatre was like spending an evening in the Ritz.

No reviewers remarked on the Lyttelton's technical failings. Scene-changes were protracted because the revolve had broken down and was being turned by hand; the air-conditioning was so noisy that it reminded Donald Sinden of a ship's engine; the acoustics in the dress circle left much to be desired. Hall confessed to the Board that this was a problem. Compared to opening the Olivier, however, it was a small problem.

Theatre Projects Ltd, the technical consultants who had conceived the drum revolve, tried to persuade the South Bank Board to open the Olivier only when it was fully operational. Hall believed this plan to be a cover-up for delays and incompetence, and insisted on opening the theatre with Marlowe's *Tamburlaine* at the beginning of October in 1976. The argument that finally convinced the South Bank Board was that the National Theatre could not survive without revenue from the Olivier.

By mid-August, Hall had accepted that the acoustics were poor in parts of the Olivier as well, but there was a more pressing difficulty. Stagehands had refused to be on call in both the Lyttelton and the Olivier, insisting on separate gangs for each theatre. The dispute went to arbitration, but the stagehands rejected the award. On 13 August 1976, the first technical rehearsal of *Tamburlaine* in the Olivier did not take place; the men had walked out.

The strike was unofficial, but when NATTKE – the union for

stagehands and cinema workers – ordered them back to work, the men stayed put. Kon Fredericks, a Trotskyite shop steward who had worked in the printing trade and been an actor before becoming a militant stagehand, exercised more control over the National Theatre stagehands than their elected national officials, and a power struggle on the South Bank suited him.

Victor Mishcon, deputed by Rayne to advise Hall and his management colleagues, did not underrate Fredericks: here was a shop steward who appreciated the difference between leading a strike in a West End theatre and a strike at the National.[8] The first would rate a paragraph in the *Evening Standard*; the second would advertise union militancy in the national newspapers and on television, and cause Rayne and Mishcon embarrassment they hated, especially when it led to questions in Parliament. So when a compromise was offered by NATTKE's general secretary, John Wilson, Mishcon lobbied hard for its acceptance. He was a practical man, concerned that a strike would damage staff morale and affect advance bookings. After some anguish, Hall sided with Mishcon against his two management colleagues, Peter Stevens and Simon Relph, who had joined the NT from the film industry to take charge of industrial relations. Both insisted that the compromise hardly disguised a defeat for the management. Both berated Hall for a craven decision. Both offered to resign. Hall persuaded them not to, but he was shaken by their opposition. Only three months after Blakemore's resignation, his management colleagues seemed to have turned on him, too.

The Olivier did open, as Hall said it would, on 4 October 1976. It had to, because the Queen had been booked for 25 October, and there was no cancelling a royal opening. The members of the inner group on the Board, the finance and general purposes committee, gave much thought to the programme and suggested two one-act plays to be set before the Queen; they even suggested the titles: Peter Shaffer's funny and ingenious *Black Comedy* and either Rattigan's *The Browning Version* or Sheridan's *The Critic*.[9] But the Board was trespassing here, and its suggestions were not welcomed by the artistic management. Hall decided instead that the Olivier should open with a seventeenth-century Venetian comedy, *Il Campiello* by Carlo Goldoni. He should have listened to the Board. *Il Campiello* was a disaster, and the only hit on the opening night was a wonderfully florid speech by Olivier himself.

The South Bank was in business at last, but Hall felt no elation. Quite the reverse. On 5 October, after the opening of *Tamburlaine*, Hall wrote in his diary that he was feeling awful and did not want to continue with this life or this job.[10] After the royal opening, his diary records some satisfaction that the theatre was open, but Hall adds that his fear was that only his successor would make a success of it. This was the authentic voice of his Pamment genes; as it turned out, that melancholy was utterly misplaced.

He did have good reason to worry about money, however. His original gamble, moving in without the money, had paid off: the Arts Council had managed to procure an extra £500,000 in 1976. There was also windfall income from Peter Shaffer's *Equus*, which was running well in the West End and on Broadway. But the deficit did not diminish, and by the summer of 1977 Rayne was worrying that the NT would have to close down within a year of its opening. Lord O'Brien, a board member who had only recently retired as Governor of the Bank of England, also worried about solvency and he raised the possibility of a collective resignation. But the Arts Council came to the rescue again in October 1977, agreeing to maintain the cash flow. At least the creditors could be paid.

When the Arts Council grants for 1978–9 were announced, the National's share was £3.7 million. This was a huge sum compared to grants in the Old Vic days, but it was still £130,000 less than they had asked for. In the crisis that followed, actors were made redundant, and planned new productions were cut from twenty-three to twenty; but this was not a fight for survival, it was a crisis of financial management of the type that was to recur year after year, as predictably as the seasons. All that was required for survival now was strong nerves, and Hall had those – in public at least.

Hall had had his quarrels with Max Rayne – about his public criticism of McAlpines, for example, and about working on *Aquarius* – but Rayne had grown to admire Hall. Years later he listed Hall's strengths: articulacy, determination, youth, strength, energy, intelligence. 'Peter was much more than a director. No one could administer as well as he did, or direct as well as he did, or work as hard as he did.' Rayne concluded that no one else could have got the National Theatre into the South Bank. Victor Mishcon agreed: 'No-one else could have withstood the strains and stresses of the early years.' Mishcon mentioned two other characteristics:

the first was courage, but the one he set above all others in the battle to open the South Bank was 'pig-headedness'. It was not always to be so, but in those years Mishcon saw this as a virtue. Whatever criticism came from the rank and file, Hall's position was protected by the support of the two most senior members of the Board. And by 1978 he needed it.

A bizarre strike in April 1977, which started when a plumber named Ralph Cooper was fired because he refused to fix two washbasins in a lavatory, confirmed Rayne and Mishcon in their judgement about Hall. The unofficial strike stopped the second-night performance of Robert Bolt's *State of Revolution*, a play about the Russian Revolution which, in the circumstances of the strike, Hall thought was too understanding of the extremists' point of view. The washbasin strike made good big headlines (THEATRE OF THE ABSURD, was the *Daily Express* line). And Hall fought the strikers through the newspapers, threatening the shut-down of the National Theatre. The *Daily Telegraph*'s report quoted him: 'We can't go on for very long without shows. Theatres are not like the water system – nobody actually needs them. The dispute is not, in essence, about the sacking of Mr Ralph Cooper. It is about abiding by agreements.' The management's offer of binding arbitration was accepted by the strikers after six days, and Hall's policy of defending the principle of the agreement was applauded outside the theatre. This time, he was on the same side as his management colleagues.

Still in an agitated state, Hall wrote a resignation letter to Rayne in January 1978, but he tore it up because to leave then would look like a defeat.[11] But his insecurity nearly caused a bad mistake over the publication of *The History of the National Theatre* by John Elsom and Nicholas Tomalin, the skilled, flamboyant journalist who had been a year behind Hall at Cambridge and was an inspired choice to write the history – reverent towards the idea, but irreverent about many people involved. He and Hall were acquaintances rather than friends, but they had stayed in touch, and Hall was looking forward to collaborating with Tomalin. Then in 1973, in a break from researching the book, Tomalin agreed to report the Yom Kippur War for the *Sunday Times* and was killed on the Golan Heights by a Syrian missile. John Elsom, who was chosen to finish the book, had a narrower interest in the theatre than Tomalin's and preferred critical analysis to storytelling. What upset Hall was that Elsom supported the Michael Blakemore concept of a National Theatre, and gave a full account of the critical paper Blakemore had presented to the associate directors in March 1976.

Having over-reacted then, when the controversy broke, Hall did so again, and threatened to ban the Elsom/Tomalin history of the National Theatre from the National Theatre's bookshop. John Goodwin warned Hall that a ban would damage him and make a martyr out of Elsom, but the idea was discussed by the Board (John Mortimer opposed the ban; Harold Hobson, a journalist himself, supported it). Harold Pinter, who asked to meet the Board, insisted that Hall's policy had the full confidence of the associates, and, instead of banning the book, the Board passed a unanimous vote of confidence in him.[12] If the intention of his opponents had been to remove Hall, it failed totally because Hobson then proposed that his contract should be extended for between two and five years to mark their support. Rayne, who understood that job security would make Hall less touchy, set about extending his contract for a further three years, until the end of 1983.

Hall's salary already needed looking at. The inflation-proof clauses in his original 1972 contract, and in the three-year extension in April 1976, meant that, during a period of unprecedented inflation between 1974 and 1977, it had now swollen to a size that embarrassed him, and he had returned a part of it. When Rayne opened negotiations for a new contract to run from 1978 to 1983, the first thing agreed was a salary of £30,000 in 1977, with automatic increases in subsequent years of £3,000 or the increase in the cost of living, whichever was lower. When the Board discussed this new contract in the summer of 1978, Hall was already earning about £35,000 a year, and one board member calculated that the deal would lead to a salary of £42,000 in 1981.[13] Hall also received two-thirds of the rent and rates on the Barbican flat, worth £2,230 in 1977 rising to £2,899 in 1981, plus a £500 annual car allowance.

The deal with Hall – or, more accurately, with his advisers, negotiating on behalf of Petard Productions Ltd – presented Rayne with a number of problems. A new member of the Board named Sir Derek Mitchell, who had recently left the Treasury where he had been second permanent secretary in charge of international finance, was concerned that the agreement

Directors of the National Theatre: Hall with his predecessor, Laurence Olivier.

First night: The Queen Mother and her daughter Margaret at the unofficial opening of the South Bank theatre in 1976 attended by Hall and the architect, Denys Lasdun.

'A masterpiece of British architecture': Hall and the building he boosted.

'Cut the camels.' Peter Hall rehearses *Moses and Aaron* at the Royal Opera House.

Teamwork at Glyndebourne: (from left to right) Hall with Raymond Leppard, the conductor, Moran Caplat, Glyndebourne's benevolent administrator, and his designer, John Bury (seated).

A Mozart debut: Hall directs Ileana Cotrubas (left), who sang Susanna in *The Marriage of Figaro* in 1973.

A growing family: (above left) with Jacky Hall and the children Jenny, Christopher, Edward and Lucy at the National Theatre, and (below) with his parents and his Aunty Gee at Wallingford.

Third wife: Hall with opera prima donna Maria Ewing and children Rebecca and Lucy (above right).

Max Rayne's farewell, with Hall and his successor Richard Eyre.

Co-conspirators: Rayne and former Treasury mandarin, Sir Derek Mitchell.

Besieged: Hall at the stage door during an NT strike.

Revealing tragedy from behind a mask: Hall rehearses *The Oresteia*.

A tragedy becomes a disaster: Hall rehearses *Jean Seberg* with Julian Barry (left) and Marvin Hamlisch.

John Bury, Peter Hall and Harold Pinter rehearsing Pinter's *Other Places* at the National Theatre in 1982.

Evidence of a golden age: Hall rehearsing *Antony and Cleopatra* with Anthony Hopkins.

She knew it was going to be thrilling: Anthony Hopkins and Judi Dench.

Young Turks and an old Turk: David Hare, Richard Eyre, Michael Bogdanov, Peter Gill, Peter Hall, Bill Bryden, Edward Petherbridge, and Ian McKellen.

Nights with the stars: Julie Walters in Tennessee Williams's *The Rose Tattoo*; Dustin Hoffman as Shylock in *The Merchant of Venice*; Vanessa Redgrave in Williams's *Orpheus Descending*; Stephen Dillane as Hall's fourth Hamlet.

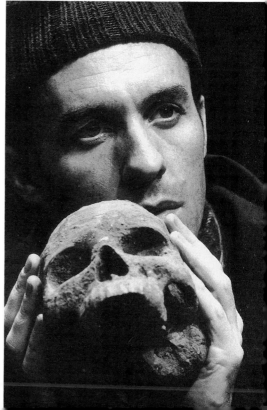

'A wonderful marriage and a tribe of children': Hall with his fourth wife, Nicki and his sixth child, Emma.

breached the government's pay policy that put a top limit on all wage increases. He and others were also concerned about the secrecy surrounding the contract, fearing that a leak revealing Hall's substantial earnings would embarrass the Board and Hall himself.

But more persistent at this time than criticism of his earnings was criticism about the amount of time Hall spent away from his job. Before this new set of negotiations began, Rayne had raised Hall's 'full-time but not exclusive' arrangement with him. Rayne had been very unhappy about the *Aquarius* episode and in November 1975 had asked Hall to think of signing a contract for his exclusive services. Rayne mentioned that the Arts Minister thought it was a good idea, too. Hall did not even discuss it; if that was a condition, he said, there would be no contract.[14]

One of the most persistent critics of the arrangement was Lady Plowden, a formidable woman who had served on a remarkable range of boards and inquiries and been vice-chairman of the BBC. Rayne offered Olivier as a precedent: he had been able to earn substantial sums from film and television appearances while he was director – so why not Hall? Lady Plowden suggested that a codicil be added to Hall's contract, defining the proportion of his time to be given to the National Theatre. That was gently repulsed by Rayne, but the unanimity on the Board that he so prized was subverted by the episode, and Rayne's support for Hall was questioned for the first time. After the board discussion in July 1978, Sir Derek Mitchell wrote to Rayne: 'Among ourselves the justification for giving way on virtually every point put to us by Peter Hall through his advisors has been that we cannot afford to lose his services. Not everyone at the Board was prepared to accept this and certainly not everyone, in or out of the profession, would accept that proposition.'[15] Rayne redoubled his energies, and by the autumn he had pacified his own Board, the Arts Council, and the Department of Education and Science where the Arts Minister was housed.

As an administrator, Hall had proved indispensable in getting the National Theatre from the Old Vic to the South Bank, although after Peter Stevens decamped to New York in 1978 he had to run the organisation with a new general administrator. Hall, with help from Derek Mitchell, chose as Stevens's successor Michael Elliott, a senior manager in the company that makes Kleenex tissues. (The RSC's unhappy experience with Derek Hornby, who had come from industry to manage the company, had not altered his conviction that a manager with industrial rather than showbusiness experience was best equipped to run a large theatre company.)

Almost indispensable as a manager, Hall was also matchless as an impresario. That combination was the basis of his reputation as a powerful man. His reputation as an artist depended on different skills, and would be judged by his work on the stage.

14

The Director as
a Conductor

'My search for classicism is not working out'

Some months after the opening of Albert Finney's *Hamlet*, Peter Hall discussed with John Heilpern, a former critic on the *Observer*, whether the production had had a point of view, and, if it had not, whether it should have had? Violently mixed reviews for Finney, and an unenthusiastic reception of his own work, had forced Hall to think about basic assumptions. Conventional opinion held that famous Shakespeare directors ought to have a point of view, especially in such turbulent times as 1976 when the domestic economy was in chaos and political passions were hot. Hall's view was that his determination to perform the text with no cuts was a point of view in itself. But if it was, it was not widely appreciated. 'What critics have grown used to in this country, and I am as responsible as anybody,' said Hall, 'is a simplistic theory grafted on each production. It makes it far easier to understand the play and far easier to criticise it.'[1]

There was the germ of an important idea here, and when it developed David Hare, a director and a playwright, called it the Theory of Directorial Neutrality.[2] As he said himself, Hall had grafted a simplistic theory on to some of his work at Stratford; his Hamlet there, for instance, had been indecisive and burdened by an inability to act in a committed way, which was thought emblematic of 1960s youth. But even before Hall settled down in Stratford, his productions of plays by Samuel Beckett and Harold Pinter had been scrupulous reproductions of the text, devoid of any imposed theories. The audience was never told what to think, and interpretation was an individual responsibility rather than a collective one. Seen like this, a play is as much like a piece of music as a work of literature. Indeed, when Hall directed Harold Pinter's *Betrayal* he used that metaphor exactly: 'The tension builds up at an enormous rate. It's not fanciful to think of Mozart . . . there's the same precision of means, the same beauty, the same lyricism, and the same sudden descents into pain which are quickly over because of a healthy sense of the ridiculous.'[3] Alan Ayckbourn, as a young actor in *The Birthday Party*, remarked that hearing the text was like listening to Stravinsky.[4]

If a play is music, the director is a conductor. Hall saw the logic of this, and liked it. If this was the case, a Shakespeare play was like a Beethoven symphony, the conductor's interpretation being based on emphasis and tempo. Meaning exists only in the mind of the listener. It is hard for a director to get more neutral than that.

Hare detects a second influence in this conversion to textual neutrality. Hall, who had directed all Pinter's new work since 1965, had come to know and admire him. According to Jacky Hall, what he particularly admired was Pinter's certainty.[5] And one of the things Pinter was absolutely certain about was the sanctity of a writer's text (an opinion he shared with Sam Beckett). Since Hall accepted without question that he could not alter a dot or comma in Harold Pinter's plays, why, then, should he do so in William Shakespeare's? This was the theory of directorial neutrality in its purest form.

Hall had plenty of opportunities to put theory into practice in the 1970s. He had taken office at the NT during a purple period in British playwriting: he invited no less than eight dramatists to write plays, and all of them delivered. The production of new writing was one of the pleasant surprises of Hall's regime, but it was not what most people thought the National Theatre had been created for. The NT's most obvious purpose was to perform the classics in a way that distinguished it from the RSC; and one good reason for appointing Hall had been that he was an accomplished director of the classics, even though he did come from the opposition. Once John Dexter left for the Metropolitan Opera in New York and Jonathan Miller had gone, Hall was, in fact, the only director of classic plays working regularly at the National Theatre. John Schlesinger returned from Hollywood to direct *Julius Caesar* in 1977, but of the four Shakespeare plays performed in his first six years as director, Hall directed three.

The vigorous, poetic style of playing Shakespeare at Stratford was the result of his fruitful competition with Peter Brook, and the close support of John Barton and Michel Saint-Denis. Though he was surrounded by associate directors at the NT, Hall discovered no one he could talk to about classic texts, not even Olivier. He had hoped to persuade Olivier to play *King Lear*, directed by him if possible, but Olivier did not feel generous towards his successor and there was no collaboration of any kind between them.

Hall's first production at the National Theatre was *The Tempest*, one Shakespeare play he had not directed at Stratford; his approach was to make it look as authentically Jacobean as possible. He drew on his recent experience of baroque theatre while directing Monteverdi at Glyndebourne, and the feel of the production was inspired by the masques of the period designed by Inigo Jones. John Gielgud, performing at the National Theatre for the first time, was Prospero. Hall thought Gielgud was probably too gentle and too nice for the part, but he was starting as he intended to go on: he did not want to reproduce the Stratford ensemble style, and proposed relying on star players for the leading roles in his productions of classic plays.

Hall had intimations of *The Tempest*'s failure before it opened at the Old Vic in March 1974. The sets were heavy and expensive. He was dreadfully lonely. Unlike his former colleagues in Stratford, none of his new associates offered help and he was too shy to ask for it. He felt vulnerable, and rightly so, because when *The Tempest* opened Michael Billington in the *Guardian* called it one of the four worst Shakespeare productions he had ever seen. (Hall said he was unable to comment on this because he had not seen the other three.)

Years later David Hare, generalising boldly, observed that the critics do not respect a director's work while he is also playing the role of impresario, as Hall was. By 1974 there was some evidence to support that. Hall's next classic production was one of the plays that would open the South Bank theatre. As Olivier had done in 1963 when he opened the National Theatre at the Old

Vic, Hall decided on *Hamlet*. Olivier's Hamlet was Peter O'Toole.
Hall's was Albert Finney, the actor who had turned down the film
role of Lawrence of Arabia before it was offered to O'Toole. Hall
thought Finney might be five years too old for Hamlet, but still
wanted to see what he would make of it. As a motive, that was
weak. It was only ten years since David Warner's famous student
Hamlet, and Hall felt no real compulsion to do another.

He was fascinated, however, by the constant evolution of
Hamlet, and he had decided which new direction he wished to
take. The diary for 29 July 1975 leaves no room for interpretation:
from now on, the text's the thing. He wrote:

> It seems to me that we have come some distance in the last 25 years in
> understanding the rhythm of a Shakespeare play, how it operates, how one
> segment reacts on another. We have also come some way in understanding
> how to speak the verse. But we still cut the text like barbarians. Do we know
> what *we* cut? And don't we normally cut either to fit some preconceived
> theory for the production, or because we simply can't make the passage
> work? I think my future direction in Shakespeare must be to reveal the
> total object as well as possible. I feel in my blood that I know how.[6]

Some colleagues had cast doubt on Finney's credentials as a
classical actor, but Hall was anxious to sign up another star,
and it was time for Finney to do some serious acting. Finney
is an ebullient actor who slips easily into the role of company
leader. His contemporaries regarded him as the next leader of the
profession, and, as Hamlet at the National Theatre, he seemed to
have found his proper place at last.

In rehearsal, Hall found Finney powerful, passionate, sexy and
responsive, and was excited by the way their discoveries spread
through the cast. He himself was learning how Shakespeare wrote
scenes to expedite entrances and exits, and how a thematic line five
or six lines into a speech usually explains what it is all about. He
also thought he had established a uniform style of verse-speaking
which was less intellectual and more emotional than he had been
used to at Stratford. When it first opened (at the Old Vic, before
going on to open the Lyttelton) Hall thought his undecorated and
uncomfortable *Hamlet* was the closest he had ever got to the heart
of a Shakespeare play. The audience liked it too, but few critics
appreciated Hall's passion for the text. (One curiosity was that,
although Hall had cut 730 lines from his Stratford *Hamlet* with
David Warner, his uncut National Theatre version ran for only

five minutes longer; some critics complained that it was spoken too rapidly.)[7]

Hall's new theory was not strictly adhered to in his next production of a classical play, Christopher Marlowe's *Tamburlaine the Great*, which opened the Olivier Theatre. This was a play Hall had wanted to do from the outset at the National Theatre, and in rehearsal he explored the text so thoroughly that he decided no scholar had yet properly understood its precise structure. He also developed his analogy between plays and music, describing the actors as being like opera singers, each having specific solos.

Tamburlaine comes in two parts, and Hall insisted that both should be played on the same evening, even if the curtain rose at 6 p.m. But doing both parts meant that the text could not be treated as sacred; Hall cut twenty-five minutes, and changed the order of the scenes in Part II.

John Bury was the designer and their relationship was now so close that they spoke in shorthand. ('I just showed [Peter] my scribbles; he whacked his thigh and announced: "Yes, that'll be all right."')[8] The play, in fact, presented fewer problems than the actual theatre. Hall's anxiety about when the Olivier would be ready was interfering with his work: 'To be open when you work, to discover, you have to be quite relaxed. I'm not. I can't feel what the actors think.' The first strike on the South Bank forced the actors out on to the terraces in front of the theatre to rehearse, which actually raised morale. But Hall worried that he was not giving Finney enough help. Marlowe's bleak melodrama of an evil and ruthless tyrant suited Finney's exuberant style ('He makes it credible that he would use the Turkish emperor as a footstool,' wrote Milton Shulman in the *Evening Standard*), and the rest of the cast was out of the National's top drawer. The lavish production, all red and gold and silk, was deservedly well reviewed.

The final act of collaboration between Hall and Finney was *Macbeth*, which opened in the summer of 1978. Finney was eager to do the part, and bullied Hall into directing it, which he did out of recognition and gratitude for Finney's loyalty to him. At the outset of rehearsals, Hall reiterated his commitment to the classic virtues, confessing that he was militant about them. They would use only the vigour of the play and the richness of the text, he pronounced.

The first person on whom it dawned that such a purist approach

was not working was Hall himself. He now worried that he and
Bury had become stuck in a *Wars of the Roses*-type realism which
had become old-fashioned. By the opening night, he judged that
his *Macbeth* was ordinary. The critics felt more strongly than that.
Hall thought the notices were as terrible as he had ever had.
He wrote: 'It was a failure because it was unfashionably simple,
unfashionably contradictory, and because it's directed by me – and
I am out of fashion too.'[9] Finney thought his *Macbeth* failed because
it was 'dreadfully operatic', though he blamed the auditorium not
the director. The production ended their relationship, however:
'People thought we would make a good combination of brawn and
brain – I was the emotional actor, he was the academic director.
But I don't think it ever caught fire,' Finney said later.[10]

Hall's fortunes with other classic texts in the 1970s were mixed.
William Wycherley's *The Country Wife* was his first attempt at
Restoration comedy and he realised in rehearsal that it was not
his sort of play; he wrote that he was bringing to it the same
inspiration that he would to a game of draughts. He did not
resent the bad notices, but they hurt, and caused him to question
his new militancy: 'My search for classicism is not working out,'
he said in a melancholic mood.[11]

Besides *Tamburlaine*, however, there was one more success
with a classic play, and it brought another desirable name to
the National's bill of stars. Hall had yearned to direct Paul
Scofield ever since he was the boy-director at Stratford, where
the results had been mixed: Scofield came up with the best Lear for
at least a generation with Peter Brook, followed by one of the worst
Macbeths with Peter Hall. For the National Theatre, they settled on
a less ambitious property: Ben Jonson's *Volpone*. Rehearsals were
encouraging, and Hall felt secure: 'I have it inside me,' he wrote.
(The only thing he was unsure about was where to cut it.)

Since doing the classics had in general exposed Hall to
volleys of criticism, he now took refuge in new plays, and
in reviving modern masters like Ibsen and Chekhov. One
of the eight writers he had asked for a new play was Alan
Ayckbourn, who had written a string of brilliant commercial
hits for the West End. When Ayckbourn expressed doubts about
his credentials, Hall flattered him outrageously: 'You can easily
do without the National Theatre, but can the National Theatre
do without you?' he asked. Ayckbourn was encouraged by the
discovery that Hall liked his plays: 'He had seemed to me a

severely classical man who would not have truck with the likes of us.'[12]

When Michael Codron, Ayckbourn's West End producer, saw an early performance in Scarborough of the play chosen for his début in the subsidised theatre, he muttered that Hall was 'a lucky old knight'. The play was *Bedroom Farce*, which transferred to Broadway as well as to the West End, and turned out to be one of the National's biggest hits.

Ayckbourn was used to directing his own plays at the Stephen Joseph Theatre in Scarborough, but Hall suggested that, since working in the Lyttelton was still tricky, and because the cast would come mainly from the pool of National Theatre actors, they should co-direct *Bedroom Farce*. Having agreed to this, Ayckbourn discovered that besides Hall and himself, there were also Hall's assistant director and a National Theatre staff director – four in all, or one director for every two members of the cast.

Hall started rehearsals by running the play through with the actors, and once it was clear that Ayckbourn was capable of dealing with the mechanics of farce, he slipped away for a week, reassuring Ayckbourn by saying he'd be next door if he needed him. When Ayckbourn looked puzzled, Hall explained that he would be in the next-door rehearsal room where he was directing *Volpone* – a classic example of Hall's ability to do two things at once. When they did work together, Ayckbourn noticed stylistic differences between them. He himself was always afraid of taking a comedy apart in case he could not put it together again, but Hall broke it down into its component parts and rehearsed them separately, as though it were Shakespeare. Hall gave his notes in the form of questions ('Where do you think your character would go for holidays?'), while Ayckbourn explained the characters he had written by reminiscing about people he knew.

The success of *Bedroom Farce* in March 1977 happened at a time of deep gloom at the National Theatre, and it put a spring in the stride of people working on the South Bank. 'Let's do it again,' Hall said to Ayckbourn. The relationship was important to both of them. In the West End, Ayckbourn was a superior practitioner in the giggle business. At the National he was a social satirist in the tradition of Ben Jonson. Hall relished Ayckbourn's writing, which was hardly less precise than Pinter's. Like Pinter, Ayckbourn had been apprenticed as an actor, and theatricality is a quality they share. The theory of directorial neutrality worked well with both of them.

Pinter's *No Man's Land* was the first National Theatre production to transfer to both the West End and Broadway. It was vintage Pinter. The leading parts were played by Ralph Richardson and by John Gielgud, who found that in Pinter he could manipulate the audience as he could in high comedy by Wilde or Congreve. Hall's ear had become so attuned to Pinter that he could distinguish between pauses that were primarily about sex (in *The Homecoming* and *Old Times*) and pauses that were a matter of threat and tension (as in *The Caretaker* and *No Man's Land*). The Old Lions served Hall well, and the play had 378 performances.

The alliance between fine texts and bright stars was common to all Hall's early successes. Since his first days at Stratford he had wooed Peggy Ashcroft, and when he joined the NT he wooed her again. Having overcome her initial resistance, he persuaded her to play Winnie in Samuel Beckett's *Happy Days*. Richardson and Ashcroft appeared together in a difficult late Ibsen play, *John Gabriel Borkman*, during rehearsals of which Richardson claimed he had got the John and the Borkman, but the Gabriel was still eluding him. He found it in time to prevent Hall experiencing another setback, at a point early in 1975 when he thought his reputation might not have withstood it.

If *Borkman* was a high on Hall's emotional rollercoaster in the 1970s, *The Cherry Orchard* took him to the depths. By now he was tired, depressed and overworked. His opening address to the cast – a wonderful confection of Dorothy Tutin, Ralph Richardson and Albert Finney – accurately echoed what Michael Frayn, who had translated the play, had told him about it the night before. During rehearsals he wondered if he was trying too hard, or whether his creative talent had gone, leaving him with nothing but technique. He was sure that Chekhov should be funny and passionate, rather than characterised, as was then customary, by gentle pathos. When the play opened and his theory seemed to have worked, Hall was so relieved that he almost burst into tears when he thanked the cast: 'Not my best work, but good,' was his judgement, and, with the exception of Bernard Levin in the *Sunday Times*, who found it hard to say a good word about the National Theatre, the critics thought so too.

Harold Pinter fed Hall's self-esteem and his creative appetite later in 1978 with his new play, *Betrayal*. As soon as he read the script, Hall saw that this bleak and disturbing piece about infidelity was another top-quality Pinter play. Since Pinter himself had just left Vivien Merchant, and Hall was constantly thinking of leaving Jacky, both were emotionally engaged in the subject; but the external events that made it hard for him to concentrate had more to do with labour than with marital relations. Rehearsals were disturbed by the rumblings that were the prelude to more industrial action at the National Theatre, and Hall was so tired by the constant round of meetings and negotiations that he would occasionally drop off to sleep in front of the cast. But it made no difference in the end: Pinter told Hall that *Betrayal* was the best piece of work they had done together. Fresh from the disaster of *Macbeth*, this was exactly what he needed to hear. 'I've respected my own work again,' he wrote.[13]

None of the plays Hall chose to direct in his first five years at the National provided a hint of evidence to support Jonathan Miller's suggestion that Hall was 'assertively middlebrow'. The reverse, rather. The one thing Hall and Miller have in common is that both are snobs about art. David Hare notes that Hall's selection of a late Ibsen play like *John Gabriel Borkman* is an example of his taste in refined high art, which is also to be found in the music and the paintings that he likes. Hall took no pleasure at all in Gilbert and Sullivan, for example (unlike Miller, who directed an electrifying *Mikado* for the English National Opera); and his treatment of *Bedroom Farce* led Ayckbourn to suspect that comedy might not be his forte either. The closest Hall's taste came to middlebrow was Peter Shaffer, and *Amadeus*. When Hall directed this in 1979 he showed that, confronted by an unusual opportunity, his rule about sticking to the playwright's text could be broken for the time being.

Shaffer's working method was quite different from Pinter's or Ayckbourn's, both of whom present scripts as they are intended to be performed. Hall describes Shaffer's first drafts as slapdash and excessive, like vast oil sketches. In the case of *Amadeus*, however, there was an epic drama even before rehearsals began.

Hall's original interest had been as an impresario. Shaffer had let him read a first draft when the play was still called *Salieri*. Hall immediately decided he wanted the play for the National Theatre, and that it should be directed by John Dexter, who had worked intimately with Shaffer on *Equus*; together, Hall said, they were 'sweet and sour and plenty of bitch'. (Hall's early support

for *Equus* had helped overcome Olivier's and Tynan's opposition
to the play at the National Theatre.) Reading a later version, now
titled *Amadeus*, in January 1979, Hall judged that, in showing
Salieri destroying Mozart and being himself destroyed by Mozart's
genius, Shaffer had written one of the most remarkable new plays
he had ever read. Some of his colleagues had reservations, as
they had had with *Equus* (Michael Rudman called *Amadeus* 'the
longest sleeve-note ever written'), but they did not deflect Hall.
He declared an absolute child's lust to direct it. But *Amadeus* had
been offered to Dexter, who took it for granted that he would be
the director, and who was involved in byzantine negotiations to
secure a generous deal for himself.

In theory, Hall should have appreciated Dexter's position.
Putting on a play by Peter Shaffer meant directing the author
as well as the actors. Dexter had found it galling that though the
stage directions in the published version of *Equus* were his work,
all the royalties went to the writer. Consequently, he wanted a
percentage of the royalty on all productions of the play that were
put on after his own production had opened. Hall found this a bit
cheeky. His productions of Pinter's work had influenced the way
they were performed all over the world, he said, but he would
not dream of asking Pinter for a share of his percentage. Dexter's
reply, in his posthumous autobiography *The Honourable Beast*, was
that Pinter's plays might be hard to do, but they were finished:
'Check the black [original] script of Equus for comparison.'[14]

Throughout these negotiations, Shaffer, or 'Ruby' as Dexter
called him – he was the sweet part of the sweet-and-sour cocktail
– insisted that he wanted to reach agreement but that, as the
playwright, he was not prepared to pay for the services of the
director. After a concentrated bout of hysterical negotiation ('I'm
beginning to wish this play had never come to us,' said Hall after
a prolonged conversation with Dexter in a cold telephone box at
Glyndebourne), talks broke down, with Dexter swearing never to
speak to Ruby again.

Hall tried to remain impartial, but Dexter thought him an
interested party, which explained, in Dexter's view, why he did
not try very hard to break the deadlock. The evidence does not
support that charge, and David Hare recalls how focused and
purposeful Hall was about securing *Amadeus* for the National
Theatre, not for himself. When Shaffer did ask him to direct
it, Hall was overjoyed – though the Pamment in him thought

that, because the subject was a classical composer, it might not be a great commercial success. The Hall in him, however, sensed that he might have hit the jackpot: 'If I am to do Amadeus [on Broadway] it may be one of my last chances of making money, real money.'[15]

Paul Scofield agreed to play Salieri, Simon Callow was Mozart and Felicity Kendal his wife Constanze. Rehearsals were scheduled to start in September 1979. Before that, Hall and Shaffer had plenty to do. When the rewrites started to arrive early in August, Act I was still at least half an hour too long. Hall wanted Shaffer to make the play more profound by making Salieri's confrontation with God the play's principal theme, and his way with the writer was a complete contrast to Dexter's. To get themselves in the right frame of mind, Hall and Shaffer travelled together to Vienna and Salzburg, becoming steadily more intimate, with Hall confiding in Shaffer about grave convolutions in his marriage. Dexter had bullied Shaffer; Hall flattered and coaxed him.

At the outset of rehearsals, Act I still lasted an hour and fifty minutes, but Shaffer was behaving like a trouper, cutting whole speeches rather than just lines. In his diary, Hall says that Shaffer describes the process as carving out a play with actors, and had said to Hall that he must find it a strange way to evolve a play, especially after working with Harold Pinter's hard, finished texts.

The actors found that the constant cutting and rewriting made learning the lines hard; and Hall also insisted on a difficult style of acting in which Shaffer's torrents of words were played very fast. But the actors enjoyed themselves. Callow, for instance, was one of a new generation of actors who had no strong prejudices about Hall, and enjoyed his first experience of working with him. It was a refreshing change from Dexter's openly authoritarian style. Callow wrote: 'Hall has great sensitivity to the text, and fine taste in terms of acting. He was wonderfully helpful in judging between one invention and another. He creates, too, a relaxed and genial atmosphere which is very productive. We laughed a great deal. It was delightful.'[16] Harrison Birtwistle found an ingenious way of keeping Mozart's music in the background by arranging it electronically. John Bury overruled Hall's objections and put a proscenium arch at the back of the Olivier stage to frame the court scenes. The production looked and sounded wonderful.

Callow emphasised the contradiction between Mozart's prodigious musical talent and his scatological language and manic activity, and by doing so found a way of portraying a genius as a human being. 'Shaffer's is a theatre of gesture . . . The wig, the giggle, the little hop,' he wrote. Scofield's Salieri had to convince the audience that he was jealous enough to be capable of poisoning Mozart. That both succeeded brilliantly was clear as the curtain came down on the first preview: 'There was never any question, whatever the critics might say, that the effect of the play on the public was going to be enormous,' said Callow.

The critics had a lot to say. *Amadeus* was generally praised as a magical theatrical spectacular, but the text produced violent reactions. The revewiers made much of the fact that there was no evidence at all that Salieri murdered Mozart. Several minded Mozart's swearing quite so much. The worst review of all was by James Fenton, the poet and former war correspondent who had recently become the theatre critic of the *Sunday Times*. Fenton wrote that Shaffer was perhaps the worst English playwright since John Drinkwater, which made him the worst for fifty or sixty years, and that *Amadeus* was 'a nauseating load of – to use a word much loved by Peter Shaffer – shit'. Each week the *Sunday Times* carried a paragraph in its Theatre Guide repeating the adjectives 'appalling' and 'plasticated' and 'mediocre'. But, despite the size of his readership, Fenton had profoundly little effect on the audiences, or on the people who gave out awards, of which *Amadeus* won thirteen in all. But Fenton's review made Hall angrier than anything said about his work before or since; he described it as 'terrorism'.

In the strength of Hall's reaction it is possible to detect an unusually sharp sensitivity about *Amadeus*. Shaffer's plot did bear a closer resemblance to melodrama than to history, and Hall's attempts to balance melodrama with theology only partially succeeded. To meet some of the objections, Hall and Shaffer continued to work on the text (reducing the number of swear-words, for example), and the Broadway production was different in many respects. Although the drama was splendid, the heart of the play remained the same shallow piece. But Hall, a man wedded to high art who regarded Mozart as a god, had, for the first time, directed a great public entertainment and he did in fact make some real money.

*   *   *

The one place where critics and audience were unanimous about Hall's work was the opposite of great public entertainment. The festival opera at Glyndebourne was a rare mixture of high art and high society, and Hall became a favourite with the devotees of both.

Hall had served his Glyndebourne apprenticeship directing little-known seventeenth-century baroque operas by Cavalli and Monteverdi. Then, from 1973 to 1978, he directed all three of Mozart's best-known operas with librettos by da Ponte, the former Venetian priest and man of the world. He started with *The Marriage of Figaro*, and immediately challenged the received opinions of it by applying to the opera the same rules that he applied to his Shakespeare at the National Theatre. He went back to the original score and ruthlessly eliminated the mass of stage directions that had encrusted the work over the years; he restored arias that were normally cut (one by Marcellina was heard for the first time at Glyndebourne); recitatives were sung at the tempo of normal conversation; and he corrected the order of various scenes so that they were played as Mozart intended. Spike Hughes, Glyndebourne's distinguished historian, had known the opera for fifty-five years by 1973, and this was the first textually complete performance he had ever heard. In his history of Glyndebourne, he wrote: 'In this way, many subtle points in the text which had been obscure now became clear.'

But the text was only the beginning. Hall wanted the singers to release the pain and sexuality in *Figaro*. This they found difficult at first, but an outstanding cast was so sympathetic to Hall's ideas that eventually there were memorable performances, especially from the women – Ileana Cotrubas, Frederica von Stade and Kiri Te Kanawa. John Pritchard, who had learned to conduct Glyndebourne's light musical style of Mozart playing from its originators, Fritz Busch and Vittorio Gui, sometimes found it difficult to concentrate in rehearsals, but he listened carefully at all of Hall's and conducted with energy and commitment. Spike Hughes wrote that he enjoyed this *Figaro* more than any he had seen. The only person who seems not to have been so sure was Hall, who thought the production was only just all right: 'The heart of the matter is true and good, but not the details,' he said.[17]

The next collaboration between Hall and Pritchard was *Don Giovanni* in 1977, and, once more, Pritchard looked forward to rehearsals. But this time they coincided with a strike at the

National Theatre, and Hall missed a number of them. He finally arrived, with a psychology text underneath his arm, to announce that the company was about to begin a voyage of exploration; Pritchard preferred directors starting rehearsals to have arrived in port.

Don Giovanni is a *dramma giocoso*, by which Italians mean that it is a comic opera that includes dramatic and tragic episodes. Hall concentrated on the latter. John Bury's dark set was inspired by Goya; in this Seville it was always raining. Hall's *Don Giovanni* was 'a theatre of madness, of impulse, of mistaken identities, dark black shadows, and dangerous games of hide and seek'. Pritchard's *Don Giovanni*, on the other hand, was lighter and more conscious of the comic element. Their previous rapport was not revived, but that summer was Pritchard's last as Glyndebourne's music director; he shared the podium with his successor, the young Dutch conductor Bernard Haitink, whose passionate approach to Mozart Hall found much more to his liking.

A striking feature of Hall's *Don Giovanni* was that arias and ensembles which revealed the characters' private thoughts were sung straight to the audience. He instructed the singers not to try to recreate real conversation on stage at those times by singing to each other; concentrate on telling the story instead, he said. Hall believed that the proximity of stage and audience at Glyndebourne allowed the freedom for such direct communication: the singers could then give an authentic account of what they were thinking and the reasons for their actions. Hall's idea was that the more boldly theatrical they were, the more real they would be. The audience quickly accepted this new convention, but some singers found it hard to overcome a lifetime habit of singing to each other. (Two years later, the suggestion initially reduced Elisabeth Söderström, as Leonora in *Fidelio*, to tears.)

Audience and critics were overwhelmed by Hall's *Don Giovanni*. 'Disturbing' and 'challenging' were the most-used adjectives; and some spectators claimed to be so emotionally overwrought that they were unable to enjoy their interval picnic. The only note of doubt came, again, from Hall himself. Conscious of the rehearsal time lost, he said: 'I know I am capable of a definitive *Don Giovanni*. I fear in these circumstances I may not have quite done it.'[18]

When Hall returned the following summer for *Così fan tutte*, he was totally confident of his method, making straight for Mozart's first version, even removing a substitute aria that Mozart himself had written for Guglielmo and restoring the original. Spike Hughes observed: 'It wasn't just a wind, but a tempest, of change that blew away the smog of slovenly tradition and left the atmosphere fresh, stimulating and clear enough to see the wood as well as the trees for perhaps the first time in one's experience.'[19]

Over the years *Così*, a sad and serious opera about sexual deception, had been turned into a comic piece. Hall exposed its deeply melancholic and cynical qualities (the title, after all, means 'Women are all like that'). As with his other revisionist versions of Mozart, the story was now abundantly illustrated and coloured by the score. The cast, which included a young American soprano called Maria Ewing as Dorabella, responded enthusiastically, and Haitink's musical interpretation complemented Hall's direction. As personalities, Hall and Haitink did not blend easily. Haitink was a solitary figure, preferring to spend time in the library rather than chatting in the restaurant, but their relationship flourished through their instinctive appreciation of each other's skills. Hall's Mozart, successfully launched with Pritchard, was at its most brilliant with Haitink.

On *Così*'s first night, Hall felt great grace, elegance and seriousness, and attributed the triumph to Haitink. He himself, of course, felt that 'it could have been better if I'd pushed it further', although he did concede that Desmond Shaw-Taylor's review of *Così* in the *Sunday Times* was probably the best notice he had ever received.[20]

Rehearsals of *Fidelio* in 1979 were interrupted by another strike at the National Theatre, and his absences became so regular that he felt that the company was suffering through lack of leadership (Söderström threatened to return to Sweden until Hall was free to attend). He also felt his own work was conventional. But Moran Caplat knew that conventional work from Hall was likely to be better received than inspired work from anyone else, and, when Hall mentioned resignation, told him to forget it. Caplat's confidence was justified by a reception that Hall described as riotous and ecstatic, although again he was not satisfied: 'I think I have done it right, but not fully.' When the good notices appeared, he commented: 'I got away with it.'

The 1979 Glyndebourne season was like a summer festival of

Hall's work. Besides *Fidelio*, there were revivals of *Così* and his 1972 production of Monteverdi's *Ulysses* – all works that showed Hall at his most radical, expert and confident. While he was directing *Così* in 1978, after the disaster of *Macbeth* at the National, Hall had a long talk with Caplat. The diaries report: '[Moran] said that in a sense it grieved him to think my best work was being done at Glyndebourne.'[21] But it was not surprising. Opera united Hall's rare experience of, and love of, music and the theatre, and he had been excavating works by Mozart that he loved and knew well and was directing for the first time. In an interview in 1980 Hall said: 'If you put me up against a wall and said "What are you good at?" I would say I'm a good opera director. I don't have any doubt about that.'[22]

Caplat's advice to Hall was that he should let someone else run the National Theatre and concentrate on being an artist. But he chose not to act on it. After six years at the National Theatre, as its director and its leading director, Hall still wanted to have his cake and eat it. To have accepted anything less would have been to surrender power, and he was always reluctant to consider that.

15

Exit Jacky; Enter Maria

'I felt perfect, as though we were one'

As director of the National Theatre Peter Hall was a public figure. He was recognised in the street; he was able to attract the attention of political leaders; and he was a controversial, even feared, figure in his own profession. In June 1977, aged forty-six, there was confirmation of his prominence when he became Sir Peter. He wrote in his diary that he was too young to become a member of the establishment, and did not really want a knighthood, but he took it because 'it would help combat mischief-makers and the horrors at the National Theatre'.[1] The reasoning was odd, but the decision pleased his parents, and his wife Jacky, now Lady Hall.

Hall had become so well known, in fact, that curiosity about him went beyond his public persona. This touched a raw nerve in Hall because, as always, the private matters that were really interesting to the public were money and sex, and these were the cause of constant turmoil in his life. But Hall was not discreet. On the contrary; when his diary covering the years 1972 to 1979 was published in 1983, clues about his domestic life and his family finances were scattered throughout the text. The diary is remarkable. It contains melancholic self-analysis as well as shrewd advice on running a large organisation and directing actors and singers. Many of those who feature in the diaries question details of Hall's account of his times, but when he is talking about his life (the original diaries were dictated into a tape-recorder, and most of them were transcribed by his personal assistant Sue Higginson) it is hard for anyone, except perhaps a former wife, to question their accuracy. The diaries are a revealing document about the state of his mind, and for the period 1972 to 1980 they are a priceless source for a biographer.

Hall's financial troubles run like a thread through the diaries, and the thread is always coloured red. When he originally negotiated his contract with Max Rayne, Hall was pleased to discover that he would be doing the job for money as well as love (an inflation-proof £20,000 a year, plus two-thirds of his rent, and a car allowance). But that money was not enough. In November 1973, appearing in a film in Munich, he said that he thought he could honestly say that it was the first thing he had ever done for money. The fee was £5,000; not enough either.

In July and August 1974, Hall paid three visits to his accountant, Bernard Kimble. On the first he was 'faced by a disastrous situation': all his personal accounts were overdrawn, and he discovered his freelance earnings, over and above his salary, needed to be between £10,000 and £12,000 a year. The next meeting with the accountant reduced Hall to 'standard despair'; he was told to cut down or earn more, and needed £7,000 quickly to keep the family afloat. The third meeting was 'a dreadful hour' with Kimble, when he accepted that something had to go. But he could not sell Wallingford because the property market was depressed. It was particularly galling, then, that Dimitri de Grunwald had offered to pay Hall £75,000 – enough to settle all his problems at a stroke – to direct Roger Moore and Sophia Loren in a film of a Moss Hart play. But some of the filming would be in Paris, and not even his financial crisis could justify his spending that much time away from the National Theatre.

By April 1975, Hall could see that his hard work earned the money to create the environment he desired, and that he never had the time to enjoy it. But he also confessed in the diary that he needed his possessions, because they reassured him. Wallingford was important to him because it was an emblem: it proved that he had arrived. When he saw Kimble next, in June 1975, Hall decided that only a millionaire could afford to run three houses as he did – two in the country (one of them for his parents) and one in town. In January, his eldest son, Christopher, got a place at Cambridge, and Hall found he would have to earn another £7,000 or £8,000 before tax to meet the £1,500 it cost a parent not eligible for government grants to send a child to university. And there were three other children who would presumably go to university, plus his parents and his Aunt Gee, never mind his wife. After a further meeting with Kimble in November 1977 he was 'more than a little depressed' to find that after nearly twenty-five years as a successful director he had no security, no savings and no assets; 'I have never been sufficiently interested in my own finances,' he wrote. Of course, Wallingford was an asset, but one that was costly to maintain.

The only action he actually took to stanch the flow of money into the upkeep of his possessions was to move to a smaller flat in the Barbican in 1978. Despite a diary entry recording that Hall felt 'no regrets', Jacky Hall claimed, years afterwards, that the move, in fact, made him weep. Since the three-storey penthouse had, like Wallingford, been an emblem of his escape from a working-class childhood, Hall saw the move as a defeat. But he went on living like a millionaire.

Peter and Jacky and their children, Edward and Lucy, now aged twelve and ten respectively, could have lived perfectly comfortably in the Barbican, but Hall liked to nurture the country roots that had sunk so deep during his few months when his father was the stationmaster at Barnham in the north of Suffolk. At Wallingford he had a large lake and eleven acres of grassland to wander in. His parents now lived there too. Reg and Grace had been in Kessingland for almost a decade and the shop was becoming a burden to them. They could have retired in Suffolk, but Jacky persuaded them that the better choice was to do up a cottage in the grounds by the lake, not far from the main house. It was comfortable, more a house than a cottage, with a new kitchen and old beams; there was enough room for Grace's sister, Peter's Aunty Gee, to join them. Jacky wanted to have them nearby in case they fell, or had to go to hospital; Reg was now in his mid-seventies, after all. But Grace was suspicious. She claimed at first that Peter and Jacky wanted them there as unpaid caretakers, at the bottom of the garden, and she wailed that she was too old for such upheavals.[2] The elder Halls, though lonely to begin with, settled in. Reg made friends in the pub. Grace found Edward and Lucy a continuing pleasure, and she loved them almost as much as she loved her son.

Bedales proved a remarkable success, providing Christopher and Jenny with a decent education as well as a secure environment. In 1976, Christopher won an exhibition scholarship to his father's college, St Catharine's, and the following year Jenny won a scholarship to Newnham College, also in Cambridge. But Hall was not only proud of his elder children; the diaries make clear that he enjoyed their company. The tension created by his divorce from Leslie Caron had long since disappeared, and the two children flew regularly to France or the United States to see her.

Jenny, who went to university in 1977, wrote later that when she left school aged eighteen, the security it had offered deserted her. As an undergraduate, she was a talented actress, and Hall went to see her in *The Tempest*, *The Seagull*, and George Farquhar's *Man of Mode*, but towards the end of her time at university, Hall wrote in his diary: 'Jenny is wondering whether to be an actress after all. She will blow hot and cold like this all her life.' It was already clear that Jenny had inherited the family's Pamment genes. Christopher, on the other hand, dealt with life competently from the start. His degree was no better than his father's, but good enough to enable him to go on to Bristol University as a film student. The trust Hall had for his eldest son was best illustrated in February 1980, when Christopher became a director of Hall's company, Petard Productions, at the age of twenty-two, while he was still a student.

The two younger children moved from their state infants' school to private day schools, Edward to St Paul's, and Lucy to the City of London School for Girls, which was conveniently situated in the Barbican. Lucy showed talent as a pianist, but neither child enjoyed school as much as Christopher and Jenny had liked Bedales, and at the end of the 1970s their parents decided to send Edward and Lucy there too.

Until the salaries of the directors of the four leading subsidised theatres and opera houses were eventually made public in 1983, Hall's exact salary remained a secret. But anyone who visited Companies House and asked to see the annual return of Petard Productions Ltd could get a shrewd idea of Hall's earnings from the National Theatre.

Petard had been established by Bernard Kimble in 1966 to take over the management of Hall's finances from Fontped Securities Ltd of 32 Sloane Street, the company that arranged Leslie Caron's and Peter Hall's tax matters. Bernard Kimble was a partner in Stanley Gorrie, Whitson and Co., chartered accountants of 9 Cavendish Square in the West End, and he was a celebrated figure among well-paid actors and musicians. He was expert in ingenious schemes, not for evading taxes but for avoiding them, and, as well as Hall and Leslie Caron, his client list included Hayley Mills, Julie Christie, Albert Finney and Tommy Steele.[3] These schemes, based on trusts, were of a complexity that defies description, but the objective was clear enough: to reduce tax liabilities to the very lowest permissible level.

When Hall signed his contract with the Shakespeare Memorial Theatre in 1959, his salary was paid to Fontped Securities in Sloane Street because it owned the exclusive rights to his services, although the directors of the company were a solicitor and a chartered accountant rather than Hall and Caron themselves. Fontped was a shelf company with no other purpose than to manage the tax affairs of a number of clients of Stanley Gorrie, Whitson, including Hall and Caron, and it was not dissolved until June 1976, but the company's reports show that the participation of Hall and Caron ceased abruptly on 12 May 1964, five weeks after their separation was announced. Following the divorce, Fontped had been disposing of its stock, but in 1971 it still had shares in 'subsidiaries' worth £28,940. Fontped's sales between June 1959 and May 1964 amounted to millions of pounds, and the Hall family's contribution was mostly from Leslie Caron's film work. Hall's income at Stratford began at £5,000 a year and he was then doing no freelance work, but in those unenlightened times the Treasury was not interested in whether a wife earned more than a husband. For tax purposes, the two were one, and the bills went to the husband.

A note in Fontped's 1971 accounts states that the Inland Revenue had served tax assessments on the company for 'very substantial sums' for 1958–9 to 1964–5, but these must have been settled because the Inland Revenue had no objection in 1976 when the company was wound up and the remaining assets of £3,993.80 were distributed among the shareholders – i.e. the solicitor and the accountant.[4] (This did not sever all financial links between Hall and Caron. A second company named Vancollin Ltd, set up by Bernard Kimble in 1958 to invest in theatrical and film productions, remained in business until it was dissolved in 1983. But, to take 1973 and 1976 as typical years, it made small losses on

a small turnover and carried over small loan accounts of around
£4,000 for Leslie Caron and £3,000 for Peter Hall.)

From 1970 until 1983 Petard Productions became the only
publicly available guide to Hall's earnings from the National
Theatre. The company had been established for another client
of Kimble's named Peggy Goddard, and the name derived from
hers. The annual report for the year ending 30 November 1970
states that the principal activity of the company was to trade as
impresarios, and this is exactly what it did in that year, having
invested £1,250 in a play called *Dutch Uncle* and recorded a small
loss. The following year it became Hall's exclusive vehicle, and
the shareholdings were adjusted so that Mr P.R.F. Hall owned
50 A and 49 B ordinary shares. (The other one is owned by
the company secretary.) Fees receivable were still only £4,293,
and a small loss was shown. Obviously, this annual report does
not reflect Hall's earnings; the first that does so is for the year
ending 30 November 1973 when, in the language peculiar to
annual reports, 'Emoluments of Highest Paid Director amounted
to £20,000.' That was Hall's salary, paid by the National Theatre
to Petard.

After paying Hall's emoluments and the accountants their fees,
Petard still made a net profit of £5,500, so some of Hall's freelance
earnings were also being paid to the company. (It was, of course,
perfectly possible for him to be paid directly and to declare those
fees as personal income and to be taxed accordingly.) From
1973 until the end of the decade, Petard declared its income as
follows:[5]

Year	Net income*	Surplus**	Hall's fee	Dividend
1973	£27,755	£2,526	£20,000	none
1974	£24,017	£421	£20,000	none
1975	£33,192	£5,485	£22,500	none
1976	£42,376	£11,164	£27,500	£1,900
1977	£42,228	£14,778	£27,500	£1,500
1978	£44,847	£11,604	£27,500	none
1979	£63,598	£11,919	n/a	none

* from 1978 net income = net fees
** after taxes and dividend

A change in company reporting practices in 1978 meant that

Petard had to present a breakdown of its spending. After salaries of £29,666, came the incidental expenses: £3,656 on office, rent, administration; £1,157 on printing, stationery, books, magazines; £2,276 on travelling expenses; £2,241 on entertaining. On top of that were costs of his cameras, his motor car, his clothes, and general expenses, which, when added up, produced a deficit for the year of £4,818.

Petard's annual reports can only be taken as a very rough guide to Hall's earnings, especially in the early and mid-1970s. When accounting practices change and net fees are declared, the returns yield a more accurate picture. It is clear that Wallingford was still being used as an office, for example. They also show that, if Hall was not exactly a millionaire, he was making a very commendable living by 1979. Expressed in terms of comparable 1994 purchasing power, Hall's income topped £160,000 that year.

In the middle of the decade, his income had been boosted by his percentage of the profits from the West End transfer of *No Man's Land*. At the end of the 1970s the transfer of Alan Ayckbourn's *Bedroom Farce*, to the West End and to Broadway, propelled his income sharply upwards. The earnings bonanza was still to come, and, when it did, there was plenty to spend it on.

His marriage is the second thread running through Hall's diaries, and this is coloured blue. As early as August 1974 'the walls appear to be moving in on me'; the following October, on the eve of his seventh wedding anniversary, he is 'standing at several crossroads', including that of his marriage. He records only one row with Jacky Hall: in August 1976, when he fails to meet her and the children at the airport. In December that year 'things cannot go on as they are on the home front': he says he is approaching a big crisis. In January 1977 he reports that the break-up of his marriage is 'looming'. That summer, 'things could not be worse' on the personal front. By Christmas 'things are now finally breaking up'.

Although Jacky is rarely mentioned by name, except as a travelling companion, there is a revealing entry for 10 November 1978. The two went together to see *Betrayal*, Harold Pinter's play about adultery, deception and domestic cruelty. Hall remarked that he thought *Betrayal* was very accurate and he records Jacky as replying tartly: 'You should know.'[6]

Having a home in the country did not bring the family together;

rather, the reverse. When Wallingford was their principal residence in the early 1970s, Jacky Hall remembers the telephone
calls from Hall at 8.30 p.m., when the dinner was ready, saying
that he was just leaving London. When they lived in the Barbican
during the week, matters did not improve. The National Theatre
never gave Jacky Hall the same sense of belonging she had had
in Stratford: 'People at the National regarded me as someone
from outer space. I felt extremely isolated.' There seemed to be
a pattern of separation in their lives, even at the weekends. Hall
often arrived exhausted at Wallingford late on a Saturday; Jacky
and the children would pack up and leave for London, where the
children were at school, on Sunday afternoon, leaving Hall alone
in the country to read and walk and listen to music.

Jacky Hall did not suspect that she had a rival until the summer
of 1978. It was the school holidays. Hall was in London, and since
the children and their grandparents were getting on her nerves
in Wallingford, Jacky decided to join him there. She recalls a
nightmarish journey slowed by a fatal road accident, and she
finally arrived at the Barbican late in the evening to find no
one at home. No one came home at all that night. The following
morning, when Hall learned that Jacky had returned to an empty
flat, he offered to come round right away. She told him not to
bother: 'I really did credit him with some integrity and loyalty.
I couldn't believe it,' she says.

She had known, as well as anyone had known, that Hall had
not been faithful to Leslie Caron, but, because Caron had also
been unfaithful to him, she had thought that the example would
not apply to her. She had remained faithful: 'I never even had a
proposition. I was the boss's wife.' The breakdown of Peter and
Jacky's marriage occurred long before Hall met his third wife,
Maria Ewing. Jacky Hall's rival was a woman who was one of
the 'six long-term serious commitments' Hall speaks of in his
autobiography.[7] (The others were four wives and a fiancée.)
Jacky's rival was the sixth woman in Hall's life, Sue Higginson,
his personal assistant at the National Theatre. She has remained
utterly discreet about the affair, asking that Hall make no reference
to it in his autobiography.

Hall's account of the break-up with Jacky in his autobiography
is terse. Speaking of the period when his style of leadership was
being attacked by the London *Evening News* in March 1978,
Hall writes: 'At home it was lonely. Jacky never mentioned

the shock of the *Evening News*. We shielded ourselves from each other, and there was a cold silence.'[8] This concept of the 'cold silence' incensed Jacky Hall when she read it in the *Daily Mail*'s serialisation of Hall's autobiography. (She subsequently refused to read the book.) She believes that she was fiercely encouraging during the turmoil at the National Theatre. But she does not dispute Hall's assertion that the National Theatre's troubles contributed to the collapse of the marriage.

She had been surprised at the viciousness of the attack on Hall two years earlier, in 1976, and believed, as Hall did – wrongly as it happened – that Michael Blakemore fed the *Evening Standard*'s attacks, motivated by envy and vengeance. She remembers Hall coming home after being interviewed by Gaia Servadio of the *Evening Standard* in April 1976, shortly after Blakemore delivered his broadside to the associate directors, and his reaction: '"It's no good. She wants my balls. She'll publish, and it will be the beginning of the horror."' So it was, but even Jacky was startled by the intensity of Hall's reaction: 'For the first time I saw a chink in Peter's armour.' After that, Hall was obsessed by the National Theatre, getting up very early and returning very late. 'That probably destroyed our marriage,' she says. But she also felt that Hall had begun to associate her with things that were going wrong in his life. Not just the National, but the embarrassing Sandersons advertisement, and the move to a smaller flat in the Barbican: 'The failure was blamed on me, and I became part of it, but it wasn't a case of weathering it and moving on. There had to be a scapegoat.'

Doubtless the strain caused by the attacks on him exacerbated the troubles in their marriage, but Hall's diary shows that his disenchantment with Jacky had set in before the turmoil at the National Theatre began. When he left Jacky, Hall told her that he would always remember ten wonderful years, and that the divorce was not her fault – but ten wonderful years were up in 1975, more than three years before he eventually left.

The diary dates his decision to leave Jacky to August 1979. Hall was unhappy during the first weeks of rehearsals for *Amadeus*, but on 7 October he said that his 'Black Dogs' had receded, and he supposed this was because he had decided what to do about his personal life. In that case, the woman for whom at that moment he would have left Jacky must have been not his third wife, Maria Ewing, but Sue Higginson.

Hall had met, but not fallen in love with Ewing in 1978, when she was singing Dorabella in Glyndebourne's production of *Così fan tutte*. That they had met at all was chance. Because opera planning takes place years ahead, the conversation with Moran Caplat in which Hall agreed to direct *Così* was in the summer of 1975. By 1977, when the pressure of work seemed intolerable, Hall got cold feet and said he was cancelling. Had he carried out his threat, as he did with a planned production of *Idomeneo* two years earlier, he and Ewing might never have met. Only a most ingenious argument by Caplat ('he is a clever old fox') saved the day: 'Moran said that Glyndebourne would be in a worse mess if I walked out on it now than if I walked out next year – next year would be a crisis; now would be a catastrophe.'[9] Caplat and Hall were already discussing the casting in 1976, when Hall had said that Dorabella and Fiordiligi, the twin sisters who are deceived by their lovers, should be feminine in the best possible way – 'warm and sexy'.[10] Among the singers mentioned in 1977 as possibles for the role was an American soprano called Maria Ewing. There was a suggestion that she might sing the maid, Despina, but Hall thought she should sing the better part of Dorabella.

Maria Ewing was only twenty-seven when she and Hall started rehearsals at Glyndebourne. All she knew of him was from a television programme about the Royal Shakespeare Company she had seen in New York City a couple of years earlier. She had found him 'fascinating', but not so much so that she jumped at the chance to join him at Glyndebourne. Ewing had had a big success as Cherubino in *The Marriage of Figaro* at Salzburg in 1976 and was beginning to receive attractive offers from international opera houses. She could see that *Così* done by a Shakespeare director might be good for her career, but her first thought was that Glyndebourne would be English and stuffy. Only after her agent insisted that the chance was too good to pass up did she say yes.

She found that, far from being stuffy, Glyndebourne was relaxed and well organised. At the outset of rehearsals, one of her fellow-sopranos told Ewing that everyone fancied Peter Hall, especially when he was directing and was exuding maximum charm and sexuality. Hall had noticed her too: he thought her 'wide-eyed and with the absolute beauty that can come of mixed race'.[11] But what Ewing liked first was his intelligence, which released her own: 'I never felt he was trying to get me to do it his way; he wants the performance to come from you and who you are.'[12] In the relaxed atmosphere of the piano rehearsals, they found that they approached opera in the same way, as music drama with strong theatrical content. Ewing was fascinated by Hall in the flesh as well, and felt a spark ('more than a spark') as they rehearsed. Hall admired Ewing too, later berating a reviewer for failing to notice that the one undoubted star performance in an elegant, dark production of *Così fan tutte* was hers.

Hall helped her with her heavy luggage when they travelled back in the train to London at the end of the season, and during the journey Ewing told him that when she sang *Carmen* she would like him to direct it. She did not appear in the revival of *Così* the following summer, so the next time they met was in Salzburg, where Hall was working with Peter Shaffer on the script of *Amadeus* and she was singing Cherubino. Then in mid-November 1979 when Hall arrived in New York to rehearse the Broadway production of *Betrayal*, he telephoned her to say that he had a pair of tickets for Donizetti's *Don Pasquale* at the Metropolitan Opera. It was chance that she happened to be in the city, and that she was free. They liked the opera so little and their own company so much that they left after the first act. The affair that began shortly afterwards was so passionate and absorbing that Hall did not return home to his family for Christmas.

On 25 December, he wrote in his diary: 'I have always kept this diary professional and unpersonal, but now it's beginning to seem ridiculous if I cannot say – or will not say – what's in my heart. I am deeply in love with Maria Ewing, and have been here with her. We plan to make our life together in the new year when she will come to London.' (One consequence of their affair was that Hall stopped keeping his diary; after his Christmas Day confession, only fourteen more entries appear.)

Hall and Ewing were besotted with each other: 'He said to me "I want you and I'll pay any price", and I felt perfect, as though we were one, bound together.' By falling completely in love, Ewing had surprised herself. Part of her was a committed loner who insisted on having time to herself. Another part of her resisted marriage because of the friction she had observed in her own home. The youngest of four sisters, she came from a working-class family from Detroit, where her father was an engineer. Her parents contributed to an exotic cocktail of racial ingredients. Her American father had blood from Scottish, African and Sioux

Indian forebears, and her mother was Dutch: 'a temperamental, passionate lady who tended to get very emotional. There was a lot of laughter and some of it was hysterical.'

As Ewing had guessed in Glyndebourne, she found Hall sexy ('He is a very, very sexy man, take my word for it'). But Ewing was afraid – not because of his previous life, about which she knew little, but because of hers. She was afraid that the emotional instability of her parents' marriage might affect her own.

At the beginning, they simply delighted in the discovery of things they had in common: a working-class background, for example, a loving father, and an emotional mother. 'Despite the fact that Peter had gone to the university and I hadn't – and was in many respects self-taught – our backgrounds were similar enough to create a very strong bond between us. I never felt any difference in class between Peter and me,' says Ewing. The joy of being together overcame her fears, and she planned her move to London.

A cyclical pattern was developing in Hall's domestic relations. A star (Leslie Caron) was replaced by a personal assistant, or assistants (Jacky Hall and Sue Higginson), who were, in turn, replaced by another star (Maria Ewing). The personal assistants were sometimes like surrogate mothers, fiercely supportive and caring at home or work, looking after the children, and keeping the finances and the hectic work schedule in some sort of order. Having grown up with a protective mother, a part of Hall prompted the mothering instinct, and responded to it. That half of him had enjoyed concurrent relationships with Jacky and Sue, and he was never able to choose between them. Hall's other half craved excitement, risk and unpredictability. His stormy, dramatic relationship with Maria Ewing satisfied that need. She was his most passionate lover, his most fulfilling collaborator, and his severest critic.

16

The Eighties: Part One

A Religion Abandoned

The last year of the 1970s was crucial for Peter Hall. Having agonised for years over leaving Jacky Hall for Sue Higginson, he had resolved his dilemma by falling in love with Maria Ewing. But the end of uncertainty meant the beginning of turmoil.

The politics of the decade had also reached a climax. After years of being mesmerised by the capricious behaviour of trade unionists, organisations like the National Theatre began to fight back. This mood was reflected nationally in the election of Margaret Thatcher, and Hall was part of the swing to the Conservatives.

Hall's basic loyalty to the Labour Party had remained intact through the disappointments of Harold Wilson's administration from 1964 to 1970. But his disenchantment with Wilson himself had increased. During the miners' strike and the three-day week in January 1974, Norman St John Stevas, the Minister for the Arts, asked Hall if he was still a Labour man; he replied that he was, but that he could not vote for Wilson. In particular, he objected to Wilson's opposition to the European Economic Community; Hall disliked Little Englanders.

In the February 1974 general election Hall, who was registered to vote in Wallingford, was relieved to find himself in London. He could not face voting Tory; it would be, he thought, like a Catholic abandoning his religion. In the election that followed in

October 1974, he did in fact vote Labour; but by the election of 1979 he had come to believe that the Labour Party's association with the trade unions meant it protected pressure groups and bully boys. On 3 May, Hall found that voting for Mrs Thatcher's Conservative Party actually made him feel good.[1]

In a profession where politics are conventionally left of centre, Hall's vote for Mrs Thatcher was regarded as a defection, a betrayal even, and he did not feel good about voting for her for long. But his vote was not hard to understand: while the 1979 election campaign was in full swing throughout the country, the National Theatre was experiencing its fifth strike in four years. In mid-March, when Hall heard that stagehands were threatening to strike, he hoped they would go ahead: 'We can't continue teetering on the precipice.'[2] The stagehands and workshop staffs received letters on 16 March telling them they would be sacked if they went on strike, so they struck.

To begin with, ticket-holders were given their money back, but, since that seemed a feeble way of supporting the principle that agreements ought to be upheld, stage performances began again, without scenery and at reduced prices. When John Galsworthy's play *Strife*, which was about an industrial dispute, rejoined the repertory, the strikers found it provocative and demanded that it be taken off. (That was the way strikers thought in the 1970s.)

On 5 April, all seventy-seven strikers were dismissed, a gamble that did not end the strike but did not provoke its escalation either. After five weeks, and only a few days before the general election, the strikers cleared the picket lines and faded away. Someone on the Left must have noticed that the behaviour of the strikers on the picket line was politically counterproductive – Michael Redgrave, who had Parkinson's Disease, was forced to get out of his cab and shuffle a hundred yards or so to the stage door, for example.

The strikers were given the option of reapplying for their jobs, but of seventy who did only ten were re-employed. Manning levels on stage crews fell immediately. The cost of the dispute was £510,000 in lost income, and four productions were dropped, but that was, as it turned out, a small price to have paid. Box-office successes like *Death of a Salesman* with Warren Mitchell, and Peter Shaffer's *Amadeus*, quickly restored audiences to pre-strike levels. After the summer of 1979, the National Theatre had difficulties with the law, with the government, and with the Arts Council, but for eight years there were no more labour disputes in its own back yard.

During the strike, Hall had confided to his diary: 'My heart is no longer in this shit-heap.'[3] The statement, made when he was out of sorts in the middle of another industrial dispute, was extravagant, but there was genuine and lasting feeling in it. After 1979, his commitment to the National Theatre was rarely as single-minded as it had been in the previous seven years. His concentration, which had hardly wavered during the fight to get into the South Bank and then to make a reputation for the new theatre, began to falter.

A number of consequences flowed from his affair with Maria Ewing. Sue Higginson, the efficient head of his private office, quit, and other senior colleagues left at the same time, breaking the continuity of seven years. Hall was less in evidence in the building. In the 1970s, he had been absent when he was directing at Glyndebourne, or when he took Pinter's *No Man's Land* and Ayckbourn's *Bedroom Farce* to the United States. But the opera house was only an hour away from the NT by train, and the touring companies had comprised original casts that needed a minimum of re-rehearsal.

The Broadway production of *Amadeus* signalled a change. Because the American actors' union would allow only one English actor to work in the show in the US – Ian McKellen played Salieri – Hall was forced to spend time auditioning and rehearsing in New York. Besides, Maria Ewing was there, and his heart, having flown the shit-heap, was now where she was.

Wherever Ewing was singing, Hall would try to join her for the weekend. This naturally affected the attention he gave to his rehearsals and to advising his fellow directors, but his travels were not only expensive in terms of time. They cost him money he did not have. He had not stopped supporting his extensive family when he left Jacky Hall: she was in Wallingford, and so were his parents; two children were still at school. Now he was paying for one more household, and it was not a frugal one.

The compulsion to earn reduced further his commitment to the National Theatre. Money was not at the root of his decisions – he was not disloyal to his art – but it did play a part in his determination to hold on to his permanent job at the National Theatre, and to supplement that full-time salary by becoming the artistic director of Glyndebourne's Festival Opera, and by taking on ambitious, time-consuming projects like directing Richard Wagner's *Ring* in Bayreuth. What governed his life was the art of the theatre and a love of being in love, but the money he required, and the time it took to earn it, also had a profound influence on Hall's life in the 1980s.

An Impulsive Patron

Peter Hall was a committed, courageous, and sometimes reckless patron of new writing. His early commissions at the National Theatre were for plays from established writers like Harold Pinter and John Osborne. Work by Tom Stoppard was revived; and Robert Bolt and Alan Ayckbourn were persuaded to desert the West End. But new names joined Hall's school too: Stephen Poliakoff, David Hare and Howard Brenton.

The commitment of Hare and Brenton was significant. Both were left-wingers who had come in from the fringe, and each had encountered hostility from former colleagues to whom the sprawling, state-subsidised National Theatre was an offence. But Hare and Brenton saw an opportunity to create a popular theatre performing new plays by a new generation of writers – their generation.

At Stratford, Hall had felt most comfortable with people like Brook and Saint-Denis, who were older than him and not a threat. At the National Theatre he drew a number of ambitious theatre people who were too young to threaten him. Hare, for example, was exactly the kind of writer and director Hall wanted on his side. Hare claims that everyone in the theatre has a favourite Peter Hall story, and, in telling it, they reveal what they think of him. Hare's favourite story is about the production in 1978 of his play *Plenty*.

The reviews were not very good, and to begin with *Plenty* was playing to houses of only 60 per cent, which was below the NT's break-even point. It should therefore come off. (John Osborne had been a victim of the 60 per cent rule.) Max Rayne asked when the Hare play would be coming off, but by 1978 Hall felt confident enough to say that unless the National Theatre did the plays it believed in, it would not find the audience it wanted. *Plenty* stayed in the repertory and, because word of mouth was good, the audience began to build. By the end of the run, the Lyttelton

Theatre was full and the play transferred to New York. 'How then could I not love Peter for life?' says Hare.[4]

The affair that earned Howard Brenton's loyalty was Hall's promotion and defence of *The Romans in Britain*. This was a classic example of Hall's artful relationship with the National Theatre Board; of his relish for controversy; and of his uncompromising defence of an artist under attack.

Howard Brenton had come from the Royal Court with a public reputation as a fierce left-wing polemicist. In private, he was like a friendly bear, obliging and unpretentious, and when he first visited the National Theatre and was shown around the Olivier by Hall, Brenton was a little in awe of him.[5] Brenton's father was a policeman who became a Methodist minister, and, like Hall, he had gone to Cambridge; he felt that each instinctively understood the other's background.

One of the first new plays to be performed in the National Theatre in July 1976 was Brenton's *Weapons of Happiness*, directed by Hare, a political play about varieties of left-wing experience. After it opened, Hall asked Brenton to write him another. There were teething troubles; the work came slowly and when it arrived Hall wanted it rewritten. More than two years went by before Hall showed Brenton's script to the associate directors. When he did, Harold Pinter hated it; among the other associate directors, Bill Bryden was unenthusiastic, and David Hare did not want to direct it himself.

But Hall was not listening. 'I am determined to get this play on,' he wrote.[6] Brenton hoped Hall would direct it himself, but he did not have the time and eventually the job went to a young Irish director called Michael Bogdanov, who had had a success with a clever production of *Hiawatha*. *The Romans in Britain* was scheduled to open in October 1980.

Before it did so, Hall gave notice at the July board meeting that, by drawing a parallel between the problems in Ulster and the Roman occupation of Britain, there was 'an element of risk' in the play.[7] This was curious, because politics was not one of the controversial issues about which Hall had promised to warn the Board before a first night.

Max Rayne had not tried to imitate Lord Chandos, who was sure he knew best and did not hesitate to censor plays when they gave offence to him, such as *Spring Awakening* and Rolf Hochhuth's *The Soldiers* (which suggested that Winston Churchill had had a hand in the death of the Polish wartime leader, General Sikorski). Rayne had conceded artistic control to Hall without a fight, his only condition being that the Board should be forewarned about obscenity, *lèse-majesté* or blasphemy.

This enlightened regime survived its first test with only a murmur. When Hall demonstrated his independence by putting on *Spring Awakening* in 1974, there were no complaints from the Board about the London production (though when a tour was planned, Victor Mishcon did wonder aloud whether the group masturbation scene as presented at the Old Vic in London was suitable for audiences in the provinces).[8] While Hall felt that the Board deserved advance warning about Brenton's play, he omitted to mention that in one scene in *The Romans in Britain* a Roman soldier buggers one of the native Celts.

Before the company, which included experienced actors like Michael Bryant and Stephen Moore, left the rehearsal room for the Olivier stage, a run-through before an audience of colleagues from the National Theatre was a great success: 'The studio audience thought the male-rape scene was terrific,' says Brenton.

After Hall had flown in from New York to watch a preview he took Brenton and Bogdanov to dinner and told them that if they cut some bad language and played the rape scene behind a tree, they would have a 1960s-type hit. Brenton recalls: 'Being good 1960s-type men, we said no.' Hall, accustomed to having his suggestions accepted by other directors, did not grumble in this case when they were ignored; nor did he now move in on another director's production, as he had done at the RSC to John Barton and Bill Gaskill.

He did, however, take the precaution of warning the Board three days before the first night that misunderstandings might arise because, as a metaphor of colonialism, a Roman soldier violated a British youth. This worried Mishcon, who argued that the National Theatre should be a guardian of good taste. Hall replied that it ought to be the guardian of good art, and that *The Romans* was a flawed but important play which would probably not draw large audiences. 'In the Director's view, [the rape] scene was handled with discretion,' the minute reports.[9] If that was the case, Hall was in a tiny minority.

The rape scene caused an uproar. On the guest night, which preceded the press night on 16 October, two prominent Conservative members of the GLC walked out in the interval. Sir Horace Cutler,

the leader of the GLC, called *The Romans* a disgrace to the National
Theatre and denounced Hall's 'singular lack of judgement'. The
Tory chief whip in County Hall, Geoffrey Seaton, told Hall that
many members felt the GLC grant to the NT should be suspended
forthwith. Since this was £650,000 a year, it was not a threat to
treat lightly.

Hall's difficulty was compounded by a chorus of disapproval
from board members and the critics. Even boardroom allies
like Sir Derek Mitchell found the piece 'nasty and second-rate'.
Benedict Nightingale in the *New Statesman* put the general dissent
more pungently: 'The real trouble is that the plaint it [the rape]
is designed to italicise is hardly more sophisticated than that
imperialism is a crying shame, not to say a pain in the arse.' In
the *Sunday Times*, James Fenton took another tilt at Hall himself:
'If I were Sir Peter Hall and had instigated such a production, I
would take myself out to dinner and very tactfully, but firmly,
sack myself over the dessert.'

Brenton was disappointed, with himself as much as anything
('we got the show wrong months before the first night'), but
thought the production improved as time went by. Seaton told
the Board that, if they wanted to secure the GLC's grant in the
coming year, the sooner the play came off the better. But they
resisted blackmail, deciding that *The Romans* must run until March
1981, as scheduled: 'It would be impossible to justify to the author
any decision to take the play off earlier because the production was
playing to a serious theatre audience,' said Hall.[10]

But the controversy suddenly ceased to be about taste or art
when Mary Whitehouse, Britain's self-appointed moral arbiter,
brought a private prosecution against Bogdanov for 'procuring an
act of gross indecency' under the Sexual Offences Act. No other
opponent of the National Theatre had thought of this manoeuvre,
and it transformed the argument about the merits of the play into a
matter of principle involving censorship and freedom of speech.

Although the rule of the Lord Chamberlain had ended in 1968,
the publicity meant that the National Theatre had still braced itself
for a visit on the first night from the Metropolitan Police's Obscene
Publications squad. But the Director of Public Prosecution had sent
an anonymous lawyer to have a look instead, the upshot of which
was that the government's law officers decided the law had not
been broken. Brenton and Bogdanov, who had feared a vengeful
attack on the subsidised theatre by the forces of reaction, thought

they had seen off the opposition. Then Mrs Whitehouse's solicitor called Bogdanov out of a Christmas party to issue him with a writ. He was due to appear in Horseferry Road Magistrates' Court on 30 June 1981, a couple of months after *The Romans* ended its run.

It went unrecorded at the time, but the case proceeded because the National Theatre decided that it must, for reasons not of principle but of money. Throughout the spring of 1981 Mary Whitehouse's solicitors were suggesting that, since there were no plans to revive the play, they might drop the action if each side paid its costs. The National Theatre's negotiators replied that Mrs Whitehouse must offer to pay a proportion of the NT's costs. Ahough Victor Mishcon reported in April 1981 that 'everything possible was being done to arrive at a solution without recourse to a court case', there was in fact too much pride at stake, and neither side would back down far enough.[11]

Because Lord Hutchinson, appearing for the National Theatre, asked that reporting restrictions be lifted, the magniloquence of Hall's performance at the committal proceedings was widely reported, especially as he managed to draw a parallel between Brenton's *The Romans* and Shakespeare's *Lear*: 'I thought [the rape scene] would be found horrifying, just as the gouging out of Gloucester's eyes in King Lear is horrifying. But the scene is in my view a precise and inevitable metaphor about the brutality of colonialism, where the other side, the other race, becomes not human at all, but simply plundered.'[12]

There was one detail in Hall's evidence, however, that did not quite accord with the account of other participants. The *Daily Mail*'s report states: 'Sir Peter said that during rehearsals Mr Bodganov asked whether it was right to do the scene in full light. "I said it was right because the scene was meant to horrify and if it had been done in half light behind a tree, it would have titillated."'[13] But Hall's loyal revision of the play's production history was no help. The magistrate was not unsympathetic, making the legal point that, since the Sexual Offences Act applied only to men, the prosecution would have failed if the play had been directed by a woman. But he felt there was a case to answer, and Bogdanov was committed for trial at the Old Bailey.

The National Theatre's lawyers were uncommonly generous about their fees, but in the judicial system nothing costs nothing. Despite the solicitors reducing their charge from £13,750 to £5,000, costs up to the committal hearing were already £11,489.

In September 1980, no less than £72,000 was budgeted from the National's central funds for Bogdanov's defence, and the chairman of the Arts Council, Kenneth Robinson, was expressing his concern to Rayne about the diversion of public funds to pursuing the case, especially when these were short.[14] (In fact, public funds were to be stretched even further when Bogdanov was awarded £20,000 in legal aid.)

At the first day's trial proceedings in March 1982, Mr Justice Staughton seemed so unsympathetic that Brenton was overcome by horror at the notion that it was the director rather than the writer who would be found guilty and might go to jail. Then, quite suddenly, in a moment that would have graced the climax of any courtroom drama, the Attorney-General stopped the show. Prompted by Mrs Whitehouse's own counsel, he issued a *nolle prosequi*, meaning that he did not wish the case to be pursued. The principle involved – whether simulation of a sexual act on stage is subject to the same laws as sexual acts committed in real life – was unresolved, but Hall declared that the NT had won, and no one argued.

After the case was over, Hall gave Brenton some sound career advice: 'Don't dine out on it,' he said, 'or you'll become known as the man who wrote that rape play.' (Brenton took the advice, and became known as the co-author, with David Hare, of the astonishingly successful *Pravda*.)[15] For its part, the Board had some advice for Hall after the trial. When he thanked its members for their support, three of them said that next time they hoped to be told exactly how explicit and controversial a play was going to be.

Hall's impulsive and generous patronage of new writing had led him to display and exploit the whole range of his stubborn authority. As impresario, he had overruled his colleagues; as chief executive, he had, whether deliberately or not, misled the Board; and, as distinguished public figure, he had appeared to be economical with the truth in the courtroom. Hall had also displayed three of the essential qualities of a leader: courage, determination and loyalty. It was a good performance.

Bearing Gifts to the Greeks

Tony Harrison, the Leeds-born poet, had done the National Theatre good service. His translation in witty rhyming couplets of Molière's *The Misanthrope* had brilliantly transposed the play into the Elysée Palace of Charles de Gaulle and caused Laurence Olivier to kiss Harrison's mother after the first night, and say: 'You must be very proud of your little boy.'[16] For the first time in her life, Harrison's mother later said, she was glad her son had chosen to become a poet and not a schoolteacher. Harrison had next transformed Racine's tragedy into *Phaedra Britannica*. When Peter Hall took over at the National Theatre, he treated Harrison as a most valuable part of his inheritance.

Harrison was a linguist; besides French, Czech and Hausa, he read Greek fluently. He was also a poet with a single-minded commitment to his art in the theatre. Soon after taking over, Hall asked him to maximise both these talents by writing a new version of Aeschylus' bloody trilogy known as *The Oresteia*, after Orestes, the son of Agamemnon and Clytemnestra, who kills his mother to avenge her murder of his father. Translations of Greek drama had so far been the monopoly of professors of classics like Gilbert Murray, but what Hall wanted from Harrison was a text that respected the poetry while being accessible to the National Theatre audience.

By March 1976, Hall had decided that the three plays should be done simultaneously, as 'one brave gesture'. By Christmas, he declared that *The Oresteia* was the most exciting project he had ever contemplated. Early in 1979, shortly before the first experimental workshop for these Greek plays, Hall confided that he thought that in getting the National Theatre launched, he had won the greatest battle of his life: 'Now I bloody well want to enjoy it.'[17] *The Oresteia* was the prize; the first production of the complete trilogy in English since it was written, almost 2,500 years before.

Harrison was having a bumper year in 1979. He had also been asked to write a modern version of the York Mystery Plays. Known collectively as *The Mysteries*, and directed by Bill Bryden, they became one of the most memorable productions in the history of the National Theatre. His version of *The Passion* was already playing to packed, admiring audiences, and previews of *The Cresteia* were due to begin in April. Then the stagehands' strike began, and although it did not halt all performances – *The Passion* was played on the terrace in front of the theatre – it did hobble much of the new work. *The Oresteia* was the most notable casualty: its acting company was wound up at the end of April, and Hall directed Peter Shaffer's *Amadeus* instead.

But the basic decisions had been taken by Hall, Harrison and Harrison Birtwistle, the National Theatre's director of music, who was composing the score. The first was that Harrison's translation would absorb the craggy, dense sounds of Old English, and the vowels of his native northern speech. A slew of new words were invented by Harrison for the purpose: bloodright, bloodgrudge, bondright, doomgroom (for Paris), clanchief (for Agamemnon) and she-kin (Elektra). The four-pulse beat in each line was so regular that the verse was spoken at precisely ninety-two crotchets to the minute.

The second decision was that Birtwistle's music would be percussive, a driving accompaniment to the verse, establishing the rhythm and the pulse. The music would also provide the completely modern component. The third decision was to confirm the lineage from ancient Greece by using masks that entirely covered the actors' faces. Hall intended to emphasise the ritual element of Greek drama.

Hall was fascinated by masks throughout the 1980s. After *The Oresteia*, he did a version of George Orwell's *Animal Farm* in masks, and in 1990 he got as near to a theory of artistic performance as he ever did by defining performing arts in terms of masks. (The theory of directorial neutrality was David Hare's, not Hall's.) The occasion was the Goodman Lecture at the Royal Society entitled 'The Mask of Truth', and Hall took as his text a line from the comedian George Burns: 'The important thing about acting is honesty. If you can fake that, you've got it made.'[18]

Hall's case was that it is impossible for an actor to perform great passions of birth, death or making love in a purely naturalistic way. Naked passion is painful, repulsive almost; so the passions are filtered by an actor ('any actor will tell you that if you wish to move an audience, do not cry'). The Greeks understood this and invented the mask, to reveal tragedy rather than to obscure it, and to release the bawdy, childlike energy of comedy.

'The mask enables you to release and to deal with passion at an intensity which takes you beyond that moment of repulsion,' Hall said. 'The screaming, naked, actual face repels you. The screaming face of the mask does not. Indeed, the Greek theatre itself – keeping all fundamental or violent action offstage – is like a mask . . . So I am led to believe that any form of performance art needs the equivalent of the mask wherever it deals with huge and primeval passions.'

Hall's case led him to propose that form itself is a mask. When Shakespeare's disciplined iambic pentameters are the form, then the verse is the mask. In opera, the precise and balanced form of a Mozart aria is the mask. In dance, choreography is the form and the mask. As a stage director, he was, he said, interpreting the form: he saw this as meaning that he was more like an orchestral conductor than a film director or an actor. Hall had, in fact, arrived at the same conclusion as Hare had, by a different route.

Hall had an intellectual's education and liked to discuss ideas, but, as a practical man, he preferred putting theory into practice rather than down on paper. Lord Goodman, in the chair at the Royal Society lecture, described it as the most impressive piece of spontaneous oratory he had ever heard. What he meant was that Hall had not written his speech. There is a theatrical phrase for his performance. He was 'busking it', and doing so unusually well. Trevor Nunn first became conscious of Hall when he heard him speak at Cambridge: 'It was off-the-cuff, and yet formed and balanced, spontaneous but moving; he is formidably brilliant at expressing complex things. I don't know anyone else who has that public gift.' Behind his own mask, the question Hall was asking himself was whether he could bring off performances like this, or whether he would be found out. He had asked this same question in school at the Perse, and he had been asking it intermittently ever since. At the Royal Society, the answer was that he could still pull it off.

The Oresteia company, sixteen strong, was all-male, in the manner of the ancient Greeks. There had been a brief mutter among the actors about sexism, but Hall, backed by Harrison, insisted that Greece was a misogynist society and that Aeschylus actually celebrated the new domination of men (Orestes) over women (Clytemnestra). That was clear from Harrison's translation:

The mother of what's called her offspring's no parent
but only the nurse to the seed that's implanted.
The mounter, the male's the only true parent.

The cast had been selected after workshops in which actors experimented with masks. Some had found that, wearing a mask, they were unable to speak, or could talk only gibberish, or got headaches. The masks were designed by Jocelyn Herbert, who was George Devine's regular collaborator at the Royal Court. They were made of layers of muslin, glued together, varnished and then painted, and they forced the sixteen survivors to learn new tricks. Addressing the audience directly through a mouthpiece left no space for subtlety or irony. 'You can't hint at a performance in a mask,' says Barrie Rutter, who played the Herald.[19]

Since the actors could not hold their scripts and wear masks at the same time, they learned the lines first. The trilogy was four and a half hours long, but the biggest challenge was not the length, it was the rhythm of Harrison's verse. Rutter remembers being called for a Monday morning rehearsal and not starting work until Thursday afternoon. 'Peter had to go at the pace of the slowest member,' he explains. (Hall dealt with that problem by allocating six months to rehearsals.) Rutter, Yorkshire-born, found Harrison's vowels easier to recite than actors with southern voices, but that was Harrison's intention. He wrote to Hall in September 1981: 'We don't want Barnsley Working Man's on a Saturday night knees-up, but I have written SHORT vowels.'[20] Harrison would have preferred a whole cast from the north of England; Hall said he could not afford it. Rutter was never entirely convinced by that argument, but he was enjoying himself: 'Once I got the text right, Jocelyn Herbert could have put anything on my head.'

This company was exploring new territory. Hall discovered that it broke the mood to refer to an actor by name when he was wearing a mask: the masked actors could only be spoken to collectively. If more than two of them spoke at the same time, they became incomprehensible. The actors had no peripheral vision and could not see each other, but they formed excitingly shaped groups; yet without the masks, they instinctively formed up in boring lines.

Hinged aluminium panels provided the background; John Bury's lighting shone down from above to emphasise the mask and hide the face behind it; costumes were simple and colours were muted. Hall's production did not renounce compromise entirely. To stress the bitter sexism of the piece, Harrison had wanted to separate the audience into blocks of men and women as was the custom in ancient Greece, while Hall preferred not to draw attention away from the stage. But the production was as true to the ritual as it was possible to be 2,449 years after the first performance.

The Oresteia was scheduled to run for twenty performances and did sixty-five. Though some critics confessed that they had found it difficult to stay awake, the *Observer* (Michael Coveney) said that Peter Hall had not produced anything as interesting in the theatre for years; and James Fenton, in the *Sunday Times*, described it as a very considerable achievement. The classicists were much warmer. Oswyn Murray announced in the *Times Literary Supplement* that this was 'surely the best acting translation of Aeschylus ever written', and declared the production to be this generation's classic account of *The Oresteia* against which we would judge all attempts to stage ancient Greek tragedy. Hall satisfied the audience that this dramatic experiment was what the National Theatre was for. They could have seen it at no other theatre, not even the RSC, which had two years earlier done John Barton's version of *The Oresteia*, without masks or music.

Hall was anxious for the work to reach a wider audience, and to recoup some of the heavy costs. Jeremy Isaacs, in charge of the fledgling Channel 4, wanted to establish its artistic credibility. They were made for each other. Instead of selling the rights to a production company, Hall set up a National Theatre subsidiary to film *The Oresteia*, which allowed the National to retain the management fee and Hall to retain complete artistic control.

Isaacs was staggered by Hall's working method. He had never come across anyone who shot so much film, or used so much equipment.[21] Four cameras recorded four whole performances, or sixteen shots of every second of the performance on thirty-six hours of film, as well as making a separate sound recording of a complete performance. Moreover, Isaacs observed that, unlike most television directors, Hall had not roughly edited the material while it was being filmed, or even got an assistant to do it for him. Hall took his videotape machines home with him and edited the various tapes himself.

Hall earned his £10,000 director's fee, but his lavish use of the
the editing suite, the most expensive department in preparing
film for television, cut into the project's profits. Some months
after it was finished, Rayne and his colleagues learned that *The
Oresteia* budget had been overspent by £18,000.[22] But Hall's art
was never cheap, and it was pointless to express the value of
The Oresteia in pounds and pence. By exploiting all the resources
of the National Theatre, Hall had done work on a scale that no
other theatre could equal.

The audience response to the first television transmission was
so good that Isaacs scheduled a repeat not long afterwards. 'It
was a great and moving classic; one of the Channel 4 shows of
which I am proudest,' says Isaacs. But the Greeks themselves
offered the best compliment of all when they invited the National
Theatre to repeat *The Oresteia* in the great open-air auditorium at
Epidaurus, the first production of Aeschylus to be performed there
in English. Hall had been to Epidaurus with Denys Lasdun when
he presented *Aquarius*, and it had influenced the design of the
Olivier, but doing *The Oresteia* there was Hall's first experience
of its astonishing acoustics, which allow actors to speak to an
audience of 15,000 without raising their voices.

Hall's only disappointment came when the Greek authorities
refused his request to perform the play at dawn as the ancient
Greeks would have done. But he could live with that. He knew
The Oresteia was the best work he had done as a director at the
National Theatre.

Unable to Say No

By 1982 the Board were not the only people who were starting to fret about Peter Hall's attendance record at the National Theatre. Since doing *Amadeus* in 1979, Hall had directed only one show in 1980: Paul Scofield's *Othello*, which had been a disappointment, rather like their *Macbeth* together in 1967. The monumental *Oresteia* was his only contribution in 1981. His next production, Oscar Wilde's *The Importance of Being Earnest*, was scheduled for the autumn of 1982, with Judi Dench playing a younger-than-usual Lady Bracknell.

Apart from *The Oresteia*, the memorable work in the early 1980s was done by John Dexter (Brecht's *Galileo*), Bill Bryden (Arthur Miller's *The Crucible*), John Schlesinger (Sam Shepard's *True West*), and Richard Eyre (Frank Loesser's *Guys and Dolls*). Eyre, who had joined the National in 1981, was asked straight away to recommend the sort of popular classic he had done so well at the Nottingham Playhouse. The National Theatre had never done a show on the scale of *Guys and Dolls*, and Hall had to root about in the budget to find the money for the costumes. Hall let Eyre know that the stakes were high, but, Eyre says, 'he never made you feel as though your head was on the block or gave you advice you couldn't use; he was an exemplary producer'.[23] *Guys and Dolls*, with *Amadeus*, was the NT's biggest hit, stanching the financial haemorrhage as it had been put on to do. (As a measure of the freedom such a success gives a director, Hall told Eyre it had bought him five years' grace from criticism.)

But on 22 March 1981, a couple of weeks after *Guys and Dolls* had opened, the group that met for dinner at the Savoy Hotel still had no idea how successful the production would prove to be. *The Romans in Britain* was still uppermost of the minds of Hall, Max Rayne and a small group from the finance and general purposes committee. One of the diners was Sir Derek Mitchell, the former civil servant, who was asked to produce a minute of the meeting.

From this it is clear that, once some administrative matters had been dealt with, the bulk of the evening was spent discussing Hall and his future.

The dry, Whitehall-style minute reports the opening gambit:

> *PH was asked whether there was substance in the impression that he was increasingly diversifying away from the NT, particularly towards opera. He spoke of his superabundant creative energy and denied that he was taking on new commitments . . . He stressed that he had large and growing financial obligations and needed to make the most of his talents in the coming decade. Sympathy with his position was expressed but he was reminded that he was increasingly vulnerable to adverse comment as full-time Director of the NT (and paid as such) yet publicly active and earning outside it . . . The accountability of the Board for public funds was stressed. PH should be prepared to accept a reduction of his NT remuneration to take account of outside activity; and to do this to protect the Board as well as himself from criticism.*[24]

Sir Derek's minute reports that when Hall was asked how long he wanted or intended to remain director, he said he wanted to stay on and take a leading role for around five years, which might or might not be extended: 'The rest of the group warmly welcomed this.' A new contract would be discussed, and the group even touched on the eventual succession to Hall: 'It was noted that in the likely event that no one would so well combine the creative and administrative skills, major changes might be needed in the NT's top management.' Whether the flattery was intended or not, what Rayne and his colleagues were saying was that, while Hall did not spend enough time at the National, he was, none the less, doing the work of two top people.

Rayne was punctilious about keeping members of the finance and general purposes committee informed of the course of the subsequent negotiations with Hall and his agent Laurence Evans about the new contract; so Mitchell was amazed to learn that Hall was disregarding the warning about his outside earnings. Mitchell was particularly concerned about Hall's proposed absence of three months in Bayreuth in 1983; production schedules for the following two years were already being disrupted to make way for that. Mitchell thought the answer was half-pay for the duration of Hall's absence.

Rayne had another idea. The Board had been surprised to learn quite how much Hall had earned from the American production of *Amadeus*; Mitchell recalls that in 1980–1 Hall's share of the American gross was $165,000, but that in the following year this shot up to $690,000. Rayne decided that the National Theatre ought to be on a percentage of those outside earnings that resulted from transfer of National Theatre shows. (Rayne, incidentally, discussing this proposition with Sir William Rees-Mogg, the chairman of the Arts Council, had learned that similar problems were arising at the RSC.)

But Hall was conceding nothing. Evans, his agent, reported that he saw no reason why he should take a salary cut when he was in Bayreuth; moreover, he believed he was absolutely entitled to his fees from transfers. Indeed, he claimed that were it not for his personal deal with the Shubert Organisation in New York, it was very unlikely that the Broadway production of *Amadeus* would have taken place.

Hall was gambling again, and this time he lost. Before he entered talks with Evans, Rayne had discussed the negotiating position with his cronies on the finance and general purposes committee. Mitchell recalls that they told Rayne that they could not settle with Hall at any price: the new contract must be compatible with the Board's responsibilities as the guardian of the public interest. This message got through. By July, Rayne could report that Hall had offered to waive one-third of his salary when he was in Bayreuth (a sum amounting to about £4,000), and that he would consider a formula which gave the NT a 12.5 per cent share of any of his earnings over £50,000, rising to 17.5 per cent on more than £100,000. Hall had said this was his final offer; if it was unacceptable, he would quit when his contract expired on 31 December 1983. Rayne called his bluff and got 20 per cent on all earnings over £50,000.

The new five-year contract gave Hall a salary starting at £50,000 in 1984 (the rent and car allowances were discontinued) which would rise by the same percentage as the stagehands' pay. He was allowed to be artistic director of Glyndebourne, but the opera programme had to record that this was 'by arrangement with the National Theatre'. Hall's other outside work had to be approved by the Board, and was limited to four weeks a year. Hall also agreed to help identify his successor.

Though the contract did not formally apply until January 1994, it was stretched to include any earnings from a promising new American musical that Hall had agreed to direct at the National

Theatre in 1983. It was by Marvin Hamlisch and entitled *Jean Seberg*. The addition of this clause suggests that Hall and Rayne hoped that *Jean* would be a pot of gold to rival – even to outshine – *Amadeus*.

After years of media grumbling about the secrecy surrounding the salaries of the directors of London's four subsidised companies, these were revealed by the Minister for the Arts in March 1983. Hall came top on the list, but only just: his £47,718 for 1982–3 was £77 more than Trevor Nunn was getting. (Opera was the poor relation; John Tooley at the Royal Opera House got £37,500 and Lord Harewood £19,500 at the English National Opera.) No attempt had been made to calculate Hall's actual earnings; and, since his basic salary was higher than that of the permanent secretary to the Treasury, this was as well.

The weakness of Hall's personal position was reflected in the significant concessions he made during his wage negotiations; but they were made so reluctantly that they lost him much of his reserve of sympathy among his boardroom colleagues. Rayne still defended Hall's acquisitive nature, insisting that he was no different from his predecessor, but not all the others were so sanguine. Hall was to be more carefully watched in future.

Disenchantment with his absences from the National Theatre was not confined to boardmen, bureaucrats and busybodies. Relationships with old friends and new allies were damaged by his protracted absences. Alan Ayckbourn's experiences with his next play, *Way Upstream*, which opened in October 1982, would have made a good plot for one of his doleful comedies. The set had been designed for Scarborough with a real boat in real water in a plastic water tank. Transferring the set to the Lyttelton's bigger stage called for a bigger tank and more water. Looking at the empty tank, one of the NT's security staff remarked: 'I don't think they know how much water weighs.' He was right; the 6,000-gallon tank split and deluged the stage machinery. When the tank was fixed and the boat launched, Ayckbourn thought it looked low in the water and asked how many it was carrying; the final total was eight – five actors, one stage manager and two more from props. Beset by problems and disaster, Ayckbourn wailed that no one was in charge at the National Theatre: 'It was like a ghost ship,' he says.[25]

Hall returned to London (from New York, this time) once Ayckbourn started to cancel previews, and, because there was no show in the Lyttelton, arrived back to find the whole theatre dark on a Saturday night. Since there was not much he could do by then, he gave Ayckbourn and his stage management a drink and said they deserved awards for patience. This fleeting visit did revive their spirits, but Ayckbourn was saddened by the outcome: he thought an interesting play had been swamped by technical problems, and feared that he would never be asked back. (Fortunately, he was wrong, and *A Chorus of Disapproval*, one of his finest plays, opened in 1985.)

For Ayckbourn, *Way Upstream* was the straw that almost broke the camel's back at the National Theatre. But; there was more than one camel. By 1983 Harold Pinter was also at the end of his tether. Left with a hole in the repertory in spring 1983, Hall had asked Pinter to fill the gap by directing Christopher Fry's translation of Jean Giraudoux's *The Trojan War Will Not Take Place*. Pinter obliged, but during rehearsals he grew unhappy with his work on it, and there were problems with the sound system. 'When I started to run into trouble, I wanted Peter around. I needed a father,' says Pinter.[26] The play was opening in May, and Hall was already in Bayreuth, out of reach of Pinter's cry for help. Pinter's disappointment led to an emotional breach: 'I thought "fuck it", he's the artistic director and I want his help. We'd both become very selfish at the same point, but I wasn't just thinking of myself. I was thinking of a production at the National Theatre for which he was, finally, responsible.'

Pinter decided to jump the 'ghost ship' forthwith. He resigned as an associate director, rubbing salt into Hall's wounds by declaring that the associates' body, of which he was once chairman, had become redundant. To emphasise his displeasure, Pinter also withdrew the rights to *A Kind of Alaska*, in which Judi Dench played a woman awoken after thirty years of sleeping sickness by the new drug called L-DOPA. Dench, who thought it the most beautiful play she had ever read, gave a remarkable performance and was looking forward to a transfer to the West End.[27] But Pinter had taken offence, was implacable, and *A Kind of Alaska* never transferred.

Pinter's departure did not arouse the same volume of outraged public analysis that had accompanied Michael Blakemore's, but it was not much less significant. 'What I knew was that he had started to do far too much,' says Pinter. His colleagues among the associate directors who had stayed on thought so, too.

Richard Eyre, who had had experience of running a theatre, was especially upset that the director of the National Theatre should spend so little time in it: 'He was a big man with terrific authority and presence, so when he withdrew himself, you felt his absence deeply,' says Eyre. He was one of the associate directors involved in a mini-revolt which occurred in the autumn of 1983. Hare recalls that Hall was told that they would all resign unless he spent more time on the South Bank.[28] When news of this reached the *Guardian*, Hall said crossly at their next meeting that he understood their conversations were confidential. Since his diaries, which included intimate accounts of many of their meetings, had just been published, he was not on strong ground. The associate directors were just as confused as they were angry, asking each other why it was that Hall worked so hard. One reason, of course, was those large and growing financial obligations he mentioned at the Savoy, but another was his innate inability to say no to a challenge. He was still greedy for work.

17

The Eighties: Part Two

An Ordeal in Bayreuth

Peter Hall had had plenty of time to plan his production of Richard Wagner's *Der Ring des Nibelungen* in Wagner's own theatre in Bayreuth in northern Bavaria. The performances were to take place in the summer of 1983, and Hall had agreed to direct them in June 1980, when Sir Georg Solti suggested they do the *Ring* together as they had intended to do at the Royal Opera House twelve years earlier. At Covent Garden they would have performed two new productions of the four operas in the *Ring* in one year, and two in the next, but at Bayreuth all four were to be unveiled in a single summer. When Hall and Solti asked Wolfgang Wagner, the composer's grandson, to consider changing the habit of three generations, Wagner told them that, in the first year in Bayreuth, the work was regarded as 'a study' for a polished production a year later. Hall replied that he did not work that way: he wanted the audience to see his best work from the very beginning. But Wagner was adamant. He also told Hall that Patrice Chereau, who had directed a famous *Ring* in 1976, had dealt with the problem of four massive new productions by spending a year on the project, much of it in Bayreuth.

Hall, who had never learned to speak French, even after marrying a Frenchwoman, had an Englishman's wariness about foreigners ('I always feel somewhat frightened abroad, uneasy. It's partly not being sure of the language . . .').[1] Even so, he realised that he needed to learn German to work in Bayreuth, and in 1982 he began to take lessons from a teacher who visited him at the National Theatre. But his schedule was unusually full in the winter of 1982 and 1983. After his *Importance of Being Earnest* had opened to good reviews in October 1982 (he honoured the text, exposing the melancholy as well as playing the laughs) Hall made his début at the Metropolitan Opera, directing Verdi's *Macbeth*. Since Maria Ewing was a popular performer at the Met, this production was important to them both. If it was well received, *Macbeth* might be the first of many collaborations between them in New York.

But the audience's response to Hall's melodramatic interpretation of Verdi, complete with flying witches, sprites and goblins, was to boo, and loudly. The New York critics, who had been blind to Hall's virtues in the past, put the boot in again, and word of his unhappy experience with *Macbeth* was quickly relayed to Bayreuth. Later that winter, the audience in Geneva was more appreciative of a new version of Hall's Glyndebourne production of *Figaro*, with Ewing singing her first Susanna. Back in London, there was the musical about Jean Seberg to be worked on. No time at all for German lessons, which dropped off his schedule.

The original plan was to open *Jean* before Hall went to Bayreuth, but delays meant that the only performances done in the spring were in a studio before an invited audience. The new plan was now for a London first night in the autumn, with the Broadway opening taking place a few months later. This schedule took success for granted, and there was reason to do so. Marvin Hamlisch was the composer of *A Chorus Line*, one of Broadway's greatest earners. Hall liked Hamlisch's music and was willing to suspend his belief that musicals tend to belong at the tacky end of the theatrical spectrum. He detected a redeeming social theme in the libretto by Christopher Adler: in the absence of religion, film stars are the icons of the mass audience, and sometimes get crucified.

Jean Seberg had become a star while she was still a girl, playing St Joan in the Otto Preminger film. Having flirted with radical black political activists in America, Seberg became a target of FBI harassment and emigrated to Paris, where she committed suicide, lying undiscovered in her car for ten days. It is not a happy story. Hall recommended it to his colleagues because he insisted that the National Theatre should not feed only off the existing musical repertory with productions like *Guys and Dolls*. *Jean* explored new territory. He was so sure of its merit that he told the Board in July 1982 that it should be done, whether or not it transferred to Broadway; indeed, Hall said, he suspected it might be too serious to be a New York hit. But the money men on the Board liked the idea of the potential income flow; there was talk of profits of between one and two million pounds.[2]

The reason the financial potential was so great was because Hall had arranged that the NT had an option to become one of the main financial backers of the Broadway production. But the more fastidious members of the Board were appalled by the idea of *Jean Seberg*. John Mortimer, a consistently true supporter of Hall's, was so indignant at the idea that the National Theatre was being used to try out a Broadway production, as if it were a touring theatre in Philadelphia, that he insisted his opposition be recorded in the minutes: 'He felt [*Jean*'s] inclusion in the repertory breached an important principle.'[3] Mortimer's view was that the National should do only new plays that would not be done anywhere else; he even disapproved of Alan Ayckbourn's plays being performed at the National when there was a market for them in the West End.

Although he was none too keen on *Jean* himself, Max Rayne deflected Mortimer's opposition on the formal grounds that, as an artistic decision, this was Hall's to make; the Board's views here were irrelevant. But not all Hall's artistic associates shared his enthusiasm for *Jean*; David Hare, for example, warned him of failure.[4] Mortimer's objections were widely echoed in the newspapers once *Jean* was announced in 1983. But Hall was not listening; he had been pleased with the studio performances, and swore that Kelly Hunter, playing the young Jean, would become a star herself. His optimism was reassuring: he had committed his reputation to this commercial vehicle, and it had to be good.

Hall left London for Bayreuth on 24 April 1983, exactly three months before the opening night of *Das Rheingold*, with the other three operas following it in the next five days. He had made quick trips to Bayreuth during the winter, and these had been turbulent. Hall had actually resigned three times by April 1983, twice after arguments with Wolfgang Wagner, and once because William Dudley, the designer, had been consistently late with his costume designs. Dudley was in his mid-thirties, an exuberant, insecure Londoner who had conceived a brilliant opening for the *Ring*. This takes place under the surface of the Rhine, and Hall had decided that, since he proposed to perform the *Ring* in the naturalistic style in which Wagner had written it, there must be real water for the Rhinemaidens to swim in.

Dudley delighted in illusions and recalled a Victorian stage trick called Pepper's Ghost which made magic by the use of reflecting mirrors. For Bayreuth, the trick was to have a large tank of water on stage and fly in a mirror at an angle of 45 degrees above the stage. Seen from the auditorium, the mirror transformed the water on the stage floor into an apparently vertical wall of water, and the Rhinemaidens, moving back and forth in the tank, appeared to be swimming from the riverbed to the surface. It was a sublime *coup de théâtre* – and to crown it the three sopranos singing the Rhinemaidens agreed to swim naked.

From the bed of the Rhine, the scene changes to the top of a mountain. It is a difficult transition at the best of times, and more so with a tank full of thousands of gallons of water on the stage floor, which could not be moved until the end of the evening. A solution was found, but many of the problems that dogged Hall's production flowed from it. (Since I was in Bayreuth that summer and wrote an account of the Hall–Solti *Ring*, I am the source of most of the opinions that follow.)[5]

To cover the water tank, Bill Dudley designed a hemispherical platform, powered by hydraulics, that would provide a curved acting surface representing a mountaintop. Wolfgang Wagner's Festspielhaus did not have hydraulic power, but, after some haggling, he agreed to install it, and to build the substantial curved platform. Hall knew enough about budgets to appreciate how much this was costing, but he was not deterred. Like most English artists, he regarded the German subsidised theatre as a bottomless pit of money: 'This is going to be the most expensive production in operatic history,' he said gleefully. He was as good as his word.

Having committed so much of the budget to the platform, Hall decided to use it in all four operas. For the Ride of the Valkyries, for example, the platform started out tilted vertically at the rear of the stage, and was slowly lowered into a horizontal position while moving forward, giving an impression of the ride, and, incidentally, terrifying most of the allegedly fearless Valkyries, who were strapped on to its upright surface like fighter pilots. During the rehearsals, moving the platform smoothly and accurately into a position that would let the singers make their entrances and exists proved alarmingly time-consuming. The large steel arms that raised and lowered the platform were visible from the auditorium, and Hall had to lower a gauze and use smoke to try to hide them. The production team disliked the gauze because it blurred the stage picture; the singers hated the smoke because it made breathing difficult.

Hall had other original ideas, such as putting the two giants on stilts; like the Rhinemaidens, the giants looked magnificent, but a great deal of time was spent teaching them how to sing and walk on stilts at the same time. Much energy was spent on ideas that did not work, such as a second platform which would act as a screen on which to project films of moving clouds and billowing smoke. Only after it had been built did Hall discover that it would make top lighting impossible. The second platform was cut, and lay all summer, like a reproach, by the Festspielhaus's canteen. That was not the only piece of scenery that was first ordered, then cut. Hall's reputation was not high among the stage and production crew. For his part, Hall found their work surprisingly 'unscientific' – which meant that he felt they did not always do as he asked, as the production staff did at the National Theatre and Glyndebourne, and had done at Stratford.

While few of the stage crew understood English or had any sympathy for Hall, most of the singers did. Some of them had taken their roles because they knew of Hall's eminence as a Shakespeare director and were eager to see how he would approach Wagner. But Hall had not given himself enough time to prepare the lecture with which he had always begun his rehearsals in Stratford, and he did not know Wagner in the same way that he knew Shakespeare and Mozart. Apart from Hildegarde Behrens, who sang Brünnhilde radiantly and behaved throughout the summer like a fearless and faithful warrior, the cast and Hall had a relationship that remained tepid rather than warm. And his relationship with Reiner Goldberg, the East German who was singing Siegfried, never defrosted. Goldberg, a *Heldentenor* to whom the craft of acting was a mystery, was sacked after the *Siegfried* dress rehearsal.

Maria Ewing was stranded with their small daughter, Rebecca, in a house some way outside Bayreuth, so Hall himself was never able to relax. As soon as he had finished rehearsal, he would drive back, often to do the shopping and help prepare the supper. In Germany, Hall learned how to roast a chicken, an accomplishment unique among Hall men; his mother must have been open-mouthed.

Bayreuth's English *Ring* had some wonderful moments and

some miserable quarters of an hour. Wolfgang Wagner said his grandfather would have approved of Dudley's evocation of the Rhine; and the mood of the forest scenes was drawn beautifully from the German *Wald*. Other pluses were Behrens's Brünnhilde, and Solti's conducting, which drove on with compelling rhythm and energy. But some of the parts promised more than the whole delivered, and the first *Ring* cycle ended in a torrent of booing. The reviews from German and American critics were bad; those from London were mixed. Andrew Porter, in the *New Yorker*, tried to be kind, applauding Hall's initial plan, but he considered that it foundered on Dudley's impractically ambitious designs and Hall's 'over-confidence, misjudgement, and, perhaps, inexperience'.

Although Hall's intimates speak of his tears as a regular occurrence, they are rarely to be seen in the company of colleagues and never by journalists, but his mask slipped and tears welled up in his eyes briefly after the first cycle when he and I talked about the lessons he had learned in Bayreuth. He confessed that he had spent too much time arguing and not enough planning; and that he had been too optimistic about the skill of Bayreuth's technical staff. His conclusion was that, even if this *Ring* had been properly cast and there had been a trouble-free Siegfried, doing four massive operas in a summer was a recipe for agony.

The best guide to Hall's own appraisal of his performance was his body. On his return after the first cycle, shingles struck again in a virulent form, and he was told that unless he retired to a darkened room and did nothing he might lose the sight of his left eye. His illness prevented him from returning to Bayreuth later that summer, and, faced with another bout of the agony the following year, when he was contracted to re-rehearse the *Ring*, Hall passed the parcel to his assistant, Michael McCaffery.

Wolfgang Wagner had grudging praise for Hall's work, writing in his autobiography that Hall's *Ring* had been 'useful and necessary to Bayreuth in a general context'. Wagner pointed out that the audience seemed to like the production much more than either he or the critics had done. When Chereau's *Ring* had its last performance in 1980, the applause broke all records, receiving 101 curtain calls in 85 minutes. Hall scored 128 calls in 77 minutes.[6] But Hall was not to know that when he sought sanctuary in his darkened room. Without the technical support he took for granted at the National Theatre, and the admiration and reassurance he had grown used to at Glyndebourne, Hall found directing in Bayreuth a difficult and unrewarding occupation. *The Ring,* his most ambitious project in an opera house, had proved to be his worst defeat. And when he emerged from the darkened room early in September 1983, there was no respite. *Jean Seberg* was due to open at the National Theatre in November.

Trouble had been brewing in Hall's absence. A solicitor by occupation, Victor Mishcon sensed trouble in the book's harsh portrayal of Otto Preminger. The librettist had cleared his script with every other living person in it. Mishcon called for counsel's opinion.[7] Rayne began to fret about a possible injunction from Preminger which might close the show before it opened, and it was the Board that insisted on a rewrite which erased even the most oblique suggestion that Preminger was in any way responsible for Seberg's death.

Rehearsals were dogged by ill-luck. David Ryall, one of the principals, broke his ankle, and the first night had to be delayed. Hall and Marvin Hamlisch ceased to be friends. Costs were out of control: the original budget for *Jean* had been generously set at £241,073, but the orchestrations alone cost £61,000.

Even before *Jean* was judged a success or failure, the debate about the financial propriety of doing it was revived in the *Sunday Times* and the *Economist.* The charge was that the National Theatre was financing an American enterprise at the expense of the British taxpayer – an American enterprise, moreover, from which Hall stood to gain personally. Hall told the finance and general purposes committee that he found the *Sunday Times* 'inaccurate, slanderous and most distressing personally'.[8] What distressed Rayne, however, was that , to try and deflect criticism, Hall and John Goodwin had given to the press internal estimates of the musical's potential profits. For Rayne, this was a 'serious breach' between the Board and the executive.

Had all these difficulties been the prelude to a memorable hit, they would have been merely the dark thread in a showbusiness story with a happy ending. As it was, they were auguries of a terrible disappointment. Just before the opening night, Hall recognised them; he forewarned Rayne and the committee members on 28 November. The minute records:

The Director said the [Jean] previews had been going well. Both the level of business and the audience response were very good. He feared, however,

that the critics would not like the production. He had enjoyed directing
Jean Seberg and was glad the National Theatre had mounted it. On the
other hand, he regretted the adverse publicity and the cost factor.[9]

In his autobiography, Hall describes *Jean* as 'the most notorious
flop of my career',[10] although the reviews do not justify such a
claim. Admittedly, Bernard Levin did say that *Jean* was 'one of
the most frightful stagefuls of junk ever seen in London', but most
of the critics wrote in sorrow rather than anger: 'Not a fiasco, just
not good enough,' was *Variety*'s verdict; and the problem lay not
in Hall's direction, but in the book and the lyrics. The story-line,
they said, was risible, and the music was less good than Hamlisch's
earlier work.

After the opening, a calamity became a nightmare with Hall as
the principal victim. This show – unlike *Via Galactica*, which had
closed after five days in New York – was contracted to run for
seventy-five performances in London. Although he had learned
that he might be dumped for any Broadway production, Hall could
not take *Jean* off despite the dismal NT box-office returns; to do so
would have forfeited the National's rights to Broadway profits.
(The rights were in fact notional, because there was no Broadway
production, and there were no profits.) Poor houses meant the NT's
revenue was running well below expectations. When all the bills
were in, the total cost of *Jean* was £373,839: £132,766 over budget.[11]
Worse still, *Guys and Dolls*, the NT's most profitable hit, had been
taken off when it was still doing excellent business, to make way
for *Jean*.

By March 1984 the Board learned that the deficit for that financial
year was £472,600 and rising. Far from being the cornucopia Hall
had hoped for, *Jean* was one of the ingredients in a financial crisis
that would eventually lead to the temporary closure of the prettiest
jewel in the National's crown, the Cottesloe. In one way Hall was
right: *Jean* was the most notorious flop in his career, although, as
a piece of stage work, his *Ring* had been more harshly criticised.
But his status as a commanding figure, both inside and outside
the National Theatre, was undermined by his stubborn advocacy
of a second-rate American musical. He was fifty-three, and 1983
was the most chastening year in his life. He saw there were things
that were beyond him, and, as director or as administrator, he was
never so bold – or so rash – again.

Coffee-table Confrontation

Peter Hall's best-known public speech, which accused Margaret Thatcher and her colleagues of philistinism, was made standing on a coffee-table in the foyer of the Olivier Theatre on 7 February 1985. The curtain was rising on another financial crisis at the National Theatre. Earlier that month, Hall had gone with Max Rayne to explain to the Arts Minister – who was at the time Lord Gowrie, a lover of painting and poetry who understood and appreciated the arts – why their subsidy was not big enough. But Gowrie had talked like an unrepentant Thatcherite, and told them to raise more from private industry. As Hall reported back to the finance and general purposes committee, Gowrie indicated that their subsidy would continue to decline in real terms over the next few years. A few days later the Arts Council informed Hall that the NT's grant would rise by 1.96 per cent in the coming financial year; inflation was between 4 and 5 per cent.

Hall had called a press conference to announce the emergency measures needed to balance the National Theatre's books. It was a hard speech to make, and the grim occasion got off to a bad beginning. As he was about to perform, his personal assistant, Jan Young-husband, saw Hall in tears in his office after an acrimonious argument with Maria Ewing, who had threatened to take herself and their daughter Rebecca, who was born in May 1982, back to America if she could not have more of his time. As he climbed on to the coffee table, Hall was in an emotional state, and when he spoke, it showed.

The problem, he said, was the government's mistaken philosophy that to cut public expenditure was to do good:

I don't believe this government knows what it is doing. I don't believe the Arts Council is acting responsibly in simply carrying out the government's wishes. In the old days the Arts Council used to fight the government, and

*the Minister used to try to get more money for the Arts. Now the Minister
executes Treasury policy and the Arts Council meekly follows suit. If that
continues, we shall not have a subsidised theatre.*

Hall had made two enemies at a stroke: Lord Gowrie in the
government, and Sir William Rees-Mogg, an austere romantic
who had edited *The Times* before becoming a loyal Thatcherite
chairman of the Arts Council. (Rees-Mogg liked to argue that
Shakespeare would have voted for Mrs Thatcher.)

Clearly, someone was out of step. Was it Margaret Thatcher,
who saw no reason why the arts should be exempt from cuts in
public spending, and who also believed that organisations like
the National Theatre relied too heavily on subsidy, and should
bolster revenues by attracting sponsors from private industry?
Or was it Hall, who belonged to a generation that believed it
had a mission to civilise Britain, and, as interest in the theatre,
music and painting grew in the 1960s and 1970s, thought it
was beginning to fulfil it?

The two of them had met and talked and quarrelled about
Mozart's use of scatological language, Mrs Thatcher believing
that no one who wrote such beautiful music could have been so
foul-mouthed. Alan Ayckbourn observed that each recognised the
celebrity in the other. Afraid that he would find himself alone in
a nest of vipers, Hall had asked Ayckbourn to hold his hand at a
Downing Street reception. Standing in the receiving line, the Prime
Minister saw Hall and cried 'Peter!'[13] The director of the National
Theatre smiled broadly and answered 'Margaret!' But while they
may have been united in celebrity, they were deeply divided by
ideology.

Expressed in raw statistics, the National's case looked a good
one. During the first five years of Conservative government,
which had begun with another round of vicious inflation, the
retail price index had risen by 63 per cent, and the National's
grant was lagging well behind that. Including the contribution
from the GLC, government subsidy to the NT had risen from
£5.1 million to £7.4 million, or by only 44 per cent. To catch
up, Hall said, the National needed an additional £1.5 million
in 1984–5. The Arts Council's offer was £129,000: 'I have to put
it bluntly,' he told the journalists assembled in the Olivier foyer.
'I believe the Arts Council has betrayed the National Theatre.'

The most startling news in Hall's coffee-table speech was that the Cottesloe theatre would close, to save £500,000 a year (it cost £750,000, and raised £250,000 a year); a hundred people (20 per cent of the labour force) were to be made redundant; and NT touring in Britain and abroad was to cease unless all costs were met.

Gowrie and Rees-Mogg fought back. Rees-Mogg quoted from Wolsey in Shakespeare's *Henry VIII*: 'Oh how wretched is that poor man that hangs on princes' favours.' But it took more than a witty remark to silence Hall, and his campaign received wide and supportive coverage in the newspapers. Mrs Thatcher was not at all pleased, but nor was everyone inside the National Theatre.

David Hare said that it was no use asking for sympathy; since Hall had voted for Mrs Thatcher, he would have to live with the consequences.[14] (Hare added tartly that Hall could not campaign from Concorde.) But Rayne actively disliked the coffee-table speech; he was at home in the corridors of power, and feared that Hall's intemperate public campaign might inhibit his access. Hall now proposed to keep on the pressure by transforming it into a national campaign: he was hosting a meeting of forty-two directors from the subsidised theatre. Rayne told him that though he respected his right to express personal views, he thought the campaign was diverting effort and commitment from the NT's critical artistic and administrative challenges.[15]

Hall sent a stiff reply to his chairman. The previous three months had been his most difficult at the National Theatre, he said, yet he had received no thanks from the Board. It was essential to fight government policy in order to keep up staff morale: 'To have stayed silent . . . would have been a most damaging mistake. To have relied on behind-the-scenes pressure would have brought us, as in the past, precisely nothing.'[16]

Rayne's reply was, as always, scrupulously polite and reassuring: Hall had no cause to feel under-appreciated, but, Rayne said, he did not wish the difference with the Arts Council to become a vendetta: that was no way to do business with the government and its agencies. By May 1985 the friction between the Board and Hall was such that, in a draft letter prepared on 15 May, he resigned as director. Asking to be released from his contract 'if possible by the end of the year', he explained that he saw no sign that the Arts Council appreciated the damage it was doing, and no sign of change in government policy. He did not mind Gowrie and Rees-Mogg: 'They attacked me because I attacked them. But I think it extremely improbable . . . that the National Theatre will ever be properly financed while I remain as Director.'[17] Another round of cuts was inevitable, and he foresaw a situation in which the National Theatre, able to do no more than six or seven plays a year, would be vulnerable to another attack by the philistines.

Hall thought better of this resignation, though, and the letter was not sent. But the gulf was not bridged either. Lord Mishcon, like Rayne, thought Hall was a political innocent. This view ignored Hall's astonishing success in raising subsidies for the RSC; but the allegation that Hall's protest would backfire was a serious one.

Rees-Mogg finally changed his tune at the Arts Council, arguing that the arts were a success story that the government would be wise to invest in. He asked for an extra £55 million, or 53 per cent, and got £30 million, which was better than other departments managed. The announcement of this increase was accompanied by a specific denunciation of Hall; an anonymous government spokesman said that the Prime Minister and her colleagues had objected to his outspoken criticism and regarded the Arts Council's original demands as utterly unreasonable.[18] The implication was that Hall's criticisms had stung, and served their purpose, but it took the Minister and Rees-Mogg a long time to react. When the Arts Council announced its grants for 1986–7 the National Theatre's was only 0.1 per cent less than the rate of inflation, but that was after a year in which there had been no grant increase at all. Hall, it seems, was no more politically innocent than Max Rayne himself.

Hall's campaign could claim some modest success, but he was not immune to the spirit of the times and had to some extent fallen into step – on the question of subsidy, for example. Seven years earlier, in 1978, he had told the finance and general purposes committee that a subsidised organisation like the National Theatre should not have to seek sponsorship to do its job. The first organisations which proposed a relationship – such as Pearl Assurance, which offered £750,000 over three years – were spurned because they did not meet the NT's exacting terms. By 1985, however, valiant efforts were being made to attract sponsors and Hall, whose heart was still not in it, said they had done well to raise a quarter of a million pounds in this way, though they could do with a million.

There was, however, growing evidence that the financial crisis was not as bad as Hall had thought. On the eve of its own execution, the GLC had awarded the NT a special grant of

£350,000 to finance the reopening of the Cottesloe in September 1985. The other two theatres were doing good business. *Guys and Dolls*, which had been restored to the repertory when *Jean* closed, was pumping cash into the box-office. The profit made by the National Theatre on *Amadeus* was more than £1 million; and another Peter Shaffer play called *Yonadab* was on the way. The complete version of Tony Harrison's translation of *The Mysteries* was still being performed by Bill Bryden's company; and in May *Pravda*, a play about Fleet Street, written by Howard Brenton and David Hare, opened with Anthony Hopkins giving a star's performance as a bullying press baron; it was a sell-out. (Elliot Fruit-Norton, the impotent editor in *Pravda*, was assumed to be the NT's revenge on William Rees-Mogg.) In the summer, plays by Alan Ayckbourn and Tom Stoppard joined the repertory. By October, Hall reported to Rayne that during the period when the Cottesloe was closed, attendances were still up by 13 per cent and revenues by 23 per cent.[19]

This gave Rayne something else to worry about. He was already aware of the economic miracle on the South Bank, and was confident that a small surplus in the year ending in April 1985 could be turned into a substantial surplus in 1985–6. The obvious conclusion was that the National Theatre would not need anything like the extra £1 million that Hall was demanding. This should have been good news, but Rayne confided uneasily to Sir Derek Mitchell that he feared it would soon be said that Hall had cried wolf.

Hall had been needled by the fact that the RSC was expanding while he was cutting back. That the RSC could do this was a consequence of an inquiry into its management by a civil servant named Clive Priestley, who had worked as chief of staff to Lord Rayner, Whitehall's cost-cutter-in-chief. After Priestley concluded that the RSC was well run and deserved a more generous subsidy, the RSC got a grant increase of £1.5 million. Hall and Rayne, feeling the National Theatre was just as well managed as the RSC, commissioned their own report, and asked Priestley's boss, Lord Rayner, by now the chairman of Marks and Spencer, to do it. Rayner, assisted by management consultants from Coopers and Lybrand, submitted a report in August 1985 that was no less flattering about the National than Priestley's had been about the RSC. There were savings to be made, Rayner concluded, but they were much smaller than he would have expected to find in private industry. He identified savings in the workshops, the stage operations and the box-office, adding up to £650,000 after three years, and thought sponsorship ought to be worth another £100,000 a year. But, Rayner agreed, that was not enough to put the finances on a proper footing: 'I should record support, on this evidence, for increased government support in real terms,' he wrote.[20] (The Rayner report identified as superfluous many of the jobs that Hall declared were to be lost in the coffee-table speech.)

The report also looked at the top of the management structure, and proposed that Hall should be flanked by an associate director who would share overall responsibility for running the National Theatre. The idea was not new – Rayne and his colleagues had discussed it with Hall three years earlier – but it did have important implications. Hall, who read a draft of Rayner's report in August 1985, wrote straight away to Rayne saying that he welcomed it, believed in its philosophy, and hoped the Board would adopt it.

In the letter Hall formally placed his resignation before Rayne. This time, it was not done out of any desire to leave. Hall had calculated that the Rayner recommendations would take two years to implement, and thought that ought to be the new top-management team's job. A new structure could not possibly be in place until the end of 1986; and Hall's contract expired at the end of 1988. He had already identified a successor (Richard Eyre), and an associate director (David Aukin, who had worked with Eyre in Nottingham).

However, Hall told Rayne, he had an alternative plan which the Board might like to consider. 'I have come to it after long thought, and it represents the future I would prefer for myself. I would like to extend my contract for two or three years so that I not only have time to effect the re-organisation, but have time to enjoy some of the benefits artistically.'[21] His preference was to stay, he said; but on the other hand he would understand if the Board wanted to make a completely new start.

That was food for thought. Only three months after feeling depressed enough to draft a letter of resignation, Hall was now proposing, in another letter offering resignation, that he should actually stay on as director until 1991. This would be eighteen years after his original appointment.

One immediate consequence of the Rayner report was the

departure of the general administrator, Michael Elliott, late in 1985. The appointment of an associate director would make his post redundant, and there was no chance that he would get that new job. His temperament had alienated many of the senior administrative staff, and some, like John Goodwin, could hardly speak to him. The Rayner report provided the pretext for his departure. But he did not go without making it clear to Max Rayne and Lord Rayner how critical he was of Hall's contractual arrangements, and of the amount of time he spent away from the South Bank.

In 1986 Hall had not endeared himself to the chairman of his Board, and had offended the Prime Minister, her Arts Minister and the chairman of the Arts Council. Although all were in a position to do him some harm, none of them did so. But Michael Elliott was also in a position to wound, and, unlike the others, he was not philosophical about the rough-and-tumble of institutional life.

Trial by the Sunday Times

At Glyndebourne in 1986, Peter Hall was directing Verdi's *Simon Boccanegra* and Trevor Nunn was polishing his legendary production of *Porgy and Bess*. It was the first time in years that they had worked in the same place, and when the *Sunday Times* asked to take a photograph of them together and to discuss cross-fertilisation between the commercial and the subsidised theatre, neither was keen, but both agreed – Hall more readily than Nunn. They sat in the garden, looking relaxed, their shirts open at the neck, and with smiles big enough to reveal whole rows of teeth. Nunn thought they looked almost inane. The photograph was taken before they were interviewed by two reporters from the *Sunday Times* Insight team. When the conversation was over they had not talked much about the agreed subject and neither of them was smiling.

The picture appeared the following Sunday, 29 June 1986, over a headline across eight columns reading: LAUGHING ALL THE WAY TO THE BANK. The lead story on the paper's front page said: 'Exit Nunn and Hall in cash row.' These articles did Hall's reputation more harm than anything else that appeared during his career.

Their accuracy was challenged, and rightly, but that hardly mattered because the *Sunday Times* aroused the instinctive national disapproval reserved for people who are accused of exploiting positions of trust.

The uproar this *Sunday Times* campaign caused is hard to understand without recalling the distinctive nature of both the arts and the public service in Britain. Unlike continental theatres, where actors or directors can be leading members of a company, earning a decent monthly wage with guaranteed employment and a pension, the English theatre has always been a free market. The stars who bring in the audience are richly rewarded, but, unless they are unionised stagehands, the rest get a pittance – in subsidised theatre, especially. (There are two sorts of subsidy in the theatre: one comes from the government, the other from all the men and women who work for low wages.) Hall's ensemble company at Stratford was close to the continental model: wages were not good, but the work was interesting, and there was an *esprit de corps*. Hall was best paid, but the wage differential between him and the actors was not large. By the time he reached the National Theatre, he already had two families to support, and was part of a system in which there was one rate for stars with expensive lifestyles, and another for the majority. This entrenched inequality was hardly ever questioned.

The long tradition of public service had not affected the arts until the 1940s, when the principle of public subsidy for the arts became generally accepted and bureaucratic organisations like the Arts Council were set up to distribute the money. The public-service ethos existed in establishments like municipal art galleries, but it did not spread to the theatre until the 1960s, and Hall was, of course, more responsible for its doing so than any other single person. Yet he never had much sympathy for the mixture of motives that had kept the British Civil Service honest and hard-working for generations: the money was not very good, but the power was intoxicating, and the knighthood gave a status that few could buy.

One more tradition was in play in this episode. Over twenty years the Insight team of the *Sunday Times* had established a formidable reputation. Bright, ambitious and energetic journalists who claimed no special expertise beyond their skill as reporters liked to pit their collective skill against secretive institutions and people in authority. When Andrew Neil became the paper's editor in 1983 he thought he could do without Insight; he soon repented, and by early 1985 a new team of reporters was in place, anxious to prove that they were just as good as their predecessors at getting a victim in their grip and not letting go until the guilty party had confessed. It was a single-minded approach in which an ancillary victim was sometimes the truth.

The first six paragraphs of the front-page story on 29 June contained four errors about Hall. The first paragraph stated that he was planning to resign; on the contrary, he had told Rayne in January 1986 that he would like to stay at the NT until 1991. He was not a multi-millionaire; after leaving Jacky Hall, he was far from a millionaire. He had not made £2 million from *Amadeus*. He had not made more than the National Theatre had from *Amadeus*: he admitted he had earned £720,000 from it, but the National's share was twice that. The last claim was that some employees had quit the National Theatre in frustration over Hall's frequent absences and management style. This was a reference to Michael Elliott, who had quit, just before he was pushed, eight months before the articles appeared.

One of the two Insight reporters was a tough twenty-four-year-old from Tunbridge Wells called Rowena Webster. (The other was a new recruit called Peter Hounan.) As a girl she had interviewed Michael Elliott for the local hospital radio station and this provided her with an introduction to the main source for Insight's case against Hall.[22] Elliott had a story about Peter Shaffer's new play *Yonadab*, which had opened at the National Theatre in December 1985. (After *Amadeus*, the Shubert Organisation in New York were anxious to sign up Shaffer's next big hit and to make sure Hall directed it.) Elliott's charge was that, in the spring of 1985, Hall's New York agent, Sam Cohn, had acted for both his client and the National Theatre in secret talks from which Elliott, the general manager of the NT, had been excluded. There was a smell of conspiracy in the air.

Elliott, having claimed the negotiators had presented the National with a *fait accompli*, said: 'We managed to squeeze a bit more for the NT . . . The whole balance of the deal on *Amadeus* was wrong and the same happened in the end with *Yonadab*.' The Insight team concluded that the story showed how much the artistic development of the National Theatre was bound up with Hall's personal interest in making money and extending his career beyond the orbit of the South Bank.

Rayne and the National Theatre refused any comment to Insight's reporters, and the story is not easy to unravel. But Elliott's memory of the sequence of events did seem to fail him, and the real story was more complicated than the one Insight told. It was true to say that, on 25 April 1985, Elliott received a letter from Robert Lanz, who was Peter Shaffer's agent, outlining terms, and that, when the NT asked for changes, Cohn told Elliott that the terms were final and non-negotiable.

But the negotiations which led to the improvement in those terms had taken place before the meeting to which Elliott was not invited, not after it, as Insight suggests. Moreover, the 'final and non-negotiable' offer was already an improvement on the *Amadeus* contract. These contracts are complicated, but the basic rule is that participants in Broadway and West End shows receive two kinds of percentage from gross income: one before capital costs have been met, and one after capital costs have been recouped. In the case of *Yonadab*, the National Theatre was to receive 1 per cent before recoupment, and 1.5 per cent afterward. This compared to 0.9 per cent and 1.035 per cent for *Amadeus*; and instead of 1.8 per cent of the net profits, the National was due to get 3 per cent for *Yonadab*.[23]

Casting an eye over these terms, Rayne agreed that they might be better than *Amadeus*, but were not so good as *Jean*, and he asked for more; he wanted 5 per cent of the net profits and 1.5 per cent of the gross for all North American productions. That was the point at which Lanz said the offer was final.

At an emergency meeting of the finance and general purposes committee on 29 April, Hall explained that the reason his agent was present at talks between Lanz and the Shubert Organisation was to prevent the deal from collapsing. To save it, he said, his agent was negotiating a reduction in Hall's fee for the New York production of *Yonadab*.

This was not quite as generous as it sounded, but was certainly not a conspiracy. Instead of the customary 4 per cent of the gross before recoupment and 5 per cent after, Hall's shares had been reduced to 3.75 per cent and 4.4 per cent. (His share of the net profits stayed at 5 per cent.) But Hall would earn considerably more from the New York production than from the production at the National Theatre, where *Yonadab* would open and where, by contractual agreement, a guaranteed number of performances had to be given.

Sir Derek Mitchell, who was still on the finance and general purposes committee, remembers that Hall was so convinced that he had done a good deed by the National Theatre that his London agent asked Rayne to agree to forgo the 20 per cent share of Hall's earnings due to the National Theatre from any money he earned from the commercial exploitation of *Yonadab*. Privately Rayne was appalled by this suggestion, but he went through the ritual of consultation and replied, politely as always, that he could find no support for any such idea among his colleagues.[24]

Hall was aggrieved. He believed that the National Theatre would have had no rights at all to *Yonadab* had he not surrendered a percentage of his own commercial rights. By his standards, he had behaved honourably throughout the *Yonadab* negotiations. But a gulf had grown between his standards and those of the Board. It was not surprising, then, that Hall felt wronged when his behaviour over *Yonadab* became the centrepiece of the Insight attack on him. And, indeed, the accusation, as made, was incorrect.

Rayne did his best to repair the damage by issuing a statement denying that the Board had received any notice of resignation from Sir Peter Hall, and adding that as far as he and his colleagues were concerned, Hall's integrity was not in question. Rayne thought, innocently, that his statement might discourage further speculation and comment. Not so; this is the kind of story the chattering classes love chattering about.

Because the accusations had been made in public, Hall decided to give his version of events at a press conference.[25] (Nunn chose to say nothing.) Hall gave a robust performance; he revealed that, of ten National Theatre productions that had transferred since the opening of the South Bank, he had had a hand in only two – *Amadeus* and *Bedroom Farce*, which he had co-directed with Alan Ayckbourn, and for which he got only half the fee. (*No Man's Land* had been done at the Old Vic.) In all ten cases, the director's fee was 4 per cent before recoupment and 5 per cent after. He had not conspired with the American producers to raise his fee for *Yonadab*, he said; on the contrary, he had endangered his commercial reputation by reducing his normal fee. For that reason, his lawyers were considering a libel writ.

But Hall's candour did him no good. The following week the *Sunday Times* simply repeated the conspiracy charge, and had much fun with the £720,000 Hall had earned from *Amadeus*, even though it was only a third of the sum they had originally accused him of earning. Hall had insisted that, far from being a multi-millionaire, his only assets were 'a small house in Chelsea, and perhaps £75,000 in the bank.' Reminded later that he also lived in a rent-free country house in Sussex, he said lamely that nobody had asked him about it, and it wasn't an asset, it was a facility. But small houses in Chelsea are not cheap, and the rent-free possession of country houses is not usually described as 'a facility'.

Hall believed that the Insight article was a deliberate attempt to discredit the subsidised theatre. 'I'm not saying that the Minister and the Arts Council set it up, but they are certainly taking advantage of what is happening,' Hall said at his press conference. Victims of newspaper campaigns always look for a hidden motive, yet for young reporters a good story is an end in itself. Rowena Webster remembers it was prompted by the editor of Insight receiving a two-line memo from Andrew Neil saying that stories he had heard about Hall's and Nunn's earnings and absenteeism should be followed up. 'We had just moved to Wapping and Neil was anxious to get some big stories in the paper,' she says.[26] It was Hall's misfortune that he was radical chic, a member of the establishment, on a public-sector payroll, and liked attacking the government for being tight-fisted. He was the perfect target for Neil's angry populism: 'Wapping morality' was Hall's term for it. Nunn assumed the story was dinner-table gossip converted into a cheap shot. But the secrecy that in the 1980s shrouded the commercial activities of the subsidised theatre could as easily have attracted earlier generations of Insight reporters.

In retrospect, Hall wrote that he could not easily forgive Richard Luce, the Arts Minister, or Sir William Rees-Mogg 'for their silence, or for implying by it that there was something to investigate'.[27] Nunn felt no less strongly. The Minister, Richard Luce, who stated publicly that he was aware of growing public concern, admitted later that the evidence for this was no more than a few telephone calls. None the less, Hall's remark does reveal a streak of innocence in one with a reputation for being a shrewd politician. Despite often having accused the Arts Council of betrayal and the Arts Minister of impotence, he still thought it was their duty to spring to his defence. The fact was that he had few allies, and he was going to have to look after himself.

Hall and Nunn sued for libel, which caused more worry to Hall than to the *Sunday Times*. In the coming months he learned enough about the law to pass an exam, and discoursed with learned friends on the implications of *Bembridge v. Latimer* having been overturned by *Polly Peck (Holdings) plc v. Trelford*. As a consequence of this case, he learned that he could not fight the case on his chosen terms. He wanted to focus on the allegations about *Yonadab*, but a Master-in-chambers overruled him. The only evidence he could expect from the *Sunday Times* was the reporters' tapes and notebooks. The *Sunday Times*, on the other hand, could and would use every subject raised in the articles in their defence, which would make Hall vulnerable to questions about every aspect of his professional life – and a full-scale assault by a skilled libel barrister is difficult for anyone to combat. But the principal reason Hall eventually gave for not going ahead was the price of British justice. He flirted with the idea of defending himself, but even then a defeat might have cost him hundreds of thousands of pounds. That was more than his day in court was worth. (Nunn continued his own action for some years before settling it out of court after a grudging apology was published in the *Sunday Times*.)

Hall wrote later that, although the *Sunday Times* pieces had been a disconcerting irritant to him, he had suffered no serious lasting effect.[28] Judging a lasting effect is difficult, but Nunn thought they had both been hugely damaged. (Five years after the articles appeared, a taxi driver in Melbourne, Australia, asked Nunn if he was the bloke who'd had his hand in the till.)

One consequence of the *Sunday Times* articles was a change in the commercial arrangement for transfers from the subsidised theatre. Sir Kenneth Cork, a flourishing City accountant who had learned about the subsidised theatre as chairman of the RSC, was already conducting an inquiry for the Arts Council into the state of the English theatre, so the issues raised by the *Sunday Times* were conveniently tacked on to his terms of reference. In his report, Cork recommended that half the earnings from a transfer should go to the theatre where the show originated, so from then on the National Theatre insisted on having 5 per cent of the gross as well as the net profits. This policy was powerfully influenced by hindsight, but the inference was that the Board did indeed feel the NT had not done as well as it might in previous deals.

As far as *Yonadab* was concerned, Hall did not laugh all the way to the bank. *Yonadab* was a dog. An unlikely tale of a minor biblical figure who instigates an incestuous relationship between a son and daughter of King David, this was one of Shaffer's plays that did not benefit from comprehensive rewriting during rehearsal. *Yonadab* was guaranteed eighty performances, and since the houses were poor, it became a costly embarrassment to the National Theatre. The London losses would have been recouped if it had been a Broadway success, but the Shuberts did not like what they saw on the South Bank. As with *Jean*, there was no transfer. All for nothing.

The Insight article turned out, in part, to be a self-fulfilling prophecy. When the article appeared, Rayne and Hall were still considering his proposal that he should extend his contract for two or three years. Mitchell remembers that on 14 July 1986 Rayne told the Board that, although nothing had been agreed, Hall might stay on for an extra year. But a week later Hall wrote formally proposing Richard Eyre as his successor when his contract expired at the end of 1988. The extension of his contract was still unresolved, but Rayne must have judged that there was not enough enthusiasm among his colleagues for it. In September, Hall formally informed Rayne that he would be going when his contract expired.[29] He added that the National Theatre would be in good hands.

18

The Eighties: Part Three

Honouring Shakespeare

The British theatre's golden age had lasted for more than twenty-five years as Hall neared the end of his term at the National Theatre. The ingredients were great companies like the National Theatre and the RSC; stars like Olivier, Richardson, Gielgud and Ashcroft, whose names will still be known in a hundred years; writers like Pinter, Osborne and Ayckbourn, whose work will be revived as long a people put on plays; a generation of actors like Dench, McKellen, Gambon and Bryant, all wonderfully polished artists; new theatres; a large, appreciative audience.

Time and money were essential elements: time to rehearse and money to finance the actors, designers, musicians and lighting directors, and to commission writers. These were luxuries the London commercial theatre could not afford – which was one reason why so many productions transferred to the West End from Stratford and the Barbican, and the South Bank. The difference was subsidy.

But the lustre was starting to fade. No matter what Hall had said on his coffee table, the principle of subsidy was not in danger, but it was true that the sums involved were falling in real terms. Less money means less time, less variety and lower quality. The writers also were less fecund; Harold Pinter, for example, had not written a play for nine years. And some of the best actors were becoming more interested in winning Oscars than Oliviers.

With its star performances, its electrifying speed and detail, the musicality of its verse-speaking, and its attention to detail, Peter Hall's *Antony and Cleopatra* in 1987 defined the golden age, though it was much more like what had gone before it than what came after.

Hall's *Antony* saw the breaking of a partnership that had lasted more than twenty years with hardly an interruption. Hall had occasionally asked his university contemporary Timothy O'Brien to design productions for him, but ever since *The Wars of the Roses* in 1963 all his important productions had been designed by John Bury. Their long run ended after *Coriolanus* in 1984, which was remembered for the superb performances of the principals – Ian McKellen and Greg Hicks as Coriolanus and Aufidius – and for a device with the audience. At every performance some part of the audience was brought on to the stage before the performance began to be the citizens of Rome, and was brought to its feet by the actors when a mob was required. Hall thought this confusion of roles worked best when the production was on tour in Athens, but some of London's more reserved theatregoers found it embarrassing. For them, it was hard to know who was more uncomfortable – the audience on stage or the audience in their seats. The sets had had to be designed to make room for the band of amateur players, but they were instantly recognisable as Bury's: black, architectural and forbidding.

In 1978, when they did *Macbeth*, Hall had wondered whether their work together had become stuck in 1960s realism, but Bury had continued to turn out visually impressive productions: the most memorable were at Glyndebourne, which Bury regarded as a second home, but the partnership was also on good form in *Amadeus*, *The Importance of Being Earnest*, and *The Oresteia*, which was lit by Bury. The first notable break came when Hall chose William Dudley to design the Bayreuth *Ring*; a year later *Coriolanus* proved to be their finale.

Bury knew why he was so valuable to Hall: 'I'm a jolly good disciple,' he says, 'good at understanding what directors want and making it work.'[1] But as the years went by at the National Theatre, Bury found Hall harder to talk to. He recalls: 'Peter always said "John Bury and I only have to meet in the lift and the production's designed." But we weren't in the lift on the same day any more. There wasn't time, and it was beginning to show.'

Bury's retrospective analysis of Hall's success as a director is straightforward: because he made the actors think, they knew what they were doing. In *Antony and Cleopatra*, Hall had the time and the cast – Anthony Hopkins and Judi Dench in the name parts – to put into practice everything he knew about Shakespeare and the stage. The rehearsals lasted three months, and even after that Hall was still willing to contemplate the cancellation of previews to make sure everything was right. Unlike other National Theatre productions in which he was constantly distracted by problems, his concentration here was hardly interrupted at all. Apart from one long weekend in New York, he attended all the rehearsals.

Judi Dench recalls that at the first run-through she noticed that Hall, who had grown portly in the mid-1980s, had lost a lot of weight. She took this as a good sign, and remembers how secure she felt at the start. 'I knew it was going to be thrilling. I had that kind of trust.'[2] From the outset Hall nurtured that feeling, inviting the cast to contribute their ideas and infusing these with his own experience. The chemistry worked.

Hall began as he always did, by insisting that all the secrets of the play were to be found in the text, and by demanding proper verse-speaking: 'I'm unashamedly pedantic about this,' he said. 'It may need a beat, an elision, but every single line in Shakespeare will scan. Your business is to find and keep as close to the five beats of the iambic pentameter as possible, and then decide on what's right for you in terms of emphasis and colour.' Only he, John Barton and Trevor Nunn, Hall said, could pass on this authentic way of speaking Shakespearian verse, because they had learned it from Dadie Rylands in Cambridge, who had received it personally from William Poel, the leader of the Elizabethan revival at the beginning of the twentieth century. (We know this from a detailed and sympathetic account of the whole process by Tirzah Lowen, entitled *Peter Hall Directs 'Antony and Cleopatra'*.)[3]

Hall emphasised this scholarly approach by sitting behind a lectern, and, for a couple of weeks, keeping his eyes down and just listening. Not all actors admired such academic rigour, but all made fun of it. Judi Dench tells how she would stick her tongue out at Hall's lowered head, and he would ask why she had taken a pause. This is an old actors' tale: Maggie Smith claims to have done the same thing, and at the RSC it was a well-known way of teasing John Barton. In fact it was Barton who claimed to have done it first, as an undergraduate, sticking out his tongue at Dadie Rylands, whose head was hardly ever raised from the text.

Once the rhythm of the verse had sunk in, Hall turned his attention to the light and shade, telling Anthony Hopkins: 'Change the tone at every full stop. Come to each new thought differently.' He wanted Hopkins to catch Judi Dench's rhythm and timbre and work it into his own, to focus the sense and make better music. When characters spoke in a group, as Antony does with his guards, Hall asked them to create a choral effect by beating the lines and the pauses internally. Once the sound was correct, he wanted more colour in the characters. To Cleopatra's maids, for instance, he said: 'You've got to become more abandoned, wilder, cheeky. Make it more raunchy, sharper, wittier.'

John Bury's successor as designer was Alison Chitty. She had joined Hall in 1985 to design *Martine*, and her brilliantly coloured field of poppies and corn was one of the best-remembered things about it. She had also designed Hall's production of a Stephen Poliakoff play, *Coming in to Land*, which opened only four days before the *Antony and Cleopatra* rehearsals began. These rehearsals were so protracted that Chitty did not have to design the set until she had absorbed the ideas of the first few weeks' work. Hall's general advice to her was to remember that the central space in an Elizabethan theatre was always filled with the actors, and that one scene must rapidly give way to another so that they appear to overlap. Consequently, heavy movable scenery was out of the question. Chitty's solution was two great doors, surrounded by crumbling ruins, centred in front of a 100-foot-long cyclorama painted in blood-red stucco. The costumes were based on Veronese's Renaissance paintings of classical figures. The images were powerful, and, except possibly for the colour, they might have been designed by John Bury.

The production, in the conscious absence of a concept, was judged by the performances. Anthony Hopkins was playing Lear while rehearsing Antony, and had found the transition difficult. He is an actor who believes he knows whether he fits a part or does not at the start of rehearsals, so this made him dissatisfied with his work. But he was his most severe critic. His performance made him runner-up to Michael Gambon for the *Evening Standard*'s Actor of the Year award.

Judi Dench was also working in the evenings, playing in a

two-handed comedy with her husband, Michael Williams, but she had no problem in transforming herself into an imperious, mischievous, desolate and sexy Queen of the Nile. Her carnality was a surprise, which she attributed to working with Hall: 'He makes you feel so special and good in a part, and that becomes sexy,' she says. Hall thought Dench gave one of the best half-dozen or so pieces of character acting he had seen, and the judges of both the *Evening Standard* and the Olivier awards chose her as the Best Actress of the Year. Michael Bryant's strong soldierly Enobarbus won him an Olivier award as Best Supporting Actor. Hall was the *Evening Standard*'s Director of the Year.

Though he did not always succeed, Hall genuinely tried to remain detached from reviews, but he did admit that he was pleased that the critics understood what he had been trying to do. Michael Billington, who had declared Hall's 1973 *Tempest* to be one of the four worst Shakespearian productions he had ever seen, was becoming a fan: 'Like all great Shakespeare productions, Peter Hall's uncovers meanings in the text that may seem obvious, but have never hit one so penetratingly before.' Like other critics, Billington was enthusiastic about the verse-speaking, but none was more extravagant in his praise than John Peter in the *Sunday Times*, the paper that had described Hall as little better than a charlatan less than a year before. Peter wrote:

> *Golden ages of the theatre are usually in the past – but we may be living in one today. Peter Hall's production . . . is the British theatre at its spellbinding and magnificent best. [He] reminds us . . . that the bedrock of classical theatre is the text; that the life of the play is first and most essentially the words of the play, and that the visual splendour and the excitement of action needs to be justified by a sense that the words are felt and understood.*

After the first night, Hall said that he had never enjoyed anything more in his life and that he wished it weren't over. His *Antony and Cleopatra* was his finest Shakespearian production since the mid-1960s at Stratford, shortly after the golden age began.

A Shock in Sussex

Peter Hall's failure to appear at scheduled rehearsals for Glyndebourne's summer festivals aroused George Christie's anger, and
it was Moran Caplat's duty to pacify him. 'It's no use waving
a contract. It doesn't work,' he advised.[4] Caplat's method was to
put Hall on his honour to be in Glyndebourne when he said he
would, even though he knew that Hall would break his word. 'It
needed strong nerves to have Peter working for you, but when
he did turn up, it was full speed ahead. Two days from him were
worth a fortnight from other people,' says Caplat. Hall recognised
his debt: 'Moran gave me room to expand and work my way in
opera,' he said.[5]

Hall and the Dutch conductor Bernard Haitink had begun an
exhilarating collaboration in 1977 with a fierce and dark *Don
Giovanni*. It continued the following year with a *Così fan tutte* that
'blew away the smog of slovenly tradition'.[6] In 1979, *Fidelio, Così*
and *Ulysses* were all in the repertory, and, in the circumstances,
Caplat wondered why Hall, a guest director, did not formalise
his relationship with Glyndebourne and become its permanent
artistic director. Hall was interested in the idea; if Haitink were
to stay on, and if the money was right, it was attractive. Then
Maria Ewing, who would be singing in Glyndebourne productions
directed by Hall, decided she wanted to live in the area, and that
clinched it.

Caplat retired after the 1981 season, Hall having directed a
magical production of Benjamin Britten's *A Midsummer Night's
Dream* as a farewell present; and two more years then went
by before the announcement of Hall's new position. The deal
had to be agreed by the National Theatre Board, which wanted
to be satisfied that the post carried no administrative responsibilities, and that Glyndebourne would acknowledge that Hall
worked there 'by arrangement with the National Theatre'. He
was due to take up his duties in 1984 with a new production

of Monteverdi's *L'Incoronazione di Poppea*, in which Ewing was to star. The money was right, too: starting at £30,000 a year.[7] The Halls adapted to a rural lifestyle in a grace-and-favour house owned by George Christie in South Chailey, a few miles to the north of Glyndebourne.

It sounded idyllic: new wife, new house, extra money guaranteed. But, as well as a change in status, there was a change in Hall's relationship with the new general administrator, Brian Dickie, who had formerly been Caplat's assistant. Caplat's tone had always been mollifying: '. . . thinking about your only too reasonable request for more money'.[8] Dickie was sharper and more direct: 'It really is not good enough to fall back on the hoary old argument that artists are not subject to basic disciplines because it stifles creativity.'[9]

Hall and Dickie's bad-tempered disagreements about consultation over casting caused Christie to intervene as peacemaker. In reply to Hall's insistence, in the autumn of 1976, that he must hear all the singers who might appear in his productions, Christie wrote: 'Your letter smacks to me somewhat of distrust on your part, and lack of confidence in Glyndebourne's ability to provide you with singers of the quality that you admire.'[10] Hall replied briskly that it was he who had to direct the operas, not Brian Dickie.[11]

The two of them did not disagree about the repertory, however. Having completed the Mozart/da Ponte cycle, Hall and Haitink decided to tackle Verdi. Caplat, who had had strong feelings about the Glyndebourne repertory, had actively dissuaded Hall from experimenting with Wagner's *Tristan und Isolde* in the 1970s; and although he was no longer in charge, Caplat felt that Glyndebourne was the wrong size for Verdi's *Simon Boccanegra* and *Traviata*, and that they produced the wrong sound for the house. There was no argument about Britten: Hall's production of *Albert Herring* in 1985 was inspired by his own experience of life in East Anglia, where it was set, and the acclaimed production was the first from Glyndebourne to transfer to the Royal Opera House. His stimulating collaboration with his wife continued with a vivid production of *Carmen* including all the original dialogue; but, perhaps for that reason, it was not a hit when it transferred to the Metropolitan Opera in New York.

None the less, the constant glow Hall's work had created in the 1970s was not reproduced in the 1980s; the comparison became particularly marked when, in 1989, Hall embarked on a second Mozart/da Ponte cycle at Glyndebourne. Naturally, he opted for different colleagues; instead of Bernard Haitink, Simon Rattle was conducting the Orchestra of the Age of Enlightenment rather than the London Philharmonic Orchestra, which normally provided the music for Glyndebourne. John Gunter had taken over from John Bury as designer. Hall's new *Marriage of Figaro* was even more melancholy and bitter-sweet than his first sixteen years earlier, and the new team failed to reproduce the power of the original one.

Christie's mediation had not succeeded in appeasing either Hall or Dickie, and a number of administrative irritations prevented their relationship from growing warmer. Max Rayne was badgering Hall about the National Theatre getting a proper credit for his services, but no one at Glyndebourne seemed to understand why it mattered. There were letters of complaint about Hall's office when he was moved to inferior quarters. He was infuriated by the failure of the *Radio Times* to credit him as director of *Carmen* when it was performed at a Promenade concert. But nothing bothered him more than the concept of director's copyright.

A stage director's work is ephemeral, existing only in the memory of the audience – unless, that is, it is filmed. The work of generations of directors lingered in history only through written descriptions of it, over which the director had no control at all. Television and video recording changed that, and the concept of the director's copyright became an issue for the first time. Hall was especially anxious to retain control of his own work, and to make sure it appeared on the screen as he had done it for the stage. He also wanted the film version to pay him a director's fee.

Television companies, on the other hand, were paying good money for the rights and wanted a director they could rely on to produce a film that came in on budget and on time, and Hall's record for spending freely was legendary. By 1985, he became convinced that the BBC was trying to squeeze him out, and he counter-attacked by insisting that from 1986 he would only accept offers to work at Glyndebourne on the clear understanding that he retained director's rights. He did not mind assistant directors preparing a first draft of a television opera, but he insisted on being responsible for the final version, and on getting the credit, and the fee.

His stubborn insistence on this almost led to the cancellation of the contract to film *Simon Boccanegra* for television; he relented only because the chorus would have lost their fees. Relations between Hall and the management did not improve in 1987, when *La Traviata* joined the repertory, but they reached their lowest point after that season, when Hall and Dickie were at each other's throats again about casting. At that point Christie and Dickie began to talk seriously about Hall's role in Glyndebourne's future. Both considered the possibility of bringing in a new artistic director at the end of the 1988 season. Finally they decided that Hall's experience was preferable to any new blood they could think of, and, at the end of the 1988 season, Dickie confirmed that Hall's contract would be extended for a further three years; but at the same time it was mutually agreed that the relationship would terminate in 1992.[12]

In 1988 Hall's production of *Falstaff* concluded his Verdi cycle, and *La Traviata* was revived, but Caplat had probably been right about Verdi's being the wrong sound for the house. The Glyndebourne audience never developed the affection for Verdi that they felt for Mozart and Rossini. The Mozart cycle, conducted by Rattle, would begin the following year and a new opera by Sir Michael Tippett entitled *New Year* was to open in Houston, Texas and Glyndebourne in 1990. Dickie's calculations show that Hall's fees in 1988 were £38,100, a sum that was expected to rise to £44,635 in 1990. But in the same year that Hall was leaving the National Theatre for an uncertain future, he was being informed politely that his services as artistic director were no longer crucial to Glyndebourne.

He was not even consulted about his succession. When Dickie wrote confirming Hall's new contract, he added: 'We have given considerable thought [to the appointment of your successor] and have come to the conclusion that Nicholas Hytner has the qualities necessary . . . it is difficult to imagine the place without you, but let's not even think of it.'

As it happened, Hall lasted longer than Dickie, who took a job in Toronto in 1989, but he did not last the full term of his contract, resigning in 1991 over the kind of dispute that had bedevilled his relationship with Dickie. His decision was prompted by the fact that he was not consulted, as artistic director, about the decision by Peter Sellars, the young American director, to cut all the dialogue in the English text he was using for *The Magic Flute*. 'I couldn't stand my most central beliefs being treated so casually,' Hall wrote.[13] (Hytner, incidentally, never slipped comfortably into

Glyndebourne's ethos, and turned down the artistic directorship, which passed to Graham Vick.)

After an association of twenty years, Hall left Glyndebourne with hardly any regrets. That was his way. He even refused a placatory offer to redirect his *Marriage of Figaro* for the opening of the new Glyndebourne opera house in 1994. But his Glyndebourne period showed how his best work, in Stratford-upon-Avon and in the Sussex countryside, was done in a secure working atmosphere created for him by people like Caplat and Fordham Flower, whom he regarded as good friends and who were loyal colleagues.

The last years at Glyndebourne also show how the exercise of power had become a habit. At the National Theatre and the RSC he had grown used to having his own way. When he no longer got it at Glyndebourne, it came as a shock.

Loving and Leaving Maria

Maria Ewing, whose earnings were higher than Peter Hall's during most of their marriage, never thought of her husband as a rich man, but she did find him generous, especially in the very good years. Hall liked buying gifts for the women he loved. When the *Amadeus* money started to flow in 1981, he bought a mink coat for her ('when people wore mink coats; now I use it as a bed-warmer,' she said some years later), and a two-seater Mercedes with a retractable roof for them both.[14] Ewing never thought Hall was obsessed by money: had he been, she said, he would have directed *La Cage aux Folles* when it was offered, because that became a monumental Broadway hit.

Hall expected, though, to live in style and comfort. He and Maria moved into a restored terrace house in town at 33 Bramerton Street off the King's Road in Chelsea, and into the house provided for them by George Christie at South Chailey in Sussex with a pool and a long lawn looking across to the South Downs. The National Theatre provided his basic income: £50,000 a year in 1983, rising annually at the same rate as inflation, so that it would have been worth about £60,000 when he left. From 1984, this was supplemented by fees from Glyndebourne, where his earnings as artistic and stage director were £30,000 in 1984, rising to £40,000 by 1988, when he was on a basic income of £100,000. None the less, he felt he needed more.

The annual returns lodged at Companies House by Petard Productions, the company into which much of Hall's income was paid, showed steady growth throughout the 1980s; had it been a public company, the shares would have been considered a safe investment, as the subsequent annual reports show.

(The sudden jump in Petard's income in 1986 was made by the company's brief acquisition of the worldwide services of Maria Ewing.[15] But after 1 December 1986 only her UK income was paid to Petard, and, as an international star, she earned most of her money abroad.)

Year	Net income	Surplus*	Hall's fee	Dividend
1980	£65,598	£9,595	£40,045	none
1981	£83,512	£8,533	£56,244	none
1982	£121,272	£11,168	£80,461	none
1983	£99,181	£13,838	£59,297	none
1984	£104,862	£16,292	£26,876	£20,000
1985	£133,976	£18,836	£25,154	£34,000
1986	£340,283	£33,990	£52,836	£40,000
1987	£159,519	£32,088	£37,482	£40,000
1988	£240,949	£31,936	£71,565	£20,000
1989	£489,427	£48,476	£160,215	£60,000

* after taxes and dividend

Petard's results provide an incomplete picture of Hall's finances. For instance, the National Theatre Board learned that Hall had earned nearly $600,000 from the American production of *Amadeus* in 1980–1, and he himself said in 1986 that he had earned £720,000 from *Amadeus*, so Petard's balance sheet evidently does not include all Hall's freelance income. But there was no requirement that Hall should repatriate all his American earnings. If he did so, it could have been taxed as personal income. One reason why he might have decided to pay that personal tax, rather than corporation tax rates levied on Petard, is that the Inland Revenue refused to allow private companies (known as close companies) to retain too much income as profit. This was presumably why Hall paid himself substantial dividends in the last six years of the decade.

Yet, in his press conference after the *Sunday Times* attack in 1986, Hall said his only assets were the house in Bramerton Street and perhaps £75,000 in the bank. On the face of it, it is hard to reconcile this statement with the earnings declared in Petard's annual reports. But Hall was responsible for a family that was growing steadily more extended. His parents still lived in Wallingford, and were ageing and infirm; Reg Hall had spent time in the Radcliffe Infirmary in Oxford. Christopher and Jenny were off his hands: Christopher was learning about television as a cameraman, and Jenny, after a brief stage career, had given it up for married life. Edward and Lucy were still to be provided for, however. Although they had left Bedales, Hall financed their higher education. But the greatest single drain on his income in the 1980s stemmed from his decision to leave Jacky and marry Maria.

The divorce from Jacky Hall was an acrimonious affair. Hall had left her in possession of the house in Wallingford, taking with him only his books and his pianos; she was lonely, especially when the children were away at boarding-school, and she felt frightened, and hard up. (Her father paid for the installation of a burglar alarm, which seemed to go off regularly at one o'clock in the morning.)[16] The style of the house had fallen out of fashion and it was on the market for more than a year before it sold. Eventually, she was awarded a settlement of £1,000 a month, and one-third of the profits of Petard Productions. But neither of them was happy with this. Hall, who thought alimony a barely tolerable burden, suggested that Jacky should go back to work; she was, after all, a highly trained personal assistant. And although she was able to set up house comfortably in Richmond, and became an accomplished guide at the British Museum and a prison visitor, Jacky never felt she had a fair share of Hall's income. His new style of life put further strain on the family finances. Ewing travelled widely to sing and, whenever he could, Hall joined her.

In the early years of their marriage, they were addicted to each other. She was in her early thirties, twenty years younger than Hall, active and ambitious. She was also highly strung, and before long stories began to circulate among his friends about her tempestuous nature. Her threat to return to the United States taking Rebecca with her was one made frequently enough. In 1985 they received unwelcome publicity when a couple they had hired to help them in South Chailey were given fourteen days to quit by a local county court, after claiming that Ewing had treated them like dirt. (She complained that the garden was not properly weeded.)[17]

His friends liked Ewing's infectious laughter, and were fascinated by her dedication to singing; but some did wonder why he had committed himself to a third marriage. Judi Dench was sure she knew the answer: it was because he was fifty, and, like her, afraid of death (they once confessed to one another that they thought about it every day). 'That's why he procreates and gets married. Love is a young man's activity,' she says.[18] If that was the case, he behaved true to form: his fifth child, Rebecca, was born in 1982.

Hall and Ewing did not work together again until the Glyndebourne production of Monteverdi's *Poppea* in 1984; then he directed her as *Carmen* in 1986. In Los Angeles that same year he directed her in Richard Strauss's *Salome*, in which Ewing caused a sensation by completing the dance of the seven veils without a stitch on. In each of these shows Ewing displayed her remarkable emotional intensity. That was her true nature, on and off the stage. Strong emotions ruled the marriage: 'It was highly charged from the beginning. In certain respects, it was almost violent; though not physically – Peter was never a violent man. But all the typical husband-and-wife problems came into the picture,' she says. Ewing was infuriated, for instance, by Hall's refusal to take a deep breath between engagements and free himself from the pressure of work. 'Like me, he worries,' she says.

Unlike him, however, Ewing does not recall details of her own temperamental behaviour. Reminded of the occasion when she threw a copy of Hall's *Diaries* across the room because she thought a photograph of her looked like Leslie Caron, Ewing giggles, and wonders why it is that her behaviour should remain so vividly in his mind that he should refer to them in his autobiography. Her conclusion is: 'All these memories are very close to the surface, because of his make-up, which is very delicate indeed.'

To his wives, Hall would reveal an indecisive streak in his nature, and, looking back, Ewing could see that her impatience often triggered rows between them. 'Several times he could not make up his mind, so I just said "Go and do it." But that's no reason to have gone as far as I did.' She eventually understood that Hall needed constant reassurance, and realised that her criticism of his work had been too frank. 'A person doesn't want honest criticism all the time, but love and affection. It's unfortunate, isn't it, that you don't learn how far you should go, and how far you shouldn't, until you're older.'

The relationship was too intense to last. Ewing blames herself for the break-up: 'I was the one who was hysterical and if there was any friction between us, it was always my fault. He was so vulnerable to my every mood.' As he had done with Leslie Caron, Hall started to worry that Ewing would leave him.

I think he thought that I didn't love him any more. I never stopped loving him, but I was ridiculously frightened of things happening to him at the National Theatre, or of him being run over by a bus; and that made me want to run away. If you're pushed right to the brink, it affects your psychological balance. I don't know why, but almost every month I'd say I didn't want to be around and I was going to leave. Peter didn't want us to break up and he became very depressed. He used to say 'If I lost you and Rebecca I'd commit suicide'. I suppose

I destroyed his confidence, and then I decided it was time to leave. I turned my back.

In the end, though, it was Hall who left Ewing. In 1988 when he was preparing three late Shakespeare plays for his farewell to the National Theatre, the publicity was being managed by a young woman from the press office called Nicki Frei, who had already worked with him on his three previous productions, including *Antony and Cleopatra*. She was tall, slim, cool and calm, with big brown eyes and long, honey-coloured hair. Hall fell in love with her.

She had surprised herself: 'I didn't have a history of dating older men, and if it hadn't happened gradually, I don't think it would have happened at all.'[19] Like all his other wives, Frei was in her late twenties when their affair began, having been born in Epsom in 1958, one of three children of parents of mainly Swiss and German ancestry. When she went to King's College, London, she chose a course designed to lead to a sound professional occupation and studied law. By the time she graduated, however, she had decided the legal profession was too public-school and masculine for her taste: 'I thought I'd go back to the law when I was thirty and cynical,' she recalls.

She decided to try the theatre instead, and took a menial job at the Riverside Theatre in Hammersmith; since the management had trouble finding the wages, most of her colleagues had to leave and, within weeks, she was press and publicity officer, looking after exotic figures from the theatrical avant-garde like Dario Fo. She moved on to a West End public relations company, specialising in looking after stars, but when a vacancy occurred in the National Theatre press office, she was glad to get the job: 'The fun in public relations is not holding a film star's hand, but in getting an audience to something they didn't know they wanted to see.'

The affair took its timing from the work they did together. There had always been a rapport between them, but she first noticed the flare of sexual interest while Hall was directing *Entertaining Strangers* in the autumn of 1987. They managed to keep their affair secret during the spring and early summer of 1988 by denying it, but it caused Hall another bout of severe emotional turmoil. By now there were so many people whom it would hurt: two parents, three wives, and five children. In June he and Nicki spent one

week in Le Cannet on the hill behind Cannes in a flat owned
by John Goodwin, and during their stay Hall became seriously
depressed: 'Peter was actually coming apart at the seams, and
I knew the only way he'd come out of it was to come home.'
Since he was in no condition to do so, she drove them the whole
way back. Hall writes that he thought of suicide once again, and
Nicki Frei does not think he was exaggerating.[20] 'He hadn't told
Maria that we were together, and he didn't think he had behaved
honourably. I don't think he handled it terribly well.' His doctor
thought that a spell in a clinic might be necessary, and Frei was
convinced that he was on the brink of a nervous breakdown. He
was distraught at the prospect of losing Rebecca, and before long
told Frei that their affair could not continue.

As for Ewing, when she discovered he was seeing Frei she
was devastated: 'It was dreadful.' Hall had told her he wanted
to leave a number of times: 'I'd think he was really going to go;
and then when he came back, I'd say "Well, go"; but when he
did, it was "Oh my God, he's gone."' Hall's final decision was
communicated to her by his lawyers: 'The minute that happens,
the marriage really crumbles, it falls into the pits. If he had not
made the decision by then, by golly, I'd have made it for him.'

After ten days apart from Frei, Hall telephoned and told her
he wanted to come back. He added that the *Daily Express* was
about to reveal their secret, there were reporters on the doorstep
in Bramerton Street, and outside Frei's flat in Islington in no
time at all. The tabloids relished the story: SAD SALOME DRAWS
VEIL OVER ANGUISH, said *Today*. On the run from reporters,
they hid away in Alan Ayckbourn's flat in Docklands before
deciding to flee together to Greece, where Hall's National Theatre
productions of Shakespeare's late plays were being performed at
Epidaurus. Since he knew the tabloid reporters would follow
Hall there, John Goodwin had advised Frei not to go, but she
was tired of hiding out, and the tabloids finally hunted them
down in Greece. *Today* surpassed itself: 'Sir Peter looks like
a pot-bellied Falstaff but he is a Romeo to his lovely Juliet.'
His Juliet was more concerned about the reaction of Hall's
Jenny, his eldest daughter, who was playing Miranda in *The
Tempest*. But this was not a new experience for Hall children,
and, when they were introduced, Jenny put Nicki at her ease.
She was, after all, the elder of the two. (Having caught their
quarry, the tabloid reporters left again, for London, and Hall

joined an audience of 25,000 people over three nights to watch Shakespeare.)

Ewing's lawyers wasted no time in giving Hall notice of her rights of occupation at 33 Bramerton Street under the Matrimonial Homes Act.[21] They were unlikely to bump into each other there, but when Hall went to Los Angeles to rehearse *Così fan tutte*, the Dorabella was Maria Ewing. Each survived that drama. The *Daily Mail* reported a reconciliation, and although there was no truth in that, they quickly re-established a working relationship. After the *Così fan tutte* in Los Angeles, the production of *Salome* was to be seen in Chicago. Ewing relented about Bramerton Street; Hall and Frei set up home there in the autumn.

Grace Hall had not approved when he had left Leslie, or when he left Jacky. She had grown fond of Maria, who encouraged Hall to take Rebecca to see her grandmother, and would not have approved of Hall's decision to leave her either. Ayckbourn tried to cheer Hall up by inventing a press headline about his mother's discovery of the news: 'SON RIGHT OFF THE RAILS, says Railway Wife.' Both his parents were unwell when Hall went to Wallingford to tell them about Nicki, but the news was so familiar to them by now that his mother did not appear particularly upset; resigned to it, rather.

Pardon's the Word

John Mortimer, who sat on the Board of the National Theatre throughout Hall's term as director, claims a little fancifully that Hall's political skills are even more impressive than his understanding of Shakespearian verse. In his last two years at the National, when he knew he was leaving, Hall did not lose his political touch so much as his concentration. He no longer took the trouble to win the Board over to his side. Victor Mishcon observes: 'It wasn't very easy, in the last years particularly, to persuade Peter to follow a line which he did not like.'[22]

David Hare, still under forty, and already a veteran observer of the National Theatre, thought Hall's reputation as a manipulator was overrated. He describes a scene that took place in Hall's office, when he asked each of the associates about their plans, noting down their replies on postcards for future reference. Hare claims to have glanced at Hall's cards after the meeting, and found the notes read 'more cigars' and 'collect laundry'.[23] The story's authenticity is dubious because of the unlikelihood of Hall's ever collecting his laundry, but it has a poetic truth. Hall had become less enthusiastic about formal consultation procedures. After 1985, five different groups – led by directors such as Ayckbourn, Eyre and Hare – each produced three plays over a period of two years or so, and, once Hall had agreed to their programme, he let them get on with it.

Hare also recalls an occasion at which he was shocked by Hall's estimation of his own public reputation. At the wedding of Hall's eldest son, Christopher, Hare told Hall that the reason he felt so moved by it was that Christopher was such a nice person. 'You mean, how could a shit like me produce such a nice person?' Hall commented. Being criticised as a shit was by then so much part of his public persona that Hall seemed to believe it himself. Though his colleagues at the National Theatre no longer had any illusions about Hall, they had a mature and fond relationship with him, and they certainly did not think he was a shit. They treated him a bit like a grand old man. He might have preferred to be thought a shit.

Young directors like Bill Bryden, Richard Eyre, Michael Rudman and Hare himself were at this period producing consistently interesting work. Not only was Ayckbourn back, but a company formed by Ian McKellen and Edward Petheridge brought together an ensemble that was reminiscent of the Old Vic days. Judged by the awards it received, the National Theatre was on marvellous form: twenty in 1985 and twenty-two in 1987.

As for the Board, Hall humoured them when he felt like it, and ignored them when he did not. There was another outbreak of hostilities with Rayne in 1987 after Hall had written a rude letter to *The Times* accusing Mrs Thatcher of mean-spirited philistinism, and Rayne disassociated the Board from it. 'I'm afraid we will just have to agree to disagree,' Hall wrote to Rayne. 'You will accept that I have had the interests of the National Theatre at heart for nearly as long as you, and I am satisfied that things would be much worse if we had just kept quiet and allowed ourselves to be kicked around like a football.'[24]

But in another skirmish with the Arts Council they were on the same side. Though Rayne and the Board agreed with Hall that his successor must be Richard Eyre, the Arts Council insisted that the job should be formally advertised. Infuriated by such bureaucratic interference, Rayne wrote to Luke Rittner, the Arts Council's secretary-general: 'If you want to run the National Theatre, you are welcome to do so. By the same token, if you want an office boy to serve as chairman of the National Theatre Board, you'd better advertise for one, in the secure knowledge that I shall not apply.'[25] Hall could not dislike the man who wrote that.

Rittner was making a nuisance of himself again in the spring of 1988, telling the Board that ministers had suggested that the National Theatre was getting too much money, not too little: 'The government are not going to be persuaded by us or by anyone that the National Theatre faces financial difficulties for so long as you show a healthy accumulated surplus,' Rittner wrote.[26] Neither the government nor the Arts Council need have worried. Hall had a method of dealing with accumulated surpluses. First at Cambridge and then at Stratford, the cupboard had been bare when he left. The National Theatre was to be no exception.

Hall left the National Theatre the hard way, by directing three plays by Shakespeare simultaneously, including *The Tempest*, with which he had begun at the Old Vic in 1973. But among students of showbusiness the thing Hall's late period at the National was famous for was his sacking of the film actress Sarah Miles.

The three late Shakespeare plays were due to open in May 1988, and the cast of thirty was given plenty of time to rehearse. A number of actors, such as Michael Bryant, Tim Pigott-Smith, Sally Dexter and Daniel Thorndike, had been in *Antony and Cleopatra*, and were confident about speaking the verse. For the leading women's parts of Innogen in *Cymbeline* – Hall declared the more familiar 'Imogen' was a First Folio printer's error – and Miranda in *The Tempest*, Hall cast a vivid young actress called Wendy Morgan who had worked well with him in 1985 in a translation of a play by Jean-Jacques Bernard called *Martine*. (Hall's work on *Martine* so impressed Harold Pinter that, by dropping Hall a card, he resumed their friendship.)[27]

But Wendy Morgan's decision to spend time with her three-month-old baby instead had fateful implications for Hall. Searching for a replacement that Christmas, he met Robert Bolt at a party. Bolt was an old friend, and one of the eight writers whom Hall had asked for new plays when he started out at the National Theatre. He was married to Sarah Miles, a waif-like and highly emotional actress, who had had a couple of recent film successes, like *What Mischief*. She and Hall had met years before, and after a short conversation, Hall impulsively asked her if she would like to play Innogen. Miles, keen to revive her stage career, auditioned successfully and started work in January. Hall's choice of his daughter Jennifer Hall for Miranda was no less startling.

He was taking two huge risks. Miles had not acted on stage for a long time, and she was working alongside skilled verse-speakers on top form. Before long, Hall realised his gamble was lost. He was reluctant, however, to fire Miles: he always told his fellow-directors at the NT that they should live with their casting errors, and he had already broken his rule once on this production – letting seventy-nine-year-old Robert Eddison go because he wanted to speak verse in a different style, and was having trouble with the lines.

Only when there was just a month left did Hall act decisively and fire his leading lady. At the time he said: 'If you've got a dead play on your hands, you've got to do something about it. It's tragic in human terms, and I'm not proud of it, but, because I wanted to be fair, I endangered the production and the company by leaving it to the very last moment.'[28] The NT press office and Miles's agent agreed to a form of words that had them parting by mutual consent, but the wound was deep and Sarah Miles was determined to show it. A change of cast at the National Theatre became a tabloid sensation, and produced some mawkish journalism. Miles appeared across two pages of the *Daily Mail* under a long headline which read: TO FIRE ME LIKE PETER HALL DID IS DEEPLY INCORRECT . . . IF HE WANTS TO DESTROY ME WHAT IS HIS MOTIVE . . . HE WAS SO COMPLIMENTARY. WHAT A SCHMUCK I WAS TO BELIEVE HIM. The article was accompanied by pictures of Hall looking predictably sinister. Those facets of his personality that were actually revealed by the Miles affair were impulsiveness, risk-taking and indecisiveness, none of which is unsympathetic. The feeling that the newspapers left lingering was, however, that he was a bit of a bully.

Hall was lucky that Geraldine James was available to take Sarah Miles's place. Within a month she had emerged 'superbly as a tough, strong-jawed woman full of irony and anger', according to Michael Billington in the *Guardian*. Hall had not been entirely free to concentrate on rehearsing her either; he had to spend time at the Royal Opera House rehearsing Maria Ewing in *Salome*, and there were grave distractions in his personal life and his family's. Some members of the company had denounced the casting of Jennifer Hall as nepotism. So it was, for Hall never missed an opportunity to put work in the way of his immediate family, and never apologised for it either. Jennifer had acted at Cambridge and intermittently during her twenties. Now, having given a decent account of Miranda, she left the cast towards the end of the run without explaining why. Her father was embarrassed and angry.

The Winter's Tale was a first attempt, and the *Cymbeline* was his first for thirty-two years, but the play that fascinated him most was still *The Tempest*, in which Prospero was this time not to be played by an imported star, but by Michael Bryant, a masterly company man. Having reacquainted himself with the text of the play, Hall arrived at a new and profoundly unsentimental interpretation: his Prospero was a man who had the chance to play God, and relished his power to perform God-like acts – to open graves and resurrect the dead; to torment and terrify. When Michael Bryant at the end of the play finally called for heavenly music and broke his magic staff, Hall's view was that Prospero was asking God's forgiveness for having usurped him. Irving Wardle in *The Times* commented: 'It is thrilling to witness this tortured human emerging from the anonymous shadow of stage tradition.' The late Shakespeares were well received ('A majestic end to one of Hall's careers': John Peter, *Sunday Times*). But, perhaps expectations had been too high, and there were too many mishaps, because the plays did not jostle for a place in the canon of Hall's finest work.

Hall's farewell was intended to be lavish, even though the three plays were originally scheduled to be performed only in the Cottesloe, and thus would be seen by no more than 400 people a night. The first working budget of £442,095 for all three was partly offset by £80,000 in sponsorship. A month before the plays were due to open, the estimated costs had risen to £473,719, a fairly modest 7 per cent increase. That was the point at which chaos set in. The sets and costumes had been subcontracted out, supposedly as an economy measure. In all three plays the stage was dominated by a mobile circular steel frame, decorated with stars and planets; it was a complicated (it got stuck on the first night) and expensive piece of stage machinery. Because the sets were late, five previews had to be cancelled before the opening on 18 May, and by that time costs had gone almost out of control. They were now £639,873, 45 per cent over budget, and the impact on the theatre's finances was catastrophic.[29]

It had been a bad summer in general at the box-office, and income from catering and sponsorship had not met expectations. By June the general reserve was being used to stanch the cash drain, starting with £527,787 to meet the initial capitalisation of Hall's three plays. In July, the Board learned that the whole of the general reserve had been used, and there was still a budgeted deficit for the year of £129,916. The full implications were not spelled out until October, when it was learned that the sum taken from the general reserve had been no less than £811,000. On discovering the deficit he inherited, Richard Eyre recalls feeling 'as sick as a parrot': 'I felt wrong-footed. It's hard at a moment of maximum lack of confidence to have it exacerbated by the financial position,' he says.[30]

The late Shakespeares did play to a larger audience than the Cottesloe held, touring to Moscow and Georgia, then to Japan and Greece, before returning to London for a season in the Olivier. John

Mortimer was in Moscow at the same time as Hall, and, although Hall claims to have detected in Russia a feeling that change was in the air, Mortimer recalled that Moscow seemed to Hall to be everything that he had escaped in his marvellously organised flight from the small town where his father was a stationmaster – 'the single bar of an electric fire to study by, and the relations who called birth a "happy event" and death a "merciful release"'. Mortimer reports that Hall found Moscow irredeemably working class. Their Moscow hotel breakfast of pork and roast potatoes, rice pudding, buttermilk and cold soft-boiled eggs did not appeal to Hall at all; and his work did not appeal to the Marxist theatre critics, who were disappointed not to find a social message in his Shakespeare. Mortimer writes that Hall contrived a second escape, by taking a taxi to the airport and a plane back to London: 'He left the Russians a marvellous production of *Cymbeline*, which had no message except its story of past injustices and old brutalities forgiven. As the king at the end of the play says, "Pardon's the word to all."'[31]

Hall actually had a more pressing reason for leaving the cast in Russia. It was the usual one: there was Verdi's *Falstaff* to direct at Glyndebourne, and a new career to begin in the commercial theatre. After the final decision to leave the NT in September 1986, Hall did not waste any time in planning his future. By November he was telling colleagues that he proposed to go into partnership with two producers, Duncan Weldon in London and Jerome Minscoff in New York; and the Peter Hall Production Company Ltd was registered at Companies House in March 1987. Hall had 50 per cent of the shares, and his partners the other 50 per cent.

Hall left the National Theatre before his contract formally ran out at the end of December 1988. Parties were given for him and for Max Rayne, who was succeeded by Mary Soames, Winston Churchill's daughter. Despite their differences and arguments, Hall had generous words for Rayne. At his farewell dinner, Hall said: 'He was always totally loyal, and this needs stressing. It is easy for amateur boards and amateur chairmen, who are necessarily part-time and who are thought to be disinterested, to be, on the contrary, interfering, mucking up the professionals, being silly. That has never been so in my time. That is Max's gift to us.'[32]

The Board's gift to him had been organised some time before:

a specially made garden seat decorated with his initials and Maria Ewing's. But by the time he was ready to receive it, there was no garden and no Maria. That was the official present. A collection among his friends and colleagues went towards an expensive camera. Hall had asked for a Hasselblad; and when Lord Snowdon found out that it cost more than the collection had raised, Samuel Beckett made up the difference. These exchanges involved as many famous names as could be found in a well-informed gossip column on a good day – Hall, whose first reputation was as a young prodigy, had been working in the professional theatre for thirty-three years, and he knew a lot of people. Having masterminded the expansion of the RSC and the National Theatre's move to the South Bank, he had become an institution himself.

The chattering classes still regarded him with suspicion, and he was a target for the bitchiness of main actors who felt that, by emphasising his own part in productions as the director, Hall had ruthlessly subordinated the role of the actor. But no one had done as much to develop the subsidised theatre in which virtually all clever British writers, original directors and talented actors worked at some time in their lives. He had been around for so long that his virtues were taken for granted, and his faults tolerated.

19

Our Theatres in the Nineties

'I don't know how to say no'

In the autumn of 1988 Reg Hall had spent a few days at the Radcliffe Infirmary in Oxford. Soon after he returned home, Grace went into the hospital, and in October, cancer was diagnosed. Hall believed that, once Reg knew her illness was fatal, he decided not to go on living. He died at home in Wallingford, on 5 November 1988, shortly after his eighty-seventh birthday, of a heart attack during his afternoon nap. Grace died soon after Reg's funeral, on 11 November, without knowing of his death. Hall suffered all the feelings that overcome children when their parents die. He had never realised how much he would miss having a home to go to, or how conscious he would be that he was next in line.

But work provided a distraction from grief. Tennessee Williams's *Orpheus Descending*, the first production of the Peter Hall Company, was due to open in Bath in November. His future in the theatre and opera in the West End, Broadway and Epidaurus, the Royal Opera House and Glyndebourne, and opera houses in Florence, Los Angeles, Chicago and Houston, was being constantly renegotiated. The Peter Hall Company had an office in Exeter Street, directly across Waterloo Bridge from the National Theatre, but Hall was rarely there. When he was, he was affronted by the sight of his beautiful glass desk, which had been cracked during the move.

Every evening Hall would receive a list of his messages and appointments, and early each morning he dictated letters and messages into a tape-recorder. These would be acted upon in Exeter Street, which was Peter Hall's communications hub. An indication of how hectic his life had become can be gauged from his messages, letters and appointments for 14 November 1988. There are fifty-two items on the list.[1]

Hall was in Bath that day, where he started lighting *Orpheus Descending* at 8 a.m., and he would be there all week, which meant missing the *Evening Standard* awards on Friday, where an award was being made to him to mark the National Theatre's twenty-fifth anniversary. A proposed trip to Chicago, where Maria Ewing was opening in his production of *Salome*, was out; he would not even be able to take tea with the cast of the late Shakespeares at the end of the run. One appointment was to be untouchable, however: a family dinner for his son Edward a couple of weeks later.

Casting was a preoccupation. Hall had met and liked Alex Jennings for Bassanio in *The Merchant of Venice*, planned for the following spring with Dustin Hoffman as Shylock. ('Please could we try to do a deal today? It is very urgent.') He had dictated a letter to Hoffman, saying he would shortly receive a second tape explaining Hall's view of Shylock; Hall also wanted Hoffman to think about transferring the *Merchant* to Broadway, possibly later in 1989. Hall had auditioned a soprano for Sir Michael Tippett's *New Year* ('I thought she was ideal'), which was to have its first performance in Houston in spring 1989, before transferring to Glyndebourne. His own agent, Laurence Evans, was gently pushing a couple of his other clients for small parts in a BBC film of a Stephen Poliakoff play, *She's Been Away*, starring Peggy Ashcroft, which Hall was to direct in February 1989.

Clashes in the schedule had to be sorted out: between Berlioz's *The Trojans* in Florence and *Così fan tutte* in Glyndebourne; between *The Trojans* and Richard Strauss's *Elektra* in Los Angeles; and between the conflicting claims on the time of his Glyndebourne assistant, Stephen Lawless ('I am desperate about the news . . . I can't lose him from *Figaro*').

The appointments diary had to be rearranged so that Hall could fly to Greece in mid-December to discuss a production of a tragedy in masks at Epidaurus in daylight; from Athens to Florence (*The*

Trojans to be planned); and then direct to New York to discuss casting Peter Shaffer's *Yonadab*. Shaffer was among the people Hall must see; so was Trevor Nunn's solicitor about Nunn's libel action against the *Sunday Times*.

He instructed Jan Younghusband, his personal assistant who had followed him when he left the NT, to keep an eye on Jason Carr, a young composer working on *Born Again*, an adaptation Hall had done with the American writer Julian Barry of Eugène Ionesco's *Rhinoceros* ('Ask him if he needs a meeting with me'). Hall was constantly trying to persuade David Hockney to design *Born Again*. (The job eventualy went to Gerald Scarfe.)

Hall was anxious to see a video of *Elektra*, and wanted tickets for *Mrs Klein* at the National Theatre. There were eight letters to be written, including his acceptance of the presidency of the Eastern Arts Association ('I cannot be very active because of the demands of my own career'); he wanted the playwright Simon Gray to pursue his translation of Molière's *Tartuffe*; he turned down an invitation to stay with the British ambassador in Rome. A painter called Matthew Hayward had asked to do his portrait ('I don't know how to say no. What do you think?'). He wanted an appointment for a Shiatsu massage; some pills in case his sinuses caused trouble; and a biography of Charles Dickens.

His other preoccupation was the harrowing matter of his mother's funeral: the place, the time, the wake, the announcement in *The Times* and the *Daily Telegraph*, ringing round the children and the relatives, retrieving her belongings from the hospital.

A little less than four months earlier, Hall had been on the verge of a nervous breakdown. Having recovered from that, he was now, Nicki Frei found, 'completely solid'.[2] He had trouble sleeping and his sinuses bothered him; he was almost fifty-eight and his grey beard and balding head betrayed his age. But the appetite for work and the restless drive shown in just one day's messages are those of a person who had never lost his passion for art, or for action.

'I doubt whether a compromise is possible'

When Peter Hall, leaving the National Theatre, asked Alan Ayckbourn to join him in his West End adventure, Hall told him he wanted to start a repertory company in the centre of London doing the equivalent of the NT's work, but on a commercial scale. Ayckbourn said later that if a lesser man had made him the offer, he would have said he was talking bollocks.[3] At the time, however, he thought the combination of Hall's realism, his own cynicism, and the pessimism of Duncan Weldon, his partner, gave them a good practical basis for success.

Duncan Weldon had created a comfortable niche for himself as a commercial producer by putting on revivals of classic plays with star names at the loveliest theatre in the West End, the Theatre Royal, Haymarket. Weldon's father owned camera shops in Manchester, and Weldon had worked his way into the theatre as a photographer. By 1988 his company, Triumph Theatre Productions, had produced forty-five plays in seventeen years.[4] He and Hall had met by chance in Los Angeles in 1986, when Weldon had said that if Hall was setting up a commerical production company, he would like the Theatre Royal to become its home. But working with a legendary figure from the subsidised theatre was a new experience for Weldon. Indeed, it proved to be a steep learning-curve for both of them.

Hall had accepted some curbs on his original idea. Instead of playing in repertory, there would be no company, no large casts; if a play was not an immediate success, it would close, because there would be neither time nor money to nurse it. 'All this makes us a mite more cautious,' Hall said at the time.[5] Weldon had already been a mite cautious on his behalf, and with his partner, Sir Ronald Miller, had thought up a scheme for raising money that would make it easier for Hall to work in the style to which he was accustomed. (Miller was the playwright and scriptwriter who had subtly transformed a play title of Christopher Fry's into the slogan:

'The lady's not for turning.') Weldon and Miller proposed selling associate memberships in the Peter Hall Company at £4,000 a time. They hoped to persuade 300 companies to part with this sum in return for tickets they could use for company entertaining. Miller thought it was feasible to talk of raising £1.2 million: 'The scheme's kosher, and it couldn't be better,' he declared before the company opened. The pessimistic Weldon commented: 'If we don't get it, we can survive without it.'

There were departures from the original plot. Hall had hoped that Ayckbourn's first contribution would be a new play by him, but he was sharply disabused: Ayckbourn had promised his next new play to Weldon's rival, Michael Codron. He did, however, agree to translate an unfamiliar French satire called *Les Corbeaux* (The Scavengers) by Henri Becque, which he entitled *Wolf at the Door*. That was to be the second show of the Peter Hall Company, which was to be launched with Hall's production of Tennessee Williams's *Orpheus Descending*. Vanessa Redgrave was the star, and her presence meant that the production conformed to Ayckbourn's general rule about the London commercial theatre: 'I learned my lesson years ago. You can't go into the West End without the protection of a few famous names,' he says. But Ayckbourn was ignoring the lesson of his own experience.

Hall had said that the choice of plays and 'make or break' casting would be decided by Weldon and himself, but, after they had agreed to do it, Weldon began to show a marked lack of enthusiasm for *Wolf at the Door*. Jan Younghusband's budgets seemed to him to deny conventional theatre economics: Weldon wanted them reduced and Hall asked Younghusband to see what she could do. 'I wish we could get them down some more because the cost each week is too high for a play without stars,' he told her.[6]

Having accepted smaller budgets, Hall thought that Weldon had agreed to proceed with all systems go on *Wolf*. But that was not what Weldon thought. He wrote to Younghusband on 17 October 1988, saying that only after further new budgets had been prepared would *Wolf* be considered – 'against the best potential star value we can give the attraction'. Ayckbourn had never intended *Wolf* as a star vehicle, while Weldon believed it could not run without them. 'We were doing all the things that, when we first talked about it, we said we weren't going to do,' says Ayckbourn. Learning of Weldon's obduracy, Ayckbourn fired off what he describes as 'one of my ill-judged faxes'. (Apparently it contained some highly unflattering remarks about the reputation of Weldon's Triumph Theatre Productions.)

Hall tried to make peace through Miller on 21 October, but Weldon was adamant. *Wolf* was to be dropped. Hall wrote to him on 26 October: 'I had a long conversation with Ronnie in which we agreed that he would try to persuade you to do *Wolf at the Door* if I got Alan to withdraw the abusive letter he sent you . . . I rang Alan and got him to withdraw his letter . . . what I thought we were doing was producing the situation where *Wolf* might happen; not where it was being cancelled.'[7] For Hall it was a harsh lesson: at the National Theatre and the RSC, no one had had the power to tell him he could not put on a play. Because he had ultimate control over the budgets, Hall was the impresario. That baton had now passed to Weldon.

Weldon's immediate response to Hall's letter was evidently unsatisfactory, because he wrote a second letter on the same day, 26 October: 'I do not consider my position to be a tenable one and I must therefore ask whether there is any way I can be released from my contract. To pretend we can go on as if nothing had happened is not a solution to the problem; and, much as I would like one, I doubt whether a compromise is possible.' The exchange took place three weeks before the press night of *Orpheus Descending* at the Theatre Royal; even before Hall's company had moved into its new office. Hall's well-publicised relationship with a commercial producer had ended in an acrimonious disagreement about policy and standards almost before it had properly begun. Ayckbourn formally resigned from the Peter Hall Company before the end of the month: 'It had all become a nonsense, but it was rather sad,' he said, some years later.

Weldon would not release Hall from his contract, perhaps because *Orpheus Descending* was a critical success and Hall was to direct Dustin Hoffman as Shylock in the spring. The annual report of the Peter Hall Company showed that, although *Orpheus Descending* made a loss, it had proved profitable to the partners: Hall's fee as director was £58,333, and Triumph received £42,500 in management fees.[8] But whatever hope and warmth they had invested in the partnership had evaporated. Some months later Weldon asserted: 'The problems were caused by a bit of insecurity on Peter's part about working with a commercial company.' But they went deeper than that; any illusions that Hall brought with him from the South Bank to Shaftesbury Avenue had been lost. Three more productions were to be done with Weldon, although none of them appeared at the Theatre Royal, and Hall ended the relationship as soon as the lawyers would let him.

'They are from different ends of the world'

When Dustin Hoffman was in London in the summer of 1988, he had sought out Peter Hall and asked whether he thought he could play Hamlet. 'You've left it a bit too late,' Hall replied.[10] *The Merchant of Venice* was a different matter: Shylock is an outsider and a Jew, and Hall thought the part would suit Hoffman perfectly. Moreover, since Hall had not done the play before, he was keen to direct it himself. The deal between them was done early in October, and Hall recorded the terms for the company files.[11]

Rehearsals will commence 27th March 1989. This moves the project a week later but Dustin needs it to finish a film.
He would accept the top salary of the company – whatever that is. I did not mention figures, but said it would be the same as Vanessa [Redgrave's].
He wants no billing. Indeed he insists on alphabetical billing.
He will play until the end of the first week in September.
He may then make another movie.
If the production goes well, it is our intention to play it for a short season in New York. I would prepare an American cast without him and then have him come and join us.
His lawyer thought that billing would be appropriate in New York.

The collaboration proved remarkably successful. In rehearsal Hoffman became an ardent convert to the rhythm of the iambic pentameter, clicking his fingers at the end of every five-beat line. Hall drummed into him the same instruction that he had given to actors for almost four decades: keep the line as smooth, light and whole as possible. Hoffman responded enthusiastically: 'I'd love to get to the point where Peter can't nail me,' he said.

Working with a Hollywood star intrigued Hall. 'Most actors cook slowly, taking three or four weeks to get to a point, but Hoffman goes from nothing to total creation. He can do a scene 10 different ways. He's almost too inventive.' Hoffman learned the lesson about speaking directly to the audience ('the aside is not kosher'), and about containing emotion. He described playing Shylock as like being on a hot date, and was impressed by Hall's impartiality: 'I never felt he had a preconception of what he wanted me to feel, and that's one of the nicest gifts an actor can get.'

Duncan Weldon did not make the Theatre Royal, Haymarket available after all, so *The Merchant* opened at the unfashionable Phoenix Theatre off Charing Cross Road. But the location did not count. *The Merchant* was a hot ticket, described as the theatrical event of the year, and it sold out throughout the run. Hoffman justified the hype, too, though the production was so tightly focused on him that many members of the cast seemed to lose their concentration, and it sometimes looked faded at the edges. The New York transfer did take place and Hall thought that, by the end of the run there, Hoffman's Shylock was among the most accomplished pieces of Shakespearian acting he had seen. They fell out, however, over Hoffman's wish to film the last few performances and piece together a video. That was too haphazard a method for Hall. After he refused his permission, they never spoke again.

Hall did two more plays in partnership with Weldon in 1990: Ibsen's *The Wild Duck* and Pinter's *The Homecoming*, neither of which could be described as pandering to popular taste. There were to be no compromises in Hall's choice of plays, but in other areas some trimming was unavoidable. Commercial producers could not afford the long rehearsal periods he had been used to in the subsidised theatre. Hall himself was still incapable of doing one thing at a time, but juggling with more than one production was a harder trick once he no longer had the NT's powerful, well-oiled machine to help him. On occasion, Hall did not lavish enough time on his productions and sometimes this cruelly exposed their limitations: a ragged account of Terence Rattigan's *Separate Tables*, for example, caused Irving Wardle in the *Independent on Sunday* to lament that this was the kind of production Hall had arrived in London in the 1950s to root out.

Hall was distressed by the suggestion that he had sold out to the commercial theatre. Far from betraying his past in the subsidised theatre, he was, he said, reaping the benefits of the time he spent in it. He was drawing on a pool of hundreds of actors with whom he had worked; writers like Stephen Poliakoff had benefited from his patronage; most importantly, however, there was a substantial audience for serious plays, created by the RSC and the NT, willing to attend his productions in the West End.

When his partnership with Weldon ended, there was always another producer who did not dissent from Hall's opinion of himself: 'A number of people have put money into letting me do what I want to do,' he says.[12] Next after Weldon was the novelist and peer Jeffrey Archer, who had acquired a controlling interest in the Playhouse, a pleasantly restored theatre off the beaten track by Hungerford Bridge. He and Hall formed Playhouse Productions in 1991, so Hall could do Molière's *Tartuffe*, *Twelfth Night*, and Tennessee Williams's *The Rose Tattoo*.

A different pattern of casting became apparent at the Playhouse. *Twelfth Night* drew on actors like Eric Porter, who as Malvolio was playing a part he had first done at Stratford thirty years earlier. In *Tartuffe*, however, in which Paul Eddington and Felicity Kendal were playing, the star was John Sessions, a young comedian who had made his name on television. In *The Rose Tattoo* the leading role was played by Julie Walters, a good actress who gave a memorable performance, but whose reputation came from her film and television work.

Because he wanted strong casts, and as much time as possible for rehearsal, commercial producers never made windfall profits out of Hall's productions. Jeffrey Archer learned this to his cost, and announced the sale of the Playhouse: Peter Hall and his company appeared to be part of the fixtures and fittings. His company never had another permanent home.

Hall had flirted with the idea of repeating *A Midsummer Night's Dream*, one of his greatest RSC successes, at Stratford, working once again with John Bury as designer. But casting problems over which Hall had no control caused delays, and when he got a better offer, he cancelled the plan. He finally returned to Stratford in the summer of 1992 to direct *All's Well That Ends Well*, though without Bury.[13] The designer was John Gunter, who had worked with him in Glyndebourne, and the cast was drawn from two generations of actors: old Stratford hands like Richard Johnson and Barbara Jefford played alongside Toby Stephens, son of the actor Robert Stephens, and Sophie Thomson, the daughter of an actor who had worked in the Elizabethan Theatre Company.

This was Hall's first experience of the Swan Theatre, whose acoustics he delighted in, although he found that verse-speaking was a mystery to most of the actors. ('They know less about it than they did in the 1950s, but they are much more willing to learn.')[14] He was distracted during rehearsals by the birth of Emma, his sixth child, but the performances were a reminder of earlier days in Stratford, when good productions ran like his old Rolls-Royce.

In London again, Hall discovered a new patron. This was Bill Kenwright, and it was an unlikely alliance. Kenwright is a Liverpudlian with an ear for popular musical taste and no great knowledge of the classical theatre. 'They are from different ends of the world,' says Hall's casting director, Gillian Diamond, 'but they need each other.'[15] Kenwright and Hall had been brought together by the actor Martin Shaw, who was to appear in Hall's production of a new play by Stephen Poliakoff. It was an expensive introduction: Poliakoff's *Sienna Red* did not survive its pre-London tour, and Kenwright's first experience of Hall was a costly one.

He was not deterred, however, largely because, together, they were able to exploit a new trend in the commercial theatre. The restoration of a chain of theatres in provincial towns like Bath and Leatherhead created a niche for serious plays that were cast with a star familiar to television audiences. The presence of the star means the managements of local theatres can guarantee a return to the producer, and, in some cases, that London producers can cover the capitalisation of a production before a show reaches the West End. Since few West End plays in the 1990s run for more than fifteen weeks – owing partly to the reluctance of stars to commit themselves for any longer – this is just as well. This practical system of finance enabled Hall to direct plays by Wilde (*An Ideal Husband*), Aristophanes (*Lysistrata*), Rattigan (*Separate Tables*), Sheridan (*She Stoops to Conquer*), Lonsdale (*On Approval*), and Feydeau (*An Absolute Turkey*). In the second half of 1993, four of these plays were among five shows directed by Hall running in the West End; the fifth was a memorable performance by Elaine Page as *Piaf*.

One major difference between this line of work and Hall's repertoire in the subsidised theatre was the scarcity of new plays. The new economics of the West End does not apply to new writing. The translations of *Tartuffe* and *Lysistrata* (by Ranjit Bolt), and *An Absolute Turkey* (by Nicki Frei and Peter Hall) were original, but the only new plays Hall directed in the 1990s were by Poliakoff, John Guare – his *Six Degrees of Separation* was directed by Hall in New York – and Peter Shaffer. *The Gift of the Gorgon* was Shaffer's first play for the RSC, and Hall directed it at the Barbican late in 1992, with Judi Dench and Michael Pennington in the leading roles.

After the disappointment of *Yonadab*, Shaffer had written a delightful comedy for Maggie Smith called *Lettice and Lovage*, which ran for three years in the West End, and transferred to Broadway. The new play, however, was not at all funny, the subject being terrorism and feelings of rage and revenge. After its RSC opening, it transferred to the West End in the spring of 1993, but it was one of Shaffer's interesting failures rather than one of his entertaining successes.

Shaffer and Hall were by now thoroughly accustomed to each other's way of working, and the flow of rewritten work from Shaffer stopped only when he collapsed and was taken to hospital for a heart bypass operation. But Judi Dench, new to Shaffer's style of writing, grew tired of receiving a sheaf of revised script each morning, especially when the flow continued after the opening night.

At a rehearsal one morning Dench burst into tears, walked off the stage, and went to her dressing room. Since no one came to reassure her, she switched on the Tannoy to hear what was happening on the stage. What she heard was the understudy playing her part, so 'I thought I'd better get back and do it,' she says.[16] Between herself and Hall, Dench decided it was Hall who was the bigger star.

Hall had few illusions about the commercial theatre. 'I don't work in the West End as an aesthetic choice,' he says. As the 1990s went by, his enthusiasm was more easily aroused by film and television projects, especially if he and Nicki Hall could write the script. He also hankered after the large casts and long rehearsal periods of the subsidised theatres, and began to plot his return to work on classic texts at the RSC and the National Theatre. Shakespeare was never very far from the surface of Hall's consciousness, and in January 1994 he woke up one morning and realised that he wanted to do *Hamlet* again.

Despite the length of the text (only minor cuts were acceptable to Hall), and the size of the cast, Bill Kenwright was ready to oblige again. The production toured throughout the summer and autumn of 1994 – reaching out as far as Athens and Vienna, and testing the endurance of the actors – before opening in London. Designs and costumes were by Hall's daughter Lucy, who had trained at the Central St Martin's School of Art, and learned her trade at the National Theatre Studio and the Theatre Upstairs at the Royal Court. She made her West End début in the summer of 1994, but her father had already tried to tempt her into working with him, as her brother Edward had done. When she finally succumbed in the summer of 1994, Lucy Hall discovered that the play she was to design was not the 1930s comedy she had expected to work on, but *Hamlet*.

This was Hall's fourth *Hamlet*. The productions span forty-five years in the theatre: his schoolboy *Hamlet* in 1949; the RSC in 1965; the National Theatre in 1975; his production for the commercial theatre in 1994. His schoolboy *Hamlet* was a heavily romantic copy of John Gielgud's at the New Theatre when Hall was aged three; his middle-period *Hamlets* were preoccupied by political power; Hall's programme note claimed that his fourth production emphasised Hamlet's ambiguous sexuality.

But though Hamlet's dismissal of Ophelia was unusually harsh, the critics identified a quite different theme. Irony and mockery were the chief characteristics of Stephen Dillane's Hamlet. In *The Times* Benedict Nightingale wrote: 'The result is helplessness, ennui, and black humour, an anger turned outward in mockery and inward in self-contempt. He wanted to be a Renaissance revenger – and was doomed to become a modern alternative comedian.' Hall has said that the differences between generations are reflected in the way *Hamlet* is performed, and Nightingale's review was headlined: A PRINCE FOR THE NINETIES. But Stephen Dillane's wry comedian seemed far from the bisexual Hamlet Hall said he had in mind.

No matter; the reviews were generally gratifying. Michael Billington in the *Guardian* detected the playing style of Hall's 'late classical mode': it was visually simple, textually full, and very fast. 'No director brings out more clearly the architectural shape of a play . . . Hall is the play's invisible conductor as well as director,' wrote Billington. (Lucy Hall got mixed reviews, her sets being more admired than the costumes.)

Hall's fourth *Hamlet* marked the inauguration, in Shaftesbury Avenue, of the theatre renamed to honour the actor who had inspired his first, Sir John Gielgud. It was a bold venture, but Hall did not wait for the critical reaction. He and Nicki had been working on the final version of a film script, and before the reviews appeared in print, Hall had flown to Vancouver to direct the film.

'You've got to step back'

After living with Peter Hall for a year, Nicki Frei found she did not want to keep up with the pace of his hectic daily life. When they came back from Greece in the autumn of 1988, they set up house together officially, in Bramerton Street. She handled the press publicity for *Orpheus Descending*; she became assistant producer for its Broadway production, and, after that, for the *Merchant of Venice* with Dustin Hoffman in London and New York. But she was tiring of publicity work ('It's a bit of a cul-de-sac'). 'You have to adjust a bit to living with Peter,' she says.[17] 'If you don't establish a slight detachment, you get buffeted by it. You want to live it all, but you've got to step back.' By accident, she discovered a way of being involved in Hall's working life but not in his manic daily round. Hall asked her to help with a script based on a file of material he had received about the Italian tenor Enrico Caruso. They discovered they were natural collaborators. 'We wrote together line by line,' she says. 'To someone who went through her twenties with an abject fear of failure, he's a great confidence-giver.'

From Caruso, which had sex and music but no producer, she moved on to Feydeau's famous farce *Le Dindon*, a play that had always intrigued Hall. (When Hall asked Ayckbourn if he was interested in directing it, he said he found it too heartless.) Frei, who had intended to study English and French law, did a literal translation of the play while Hall was producing *Born Again*, his musical version of Ionesco's *The Rhinoceros* at Chichester in the summer of 1990. They decided to risk the sarcasm of the critics and call it *An Absolute Turkey*. (*Born Again* was the turkey.)

As Frei's pace slowed, she was able to consider the reasons why his never did. One had been clear to her since they first met: he truly loved directing. The rehearsal room to him is an adventure playground. Frei thinks a second reason was that Hall remains instinctively the outsider: conscious of his origins, he cannot really believe that he belongs at the top of his profession, and needs always to justify his status.

The third reason why he worked so hard was familiar to all his wives, since Leslie Caron left him in 1964. 'He was financially up a major gum tree,' says Frei. The separation from Maria Ewing increased his financial liabilities, and money was always owing to Jacky. Since Bramerton Street was infused with memories of Maria, they wanted to move, but not far; and houses in Chelsea are not cheap, especially when Hall is involved in their refurbishment. Frei quickly learned that Hall was not interested in the management or investment of his money: 'He's brilliant at earning it, but he loves spending it,' she says.

Hall's brilliance at earning money was reflected in the results of Petard Productions. In 1989, director's pay (i.e. Hall's income) was £160,200, plus a dividend of £60,000. The following year, his total pay was down slightly to £211,500, but in 1991 his earnings rose to £222,400. During those years the net fees received by Petard were £487,400 (1989), £504,700 (1990) and £445,300 (1991).[18] The fact that this was not enough to bring him down quickly from his financial gum tree indicates the scale of his obligations.

Hall and Nicki married in New York on 17 September 1990, and a little under two years later his sixth child, Emma, was born. At birth, Emma already had two nephews and a niece, and the family, having been blown apart a number of times by divorce and remarriage, was knitting together again. After an interval of a couple of years, once she was sure that Hall would not use Rebecca as ammunition in any divorce settlement, Maria Ewing became a good friend of Hall's. Leslie Caron sees him on her regular visits to London; they enjoy each other's company and keep an eye on each other's work. Both Maria and Leslie say they still love Hall. There was, however, no reconciliation with Jacky Hall, and the language of their relationship remained steeped in anger and guilt. But Jacky, too, says she still loves him a bit: 'After all, he is the father of my children.'[19]

The six children, spanning thirty-five years, bind Hall to his former wives. Nicki Hall reports that most of them telephone with their news at weekends, and one or two of them look in at the new house at World's End, down the King's Road from Bramerton Street. They are close partly because they all have an occupation in common. Hall is like the chairman of a small family business.

Christopher Hall is a television producer of popular series such as *London's Burning*, *Poirot* and *Anna Lee* (in which the heroine is played by the third wife of Hall's former colleague, Trevor Nunn). Christopher had been drawn into the family business as a director of Petard Productions while he was a post-graduate student at Bristol University. He married and is the father of Emma's two nephews.

Jenny, the mother of Emma's niece, did not have such a smooth ride. When her father cast her as Miranda in *The Tempest*, she left the play before its run ended, and he was entitled to feel let down. After the failure of her own marriage to a Devonian apple farmer whom she had met at school at Bedales, Jenny Hall wrote an article in the *Daily Mail* saying that she had married because she hoped his stable family would be the opposite of the turbulence of her own childhood after her parents divorced.

'My family life has always been a war zone,' she wrote, exhibiting a touch of the Pamment genes.

> *It meant watching with dread the birth of new siblings and hoping it would not be the same again. Also, it meant having to face up to feelings of jealousy over a newborn when you are supposed to be much too old for such things . . . When people get divorced they tend to think they have to put their failed marriage behind them and start all over again. This is a myth. You can never make a complete break. Memories haunt you, your children's dispositions, looks or talents are like your spouse's, and you can never forget it.*

Jenny Hall's *Daily Mail* article distressed both her mother and her stepmother. Leslie Caron was sad ('she has no idea what she wrote'), and she was comforted by Christopher. Jacky Hall was furious at the suggestion that she was the wicked stepmother who had burned Jenny's clothes. She was appeased by her daughter Lucy, who said that any defects in Jenny's memory must be attributed to her unhappiness as a child.

The second of the new siblings Jenny referred to was Lucy's elder brother Edward. When he was still a boy, and seemed to be a great worrier, Jenny identified Edward as an inheritor of the Pamment genes. On the contrary, when he grew up the one characteristic of Edward's that people commented on was his sunny good nature. As an adult, he seemed to be the clearest inheritor of his father's mantle. He directed his own stage productions, worked for the RSC, and when his father's *Lysistrata* transferred from the Old Vic to the West End in 1993, Edward directed that too.

Rebecca Hall became a public figure at the age of nine. While she was still small, Ewing was reluctant to let Rebecca out of her sight, and Rebecca became an *habituée* of rehearsal rooms. She was, Hall decided, by far the best of the children who auditioned for his television adaptation of Mary Wesley's novel *The Camomile Lawn* in 1991. Indeed, she performed as to the manner born, upstaging a cast that included mature professionals like Paul Eddington and Felicity Kendal.

Emma made her own début, aged two, as the baby Joseph in a film entitled *Jacob* that Hall made in the Sahara in 1994. He then claimed to be the only father with six children between the ages of two and thirty-seven, who had directed five of them (Christopher was the odd one out). But the two youngest girls were the only ones who saw much of him as children. By then he believed that making time for them was part of the process of maturing, or, as he put it, becoming more like himself.

The children and the former wives are virtually unanimous in giving Nicki Hall credit for providing a home in which the Hall family could unite. (Only Jacky Hall reserves judgement.) With Nicki, Hall saw, perhaps, a last chance of making a stable marriage, and he seemed eager to take it. As for Nicki, the media seem always to label her with her past ('a former publicist'), and to deny her a dependable future (always Hall's 'current wife', as though there will be another one some day). The demotion of her own intelligence that this involves is the price of being married to a much-married celebrity. She is able to take it in her stride.

'You can't drive yourself to be successful'

Peter Hall did not find it easy to work on his autobiography. Originally, he had intended to write an account of his experiences of directing Shakespeare, but when the advance from the publishers, Sinclair-Stevenson, was doubled to £100,000, the book became a full-blown autobiography. The tapes Hall made of his life story were transcribed, and the text was sent for editing to the NT's former publicist John Goodwin, who had edited the diaries so splendidly in 1983. Then the work had been a pleasure. This time Hall was unfocused, and seemed uneasy at having to dig deeply into his feelings about the past. When he devoted a whole month to working on the book, he dried up completely. The final account, subtitled with a phrase of his mother's – 'Making an Exhibition of Myself' – strung together an entertaining but unreflective account of his life; it was at its best when he was writing about directing and speaking Shakespeare. But it did not reveal whether in his case it was true that the older you get, the more like yourself you become.

As a man of the theatre, the opposite seemed to have happened. Hall had started out as a purist and a romantic, a disciple of visionaries like Edward Gordon Craig and Norman Marshall who foresaw a golden age in the British theatre led by a state-subsidised National Theatre with a permanent company of actors. During his life Hall had done as much as – probably more than – any single individual to make the golden age happen. Yet the third act of his career was not what he would have wished.

This was clear from the wistful tone of an interview he gave to publicise his autobiography. 'What I'd most like to do,' he told Penny Fox of the *Scotsman*, 'is have a millionaire give me a little studio theatre and enough money to examine Shakespeare with young actors. Teach them, and teach directors, and have some very high-powered actors working there, too. Judi Dench and Ian McKellen . . .'[21]

As he approached his mid-sixties, Hall despaired of the state as the fairy godmother of the British theatre; and, as for the realisation of his own dream, one millionaire would not be enough. For Hall to be a teacher ('that would be my best old age'), he would need a new millionaire each year. A few lives have such happy endings, but not – so far – Hall's. He is a splendid teacher, and a wealthy and benevolent society might well provide him with a school; but he is sufficiently a man of the world to appreciate that teaching does not pay alimony, or educate his young daughters, or provide for his wife as he grows older.

The financial imperative has governed his work in the theatres of the 1990s. He regrets it, but gets on busily with the life that is available to him. Declaring that he is a better director in his sixties, he does believe this is because he is more like himself. 'When you're young, you think that every play is your last and it has to be right. As you get older, you begin to realise that honest work and endeavour are all you can do. If people like it, good; if they don't, sad. You can't drive yourself to be successful.'[22] Like elderly painters whose work grows less disciplined and more personal, Hall is now more relaxed about his work than he used to be. At its best, it is incisive and illuminating; at its worst, it can seem shallow and occasionally sloppy.

Hall has been a man of extremes: the most charming of all (Harold Pinter's view), the most insecure of all (Gillian Diamond), or the loneliest (Alan Ayckbourn). But time has blunted the hard edges. Although he remains susceptible to the Pamment moods, and is still accustomed to getting his own way, Hall is, he says, now less prone to black depression. He judges that he is less neurotic, less self-centred, and less driven or possessed, than he once was. 'I walked over a lot of people without noticing what I was doing.'

But were those traits that made him such a formidable administrator and propagandist the real man, or has shedding them revealed him? He is in no doubt: the real Peter Hall is more generous and genial than his mask of power has been. That he is beginning to like himself more, Hall attributes to his family: 'a wonderful marriage, and a wonderful tribe of children who are all interested in the same things I'm interested in'. When he says, in 1994, that he has never been happier, there is, perhaps, a glimpse of the eight-year-old boy in Barnham riding in the shunting locomotive and playing his ukulele for the driver.

The matter can never be resolved, but a genial, cheerful Hall might never have achieved so much. The theatre-mad adolescent who was driven to free himself from his roots became the single-minded adult, determined to run his own theatres and direct the best plays in them, and to work in the world's leading opera houses. If it was his neurosis that possessed him, among the consequences are *Waiting for Godot*, *Twelfth Night* in 1958, *The Wars of the Roses*, *The Homecoming*, *The Oresteia*, *Antony and Cleopatra*, *The Marriage of Figaro* (1973), *Così fan tutte* (1978), Britten's *Midsummer Night's Dream* (1981), and the revival of *Don Giovanni* in 1982.

It is, of course, too soon to judge Hall's career. There are still plays and films to direct. Perhaps one day he will do as he would like, and teach. But it can already be said, with perfect justice, that if Hall had not been so ambitious, dedicated and ruthless, Britain would still have had either a Royal Shakespeare Company or a National Theatre on the South Bank of the Thames, but it would not have had both. These two theatre companies, which have enriched Britain's culture, are Peter Hall's enduring legacy.

Notes

Abbreviations

BBC TV   Transcriptions of interviews with Peter Hall, his family and his Cambridge contemporaries, conducted by the author and Bridget Winter, the BBC producer, for a television profile, 1974–5.

CDM   Conversations with Sir Derek Mitchell, 1993–4; during these, Sir Derek would read excerpts from his National Theatre correspondence.

FFP   Fordham Flower Papers, Shakespeare Centre Library, Stratford-upon-Avon.

GA   Glyndebourne Archive.

NTBM   National Theatre; Board Minutes.

NTFGPM   National Theatre; Finance and General Purposes Committee Minutes.

PHL   Peter Hall's Letters.

ROHA   Royal Opera House Archive, Covent Garden.

Publishing details of books referred to in the notes are to be found in the bibliography.

Prologue: 'A Dramatiser of His Own Life'

1 *The Times*, 21 November 1930.

2 Ivor Brown's review of *Antony and Cleopatra* is in James Agate's anthology, *The English Dramatic Critics, 1660–1932*.

3 Harold Hobson, *Indirect Journey*, p. 233.
4 Mark Lawson, 'Hall of Mirrors', *Independent Magazine*, 2 September 1993, p. 23.
5 Peter Hall, BBC TV, soundroll 21/4.
6 Lord Birkett, interview with the author, 1993.
7 Peter Wood, interview with the author, 1993.

Chapter 1 – An East Anglian Childhood

1 Grace Hall, interview with the author, one of two with both Hall's parents in 1987 and 1988.
2 Peter Hall, in his autobiography, *Making an Exhibition of Myself*, various entries from p. 6.
3 Jacky Hall, interview with the author, 1994.
4 Peter Hall, autobiography, p. 386.
5 Grace Hall, interview, op. cit.
6 Peter Hall, autobiography, p. 12.
7 Leslie Caron, interview with the author, 1994.
8 Reg Hall kept his copy of the family tree in the family Bible.
9 Vera Pamment, interview with the author, 1992.
10 Elsie Glading, interview with the author, 1992.
11 Grace Hall, interview, op. cit.
12 Peter Hall, interview with the author, New York, 1989.
13 Peter Hall, autobiography, p. 15.
14 Elsie Hall, interview with the author, 1992.
15 Reg Hall, interview with Bridget Winter, 24 November 1974, soundroll 2A.
16 Peter Hall, *Sunday Telegraph*, 21 June 1992.
17 Reg Hall, interview with the author, op. cit.
18 Peter Hall, autobiography, p. 31.
19 Peter Hall, interview with Anthony Clare, *In the Psychiatrist's Chair*, p. 66.
20 Derek Lawrance, interview with the author, 1992.
21 Anthony Storr, *Churchill's Black Dog*, p. 45.
22 Peter Hall, *Sunday Telegraph*, 14 July 1966, p. 6, the second of a series of three articles; Hall's first attempt at autobiography.
23 Peter Hall, BBC TV, soundroll 32/7.
24 Peter Hall, autobiography, p. 7.

Chapter 2 – Public Schooldays at the Perse

1 The Perse School, Handbook, 1940.
2 Stanley Price, interview with the author, 1992.
3 Dr John Polkinghorne, interview with the author, 1994.
4 Peter Hall, interview with the author, New York, 1989.
5 Mel Calman, interview with the author, 1992.
6 Grace Hall, interview with the author, one of two with both Hall's parents in 1987 and 1988.
7 Reg Hall, interview, op. cit.
8 Peter Hall, *Sunday Telegraph*, 14 July 1966.
9 Anthony Holden, *Olivier*, p. 194.
10 Michael Billington, *Peggy Ashcroft*, p. 115.
11 Sally Beauman, *The Royal Shakespeare Company: A History of Ten Decades*, p. 176.
12 Donald Davie, *My Cambridge*, ed. Ronald Hayman, p. 76.
13 John Tanfield, interview with the author, 1989.
14 Stanley Price, interview, 1992.
15 Douglas Brown, *The Pelican*, the Perse School Magazine, Spring 1949.
16 Mel Calman, excerpt from an unpublished diary from his schooldays.
17 *The Times Educational Supplement*, 19 February 1949.
18 Simon Raven, *Shadows on the Grass*, p. 198.
19 Peter Hall, interview with the author, New York, 1989.
20 John Goodwin, interview with the author, 1994.
21 John Barton, interview with the author, 1993.
22 Peter Hall, PHL. The notes for his speech were kept in a file along with school reports, magazines, etc. They belong with his letters.
23 Donald Davie, op. cit., p. 77.
24 Peter Hall, *Sunday Telegraph*, op. cit.
25 Peter Hall, autobiography (*Making an Exhibition of Myself*), p. 40.

Chapter 3 – Sergeant Instructor (Acting)

1 Peter Hall, interview with the author, New York, 1989.
2 Peter Hall, autobiography (*Making an Exhibition of Myself*), p. 59.
3 David Isitt, interview with the author, 1993.

4 Norman Marshall, *The Other Theatre*, pp. 226–32.
5 Lord Birkett, interview with the author, 1993.
6 RAF List, 1952.

Chapter 4 – A Cambridge Apprenticeship

1 John Vaizey in *My Cambridge*, p. 115.
2 Simon Raven, *Shadows on the Grass*, p. 196.
3 F.R. Leavis, *The Common Pursuit*, p. 258.
4 Peter Hall, interview with the author, New York, 1989.
5 Kitty Black; her autobiography, *Upper Circle*, gives an account of the Company of Four.
6 John Barton, interview with the author, 1993.
7 Peter Hall, BBC TV, soundroll 26/5.
8 George (Dadie) Rylands, interview with the author, 1989.
9 Theresa Robertson, interview with the author, 1992. (She acted at Cambridge as Theresa Moore.)
10 Peter Hall, autobiography (*Making an Exhibition of Myself*), p. 68.
11 John Tanfield, interview with the author, 1989.
12 The Very Revd Michael Mayne, interview with the author, 1992.
13 *Varsity*, 11 October 1952. Periodical Department, University Library, Cambridge.
14 *Varsity*, 18 October 1952.
15 Peter Hall, BBC TV, soundroll 37A/4.
16 *Granta*, November 1952.
17 *Varsity*, 15 November 1952.
18 *Daily Telegraph*, 13 November 1952.
19 *Varsity*, 15 November 1952.
20 Ibid., 24 January 1953.
21 *Daily Telegraph*, 13 January 1953.
22 *Varsity*, 18 April 1953.
23 Peter Hall, interview with the author, New York, 1989.
24 Yolande Bird, interview with the author, 1992.
25 Peter Hall, BBC TV, soundroll 38A/7.
26 Peter Hall, interview with the author, New York, 1989.
27 Peter Hall, autobiography, p. 89.
28 Peter Hall, BBC TV, soundroll 33/5–6.
29 Ibid., soundroll 38A/7.
30 The Very Revd Michael Mayne, op. cit.

31 Amateur Dramatic Society, Minute Book, Autumn 1953. The minutes of the Cambridge ADC are kept in the Rare Manuscript Department of the University Library.

32 *Varsity*, 10 October 1953.

Chapter 5 – At Home at the Arts

1 *Theatre World*, October 1953.

2 Mary Counsell, interview with the author, 1994.

3 Anthony Quayle, *A Time to Speak*, p. 327.

4 *Cambridge Daily News*, 20 April 1955. This clipping, along with reviews and interviews, was collected in a scrapbook kept by Grace Hall covering 1953–6.

5 *The Stage*, undated clipping in the scrapbook: probably February 1955.

6 *The Stage*, op. cit.

7 *Theatre World*, May 1955.

8 *The Stage*, op. cit.

9 *Cambridge Daily News*, 20 April 1955.

10 *The Stage*, op. cit.

11 *Theatre World*, May 1955.

12 Mary Counsell, interview, 1994.

13 Grace Hall, BBC TV, soundroll 4A/4.

14 Toby Robertson, interview with the author, 1993.

15 Kenneth Tynan, *Curtains*, p. 53.

16 Yolande Bird, interview with the author, 1992.

17 Trader Faulkner, interview with the author, 1993.

18 Anthony Hartley, *The Spectator*, 12 March 1954.

19 Peter Hall to Moran Caplat, 1 March 1954, Glyndebourne Archive (GA).

20 Peter Hall, autobiography (*Making an Exhibition of Myself*), p. 96.

21 *The Stage*, op. cit.

22 Peter Hall to Sir David Webster, 2 July 1954, Royal Opera House Archive (ROHA).

23 Ronnie Barker, *It's Hello from Him!*, p. 85.

24 Ibid., p. 93.

25 Peter Hall to Moran Caplat, 14 January 1955, GA.

26 Timothy O'Brien, interview with the author, 1993.

27 Kathleen Tynan, *The Life of Kenneth Tynan*, p. 116.

28 Ibid., p. 109.

29 Kenneth Tynan in the *Observer*, 24 April 1955.
30 *Theatre World*, September 1955.
31 Deirdre Bair, *Samuel Beckett: A Biography*, p. 479.
32 Kitty Black, interview with the author, 1993.
33 Toby Rowland, interview with the author, 1994.
34 Paul Daneman, interview with the author, 1993.
35 Alan Schneider, 'Any Way You Like It, Alan', *Theatre Quarterly*, XIX, p. 31.
36 Peter Bull, *I Know the Face but . . .*, p. 179.
37 Peter Hall, autobiography, p. 105.
38 Deirdre Bair, op. cit., p. 482.
39 Peter Bull, op. cit., p. 179.
40 Harold Pinter, interview with the author, 1994.

Chapter 6 – To Stratford, via Leningrad

1 Leslie Caron, interview with the author, 1993.
2 Peter Hall, autobiography (*Making an Exhibition of Myself*), p. 110.
3 Toby Rowland, interview with the author, 1994.
4 Peter Hall, autobiography, p. 109.
5 Sally Beauman, *The Royal Shakespeare Company*, p. 229.
6 Anthony Quayle, *A Time to Speak*, pp. 333–4.
7 *Theatre World*, September 1956.
8 John Barton, interview with the author, 1993.
9 Toby Rowland, interview, 1994.
10 Peter Hall, autobiography, p. 109.
11 Tennessee Williams to Peter Hall, 12 December 1956, PHL.
12 Leslie Caron, interview, 1993.
13 Paul Daneman, interview with the author, 1993.
14 *Theatre World*, May 1957.
15 Stephen Fay, *The Ring: Anatomy of an Opera*, p. 33.
16 Michael Billington, *Peggy Ashcroft*, p. 173.
17 Kenneth Tynan, *Tynan Right and Left*, pp. 4–5.
18 Glen Byam Shaw to Peter Hall, 1 July 1957, FFP.
19 Glen Byam Shaw to Fordham Flower, 10 December 1957, ibid.
20 Peter Hall, autobiography, p. 117.
21 Dorothy Tutin, interview with the author, 1994.
22 Glen Byam Shaw to Peter Hall, 22 April 1958, FFP.
23 Ivor Brown, *The Shakespeare Memorial Theatre 1957–59*, p. 11.

24 Peter Hall to Fordham Flower, 30 April 1958, FFP.
25 Lady Flower, interview with the author, 1993.
26 Fordham Flower to Peter Hall, 9 July 1958, PHL.
27 Peter Hall to Fordham Flower, 12 July 1958, FFP.
28 Sally Beauman, op. cit., p. 14.
29 Peter Hall to Fordham Flower, 4 November 1958, PHL.
30 Fordham Flower to Peter Hall, 17 November 1958, ibid.
31 Anthony Quayle to Peter Hall, undated, ibid.
32 Sir Patrick Reilly to Fordham Flower, 4 January 1959, FFP.
33 Peter Hall, autobiography, p. 148.
34 Sally Beauman, op. cit., p. 235.
35 Peter Hall to Fordham Flower, 30 December 1958, FFP.

Chapter 7 – A Company is Born

1 Leslie Caron, interview with the author, 1993.
2 Peter Hall, autobiography (*Making an Exhibition of Myself*), p. 128.
3 Laurence Olivier to Peter Hall, 21 May 1959, PHL.
4 Dorothy Tutin to Peter Hall, postmarked 16 February 1959, ibid.
5 Glen Byam Shaw to Peter Hall, 2 June 1959, ibid.
6 Enid Bagnold to Peter Hall, 9 June 1959, ibid.
7 Dorothy Tutin to Peter Hall, undated, from the New Theatre, Oxford, ibid.
8 Sally Beauman, *The Royal Shakespeare Company*, p. 233.
9 Boris Aronson, *The Theatre Art of Boris Aronson* by Lisa Aronson and Frank Rich, p. 136.
10 Stanley Wells, *Royal Shakespeare*, p. 12.
11 Tarquin Olivier, *My Father Laurence Olivier*, p. 232.
12 Stanley Wells, op. cit., p. 18.
13 Joyce Cary to Peter Hall, 2 September 1959, PHL.
14 Tarquin Olivier, op. cit., p. 233.
15 David Addenbrooke, *The Royal Shakespeare Company*, p. 231.
16 Dennis Flower, interview with the author, 1993.
17 Sally Beauman, op. cit., p. 244.
18 Kenneth Tynan, *Tynan Right and Left*, p. 7.
19 Michael Billington, *Peggy Ashcroft*, p. 183.
20 Peter Hall to Fordham Flower, 26 March 1959, FFP.
21 Peter Hall, interview with the author, 1993.
22 Peter Hall to Fordham Flower, 7 April 1960, FFP.

23 Peter Hall, notes of interview with Irving Wardle, 3 August 1981.
24 Emile Littler to Peter Hall, 6 May 1959, PHL.
25 Emile Littler to Peter Hall, 2 June 1959, ibid.
26 Hugh (Binkie) Beaumont to Fordham Flower, 15 March 1960, FFP.
27 Dorothy Tutin, interview with the author, 1993.
28 Jacky Hall, interview with the author, 1994.
29 John Barton, interview with the author, 1993.
30 Rex Harrison to Peter Hall, written from Portofino but undated; probably June 1959, PHL.
31 Paul Scofield to Peter Hall, 2 January 1959, ibid.
32 Kate Flanagan, interview with the author, 1993.
33 John Bury, interview with the author, 1994.
34 Peter Hall, autobiography, p. 159.
35 Peter Hall, interview, 1993.
36 John Barton, interview with the author, 1993.
37 Lady Flower, interview with the author, 1993.
38 Glen Byam Shaw, October 1960 (no date), FFP.
39 Peter Hall, autobiography, p. 172.
40 Ibid., p. 173.

Chapter 8 – High Stakes, Imperfect Victory

1 Leslie Caron, interview with the author, 1993.
2 T.C. Worsley, *Financial Times*, 21 February 1961.
3 Kenneth Tynan, *Observer*, 16 April 1961.
4 John Gielgud to Peter Hall; this series of letters was written between 11 April 1960 and 3 June 1961.
5 Franco Zeffirelli, *The Autobiography*, p. 166.
6 Peter Hall, autobiography (*Making an Exhibition of Myself*), p. 167.
7 Rachel Kempson to Peter Hall, 19 October 1961, PHL.
8 Peter Hall to Fordham Flower, 17 February 1961, FFP.
9 Fordham Flower to Sir Gyles Isham, 23 August 1963, ibid.
10 Gerard Fay; the author's father represented the *Manchester Guardian* in resolving the argument.
11 Sally Beauman, *The Royal Shakespeare Company*, p. 244.
12 Jacky Hall, interview with the author, 1994.
13 Michael Kustow, interview with the author, 1994.
14 Michel Saint-Denis to Peter Hall, 25 December 1961, PHL.

15 Peter Hall to Fordham Flower, 20 January 1961, FFP.

16 Fordham Flower to Peter Hall, 24 January 1961, ibid.

17 Lord Chandos to Fordham Flower, 21 March 1960, ibid.

18 Laurence Olivier to Peter Hall, 3 July 1960, PHL.

19 Minutes of the Joint Council for the National Theatre, 2 September 1960, FFP.

20 Joint Council minutes, 4 November 1960.

21 Laurence Olivier to Peter Hall, 14 October 1960, PHL.

22 Laurence Olivier to Peter Hall, 10 November 1960, ibid.

23 Laurence Olivier to Peter Hall, 31 March 1960, ibid.

24 Lord Cottesloe to Fordham Flower, 16 August 1961, FFP.

25 Arnold Goodman, *Tell Them I'm On My Way*, pp. 337–8.

26 Fordham Flower, minute of Joint Council meeting on 25 September 1961, FFP.

27 Peter Hall, autobiography, p. 202.

28 Fordham Flower, Joint Council minutes, 25 September 1961, FFP.

29 Laurence Olivier to Peter Hall, 10 October 1961, PHL.

30 Lord Chandos to Fordham Flower, 4 January 1962, FFP.

31 Laurence Olivier to Peter Hall, undated, January or February 1962, PHL.

32 Peggy Ashcroft to Peter Hall, undated, probably summer 1962, ibid.

33 Fordham Flower to Lord Cottesloe, 8 May 1962, FFP.

34 Peter Hall to Fordham Flower, 7 February 1962, ibid.

35 Peter Hall to Fordham Flower, 6 July 1962, ibid.

36 Sally Beauman, op. cit., p. 261.

37 Fordham Flower to John Profumo, 25 July 1962, FFP.

38 Fordham Flower to Laurence Olivier, 22 October 1962, ibid.

39 Laurence Olivier to Fordham Flower, 23 October 1962, ibid.

40 Lord Cottesloe to Fordham Flower, 23 October 1962, ibid.

41 Sir Emrys Williams to Fordham Flower, 8 November 1962, ibid.

42 Sir Emrys Williams to Peter Hall, 29 November 1962, ibid.

43 Sir Emrys Williams to Fordham Flower, 31 October 1962, ibid.

44 Lord Chandos to Fordham Flower, 26 October 1962, ibid.

45 *Private Eye*, 9 March 1962.

46 John Goodwin, interview with the author, 1993.

47 Ralph Richardson to Peter Hall, 29 March 1961, PHL.

48 William Gaskill, interview with the author, 1994.

49 Harold Pinter to Peter Hall, 11 January 1962, PHL.
50 Harold Pinter, interview with the author, 1994.
51 Kenneth Tynan, *Observer*, 16 September 1962.

Chapter 9 – Break Up, Breakdown

1 Peter Hall to Fordham Flower, 24 September 1962, FFP.
2 Leslie Caron, interview with the author, 1993.
3 Peter Hall, autobiography (*Making an Exhibition of Myself*), p. 173.
4 Charles Laughton to Peter Hall, dated 31 March, probably 1960 or 1961, PHL.
5 Peter Ustinov to Peter Hall, undated, sent from New York, ibid.
6 Joan Littlewood, *Joan's Book*, p. 635.
7 John Bury, interview with the author, 1994.
8 Peter Hall, notes of interview with Irving Wardle, 3 August 1981.
9 Peter Hall, interview with the author, 1993.
10 Anthony Quayle to Peter Hall, 17 June 1960, PHL.
11 John Barton, in collaboration with Peter Hall, *The Wars of the Roses*, p. x.
12 John Barton, interview with the author, 1993.
13 Richard Pearson, *A Band of Arrogant and United Heroes*, p. 17.
14 John Bury, interview, 1994.
15 Lady Flower, interview with the author, 1993.
16 Jacky Hall, interview with the author, 1994.
17 Peter Hall, autobiography, pp. 177–8.
18 Donald Sinden, *Laughter in the Second Act*, p. 101.
19 Grace Hall to Peter Hall, undated, PHL.
20 Lord Avon to Peter Hall, 25 June 1963, ibid.
21 Tom Boase to Fordham Flower, 7 June 1963, FFP.
22 Tom Boase to Fordham Flower, 21 November 1963, ibid.
23 Lord Cottesloe to Fordham Flower, 30 January 1964, ibid.
24 Peter Hall to Fordham Flower, 6 February 1964, ibid.
25 Joan Plowright to Peter Hall, 21 November 1963, PHL.
26 Joan Plowright to Peter Hall, 16 February 1964, ibid.
27 Laurence Olivier to Peter Hall, 19 February 1964, ibid.
28 Joan Plowright to Peter Hall, undated, probably April 1964, ibid.
29 John Parker, *Warren Beatty*, p. 105.

30 Jennifer Hall, *Daily Mail*, 22 October 1992.

31 Peter Wood, interview with the author, 1993.

32 Peggy Ashcroft to Peter Hall, undated, presumably April 1964, PHL.

33 Donald Sinden, op. cit., p. 111.

34 Jacky Hall, interview, 1994.

35 Hugh Griffith to Peter Hall; this series of letters was written throughout the summer of 1964, PHL.

Chapter 10 – Abdication at Stratford

1 Sally Beauman, *The Royal Shakespeare Company*, p. 273.

2 Michael Kustow, interview with the author, 1994.

3 Tom Boase to Fordham Flower, 7 June 1963, FFP.

4 Lord Cobbold to Fordham Flower, 28 July 1964, ibid.

5 Sir Denys Lowson to Fordham Flower, 21 June 1964, ibid.

6 John Roberts to Fordham Flower, 25 June 1964, ibid.

7 Fordham Flower to Douglas Fairbanks Jr, undated, presumably late 1964, ibid.

8 Ivor Brown to Fordham Flower, 9 November 1964, ibid.

9 Harold Pinter to Peter Hall, 24 August 1964, PHL.

10 Harold Pinter to Peter Hall, 29 June 1964, ibid.

11 Harold Pinter, interview with the author, 1994.

12 Stanley Wells, *Royal Shakespeare*, p. 24.

13 Peter Hall, programme for RSC *Hamlet*, Stratford-upon-Avon, 1965.

14 David Warner to Peter Hall, undated scrap of paper, PHL.

15 Ronald Bryden, *The Unfinished Hero*, pp. 66–7.

16 Stanley Wells, op. cit., p. 41.

17 Peter Hall to David Webster, 2 August 1960, ROHA.

18 John Bury, interview with the author, 1994.

19 John Tooley, interview with the author, 1994.

20 John Johnston, *The Lord Chamberlain's Blue Pencil*, p. 197.

21 William Bundy, interview with the author, 1983.

22 Andrew Porter, *Financial Times*, 29 June 1965.

23 Jacky Hall, interview with the author, 1994.

24 Anthony Quayle to Peter Hall, 25 November 1965, PHL.

25 Peter Hall to Fordham Flower, 2 April 1965, FFP.

26 Arnold Goodman, *Tell Them I'm On My Way*, p. 346.

27 Arnold Goodman to Fordham Flower, 7 July 1965, FFP.

28 Fordham Flower to Peter Hall, 14 July 1965, ibid.

29 Hugh Willatt, interview with the author, 1994.

30 Sally Beauman, op. cit., p. 285.

31 Kathleen Tynan, *The Life of Kenneth Tynan*, p. 250.

32 Sally Beauman, op. cit., pp. 290–1.

33 Trevor Nunn, interview with the author, 1994.

34 David Webster to Peter Hall, 28 July 1965, ROHA.

35 Fordham Flower to Douglas Fairbanks Jr, 22 October 1965, FFP.

36 Peter Hall, *Guardian*, 11 July 1966.

37 David Brierley, interview with the author, 1993.

38 Lady Flower, interview with the author, 1993.

39 Jacky Hall, interview, 1994.

40 *Sunday Times*, 26 June 1966.

41 *Daily Mail*, 3 April 1967.

42 John Bury, interview, 1994.

43 *Nova*, August 1967.

44 Laurence Olivier to Peter Hall, 3 January 1968, PHL.

45 Peggy Ashcroft to Peter Hall, undated, presumably late 1967 or early 1968, ibid.

Chapter 11 – A Novice and Experimenter

1 David Brierley, interview with the author, 1993.

2 John Goodwin, interview with the author, 1993.

3 David Addenbrooke, *The Royal Shakespeare Company*, p. 223.

4 Christopher Morahan, interview with the author, 1994.

5 Inter-departmental memo, 25 March 1968, ROHA.

6 Garrett Drogheda, *Double Harness*, p. 228.

7 Peter Hall to John Tooley and Colin Davis, 19 January 1970, ROHA.

8 Moran Caplat, interview with the author, 1993.

9 Noel Annan to Peter Hall, 28 May 1970, and Hall to Annan 11 June 1970, PHL.

10 Janet Baker to Peter Hall, undated, ibid.

11 *Listener*, 11 June 1970.

12 Contracts are removed from ROH files; the relevant paragraph in Hall's contracts was read to the author by the archivist.

13 Peter Hall, interview with the author, 1980.

14 Garrett Drogheda, op. cit., p. 235.

15 Peter Hall to Garrett Drogheda, 12 January 1971, ROHA.

16 Peter Hall to Garrett Drogheda, 4 July 1971, ibid.

17 Lord Eccles to Garrett Drogheda, undated, probably mid-July 1971, ibid.
18 Peter Hall to John Tooley, 9 August 1972, ibid.
19 Arnold Goodman to Garrett Drogheda, 14 July 1971, ibid.
20 Arnold Goodman, *Evening Standard*, 8 July 1986.
21 John Tooley, interview with the author, 1994.
22 Harold Pinter to Peter Hall, 21 February 1968, PHL.
23 Harold Pinter to Sir George Farmer, 27 February 1968, ibid.
24 Harold Pinter to Peter Hall, 9 July 1969, ibid.
25 Peter Hall, *Diaries: The Story of a Dramatic Battle*, p. 333.
26 John Bury, interview with the author, 1994.
27 Peter Hall, *Diaries*, p. 21.
28 Ronald Blythe, interview with the author, 1989.
29 Peter Hall, *Diaries*, p. 261.
30 Jacky Hall, interview with the author, 1994.

Chapter 12 – Début at the National

1 Jonathan Miller, interview with the author, 1994.
2 Lord Rayne, interview with the author, 1994.
3 Lord Rayne, interview, 1994.
4 John Mortimer, interview with the author, 1994.
5 Lord Mishcon, interview with the author, 1994.
6 Michael Blakemore, interview with the author, 1994.
7 Trevor Nunn, interview with the author, 1994.
8 Laurence Olivier, *Confessions of an Actor*, p. 247.
9 Peter Hall, *Diaries: The Story of a Dramatic Battle*, p. 3.
10 National Theatre, Board Minutes (NTBM), 18 April 1972.
11 Kathleen Tynan, *The Life of Kenneth Tynan*, p. 314.
12 Ibid.
13 Peter Hall, *Diaries*, p. 40.
14 NTBM, 14 May 1973.
15 Hugh Willatt, interview with the author, 1994.
16 Peter Hall, *Diaries*, p. 52.
17 Companies House, Angle Films, annual reports.
18 Jacky Hall, interview with the author, 1994.
19 John Dexter, *The Honourable Beast*, p. 93.
20 NTBM, 25 September 1975.
21 Peter Hall, *Diaries*, p. 111.
22 Harold Pinter, interview with the author, 1994.
23 John Dexter, op. cit., p. 55.

24 Richard Eyre, interview with the author, 1994.
25 Jonathan Miller, interview, 1994.
26 Peter Hall, *Diaries*, p. 15.
27 John Elsom and Nicolas Tomalin, *The History of the National Theatre*, p. 310.
28 Peter Hall, interview with the author, 1988.

Chapter 13 – A Concorde of Culture

1 Lord Rayne, interview with the author, 1994.
2 NTBM, 14 October 1974.
3 Peter Hall, *Diaries: The Story of a Dramatic Battle*, p. 148.
4 Ibid., p. 153.
5 NTBM, 14 April 1975.
6 Peter Hall, *Sunday Times*, 20 October 1974.
7 NTBM, 4 July 1977.
8 Lord Mishcon, interview with the author, 1994.
9 National Theatre, Finance and General Purposes Committee Minutes (NTFGPM), 24 May 1975.
10 Peter Hall, *Diaries*, p. 262.
11 Ibid., p. 334.
12 NTBM, 17 April 1978.
13 Sir Derek Mitchell, conversation with the author (CDM).
14 Peter Hall, *Diaries*, p. 193.
15 CDM.

Chapter 14 – The Director as a Conductor

1 Peter Hall, *Diaries: The Story of a Dramatic Battle*, p. 239.
2 David Hare, interview with the author, 1994.
3 Peter Hall, *Diaries*, p. 382.
4 Alan Ayckbourn, interview with the author, 1994.
5 Jacky Hall, interview with the author, 1994.
6 Peter Hall, *Diaries*, p. 177.
7 Stanley Wells, *Royal Shakespeare*, p. 36.
8 John Bury, interview with the author, 1994.
9 Peter Hall, *Diaries*, p. 356.
10 Peter Lewis, *The National: A Dream Made Concrete*, p. 132.
11 Peter Hall, *Diaries*, p. 323.
12 Alan Ayckbourn, interview, 1994.
13 Peter Hall, *Diaries* p. 390.

14 John Dexter, *The Honourable Beast*, p. 220.

15 Peter Hall, *Diaries*, p. 447.

16 Simon Callow, *Being an Actor*, p. 116.

17 Peter Hall, *Diaries*, p. 47.

18 Ibid., p. 299.

19 Spike Hughes, *Glyndebourne: A History of the Festival Opera*, p. 269.

20 Peter Hall, *Diaries*, p. 364.

21 Ibid., p. 359.

22 Peter Hall, interview with the author, 1980.

Chapter 15 – Exit Jacky; Enter Maria

1 Peter Hall, *Diaries: The Story of a Dramatic Battle*, p. 295.

2 Jacky Hall, interview with the author, 1994.

3 Nigel Tutt, *The Tax Raiders*, pp. 7, 120.

4 Companies House, annual reports of Fontped Securities.

5 Companies House, annual reports of Petard Productions Ltd.

6 Peter Hall, *Diaries*, p. 389.

7 Peter Hall, autobiography (*Making an Exhibition of Myself*), p. 97.

8 Ibid., p. 290.

9 Peter Hall, *Diaries*, p. 306.

10 Peter Hall to Moran Caplat, 21 January 1976, GA.

11 Peter Hall, autobiography, p. 239.

12 Maria Ewing, interview with the author, 1994.

Chapter 16 – The Eighties: Part One

1 Peter Hall, *Diaries: The Story of a Dramatic Battle*, p. 434.

2 Ibid., p. 421.

3 Ibid., p. 430.

4 David Hare, interview with the author, 1994.

5 Howard Brenton, interview with the author, 1994.

6 Peter Hall, *Diaries*, p. 412.

7 NTBM, 14 July 1980.

8 Ibid., 8 July 1974.

9 Ibid., 13 October 1980.

10 NTFGPM, 24 November 1980.

11 NTBM, 30 March 1981.

12 *The Times*, 30 June 1981.

13 *Daily Mail*, 30 June 1981.
14 CDM.
15 Howard Brenton, interview, 1994.
16 Neil Astley, *Tony Harrison*, p. 246.
17 Peter Hall, *Diaries*, p. 416.
18 Peter Hall, 'The Mask of Truth', the Goodman Lecture at the Royal Society, London, 9 July 1990.
19 Barrie Rutter, interview with the author, 1994.
20 Neil Astley, op. cit., p. 279.
21 Jeremy Isaacs, interview with the author, 1994.
22 NTFGPM, 22 November 1982.
23 Richard Eyre, interview with the author, 1994.
24 CDM.
25 Alan Ayckbourn, interview with the author, 1994.
26 Harold Pinter, interview with the author, 1994.
27 Gerald Jacobs, *Judi Dench*, p. 109; also Judi Dench, interview with the author, 1994.
28 David Hare, interview with the author, 1994.

Chapter 17 – The Eighties: Part Two

1 Peter Hall, *Diaries: The Story of a Dramatic Battle*, p. 161.
2 NTBM, 12 July 1982.
3 NTFGPM, 25 October 1982.
4 David Hare, interview with the author, 1994.
5 Stephen Fay, *The Ring*.
6 Wolfgang Wagner, *Acts*, p. 192.
7 NTBM, 11 July 1983.
8 NTFGPM, 31 October 1983.
9 Ibid., 28 November 1983.
10 Peter Hall, autobiography (*Making an Exhibition of Myself*), p. 320.
11 NTFGPM, 23 January and 12 March 1984.
12 Peter Hall, tape of press conference speech, 7 February 1985 (from National Theatre press office).
13 Alan Ayckbourn, interview with the author, 1994.
14 David Hare, interview, 1994.
15 CDM.
16 John Goodwin, National Theatre file.
17 Ibid.
18 Peter Lewis, *The National*, p. 180.

19 NTFGPM, 28 October 1985.

20 CDM.

21 CDM.

22 Rowena Webster, interview with the author, 1994.

23 CDM.

24 CDM.

25 Peter Hall, tape of press conference, 28 June 1986.

26 Rowena Webster, interview, 1994.

27 Peter Hall, autobiography, p. 337.

28 Ibid., p. 338.

29 Peter Hall to Lord Rayne, 4 September 1986; John Goodwin, National Theatre file.

Chapter 18 – The Eighties: Part Three

1 John Bury, interview with the author, 1994.

2 Judi Dench, interview with the author, 1994.

3 Tirzah Lowen, *Peter Hall Directs 'Antony and Cleopatra'*.

4 Moran Caplat, interview with the author, 1994.

5 Peter Hall, autobiography (*Making an Exhibition of Myself*), p. 238.

6 Spike Hughes, *Glyndebourne: A History*, p. 269.

7 Brian Dickie, internal memorandum, 25 April 1984, GA.

8 Moran Caplat to Peter Hall, 28 September 1971, ibid.

9 Brian Dickie to Peter Hall, 23 April 1987, ibid.

10 John Christie to Peter Hall, 7 November 1986, ibid.

11 Peter Hall to John Christie, 17 November 1986, ibid.

12 Brian Dickie to Peter Hall, 4 August 1988, ibid.

13 Peter Hall, autobiography, p. 256.

14 Maria Ewing, interview with the author, 1994.

15 Companies House, annual reports of Petard Productions Ltd.

16 Jacky Hall, interview with the author, 1994.

17 *Daily Telegraph*, 24 August 1985.

18 Judi Dench, interview, 1994.

19 Nicki Hall, interview with the author, 1994.

20 Peter Hall, autobiography, p. 351.

21 Land Registry; 33 Bramerton Street, London SW, title number NGL305527.

22 Lord Mishcon, interview with the author, 1994.

23 David Hare, interview with the author, 1994.

24 Peter Hall to Lord Rayne, 9 April 1987; John Goodwin, NT file.

25 Lord Rayne to Luke Rittner, ibid.
26 CDM.
27 Harold Pinter, interview with the author, 1994.
28 Peter Hall, interview with the author, 1988.
29 NTFGPM, 23 May 1988.
30 Richard Eyre, interview with the author, 1994.
31 John Mortimer, *Murderers and Other Friends*, p. 185.
32 Peter Hall, tape of his speech at Lord Rayne's farewell dinner, 1988.

Chapter 19 – Our Theatres in the Nineties

1 Peter Hall, telephone messages, 14 November 1988; Jan Younghusband's Peter Hall Co. file.
 2 Nicki Hall, interview with the author, 1994.
 3 Alan Ayckbourn, interview with the author, 1994.
 4 Duncan Weldon, interview with the author, 1988.
 5 Peter Hall, interview with the author, 1988.
 6 Peter Hall to Jan Younghusband, JY's Peter Hall Co. file.
 7 Peter Hall to Duncan Weldon, 26 October 1988, ibid.
 8 Companies House, annual report of The Peter Hall Co.
 9 *Daily Telegraph Magazine*, 28 May 1989.
10 Peter Hall, *South Bank Show*, London Weekend Television, 29 May 1989.
11 Peter Hall, memorandum in JY's Peter Hall Co. file, 12 October 1988.
12 Peter Hall, interview with the author, 1994.
13 John Bury, interview with the author, 1994.
14 Peter Hall, column in the *Guardian*, 20 June 1992.
15 Gillian Diamond, interview with the author, 1994.
16 Judi Dench, interview with the author, 1994.
17 Nicki Hall, interview, 1994.
18 Companies House, annual reports of Petard Productions Ltd.
19 Jacky Hall, interview with the author, 1994.
20 Jennifer Hall, *Daily Mail*, 22 October 1992.
21 *Scotsman*, 11 October 1993.
22 Peter Hall, interview, 1994.

Bibliography

Addenbrooke, David, *The Royal Shakespeare Company: The Peter Hall Years*, William Kimber, London, 1974.

Agate, James (ed.), *The English Dramatic Critics: An Anthology 1660–1932*, Arthur Barker, London, 1932.

Annan, Noel, *Our Age: The Generation that Made Post-war Britain*, Fontana, London, 1991.

Astley, Neil (ed.), *Tony Harrison*, Bloodaxe Books, Newcastle upon Tyne, 1991.

Bair, Deirdre, *Samuel Beckett: A Biography*, Vantage Books, London, 1990.

Barker, Ronnie, *It's Hello from Him!*, New English Library, London, 1989.

Barton, John, in collaboration with Hall, Peter, *The Wars of the Roses*, British Broadcasting Corporation, London, 1970.

Beauman, Sally, *The Royal Shakespeare Company: A History of Ten Decades*, Oxford University Press, Oxford, 1982.

Billington, Michael, *Peggy Ashcroft*, John Murray, London, 1988.

Black, Kitty, *Upper Circle*, Methuen, London.

Blakemore, Michael, *Next Season*, Faber and Faber, London, 1988.

Brown, Ivor, Introduction to *The Shakespeare Memorial Theatre, 1954–56*, Max Reinhardt, 1956.

—— Introduction to *The Shakespeare Memorial Theatre, 1957–59*, Max Reinhardt, London, 1959.

Bryden, Ronald, *The Unfinished Hero*, Faber and Faber, London, 1969.

Bull, Peter, *I Know the Face, but . . .*, London, 1959.

Callow, Simon, *Being an Actor*, Penguin Books, London, 1984.

Caplat, Moran, *Dinghies to Divas or Comedy on the Bridge*, Collins, London, 1985.

Clare, Anthony, *In the Psychiatrist's Chair*, Heinemann, London, 1992.

Conway, Helen, *Sir John Pritchard: His Life in Music*, André Deutsch, London, 1993.

Craig, Edward Gordon, *On the Art of the Theatre*, Browne's Bookstore, Chicago, 1912.

Davie, Donald, *My Cambridge*, ed. Ronald Hayman, Robson Books, London, 1977.

Dexter, John, *The Honourable Beast: A Posthumous Autobiography*, Nick Hern Books, London, 1993.

Drogheda, Garrett, *Double Harness*, Weidenfeld and Nicolson, London, 1978.

Elsom, John and Tomalin, Nicholas, *The History of the National Theatre*, Jonathan Cape, London, 1978.

Esslin, Martin, *The Theatre of the Absurd*, Penguin Books, London, 1980.

Fay, Stephen, *The Ring: Anatomy of an Opera*, Secker and Warburg, London, 1984.

Findlater, Richard (ed.), *At the Royal Court: 25 Years of the English Stage Company*, Amber Lane Press, Ambergate, Derbyshire, 1981.

Goodman, Arnold, *Tell Them I'm On My Way*, Chapmans, London, 1993.

Goodwin, John (ed.), *The Royal Shakespeare Company, 1960–1963*, Max Reinhardt, London, 1964.

Goodwin, Tim, *Britain's Royal National Theatre: the First 25 Years*, National Theatre in association with Nick Hern Books, London, 1988.

Hall, Peter, *Peter Hall's Diaries: The Story of a Dramatic Battle*, Hamish Hamilton, London, 1983.

Hall, Peter, *Making an Exhibition of Myself*, Sinclair-Stevenson, London, 1993.

Hiley, Jim, *Theatre at Work: The Story of the National Theatre's Production of Brecht's 'Galileo'*, Routledge and Kegan Paul, London, 1981.

Hobson, Harold, *Indirect Journey: An Autobiography*, Weidenfeld and Nicolson, London, 1978.

Holden, Anthony, *Olivier*, Weidenfeld and Nicolson, London, 1988.

Hordern, Sir Michael, with England, Patricia, *A World Elsewhere: The Autobiography*, Michael O'Mara Books, London, 1993.

Hughes, Spike, *Glyndebourne: A History of the Festival Opera*, David and Charles, Newton Abbot, 1981.

Jacobs, Gerald, *Judi Dench: A Great Deal of Laughter*, Weidenfeld and Nicolson, London, 1985.

Johnston, John, *The Lord Chamberlain's Blue Pencil*, Hodder and Stoughton, London, 1990.

Leavis, F.R., *The Common Pursuit*, The Hogarth Press, London, 1984.

Lewis, Peter, *The National: A Dream Made Concrete*, Methuen, London, 1990.

Lewis, Roger, *Stage People*, Weidenfeld and Nicolson, London, 1989.

Littlewood, Joan, *Joan's Book*, Methuen, London, 1994.

Lowen, Tirzah, *Peter Hall Directs 'Antony and Cleopatra'*, Methuen Drama, London, 1990.

McMillan, Dougald and Fehsenfeld, Martin, *Beckett in the Theatre*, volume 1, John Calder, London, 1988.

Marshall, Norman, *The Other Theatre*, John Lehmann, London, 1947.

Mortimer, John, *Murderers and Other Friends*, Viking, London, 1994.

Olivier, Laurence, *Confessions of an Actor*, Weidenfeld and Nicolson, London, 1982.

Olivier, Tarquin, *My Father Laurence Olivier*, Headline, London, 1992.

Page, Malcolm, *File on Pinter*, Methuen Drama, London, 1993.

Parker, John, *Warren Beatty: The Last Great Lover of Hollywood*, Headline, London, 1993.

Pearson, Richard, *A Band of Arrogant and United Heroes: The Wars of the Roses*, The Adelphi Press, London, 1990.

Quayle, Anthony, *A Time to Speak*, Barrie and Jenkins, London, 1990.

Raven, Simon, *Shadows on the Grass*, Sphere Books, London, 1983.

Sinden, Donald, *Laughter in the Second Act*, Hodder and Stoughton, London, 1985.

Storr, Anthony, *Churchill's Black Dog and Other Phenomena of the Human Mind*, Flamingo, London, 1991.

Tutt, Nigel, *The Tax Raiders: The Rossminster Affair*, Financial Training, London, 1985.

Tynan, Kathleen, *The Life of Kenneth Tynan*, Weidenfeld and Nicolson, London, 1987.

Tynan, Kenneth, *He That Plays the King*, Longman's Green, London, 1950.

—— *Curtains*, Longman Green, London, 1961.

—— *Tynan Right and Left*, Longman Green, London, 1967.

—— *The Sound of Two Hands Clapping*, Jonathan Cape, London, 1975.

—— *Profiles*, Nick Hern Books, London, 1989.

Wagner, Wolfgang, *Acts: The Autobiography*, Weidenfeld and Nicolson, London, 1994.

Wardle, Irving, *The Theatres of George Devine*, Jonathan Cape, London, 1978.

Watson, Ian, *Conversations with Ayckbourn*, Macdonald, London, 1981.

Wells, Stanley, *Royal Shakespeare: Four Major Productions at Stratford-upon-Avon*, Manchester University Press, 1977.

Whitworth, Geoffrey, *The Making of a National Theatre*, Faber and Faber, London, 1951.

Zeffirelli, Franco, *The Autobiography of Franco Zeffirelli*, Weidenfeld and Nicolson, London, 1986.

Index

The following abbreviations are used: NT = National Theatre; PH = Sir Peter Hall; RSC = Royal Shakespeare Company